LOST APOSTLES

LOST APOSTLES

Forgotten Members of Mormonism's
Original Quorum of Twelve

William Shepard
H. Michael Marquardt

Signature Books | Salt Lake City | 2014

For more information, consult www.signaturebooks.com.

Jacket design by Ron Stucki.

18   17   16   15   14   5   4   3   2   1

LIBRARY OF CONGRESS CATALOGING-IN-PUBLICATION DATA

Shepard, William.
  Lost apostles : forgotten members of Mormonism's original quorum of twelve/
  by William Shepard and H. Michael Marquardt.
      pages cm
  Includes index.
  ISBN 978-1-56085-228-5 (alk. paper)
  1. Church of Jesus Christ of Latter-day Saints–History. 2. Mormon
Church–History. 3. Mormon Church–Apostles–History. 4. United States–
Church history. I. Title.
  BX8611.S45 2014
  289.3092'2—dc23
                    2013050197

To John Boynton, Luke Johnson,
Lyman Johnson, Thomas Marsh,
William McLellin, and William Smith

CONTENTS

INTRODUCTION

Latter Day Saints today enjoy a sense of continuity and stability that is a hallmark of Mormonism, whether in Utah or in any of the other major branches of Joseph Smith's Restoration Movement. All of these churches choose individuals for leadership who have been proven over the years as church employees or prominent business heads, educators, or diplomats. It was not always so. In the early days, a charismatic convert might be promoted to the top of the hierarchy, fill a short and stormy tenure in office, and leave with as much speed as he appeared. There were public disagreements among the apostles. Joseph Smith tried to stem the chaos by making adjustments to the church structure and personnel in what was a fluid sea of shifting tides.

Compare that with the current situation where members of the Utah church rest assured that when a member of the hierarchy dies, his replacement will be announced at the next semi-annual general conference with the precision of a Swiss watch. The new apostle or president will generally be as steady and predictable as the last one. It is the same in the Missouri-based Community of Christ, even—or perhaps especially—in the case of the women who have been named apostles beginning in the late 1990s. The other churches that trace their origin to Joseph Smith include the Church of Jesus Christ in Monongahela, Pennsylvania, where a Quorum of the Twelve leads the church without the need for a separate presidency. The Remnant Church of Jesus Christ of Latter Day Saints in Missouri has a president and seven apostles. All these men are reliable and tested even if they engage in experimentation in community planning. The Church of Jesus Christ of Latter Day Saints Strangite, headquartered in Wisconsin, and the Restoration Church of Jesus Christ in Missouri do not have quorums of apostles but nonetheless assume that the founding twelve in Joseph Smith's day labored reliably to spread the Restored Gospel.

For those of us who were raised in the post–World War II world, it is hard to imagine the degree of uncertainty and turmoil that existed during the founding years of the Restoration. The first converts were opposed to dogmas and hierarchies. Joseph Smith was known as the First Elder, and Oliver Cowdery as Second Elder, and that was that. However, within two years Sidney Rigdon and Jesse Gause were named to a First Presidency that quickly overshadowed Cowdery. The office of Presiding Patriarch was created for Joseph Smith's father, and Cowdery's position was redefined in 1834 as that of an Assistant to the President, a position that was mostly ceremonial. When Cowdery was excommunicated, he was not replaced and the position was eliminated. As branches and stakes were created, they needed leaders. Joseph would become enamored with someone, become disillusioned with his performance, find a replacement, and leave bad feelings behind.

Consider the case of Jesse Gause, who was baptized in late 1831 and a few months later, in March 1832, appointed to the First Presidency. Only nine months transpired before he was excommunicated and disappeared from church history.[1] Following a similar pattern was John C. Bennett except that he did not go quietly, instead choosing to publish a divisive report of his experiences. In 1837, after the fall of the Kirtland Safety Society Bank, Frederick G.

---

1. Despite good but brief treatments of Gause in D. Michael Quinn, *The Mormon Hierarchy: Origins of Power* (Salt Lake City: Signature Books and Smith Research Associates, 1994), 40–42; Erin B. Jennings, "The Consequential Counselor: Restoring the Root(s) of Jesse Gause," *Journal of Mormon History* 34, no. 2 (Spring 2008): 182–227, Gause still remains a mystery.

Williams of the First Presidency left, joined by Oliver Cowdery and the entire Whitmer family. Another of the original founders, Martin Harris, left and stayed away for three decades. Polygamy tested the perseverance of William Law of the 1840s First Presidency. Like Bennett, he broadcast his dissatisfaction, this time by founding an alternative newspaper, the *Nauvoo Expositor*. When Joseph tried to quash this irritant, it was one of the snowballing events that led to his tragic incarceration and assassination less than a month later.

Six Men

The original Twelve Apostles who were called in 1835 were asked to lead the missionary effort throughout the world but were forbidden by revelation from exercising any authority at the church's headquarters or environs. The first twelve, ranked oldest to youngest, were Thomas B. Marsh, David W. Patten, Brigham Young, Heber C. Kimball, Orson Hyde, William E. McLellin, Parley P. Pratt, Luke S. Johnson, William Smith, Orson Pratt, John F. Boynton, and Lyman E. Johnson. Most of these men, with the exception of Heber and Brigham, clashed with Joseph Smith to the point of temporarily severing their relationship with him. Three of them—McLellin, Boynton, and Lyman Johnson—would not return to the fold. Two others—Marsh and Luke Johnson—returned to the Utah church but without being restored to their former standing as apostles. Joseph's brother William would find his way back to church under the leadership of his nephew, Joseph Smith III. Five of William's former colleagues would stay more or less together in Utah: Brigham Young, Heber Kimball, Orson Hyde (who returned in 1839), Parley Pratt, and Orson Pratt and would continue to argue over doctrine and standing as they had in Ohio and Illinois.

It is a matter of perspective that allows us to label six of these men as "lost" because they would not have described themselves that way, and from the perspective of the Reorganized LDS Church in Missouri, the Utah apostles were lost, and vice versa. Some readers will assume that we, the authors, have similarly lost our way, depending on where the reader stands. One of us, Bill, was born in a Strangite community in Burlington, Wisconsin, and has remained generally loyal to it. He is the church historian and trustee of the community land encompassing the most important areas of the settlement that was once called Voree. It was founded by James J. Strang a century and a half ago under Joseph Smith's direction. Strang led the settlement on a separate but compatible journey to that of Brigham Young and Sidney Rigdon.

The other of us, Mike, converted to the LDS Church as a teenager growing up in San Francisco but now describes himself as an independent historian. The two perspectives should satisfy suspicions readers might have that we come to this project with an agenda and do not understand their viewpoint as either a believer or non-believer. One of us believes deeply in the divinity of the Restoration and the other harbors doubts. What we share in common, besides a long-standing friendship, is a passion for finding out new information about our shared past.

The purpose of this book has been first and foremost to report on what our research has turned up. Although we have a point of view, we do not insist on it. We would very much like to correct the injustice we feel has been done to the memory of these men, but the final judgment rests with the readers. Our disappointment is over the embarrassment the churches today feel over the apostles' perceived betrayal, which makes it almost impossible to quote these men as authorities on doctrine or history. What little mention is made of them is usually in the service of cautionary tales about what happens if you disobey the prophet, exhibit pride, or fail to follow the commandments. Around the globe, Latter-day Saints of all stripes (those who put a hyphen in their name and those who don't) shake their heads over these men, wondering how it is possible that they could have left the faith after everything they knew and experienced. And so they have been mostly forgotten and are scarcely understood.

Where we find mention of the six is in the lists of early members. Their names are given but not their individual characteristics or backgrounds, and they are skipped over the way the New Testament treats Jesus's disciples, as having been more important for their roles than for their backstories or pathways. Consider Doctrine and Covenants 64, where it states that Christ's disciples (apostles) "sought occasion against one another" without sharing details behind this provocative statement. In the Bible and in church history, the attention is focused on the main character. The apostles provide anecdotes about human contrariness and are useful for drawing morals from bad behavior. In a college-level manual for LDS Institute of Religion classes, Luke Johnson's baptism is mentioned but Lyman's is not, probably because Luke rejoined the church and Lyman did not. There is a brief entry, "Several Deny the Work of the Lord," that discusses apostates without affording them the respect one might think would be extended to founders. They are instead shown as destroyers of God's work. Luke Johnson and Thomas Marsh, who later confessed their errors, receive some attention. Space restrictions preclude adding too much in the way of gray areas to a lesson manual, but the fact that the dissidents have been hidden from view is also obvious.[2]

Sometimes the apostles are openly ridiculed in Sunday school manuals. Thomas Marsh left in a huff, we are told, over his wife's conflict with a neighbor over milk strippings. One could hope for a more balanced portrait of the senior apostle. Given the sheer number of men who clashed with Joseph Smith, perhaps the real question is why anyone would have joined the church in the first place, not why they would leave. What was the attraction behind the Restoration Movement? How did the prophet, whose visionary talent made him like an Old Testament figure, touch peoples' hearts?

---

2. *Doctrine and Covenants Student Manual, Religion 324-325* (Salt Lake City: Intellectual Reserve, 2001).

Things did not go exactly as we have been told. The impression we are sometimes left with is that the church brought peace and harmony to people's lives. In most cases, the opposite is true! As an example, the Johnson family was by all accounts exemplary before they embraced Mormonism, and then they became quarrelsome and dissatisfied, engaging in rancorous arguments. One can detect this pattern in other converts. Nearly all the first apostles experienced extreme turmoil. Orson Pratt thought Joseph had seduced his wife and refused, for a time, to endorse the prophet. Pratt finally concluded that the church was more important than his own petty concerns. The outliers were Brigham Young and Heber Kimball, but this is not to say that they did not have their own, more private disagreements with Joseph Smith or with the church generally. Uncertainty and discontent were ubiquitous, and there was little harmony or peace.

It was no doubt the depth of feeling people had for Joseph Smith and his doctrines that created the degree of anxiety they experienced when they had honest disagreements with policies and teachings. This does not mean they moderated their affection for Joseph himself. It was often quite the contrary. Where LDS commentators have pointed to affirmations of faith by apostates to show the rightness of Joseph's actions and correctness of the Book of Mormon, the statements are also testaments to the honesty and strength of character of the apostates themselves.

The seed for this book was a visit Bill received from LDS missionaries when they knocked on his door in Burlington one day and accepted his invitation to attend church. Afterward one of the missionaries mentioned that he had seen Lyman Johnson's grave in Prarie du Chien on the other side of the state. Bill was intrigued enough that he drove two hundred miles east to that picturesque spot on the Mississippi River. It was easy enough locating Johnson's badly weathered tombstone in Evergreen Cemetery, but the surprise was discovering, after laboring to read the date of

December 20, 1859, that Lyman died three years later than traditionally assumed. This was the first of many object lessons in being cautious in accepting facts from official histories.

One thing led to another as we were drawn into an ever-expanding project, first looking into the life of Lyman Johnson and then researching his colleagues' experiences. One conclusion we came to was that historical facts have value outside of interpretation—or at least that whatever conclusions one might draw, there is more to the story than meets the eye and that the more we learn, the less like their stereotypes the apostles seem to be. We wonder how anyone could have made so many assumptions about these men with so little evidence to go on. It is nice to be able to see the larger picture, the bad with the good. Each individual proves to be unique despite some obvious commonalities.

As we formulated a plan of attack, we realized that we had both visited the restored home of John and Elsa Johnson in Hiram, Ohio, and both of us were struck by the lavish praise the tour guides heaped on John Johnson Sr., patriarch of the Johnson family. His generosity helped facilitate the growth and stability of the Restoration Movement. We agreed that he had filled a key role, of course, and it is not that we were unaccustomed to the standard fare for simplicity and exaggeration at LDS visitor centers. But in this case, the guides seemed unable to moderate anything they said about the Johnson family's involvement in the church's founding. The Johnsons provided shelter and sustenance for Joseph and Emma Smith, as well as for Sidney and Phoebe Rigdon, in 1831-32. Elsa had lost the use of an arm that had become disabled by rheumatism, so Joseph healed it. The most famous vision in the church in the 1830s, that of the three degrees of heavenly glory in the afterlife, canonized as LDS and Community of Christ Doctrine and Covenants 76, occurred in the Johnson home in February 1832.[3]

---

3. The First Vision had not yet been announced to the church. See, e.g.,

Father Johnson supported construction of the Kirtland Temple. He defended Joseph and Sidney in March 1832 when they were tarred and feathered. As we have seen, John's and Elsa's sons, Luke and Lyman, were called as apostles in 1835. Their daughter Marinda would marry Apostle Orson Hyde and, according to her own statement, ultimately became one of Joseph Smith's plural wives.

What we were not told at the visitor center was that John Johnson became a leading dissenter in the summer of 1837, losing his place on the high council. He died outside of the church in 1843. Nor did the guides mention that mother Elsa remained alienated for decades prior to her death in Pottawattamie County, Iowa, in July 1870. We believe these facts are as relevant to her history as her miraculous healing. Within two years of joining the Quorum of Twelve Apostles, Luke and Lyman became critics and were excommunicated in 1837 and 1838. The family followed the pattern set by Jesse Gause of a quick rise to prominence, a high level of trust, and sudden collapse in their relationship with the church.

An examination of the other Johnson children is equally interesting. Olmstead did not want anything to do with the church. John Jr. was involved in savagely assaulting Joseph Smith and Sidney Rigdon in March 1832. We found no evidence that Justin ever joined the church—not in Hiram or Kirtland or Nauvoo. Even though Alice Johnson Olney died as a Mormon in Nauvoo in 1841 and was eulogized for her faithfulness, her husband, Oliver, was excommunicated for publishing works the church disapproved of. It does not appear that Fanny Johnson Ryder was a member of the church. Nor is there a record of Emily Johnson Quinn being baptized.[4] Fifteen-year-old Mary Beal Johnson

---

Kathleen Flake, *The Politics of American Religious Identity: The Seating of Senator Reed Smoot, Mormon Apostle* (Chapel Hill: University of North Carolina Press, 2004).

4. The information on Fanny Johnson Ryder comes from family tradition that Fanny had already married and moved out of her parents' home before the Smiths arrived. Our thanks to John and Carol Cluff for this insight.

died in Joseph and Emma Smith's house in 1833, and of course, Marinda Nancy Johnson married Orson Hyde in 1834 and remained faithful all her life, even though she and Orson divorced in 1870. He dissented in 1838 and was censured for supporting Thomas Marsh's denouncement of Mormon atrocities in the Mormon War in Missouri.

This amount of disunity and dissent is startling when contrasted to what seems to have been a smoothly working, united Johnson family prior to the arrival of Mormonism in Ohio. It seems the gospel message brought the sword rather than peace in intra-family fights and internal anxiety. Reconstructing this pattern and attempting to understand it are goals of this book.

Another objective has been to determine why these particular men were called. In the past it has been thought that they proved themselves during the paramilitary march on Missouri called Zion's Camp, when in fact, they were not all involved in that event. More likely it was their service as missionaries that brought them to Joseph Smith's attention as, time after time, the twelve men left their families to travel long distances to preach. After returning home and taking a brief break, they would leave on yet another difficult assignment. It is ironic to think this, but it may have been their perseverance that was most prized at the time. They sometimes became discouraged, sometimes returned home early or veered off track and had to be set straight, but they always went back to face another hostile crowd and to rely on the generosity of people they did not know, who put them up and fed them.

They were willing to stand up to respected ministers and say the existing churches were corrupt, to declare that events were in motion that would lead to the Second Coming of Jesus Christ in their lifetimes. As missionaries they testified that God had re-established his church on earth by calling Joseph Smith to be a seer and revelator and that Joseph's translation of ancient writings clarified doctrine and provided a guide for eternal life.

They preached, baptized, testified, warned people to prepare for prophetic events that would soon occur, and sealed up their congregations to eternal life.

When they were ordained, they covenanted to dedicate themselves entirely to God. Joseph Smith told them they would be expected to preach among gentiles until God told them to preach to Jews, and would begin in the eastern states on May 4, 1835. Their agenda would include ten church conferences (although one was later canceled) from May through August 28 in existing congregations in New York, Massachusetts, Vermont, Maine, and Upper Canada. Altogether it was an optimistic start, but forces were unleashed that would slowly eat away at the continuity, uniqueness, and harmony of the group. They were even criticized by the members of the existing congregations who thought it presumptuous that these men would assume to exercise authority over them.

Warren A. Cowdery, presiding high priest in Freedom, New York, said the apostles had an agenda that was wholly incompatible with the church's mission. Based on his report, the First Presidency concluded that the Twelve were loose cannons, a type of "outlaws" without any direction, and as soon as they returned home they engaged in a verbal standoff with the First Presidency. Eventually the apostles apologized for having criticized Sidney Rigdon's school in Kirtland, but they continued to complain about Joseph's preferential treatment of his brother William. Demonstrating that there was no real love lost between them, Joseph and William got into a fist fight later that year.

Several of the apostles who were young unmarried men would see their priorities change once they got married. Being away from home and missing key events in Kirtland, they would return to a changed environment. Joseph was re-editing the revelations for publication and engaging in speculative financial ventures until the national banking crisis of 1837 took down the unchartered Mormon bank. It had been founded on revelation, so members had assumed it could not fail. But it did, and spectacularly so. Nobody in the church was qualified to run a bank, nor was anyone qualified to run a school or a church, for that matter.

In their introduction to *Differing Visions: Dissenters in Mormon History*, Roger Launius and Linda Thatcher commented that converts came from "essentially the same background" as Joseph Smith, meaning families of modest means and limited education who were unhappy with the social order but unqualified to do much about it. None of them had the training necessary to handle banking. They were not teachers. The result was that all felt equally qualified to perform any task they needed to. They felt entitled to have a say in church policy too and to receive revelation.[5] Little wonder the apostles were so bold as to challenge Joseph Smith. Orson and Parley Pratt had disagreements with him in 1837. Thomas Marsh, president of the Twelve, witnessed the Mormon destruction of Gallatin and Mill Port in Missouri in October 1838 and separated himself from the church. He was excommunicated in March the next year. Orson Hyde sided with Marsh but recanted and was restored to fellowship in June 1839.

William McLellin was excommunicated in May 1838. David Patten verbally and then physically tussled with Joseph in mid-1837, and Luke Johnson was excommunicated that same year. John Boynton criticized the Kirtland Safety Society Bank and was disfellowshipped in September 1837, then restored to fellowship a week later, only to be excommunicated at the end of the year. Orson Pratt was ousted in August 1842 and restored in January 1843. William Smith was ousted in 1845.

In his ground-breaking book on James J. Strang, *The Kingdom of Saint James*, Milo M. Quaife commented on how the "worst accusations ever leveled" against Mormons by outsiders were "matched

---

5. Roger D. Launius and Linda Thatcher, eds., *Differing Visions: Dissenters in Mormon History* (Urbana: University of Illinois Press, 1994), 6.

line for line" by "similar accusations made by the Saints" against each other. "The Saints have long complained, and with justice, that the world is ever ready to believe all manner of evil against them," he wrote, "but they seem seldom to have realized that their own testimony against one another affords color to the worst of gentile accusations."[6] Launius and Thatcher suggested that belief in revelation appealed to people who did not perceive shades of ambiguity, which implied an insistence on "capitulation rather than compromise." Gordon D. Pollock, a non-Mormon historian quoted by Launius and Thatcher, perceived the existence of scapegoats on whom blame could be placed. As long as discontent was the result of "personal weakness and sin," the church was saved from introspection.[7]

Through our research, we have uncovered previously overlooked documentation about the "great missionary period" from 1832-35 (see appendix A). This was the period during which missionaries crisscrossed the eastern states. Some of these accounts will bring to life in new ways this period of history and the sacrifices the apostles and other elders made. The gentile response included curiosity, hostility, acceptance, and respect.

The greatest problems the apostles encountered occurred when they returned home and found things changed and themselves to be in a purgatory of diminished status and influence. The financial issues in Kirtland cannot be overstated. Ten of the twelve apostles decided they had had enough when they heard of reported misuse of funds. This was during the period when Father Johnson was dropped from the high council and Martin Harris was excommunicated. The Joseph Smith Sr. family was forced to leave the city for fear of their safety and relocated to Missouri where the Mormon War soon forced the membership to leave, this time to Illinois. The

---

6. Milo M. Quaife, *The Kingdom of Saint James: A Narrative of the Mormons* (New Haven: Yale University Press, 1930), 26.

7. Launius and Thatcher, *Differing Visions*, 14-15.

non-Mormons did not act, however, prior to the church setting an example by forcing dissidents out of the state.

Where did the apostles go when they were kicked out of the nest? They ended up in Iowa, New York, Missouri, and Utah. In some ways their subsequent paths are as interesting as their time in the church. One of them became an inventor, another a respected lawyer. We will look at their origins and families, as well as at their general environment at different stages of their lives.

We wish to acknowledge the assistance of the following individuals: Lavina Fielding Anderson, John and Carol Cluff, Elaine Goodell, Michael W. Homer, Erin Jennings Metcalfe, Joseph Johnstun, David Sean Muttillo, Connell O'Donovan, Ronald E. Romig, Elaine M. E. Speakman, Mark Lyman Staker, and Kyle R. Walker.

1. DISCOVERING MORMONISM

Ohio, lush and green in summertime, was frozen in early 1831. The town that would become the center of Mormonism for over six years, Kirtland, was near the banks of Lake Erie, where the wind would swirl across the lake and bring a howling chill this time of year. Snow was inevitable. Joseph and his bride, Emma Hale Smith, then five months pregnant with twins, arrived on a sleigh from New York.

Less than a year prior, Joseph had published the Book of Mormon, the scripture translated from gold plates, which an angel had revealed to him. Joseph founded the church in Manchester, New York, and was told by revelation that unnamed enemies were encircling the flock, so it was time for them to ensconce to the safety of Ohio. They were not the first New Englanders to make this migration. Nearly a million pioneers had made the move to what was then known as "the Northwest," meaning the Ohio frontier, during the first four decades of the century.

The Johnson Family

John and Alice ("Elsa") Johnson[1] were also from New England. Like Lucy Mack and Joseph Smith Sr., who were originally from Vermont, they came to Ohio from the Green Mountain region.

---

1. Milton V. Backman Jr., *The Heavens Resound: A History of the Latter-day Saints in Ohio, 1830-1838* (Salt Lake City: Deseret Book, 1983), 403n1, found that Elsa, or Elsey, was referred to as Alice in a family Bible.

Unlike the Smiths, who had experienced frustration and poverty since moving to upstate New York in 1817, the Johnsons had found that their long hours and calloused hands had paid off. They had moved to Hiram, Ohio, in 1818, a year after the Smiths moved to New York. John was an active Methodist until 1831 and owned more than 300 acres.[2] The family had a large house. Many of the neighbors considered them wealthy.[3]

Apparently the family joined with Joseph Smith's Church of Christ after Elsa's arthritic arm was miraculously healed by Joseph's touch.[4] Luke was twenty-three years old when the Smiths arrived in Kirtland, thirty miles from Hiram, and was impressed that his "mother had been laboring under an attack of chronic rheumatism in the shoulder" and "could not raise her hand to her head," but when Joseph "laid hands upon her," she was "healed immediately."[5]

Luke's brother Lyman was the fourth son of the nine surviving children. Something about the Mormon gospel spoke to him as well. He was the first in the family to profess belief in Joseph's message,[6] and he submitted to baptism at Kirtland in about February 1831.[7] His parents followed soon afterward. By April his sister,

---

2. "History of Luke Johnson, by Himself," *Deseret News*, May 19, 1858, 53.

3. For more, see Appendices 1, 2 in the current compilation and Mark L. Staker, "Remembering Hiram, Ohio," *Ensign*, Oct. 2002, 32. Staker found that of Elsa's 15 children, 9 of them (Alice, Fanny, John Jr., Luke, Olmstead, Lyman, Emily, Marinda, Justin) lived to adulthood.

4. *History of the Church*, 1:215-16n, as qtd. in Amos. S. Hayden.

5. "History of Luke Johnson," 53.

6. According to his gravestone in Prairie du Chien, Wisconsin, Lyman was born in Pomfret, Vermont, on October 15, 1813, and was forty-six when he died on December 20, 1859. Although the broken marker was repaired in 1992 by family genealogists Virginia Tims and Elaine M. E. Speakman, the text is difficult to read. Not to worry, because Speakman has a 1964 photo of the engraved text. The problem is that it contradicts the family Bible, with Lyman's birth given as October 24, 1811. Even though a family Bible record is usually accurate, one can barely imagine the year of death being so far off on a headstone, at least if it was erected at the time of death.

7. Staker, "Remembering Hiram, Ohio," 32.

Marinda Nancy Johnson, was initiated into the waters of baptism. Luke joined a few of the other children the following month, while Olmstead and Fanny declined the invitation. Marinda was fifteen when she was baptized. She later remembered how quickly the family converted. Although she omits mention of Lyman's baptism, she captures the essence of the enthusiasm most of the family felt:

> In the winter of 18[30-]31, Ezra Booth, a Methodist minister, procured a copy of the Book of Mormon and brought it to my father's house. They sat up all night reading it, and were very much exercised over it. As soon as they heard that Joseph Smith had arrived in Kirtland, Mr. Booth and wife and my father and mother went immediately to see him. They were convinced and baptized before they returned. They invited the prophet and Elder Rigdon to accompany them home, which they did, and preached several times to crowded congregations, baptizing quite a number.[8]

Lyman was ordained a priest and is listed as such when he attended a church conference on October 25, 1831, in Orange Township, northwest of Hiram, about halfway between Hiram and Kirtland.[9] Already part of Joseph's inner sphere, he became even closer to the prophet when his parents invited Joseph and Emma and their adopted twins to move in with them on September 12, 1831. The twins Emma gave birth to on April 30 died just hours after being born—the same day Julia Clapp Murdock gave birth to twins who survived, while she died in childbirth. Her husband, John, turned them over to the Smiths.[10] It was a large house and

---

8. See Marinda Nancy Johnson Hyde's account in Edward W. Tullidge, *The Women of Mormondom* (New York: Tullidge & Crandall, 1877), 403-04.

9. Donald Q. Cannon and Lyndon W. Cook, eds., *Far West Record: Minutes of the Church of Jesus Christ of Latter-day Saints, 1830-1844* (Salt Lake City: Deseret Book, 1983), 19. The original minutes from June 1830 to early 1838 were copied into this manuscript in 1838.

10. See Sunny McClellan Morton, "The Forgotten Daughter: Julia Murdock

accommodated another family, but small enough to account for the familiarity Lyman enjoyed with the prophet. It may also be the reason for the confidence Joseph developed in Lyman as he added the young man to a list of those who would be promoted in the priesthood. At the October 1831 conference, Lyman was ordained an elder under the hands of Oliver Cowdery, and then, eight days later, he was ordained a high priest in Hiram by Sidney Rigdon.[11] At the gathering in Hiram, Lyman joined with some of the other brethren in testifying that Joseph Smith's revelations were authentic.[12] The next month, Lyman and three others (Luke Johnson, William McLellin, and Orson Hyde) asked Joseph Smith what the will of the Lord was concerning them. The revelatory response was to "preach the gospel to every creature."

Lyman became an exemplary missionary for the young church. Despite significant differences among the six men we will profile, there were common threads that bound them together, among them a willingness to give up everything to leave home in the service of the church. This meant leaving family, occupations, friends, and other comforts in exchange for the uncertainty of travel and the hostility of some strangers. It took courage and commitment, and Lyman, of all the 1830s missionaries, shone brightly in the face of hardships. His first travel destination came by revelation at an Amherst conference on January 25, 1832: he and twenty-year-old Orson Pratt were directed to "take their journey into the eastern countries."[13] He was eighteen years old, neither was married.

Although the Johnson brothers are often spoken of together as a kind of package, they operated independently. Luke was older, twenty-four years old, having come into the world on November 3,

---

Smith," *Mormon Historical Studies* 3, no. 2 (Fall 2002): 37–38.

11. Cannon and Cook, *Far West Record*, 25–28.

12. Doctrine and Covenants (1981 LDS edition, hereafter LDS D&C) 68:8; Doctrine and Covenants (1990 RLDS edition, hereafter RLDS D&C) 68:11.

13. LDS D&C 75:14; RLDS D&C 75:3.

1807, at Pomfret, Vermont, but was similarly single.[14] Ten years old when his family moved to Ohio, he grew up a hard-working farm boy. In 1831 he became acquainted with Joseph Smith but waited some three months after his brother's baptism before he entered the water on May 10. Then he made up for lost time by becoming an elder by October 11. At the general conference in Orange a few days later on October 25, Luke professed to be "for God and none else[,] come life or death," saying he would "consecrate all that he had to the Lord." It was something akin to a monastic vow. In reward for this, he was ordained to the high priesthood by Oliver Cowdery.[15] "High priesthood" and "high priest" were interchangeable at the time.

Before receiving a mission assignment the next year, Luke was able to observe Joseph Smith up close as the prophet received several revelations in Luke's parents' home. In addition to that, in November 1831, church officials met in the house to outline a plan for publishing the Book of Commandments, the predecessor to the Doctrine and Covenants.[16] Joseph was also working on a revision of the Bible, so one can imagine the charged environment in the home as the word of God poured down from above into their reality, sometimes with specificity and intimacy.

Unfortunately neither Lyman nor Luke kept a diary. Luke was assigned to William McLellin as a mission companion on January 25 and sent to the southern states.[17] Heading out on February 2, they got as far as the border between Ohio and Pennsylvania and already

---

14. The modern gravestone in Salt Lake City Cemetery inaccurately gives Luke's birth year as 1808.

15. Cannon and Cook, *Far West Record*, 19, 22-23, 25; Andrew Jenson, *Latter-Day Saint Biographical Encyclopedia*, 4 vols. (Salt Lake City: Andrew Jenson Historical Company, 1901), 1:85, identifying Joseph Smith as ordaining Luke a high priest, which is incorrect.

16. Cannon and Cook, *Far West Record*, 26-31.

17. Jan Shipps and John W. Welch, eds., *The Journals of William E. McLellin, 1831-1836* (Provo and Urbana: *BYU Studies* and University of Illinois Press, 1994), 70.

encountered antagonistic crowds who, heckling them, called William "a liaar." In a small town on the eastern side of Pennsylvania, the missionaries were told to "depart out of their coasts." They did so "speedily," McLellin wrote. Rattled by this acrimonious reception, McLellin began to have second thoughts and "a query in my mind whether man or the fountain of all wisdom had called me to preach." He finally "determined to cease proclaiming until I was satisfied in my own mind." To pay his way while he deliberated, he hired out as a store clerk until the end of April and Luke returned to Kirtland. Later when McLellin returned from clerking, they were reminded by Joseph Smith that they had not yet completed their assignment.[18]

What we know about the return trip is that Luke made it at least as far as Virginia. In fact, he lingered in Huntington, Virginia, long enough to meet and marry Susan Arminda Poteet and presumably to enjoy a short honeymoon before continuing on. In those days, missions were conceived and executed differently than today, with little or no oversight or direction. Since they were the first missionaries, they had to invent the strategies that would work for them and make up the rules, in this case deciding that a mission did not imply a vow of celibacy. Presumably Susan remained home while her husband continued on; they relied on complete strangers from day to day for room and board. Typically a missionary spent the daytime hours studying the scriptures, visiting members, and even sight-seeing, but not knocking on doors. In the evenings they visited people and delivered sermons in rented halls and as guest lecturers in local churches.

Whatever the circumstances were, the wedding between the Johnson and Poteet families was performed on November 29 by the Rev. Burwell Spurlock, a Protestant minister.[19] At the end of Luke's mission, he and his wife would travel to Kirtland, where eventually

---

18. Ibid., 72-73, 78.
19. John and Carol Cluff discovered Spurlock's name.

all seven of their children would be born.[20] Other early missionaries married converts and took a honeymoon break from their mission labors. Orson Pratt converted his first wife, Sarah, while on a mission to upstate New York in 1836. After spending a three-day honeymoon with her, he resumed proselyting.[21] William Smith was so taken by Caroline Grant while on his mission to Pennsylvania in 1833 that he married her there.[22]

The thrill of being at the center of a new religious society was interrupted by two famous incidents in church history involving other Johnson brothers. Twenty-two-year-old Olmstead walked into the house in early 1832 to find that Joseph Smith had moved in. Joseph mentions this in his history written in 1843. Olmstead was dismissive of Joseph's teachings, to the extent that Joseph told him his bitter spirit "would lead him to destruction." With a note of triumphalism, the prophet wrote that Olmstead left home for the southern states and Mexico and died while traveling.[23]

The second brother to reject Mormonism was John Johnson Jr., who worshipped with the Saints for about a year and then turned against Joseph Smith. On March 25, 1832, he was among the disaffected Mormons, such as Ezra Booth, Symonds Ryder, and neighbors, including his uncle Eli Johnson, who brutally assaulted Joseph Smith and Sidney Rigdon. The mob beat the two men and covered

---

20. Their children were Mary Elsa (b. Mar. 8, 1834), Emily Susan (b. 1835), James Olmstead (b. Nov. 25, 1837), Sarah Eliza (b. Mar. 7, 1839), Fanny Catherine (b. Nov. 24, 1840), Vashtia Emily (b. Sept. 4, 1842), and Solomon Luke (b. Aug. 14, 1844), according to the family group record prepared by the Cluffs.

21. Richard S. Van Wagoner, "Sarah M. Pratt: The Shaping of an Apostate," *Dialogue: A Journal of Mormon Thought* 19, no. 2 (Summer 1986): 69-70.

22. William Smith, *William Smith on Mormonism* (Lamoni, IA: Herald Steam Book and Job Office, 1882), 21-22.

23. Dean C. Jessee, ed., *The Papers of Joseph Smith: Autobiographical and Historical Writings* (Salt Lake City: Deseret Book, 1989), 1:373-74. Olmstead's brief death notice in the LDS newspaper stated: "In Warrenton, Virginia, on the 24th of February, last, Mr. Olmstead G. Johnson, son of brother John Johnson, of this place, aged 24 years." *The Evening and the Morning Star*, Apr. 1834, 151.

them with hot pine sap and turkey feathers.[24] Sidney sustained a head injury while being dragged over the frozen ground.[25] There was collateral damage as an adopted baby, Joseph Murdock Smith, died from exposure because the door was beaten in. John Sr. did everything in his power to defend the prophet from the mob, but to no avail.[26] The motivation for this brutality was the belief that Joseph was angling to take over the Johnson farm.[27]

In a hearsay account by Luke Johnson, who was away at the time but who must have heard what happened, the mob stripped Joseph Smith "for the purpose of emasculating him, and had Dr. Dennison there to perform the operation; but when the Dr. saw the Prophet stripped and stretched on the plank, his heart failed him, and he refused to operate."[28] Whatever the motivation for the attack, Joseph and Sidney responded by moving their families to Kirtland and then escaping to Missouri for the time being.[29] The Johnsons followed suit the next year and moved to Kirtland.

In return for his devotion, Father Johnson was ordained an elder on February 17, 1833, in Kirtland. On June 4 he was made a high priest and appointed to the United Firm, confirming in a subtle way the neighbors' fears that he would lose his property. The firm was created less than three weeks before the tar and feathering to

---

24. It was said that Eli (Eliphaz) was joined by another uncle, Edward, but John Johnson's brother by that name apparently died in 1792. There was another unrelated Edward Johnson who was listed in 1831 as holding the office of priest but having "denied the faith." Cannon and Cook, *Far West Record*, 19.

25. There could have been lasting effects from this head injury, according to Richard S. Van Wagoner, *Sidney Rigdon: Portrait of Religious Excess* (Salt Lake City: Signature Books, 1994), 115-18.

26. Jessee, *Papers of Joseph Smith*, 1:374-77; "History of Luke Johnson," 54.

27. This was the conclusion of Henry Howe, *Historical Collections of Ohio* (Columbus: Henry Howe & Son, 1891), 3:111; Amos Sutton Hayden, *Early History of the Disciples in the Western Reserve* (Cincinnati: Chase & Hall, 1875), 220-21, quoting Symonds Ryder to A. S. Hayden, Feb. 1, 1868.

28. "History of Luke Johnson," 53.

29. Richard Lyman Bushman, *Joseph Smith: Rough Stone Rolling* (New York: Knopf, 2005), 180; Marvin S. Hill, *Quest for Refuge: The Mormon Flight from American Pluralism* (Salt Lake City: Signature Books, 1989), 38.

provide financial support for church leaders. The members of the firm invested what they could for the purchase of a sawmill, tannery, and printing press, then divided up the proceeds equally, thereby redistributing assets to some partners who had contributed little or nothing, as was done when the firm collapsed two years later.[30]

In addition to other factors, one probable stimulus for Father Johnson's increased interest in religion was the death of his teenage daughter, Mary, on May 30, 1833. Joseph Holbrook noted that she was fifteen years old and died at the Newel Whitney store in Kirtland. Holbrook called the store "the Prophet Joseph Smith Jr.'s home" because Joseph's wife, Emma, had moved there after leaving Hiram. Holbrook said the death "caused much gloominess at the prophet's house."[31] Mary was laid to rest in the cemetery near the Kirtland Temple site.[32]

On March 24, 1834, John and Elsa sold about 160 acres near Hiram for three thousand dollars, about half their total farmland and the equivalent of about $70,000 today.[33] About two weeks later, Joseph Smith testified in a courtroom in Chardon, Ohio, ten miles southeast of Kirtland, that Father Johnson was qualified to "keep a tavern, in the township in Kirtland," so the proceeds from

---

30. Lyndon W. Cook, *Joseph Smith and the Law of Consecration* (Provo: Grandin Book, 1985), 57-70; LDS D&C 96:6-9; RLDS D&C 93:2. On June 25, 1833, Joseph Smith wrote to William Phelps in Jackson County, Missouri: "Zombre [John Johnson Sr.] has been received as a member of the firm by commandment, and has just come to Kirtland to live." Joseph Smith Jr., et al., *History of the Church of Jesus Christ of Latter-day Saints*, 2nd ed. rev., ed. B. H. Roberts, 7 vols., 1902–12, 1932 (Salt Lake City: Deseret Book, 1959): 1:363. The members of the firm were given pseudonyms for their protection in 1835, which is reflected in the church history.

31. Joseph Holbrook, Autobiography, 26, typescript, L. Tom Perry Special Collections, Harold B. Lee Library, Brigham Young University, Provo, Utah. Joseph and Emma were living at the Newel K. Whitney store.

32. Janet Lisonbee, *In Memory of the Early Saints Who Lived and Died in the Kirtland, Ohio Area* (N.p.: By the author, 2003), 8.

33. Deed Book, Portage County, 18:393-94, recorded May 12, 1834, microfilm no. 899,069, Family History Library, Salt Lake City. The land was sold to Jude and Patty Stevens.

the farm probably went toward a drinking establishment in Kirtland. Johnson was issued a license on April 5.[34]

When Lyman took a break from church travels to start a family on September 4, 1834, he participated in a double wedding overseen by Sidney Rigdon, marrying Sarah S. Lang while their acquaintance Orson Hyde was married to Lyman's sister Marinda.[35] Lyman seems to have stayed close to home for a while but undertook several short missions throughout Ohio.[36] In Kirtland he attended a school for elders, where he studied religion, English grammar, and writing. The newlyweds were not privileged with much privacy after a homeless William McLellin imposed on them for a roof over his head. "This morning I commenced boarding with bro. Lyman Johnson," McLellin wrote on November 24, "and here I calculate to continue this winter." The women were almost entirely overlooked in such reports even though Sarah probably cooked and cleaned for their guest as well as for her husband.[37]

The Johnsons were sorely tested but chose to stand with Joseph Smith. John Sr. used his considerable means to pay the remaining mortgage for the Kirtland Temple property and donated it to the

---

34. Court Records 1807-1904, Journal of the Court of Common Pleas of Geauga County, Ohio, Journal M:181-82, 184, April 5, 1834, microfilm no. 20,277, Family History Library, found by Mark L. Staker. Oliver Cowdery reported in Joseph Smith's journal: "Saturday returned to Chardon <as witness for fath[er] Johnson> in the evening returned home," in Dean C. Jessee, ed., *The Papers of Joseph Smith: Journal, 1832-1842* (Salt Lake City: Deseret Book, 1992), 2:28n4. Susan Easton Black, *Who's Who in the Doctrine and Covenants* (Salt Lake City: Bookcraft, 1997), 153, stated: "Soon after the terrible incident [tar and feathering] Father Johnson moved to Kirtland and opened an inn near the Newel K. Whitney Store."

35. Marriage Record C:55, 64, Probate Court, Geauga County, Ohio, microfilm no. 873,461, Family History Library.

36. Rigdon told Boynton and McLellin on November 11 that "it was not wisdom for us to go so far [to preach]—But that we must Labour in the regions round about." On November 16, Lyman joined McLellin at Fairport on a preaching appointment. Shipps and Welch, *Journals of William E. McLellin*, 148; holographs in LDS Church History Library.

37. Ibid., 149.

church under the law of consecration.[38] Luke and Lyman served serial missions, the rewards of which would materialize in equal measure with new and unexpected challenges.

John Boynton

John Boynton had a personal interest in genealogy and record keeping but, strangely enough, left precious few details about his own life during his sojourn among the Latter-day Saints. After leaving Mormonism, he seemed to have little remaining interest in it and may have intentionally left that phase of his life out of the record.[39]

He was born September 20, 1811, in Bradford, Massachusetts, and was given the name John Farnham Boynton, his parents being Eliphalet and Susannah Nichols Boynton. Census records show that he stayed at home until he was twenty[40] and that he first learned the trade of shoemaking.[41] When he first heard of Mormonism, it was probably from Orson Hyde and Samuel H. Smith when they gave lectures in Bradford in August and September 1832. Elders Hyde and Smith stayed overnight with the Boynton family on August 19, Orson recording that they were hosted by the "Boyantons."[42] On the morning of August 27, the elders returned to the Boynton family to rebut Alexander Campbell's booklet, *Delusions: An Analysis of the Book of*

---

38. Roger D. Launius, *The Kirtland Temple: A Historical Narrative* (Independence, MO: Herald House, 1986), 38–39.

39. At least we have the bare facts of their lives in John Farnham Boynton and Caroline Harriman Boynton, comps., *The Boynton Family: A Genealogy of the Descendants of William and John Boynton, Who Emigrated from Yorkshire, England, in 1638, and Settled at Rowley, Essex County, Massachusetts* (Groveland, MA: J. F. & C. H. Boynton, 1897). We also appreciate information provided for this chapter by David Sean Muttillo and Erin Metcalfe.

40. U.S. Census, 1820, Massachusetts, Essex County, Bradford, 175; U.S. Census, 1830, Bradford, 20.

41. A list of church dissenters mentioned that "one of them [was] a Massachusetts shoemaker by the name of John F. Boynton, a man notorious for nothing but ignorance, ill breeding and impudence." "To the Subscribers of the Journal," *Elders' Journal*, Aug. 1838, 55.

42. Orson Hyde, Journal, Aug. 19, 1832, LDS Church History Library.

Mormon.[43] Something about the missionaries lit a spark in John, who advanced quickly after he was baptized in September. Two months later, on November 16, he was ordained an elder by Joseph Smith and sent on a mission assignment with Zebedee Coltrin.[44]

William E. McLellin

A gravestone in Woodlawn Cemetery in Independence reads: "William Earl McLellin Born in Smith Co. Tenn Jan 13. 1806 Died in Independence Mo. Mar. 14, 1883." It is a shame that so little is known about his background, since he became such a complex and difficult figure. It is probably not insignificant that he was the only Southern-born apostle, and his perspective was no doubt different than that of the Yankee converts. He also had more education than the average Mormon, his occupation being that of a school teacher. Little is known about his mother. His father, Charles McLellin, was born about 1766.[45]

BYU historian Larry Porter found that the future apostle, who had two brothers and one sister, towered over people at six feet three inches. His weight was right for his height at 224 pounds, slightly over optimum. He was said to be full of energy.[46] Two years prior to hearing about Mormonism, on July 30, 1829, he married Cinthia Ann, whose maiden name we no longer have. She became pregnant but died in childbirth, leaving William heartsick. "I was deprived of her most lovely endeavours to render me happy and agreeable, in consequence of which I spent many

---

43. Ibid., Aug. 25, 27, Sept. 3, 13, 1832. The book had just been reprinted by Joshua V. Himes.

44. Fred C. Collier and William S. Harwell, eds., *Kirtland Council Minute Book* (Salt Lake City: Collier's Publishing, 1996), 1.

45. Larry C. Porter, "The Odyssey of William Earl McLellin: Man of Diversity, 1806-83," in Shipps and Welch, *Journals of William E. McLellin*, 356.

46. Ibid., 292-93. McLellin to "my old friends," Feb. 22, 1872, in Stan Larson and Samuel J. Passey, eds., *The William E. McLellin Papers, 1854-1880* (Salt Lake City: Signature Books, 2007), 481.

lonesome & sorrowful hours," he wrote.[47] Death in childbirth was all too common at the time, but it was nevertheless a shock that probably factored into William's occasional depression and preoccupation with fate.

On July 18, 1831, according to his account, McLellin heard that Harvey Whitlock and David Whitmer were going to preach near Paris, Illinois, on their way to Jackson County, Missouri.[48] One of the elders, Whitmer, a witness to the Book of Mormon angel and gold plates, was especially instrumental in converting McLellin. The investigator closed his school where he was teaching thirty to forty students, mounted his horse, and traveled 450 miles to Independence to see this phenomenon for himself, arriving there on August 18, 1831.[49]

He was disappointed to learn that Joseph Smith had recently departed on August 9 for Kirtland, but was still touched by the message the other leaders delivered and therefore allowed himself to be baptized on August 20 in Kaw Township, fifteen miles west of Independence.[50] He was ordained an elder four days later by Hyrum Smith and Edward Partridge. In mid-October he headed north with Hyrum Smith to the conference at Orange Township on the twenty-fifth, where he met Lyman and Luke Johnson and Orson Hyde. When he was ordained a high priest at the conference, he gave

---

47. William E. McLellin to "beloved relatives," Aug. 4, 1832, in Shipps and Welch, *The Journals of William E. McLellin*, 82–83.

48. Ibid., 29. According to Lucy Mack Smith, the two men were Samuel H. Smith and Reynolds Cahoon, also missionaries, but they preached at the courthouse in Paris three days prior to McLellin's encounter with Whitlock and Whitmer. Lavina Fielding Anderson, ed., *Lucy's Book: A Critical Edition of Lucy Mack Smith's Family Memoir* (Salt Lake City: Signature Books, 2001), 541–42.

49. Richard P. Howard, "Mormonism's 'Stormy Petrel,'" in Larson and Passey, *William E. McLellin Papers*, 3–4, updated from Howard's article of the same title in Launius and Thatcher, *Differing Visions*. For McLellin's journal account of this period, see Shipps and Welch, *Journals of William E. McLellin*, 29–36.

50. This was near Kansas City, which was still twenty years away from being settled.

his promise that he would be "subject to the will of God even unto death," saying he had the "greatest reason to rejoice of any present."[51]

At McLellin's request, Joseph Smith sought a revelation about him. This resulted in a pronouncement that because he had "turned away" from his "iniquities," he was partially "clean, but not all." He was told to "repent therefore of those things which are not pleasing in my sight" and "proclaim my gospel from land to land, and from city to city," specifically in "the eastern" states. "Let my servant, Samuel H. Smith go with you, and forsake him not," the voice of God continued. "Commit not adultery, a temptation with which thou hast been troubled," declared the communiqué from heaven, which had turned personal. "Push many people to Zion," it admonished.[52]

In his journal, William recorded that, despite the sour note in the revelation, it gave "great joy to my heart because some important questions were answered which had dwelt upon my mind with anxiety yet with uncertainty."[53] The next day he preached at the Johnson home: "With confidence alone in Enoch's God I arose and addressed them about one hour and a half. And it was not I but the spirit and power of God which was in me."[54] Another missionary had been born.

Among the topics of discussion at church gatherings in November 1831 was the need to publish Joseph Smith's revelations. If anyone thought they were written by Joseph Smith himself, he disabused them of the notion by declaring in the name of God that they should "appoint him that is the most wise among you" to try to produce a better text. If anyone could do so, they would be "justified in saying" the revelations were contrived.[55] If they could not produce such a document, then they should be content with what they had from Joseph Smith. The *History of the Church* added

---

51. Cannon and Cook, *Far West Record*, 21.
52. 1835 D&C 74:2–5; LDS D&C 66:3, 7–8, 10–12; RLDS D&C 66:2–5.
53. Shipps and Welch, *Journals of William E. McLellin*, 46.
54. Ibid., 46–47.
55. 1835 D&C 25:2; LDS 67:6–7; RLDS 67:2.

scornfully that "William E. M'Lellin, as the wisest man, in his own estimation, having more learning than sense, endeavored to write a commandment like unto one of the least of the Lord's, but failed; it was an awful responsibility to write in the name of the Lord."[56]

About the same time, McLellin, Luke and Lyman Johnson, and Orson Hyde were told to go "into all the world" and "preach the gospel to every creature." They were promised the ability to discern "the signs of the times, and the signs of the coming of the Son of man." They would have authority to seal up believers to eternal life.[57] As McLellin contemplated this summons to be a modern-day Paul, he curiously took to clerking at Charles Sumner's store in Middlebury, Ohio, and pursued a relationship with Emeline Miller, whom he married on April 26, a mere four days after he met her.[58] Reasoning that he would be more useful developing Zion than preaching, he and his wife moved to Independence in May, arriving June 16, and purchased thirty-five acres of farmland. He began teaching school. Joseph Smith wrote to Emma from Greenville, Indiana, and expressed his displeasure over McLellin's marriage:

> I am not pleased to hear that William Mclelin [McLellin] has come back and disobeyed the voice of him who is altogether Lovely for a woman. I am astonished at Sister Emaline [Emeline

---

56. *History of the Church*, 1:226. This report, which is not mentioned in the minutes, was composed in 1843 after McLellin was out of the church. Its authors may have wished to stress his inferiority relative to Joseph. For our purposes, the account confirms that McLellin was better educated than most. Cannon and Cook, *Far West Record*, 26-28. See Mark R. Grandstaff, "Having More Learning Than Sense: William E. McLellin and the Book of Commandments Revisited," *Dialogue: A Journal of Mormon Thought* 26 (Winter 1993): 23-48; John-Charles Duffy, "Reinventing McLellin: A Historiographical Review," and William D. Russell, "Portrait of a 'True Believer' in Original Mormonism," in Larson and Passey, *William E. McLellin Papers*, 83-104, 105-36.

57. 1835 D&C 22:1; LDS 68:8, 11-12; RLDS 68:1.

58. William E. McLellin to "beloved relatives," Aug. 4, 1832, qtd. in Shipps and Welch, *Journals of William E. McLellin*, 82: "On the 26th of April I was married to a young Lady by the name of Emiline Miller ... the 4th day after I first even hinted to subject to my partner."

Miller] yet I cannot belive she is not a worthy Sister. I hope She will <find> him true and kind to her but have no reason to expect it his conduct merits the disapprobation of every true follower of Christ but this is a painful subject I hope you will excuse my warmth of feeling in mentioning this subject.[59]

Seven weeks later, Joseph was still upset at McLellin. He told William W. Phelps in a July 31 letter that the man who had left Ohio without specific permission should only be accepted into "fellowship & communion" if he "fill[ed] his mission to the South countries according to the commandment of Jesus Christ, I cite your minds to thise saying he that loveth Father or Mother wife & Children more than me is not worthy of me thus saith the Lord."[60] Joseph's frustration continued to simmer.

Four months later, on December 3, Joseph Smith was back in Kirtland. "Held a conference in the Evening," he wrote. "Br Jese [Gause] and … William Mclelen [McLellin] was excommunicated from the church &c."[61] As dramatic as it sounds, the excommunication proceedings were held in absentia while McLellin, who had absconded to Missouri, took a leading part that same night in a "Council of High Priests," unaware of any trouble in Kirtland.[62] On the other hand, Jesse Gause had deserted his mission in Pennsylvania, leaving his companion, Zebedee Coltrin, on August 20, 1832, never to be heard from again.[63]

Despite the seriousness of the excommunication, McLellin continued his involvement in the church as if nothing had happened.

---

59. Joseph Smith to Emma Smith, June 6, 1832, Matthew C. Godfrey, et al., *The Joseph Smith Papers: Documents* (Salt Lake City: Church Historian's Press, 2013), 2: 251, 256; terminal punctuation and initial capitals added.

60. Joseph Smith to William W. Phelps, July 31, 1832, in ibid., 262.

61. Dean C. Jessee, Mark Ashurst-McGee, and Richard L. Jensen, eds., *The Joseph Smith Papers: Journals* (Salt Lake City: Church Historian's Press, 2008), 1:10.

62. Cannon and Cook, *Far West Record*, 57.

63. Zebedee Coltrin Journal, 1832-1833, LDS Church History Library: "Brother Jesse <& I> After praying with & for each other parted in the fellowship of the Gospel of our Lord & Saviour Jesus Christ."

It is not known how the excommunication was resolved, but the chastised elder was soon called to the Twelve, raising a question about whether McLellin ever even knew he had been disciplined.

Thomas B. Marsh

Thomas Baldwin Marsh was born in Acton, near Boston, Massachusetts, on November 1, 1800, to James and Mary ("Molly") Law Marsh.[64] When he was seven, his mother died and his father moved to Westmoreland, New Hampshire. Unhappy there, Thomas took the drastic step of running away from home at age fourteen, getting as far as Chester, Vermont, where someone hired him on as a farmhand. He stayed until he was old enough to move to New York City, where a young woman two years older than he caught his eye. He married Elizabeth Godkin on his twentieth birthday, and over the next seven years, beginning in 1821, they would begin raising a family with the first of many children. After Thomas's father died in 1822, the couple moved back to Thomas's place of origin, where he worked in a foundry in Boston for six years. They affiliated with the Methodist Church, but disagreed with some of its doctrines and said they looked forward to the establishment of a purer church that would replace the existing order.

While traveling in upstate New York in the summer of 1829, Marsh heard about Joseph Smith after passing through Palmyra. He turned around and returned to Palmyra to investigate. In a brief autobiography, he wrote:

> I returned back westward and found Martin Harris at the [Grandin] printing office, in Palmyra, where the first sixteen pages of the Book of Mormon had just been struck off, the proof sheet of which I obtained from the printer and took with me. As soon as Martin Harris found out my intentions he took me to the house of Joseph Smith, sen. ... Here I found Oliver Cowdery, who gave me

---

64. *Vital Records of Acton Massachusetts to the Year 1850* (Boston: New England Historic Genealogical Society, 1923), 81. Marsh gave his own birth year as 1799.

all the information concerning the book I desired. After staying there two days I started for Charleston, Mass., highly pleased with the information I had obtained concerning the new found book.[65]

Marsh corresponded with Cowdery, telling him he would like to know more. "He wishes to hear from us and know of our wellfare," Cowdery wrote to Joseph Smith. "He says he has talked conside[r]able to some respecting ou[r] work."[66] One of the people who was most enthusiastic about the book, Thomas mentioned, was his own wife. In July 1830 he ran an advertisement in a Boston newspaper. "SEVERAL Copies of this work have recently arrived here, and on perusing it, it appears to have belonged to the ancient inhabitants of this country," the ad read. "The above work contains 588 pages and may be purchased by calling on the Subscriber, 1 door from Water Street, in Joiner street, Charlestown, or at Charles Ellms' Bookstore, corner of Court and Market Street, Boston."[67]

Even more surprising, after Marsh had run the last advertisement on August 28, he loaded his family into a wagon and moved them to the Palmyra/Manchester area, arriving at the home of Joseph Smith Sr. early in September. He later said he was baptized in Cayuga Lake by David Whitmer, but he probably meant Seneca Lake near the Whitmer farm. After his baptism, he was ordained an elder by Oliver Cowdery. Joseph Smith received a revelation for Marsh from Jesus Christ. It is significant enough to quote at length:

> Thomas, my son, blessed are you because of your faith in my work. Behold you have had many afflictions because of your

---

65. "History of Thos. Baldwin Marsh," *Deseret News*, Mar. 24, 1858, 18.

66. Oliver Cowdery to Joseph Smith Jr., Nov. 6, 1829, transcribed in 1832 into Joseph Smith Letterbook 1:8, LDS Church History Library.

67. "The Book of Mormon," *Free Press*, Boston, July 16, 1830, 3. The advertisements continued to appear in the subsequent issues of the newspaper: July 23, 30; Aug. 7, 13, 20, 28, 1830. See Appendix 3.

family: nevertheless I will bless you, and your family: yea, your little ones; and the day cometh that they will believe and know the truth and be one with you in my church.

Lift up your heart and rejoice for the hour of your mission is come; and your tongue shall be loosed; and you shall declare glad tidings of great joy unto this generation. You shall declare the things which have been revealed to my servant Joseph Smith, jr. You shall begin to preach from this time forth; yea, to reap in the field which is white already to be burned: therefore thrust in your sickle with all your soul; and your sins are forgiven you; and you shall be laden with sheaves upon your back, for the laborer is worthy of his hire. Wherefore your family shall live.

Behold, verily I say unto you, go from them only for a little time, and declare my word, and I will prepare a place for them: yea, I will open the hearts of the people and they will receive you. And I will establish a church by your hand; and you shall strengthen them and prepare them against the time when they shall be gathered. Be patient in afflictions, revile not against those that revile. Govern your house in meekness, and be steadfast.

Behold I say unto you, that you shall be a physician unto the church, but not unto the world, for they will not receive you. Go your way whithersoever I will, and it shall be given you by the Comforter what you shall do, and whither you shall go. Pray always, lest you enter into temptation, and lose your reward. Be faithful unto the end and, lo, I am with you. These words are not of man nor of men, but of me, even Jesus Christ, your Redeemer, by the will of the Father. Amen.[68]

Elizabeth gave birth to a son in March 1831 in Canandaigua, a town south of Manchester. As a sign of their investment in the new faith, they named their son Nephi. Thomas was ordained a high priest in June, and after a year and a half they moved 800 miles southwest to Jackson County, Missouri, to join a community of church members that had moved there from Colesville, New

---

68. 1835 D&C 53 (LDS 31; RLDS 30).

York. Elizabeth bore twins about the time of the conflict in Jackson County; she traveled with the other Mormon refugees across the Missouri River into Clay County at the end of 1833. In Clay County, Thomas supported his family by farming and teaching school. He was among those who received the members of Zion's Camp when the amateur Mormon soldiers arrived in June 1834. In July he became a member of the Clay County High Council.

William Smith

Historian and educator Paul M. Edwards, second-great-grandson of Joseph Smith, caught the essence of William Smith's character when he wrote: "William B. Smith was a difficult man. Like so many who feel denied power and recognition, he was probably best described as being his own worst enemy. ... William had the habit of saying what was on his mind, and as a very active and concerned man, he was often in the midst of controversy."[69] A second biographer, Kyle R. Walker, presented a similar evaluation: "By all accounts, William B. Smith was a complex person who wrestled with insecurities and fits of passion that sometimes overrode his noble desires and family loyalty. To an outsider he could be an enigma."[70] The very thing that makes William's early life the easiest to track is the same thing that would later contribute to his ongoing disputes and clashes: he was the brother of the prophet.

He was specifically the fifth son of Joseph Sr. and Lucy Mack Smith, born in Royalton, Vermont, on March 13, 1811.[71] His family moved through Vermont and New Hampshire to a New York farm, during which time he had few educational opportunities. When not working on the farm, he was more likely to be hunting

---

69. Paul M. Edwards, "William B. Smith: The Persistent 'Pretender,'" *Dialogue: A Journal of Mormon Thought* 18 (Summer 1985): 128.

70. Kyle R. Walker, "William B. Smith," in *United by Faith: The Joseph Sr. and Lucy Mack Smith Family*, ed. Kyle R. Walker (American Fork: Covenant Communications, 2005), 247.

71. Anderson, *Lucy's Book*, 265.

or fishing than sitting in a schoolroom. He later acknowledged that he "was quite wild and inconsiderate, paying little attention to religion of any kind." After his neighbors heard that his brother had dug up some gold plates with religious content, William "got into a great many quarrels and contentions with the young men of the neighborhood on the same account, but invariably came off victorious."[72] In 1883 William testified about the divine mission of his brother and the truth of the Book of Mormon in a semi-autobiography intended to provide readers with a short account of the Restoration.[73]

On June 9, 1830, when the church was two months old and numbered some twenty-five members, William attended its first conference in Fayette, New York, and was baptized by David Whitmer, as were his siblings Katharine and Don Carlos Smith and acquaintance Orrin Porter Rockwell.[74] Joseph Smith received revelations in December and January that members should assemble "at the Ohio."[75] Following the lead of Joseph and his father in late January, a company of about eighty church members departed three months later about May 1, 1831, by canal boat under Lucy Smith's leadership. Nineteen-year-old William was the only child Lucy mentioned in the group, although the family also included Don Carlos and daughters Sophronia, Katherine, and young Lucy. Mother Smith thought William had been ordained to the priesthood prior to the trip. She was probably mistaken in this.[76] William himself mentioned the trip but not any details.[77] About May 6 they arrived in Buffalo. Two days later they embarked on the steamboat

---

72. William Smith, *William Smith on Mormonism* (Lamoni, IA: Herald Steam Book and Job Office, 1883), 13.

73. Ibid. 12-14.

74. Ibid., 15-16.

75. For the command to move to Ohio, see LDS D&C 37:3, 38:32; RLDS D&C 37:2, 38:7.

76. Anderson, *Lucy's Book*, 511.

77. *William Smith on Mormonism*, 18.

Niagara across Lake Erie, and after a brief stop in Canada they arrived at Fairport Harbor, Ohio, about May 11.

On October 5, he was ordained a teacher by his brother Joseph in Hiram, Ohio.[78] When William was ordained a priest twenty days later by Oliver Cowdery, his license read: "This certifies that William Smith, a member of the Church of Christ, organized on the 6th of April, 1830, has been ordained a Priest of said Church, by authority of a conference held in Orange, Cuyahoga Co., Ohio, on the 25th day of October, A. D., 1831. This is therefore to give him authority to act in the office of his calling, according to the articles and covenants of said Church."[79]

Like other future apostles, William would make sacrifices, despite his place of privilege as the founder's brother. There would be no more lying around and watching the clouds blow by while waiting for fish to nibble. After landing in Ohio, he would join the explosion of missionary activity from elders fanning out to the east with copies of the Book of Mormon under their arms, actively recruiting converts and being met with gratitude in some instances and acrimony in others.

---

78. Anderson, *Lucy's Book*, 511n1.

79. Backman, *Heavens Resound,* 110. William's priest license is in the Community of Christ Archives, Independence, Missouri.

2. MISSIONARIES

Soon after his baptism and ordination as a priest in the spring of 1831, Luke Johnson was sent on a mission with Robert Rathburn through central Ohio. They baptized enough people in Chippewa, sixty miles south of Kirtland, to be able to organize a branch of the church.[1] After returning home, Luke was immediately sent out again in May, this time with Sidney Rigdon to proselytize among Rigdon's relatives in the Pittsburgh area. Luke recalled that Rigdon's "mother and his oldest brother, also several others in that neighborhood," were baptized and a branch organized.[2]

Thomas Marsh, after his June ordination as a high priest, was assigned to travel with Selah J. Griffin to preach in Missouri. After completing their assignment, Marsh was sent back out again in January 1832 with Ezra Thayer to New York. This became a common pattern for converts who showed any promise as speakers, to be sent out before they really knew much about the church's doctrines or policies. Grouped in twos, usually one more experienced elder with a newer convert, they fanned out over the eastern and southern states without funds or itinerary. If they baptized enough people, they organized a branch in that location. Since branch members knew even less than the missionaries, it became necessary for the missionaries to revisit the same locations, thereby providing a conduit with church headquarters. They also engaged

---

1. "History of Luke Johnson (by Himself)," *Deseret News*, May 26, 1858, 57.
2. Ibid.

in limited correspondence like Paul in the New Testament, who traveled and wrote to congregations he thought needed to be corrected for engaging in unapproved practices.

The message that the missionaries carried with them, which they delivered with a sense of urgency, was that Jesus Christ would soon return to earth to establish his millennial reign in America. The Book of Mormon was held up as evidence that Jesus was beginning his final ministry. Curiously, the Book of Mormon was seldom cited for its theological content, but rather as an exhibit to show there was a representative of Christ on earth, meaning Joseph Smith, who was bringing forth revelations.[3] Otherwise the missionaries sounded like Protestant ministers, only with a millennial emphasis. The missionaries spoke with a resounding "voice of warning," that was to be proclaimed "by the mouths of my disciples, whom I have chosen in these last days," as the preface to the Book of Commandments worded it.[4]

One of the most experienced missionaries in late 1831 was Joseph Smith's brother Samuel. He was paired with the recent convert William McLellin to serve a mission to the eastern states, and they departed on November 16, 1831, beginning in the eastern part of Ohio. Unfortunately their progress was marred by a serious cold that settled into William's lungs, resulting in his being bedridden at Weathersfield and feeling like fate had overtaken him. Joseph Smith saw it as an opportunity to demonstrate healing faith. The missionaries were still close enough to Kirtland that several church leaders were able to travel to their abode in December and bless William to be well. "Brothers Joseph [Smith], Hiram [Smith], Reynolds [Cahoon] & Lyman [Johnson] visited me," William wrote, "and

---

3. Jan Shipps and John W. Welch, eds., *The Journals of William E. McLellin, 1831-1836* (Provo and Urbana: *BYU Studies* and University of Illinois Press, 1994), 6-8, 16, 19-23.

4. Book of Commandments 1:1; Parley P. Pratt, *A Voice of Warning* (New York: W. Sandford, 1837).

Wedns the 28th in the morning Brother Joseph came to my bed side and laid his hands upon me and prayed for me and I was healed so that I got up and eat breakfast."[5] William was able to travel back to Hiram at the end of December. All told, even despite his sickness, he and Samuel baptized seven people on their short trip outside of church headquarters.[6] Between December 1831 and February 1832, when William would leave on another excursion, he baptized an additional nine children and one adult male in Kirtland.

Committed to the cause but sometimes over-confident, McLellin would later claim he received a revelation that equaled Joseph Smith's. He denied the account in the Doctrine and Covenants (discussed in chapter 1) that he had been challenged to write a revelation and had failed to. On the contrary, he said, he was told by Joseph when they were alone on January 18, 1832, that God had authorized him to receive a communication, which he did. William said he not only received and recorded the revelation but that Joseph admiringly validated it, saying, "Brother William, that is the mind and the will of God, and as much a revelation as I ever received in my life."[7] McLellin's version is probably spurious. Not only did he fail to record this signal experience in his journal, it is strange that after such an impressive accomplishment he was chastised a week later at a January 25 conference in Amherst for "murmurings." Even so, his murmurings were not severe enough to prevent his being reassigned to a mission to the South with Luke Johnson:

> Therefore verily I say unto my servant William E. McLel[l]in I revoke the commission which I gave unto him, to go unto the eastern countries, and I give unto him a new commission and a new commandment, in the which I the Lord chasteneth him for

---

5. Shipps and Welch, *Journals of William E. McLellin*, 67.

6. Ibid., 68, 413.

7. William E. McLellin to Orson Pratt, Apr. 29, 1854, qtd. in *The William E. McLellin Papers, 1854-1880*, eds. Stan Larson and Samuel J. Passey (Salt Lake City: Signature Books, 2007), 434.

the murmurings of his heart; and he sinned, nevertheless I forgive
him and say unto him again, go ye into the south countries; and
let my servant Luke Johnson go with him and proclaim the things
which I have commanded them, calling on the name of the Lord
for the comforter, which shall teach them all things that are expe-
dient for them, praying always that they faint not; and inasmuch as
they do this, I will be with them even unto the end. Behold this
is the will of the Lord your God concerning you; even so. Amen.[8]

McLellin accepted this rebuke and went on his mission, maybe
even liking the idea of traveling to the southern states. Being a
Southerner himself, he may not have seen the change of venue as a
punishment. Joseph Smith "was acknowledged President of the High
Priesthood" at the Amherst conference "and hands were laid on him
by Elder Sidney Rigdon, who sealed upon his head the blessings
which he [Smith] had formerly received."[9] On February 1, John and
Elsa Johnson hosted a farewell party for the departing missionaries,
and the next day Luke and William left in a southeastern direction,
although ultimately only visiting Ohio and Pennsylvania.[10]

In the diary William kept, he described a full schedule of preaching. The missionaries prefaced their remarks by inviting people to
give heed to "the fulness of the Gospel." They said the Christian
world had been instructed in many precious truths but that there
were more to come. The missionaries performed a healing in Weathersfield, Ohio, when Luke "prayed for" Elizabeth Everhart. He

laid hands upon her and she was immediately healed. Monday
eve[ning] old Mother Edwards told us she had had a vision and she
knew the book of Mormon was a divine revelation. She had a foot
and leg which had been struck with the num palsy. She believed

8. 1835 D&C 87:2; LDS D&C 75:6-9; RLDS D&C 75:2.
9. Elden J. Watson, comp. and ed., *The Orson Pratt Journals* (Salt Lake City:
Elden J. Watson, 1975), 11.
10. Shipps and Welch, *Journals of William E. McLellin*, 70.

we were the servants of God & requested us to pray for her. We did so and she was immediately healed.[11]

However, William was afflicted by doubts that month (as discussed in chapter 1).[12] Later in the year, he wrote that in Middlebury his "health became impaired," which caused him to feel discouraged and confused.[13] Middlebury marked the end of Luke's mission as well. In his short autobiography, he wrote that after his companion hired on as a store clerk and quit proselytizing, he "preferring not to proceed alone" and so "returned to the town of Hiram." Luke was given a new companion, Seymour Brunson.[14]

The missionaries served together for two months. Brunson recorded that "on the eleventh of March, 1832, I started with brother Luke Johnson unto the south country, and on the twenty second, we left our brethren at Shalersville, and began to preach and baptize, and arrived at Windsor, Lawrence county, Ohio, on the ninth of May, having witnessed several instances of the Lord's healing power. At this place we built up a church, which made in all that we had baptized, fifty three members. I then returned to Kirtland with brother Luke."[15]

Notice the rapidity with which the missionaries founded yet another congregation and the free-wheeling quality, seemingly implying an open-ended schedule. Brunson's upbeat report gives the impression the missionaries may have felt they had earned the right to return home; more likely, after experiencing some success, the notion of continuing farther into the unknown was daunting.

---

11. Ibid., 71.

12. Ibid., 73.

13. William E. McLellin to "beloved relatives," Aug. 4, 1832, Community of Christ Archives, Independence, rpt. in Shipps and Welch, *Journals of William E. McLellin*, 82.

14. "History of Luke Johnson," 57.

15. Seymour Brunson to "dear brethren in Christ," May 6, 1833, *Evening and the Morning Star*, June 1833, 100.

Whatever romantic notions they might have had about traveling to distant lands and converting unknown people, it was fine to venture twenty-five miles from home but when the evenings turned chilly, it may have dampened whatever enthusiasm they had experienced at home, surrounded by family and hearth. Empty stomachs, icy roads, and makeshift beds would make anyone think that a delay for slightly warmer weather would be advisable. Even though many nineteenth-century travelers relied on the good will of villagers as they traveled between cities, some who lingered too long or spoke of new scripture to rival the Bible quickly wore out their welcome.

Despite these challenges to travel, Luke's brother Lyman Johnson would outstrip all the missionaries in endurance. He and Orson Pratt first struck out together on February 3, 1832, without anything in their possession but a "change of clothing."[16] They traveled to Mercer County, Pennsylvania, on February 8, and stopped at the home of Benjamin Stokely in Cool Spring Township. At early candlelight they preached to a small gathering and told them they were sometimes called Mormonites, after the ancient prophet who descended from Lehi, a Jerusalem patriarch who "came across the water into South America." "The last battle that was fought among these parties," they explained, occurred "on the *very ground* where the [gold] plates [of the Book of Mormon] were found, but it had been a running battle, for they commenced at the Isthmus of Darien [Panama] and ended" not far from Pennsylvania in Manchester, New York. According to Stokely, Lyman testified that an angel had personally shown him the Book of Mormon plates, the same as the witnesses to the Book of Mormon:

He has left his father, mother, brothers and sisters, the farm and neighborhood of friends, to declare the will of God, and the

---

16. Watson, *Orson Pratt Journals*, 12.

revelation of John who saw the angel flying through Heaven—An angel brought the Mormonite Bible and laid it before him (the speaker;) he therefore *knows* these things to be true. Being sent to call on all to repent—he has come to fulfill the commands of Heaven: he has cleared his skirts of our blood.[17]

Stokely was amazed by what he heard:

One of the young men called himself Lyman Johnston [Johnson], from Portage county, Ohio. The other was called Arson [Orson] Pratt; no fixed place of abode. They were going North East, intending to preach the gospel to every kindred, tongue and nation:— They appeared to have very little learning, to be sincere in all they said. They had good manners—had been well raised—were decent and unassuming in every thing I saw, or heard them say.[18]

The missionaries also preached at the courthouse in Franklin, located in the adjacent county to the east. Again the elders expounded their message about Joseph Smith and the gold plates, the prophet Lehi, and the last battle. They said their founder, Joseph Smith, "repented of his sins" but had "not attached himself to any party of Christians, owing to the numerous divisions among them, and [that] being in doubt what his duty was, he had recourse [to] prayer." To modern readers, this may sound like the canonized account of the First Vision, which Joseph Smith would write about in the late 1830s.[19] But in this case, the narrative went into a rehearsal

---

17. Stokely wrote to the *Western Press* (Mercer County, PA), "As the press is a medium through which to communicate information for public use, I have sent the following for that purpose." Though the original newspaper is not available, it was republished subsequently in "The Mormonites," *The American Sentinel*, Feb. 25, 1832, 2, emphasis retained, courtesy of Rick Grunder. The article was republished as "The Orators of Mormon," *Catholic Telegraph* (Cincinnati), Apr. 14, 1832, 204-05, emphasis in original.

18. *The American Sentinel*, Feb. 25, 1832, 2.

19. Orson Pratt would be the first to explain the First Vision to the public in a Scottish missionary tract, *An Interesting Account of Several Remarkable Visions*

of how an unnamed angel appeared to Joseph to show him where the ancient records had been buried. "After retiring to bed one night," the missionaries explained, Joseph was "visited by an Angel" and was "directed to proceed to a hill in the neighborhood where he would find a stone box containing a quantity of Gold plates."

A Venango County newspaper reported:

> The balance of their discourse was on repentance, and quotations from our prophets to prove their doctrine, and the return of the Jews to Palestine, which was to be done by the gentile nations, accompanied with power from above, far superior to that which brought their fathers out of Egypt. They insisted that our Savior would shortly appear, and that there were some present who would see him on the earth—that they knew it—that they were not deceiving their hearers; that it was all true. They had one of their bibles with them, which was seen by some of our citizens who visited them.[20]

The focus on repentance and Joseph Smith's experiences offer a glimpse into the role Joseph's personal history played in shaping the message of the Mormon missionaries. A few months later, Joseph would write his earliest version of his conversion story: "I saw the Lord and he spake unto me saying Joseph <my son> thy sins are forgiven thee. go thy <way> walk in my statutes and keep my commandments behold I am the Lord of glory I was crucifyed for the world that all those who believe on my name may have Eternal life."[21]

After traversing the keystone state, Lyman and Orson looked for opportunities in New Jersey, then briefly visited New York City before concentrating their efforts in Vermont and New Hampshire.

and of the Late Discovery of Ancient American Records (Edinburgh: Ballantyne and Hughes, 1840).

20. "Mormonism," *Fredonia Censor*, Mar. 7, 1832, 4, rpt. from the Franklin, Pennsylvania, *Venango Democrat*.

21. Karen Lynn Davidson et al., *The Joseph Smith Papers: Histories* (Salt Lake City: Church Historian's Press, 2012), 1:13.

Like most of the other missionaries, they tended to avoid cities. If they could find accommodations in a village, they would remain long enough to preach and baptize all who were interested, then leave with a promise to return at a later date to ordain officers and organize a branch.

Their activities in Charleston, Vermont, were dramatically successful. They baptized future apostle Amasa Lyman and several men who would become famous colonizers in Utah: Winslow Farr and son Lorin and brothers William and Zerubbabel Snow. William recorded in the front of his journal for May 1832 that he "was baptised <on the 19th of may> under the hands of Lyman E Johnson at which time Brother Winslow Farr & his wife Olive (who had been healed of a Disease tha[t] had been upon her for ma[ny] years) & Sister Sherman was baptised."[22] The healing of Olive Farr attracted more than passing interest among the citizens of Charleston. Forty-five years later, this account appeared in the *Vermont Historical Gazetteer*:

> Orson Pratt and Lyman E. Johnson, Mormon priests, came to town in 1832, formed a large church from East Charleston and Brighton; but in a few short years this whole church with the exception of one who renounced the faith, gathered up their effects and removed to Missouri their "Promised Land." This sect professed to work miracles, heal the sick and performed all to the satisfaction of their followers. Their numbers were greatly increased through the faith of the people in the healing of a Mrs. Farr who on account of sickness had been unable to leave her bed for 3 years. After a season of prayer, the Mormon priests commanded her to "rise and walk"; upon which she immediately obeyed the injunction, declared herself healed, and the next day was baptized in the waters of the Clyde. After which she engaged

---

22. William Snow Journal, May 1832, L. Tom Perry Special Collections, Harold B. Lee Library, Brigham Young University, Provo.

in the busy avocations of active life during the remaining 3 or 4 years of her stay in Charleston.[23]

In the 1880s Edward Tullidge interviewed Lorin Farr about his early life. Lorin had since gained prominence as the mayor of Ogden, Utah. Tullidge wrote:

> In the spring of 1832, when Lorin was eleven years of age, in the month of May the family, for the first time, heard the gospel preached by Orson Pratt and Lyman E. Johnson. ... Orson Pratt commenced to preach to a crowded house, and told them the nature of his mission. ... Afterward Lyman Johnson arose and delivered one of the most powerful testimonies pertaining to the mission of Joseph Smith, and the great work of the last days, that Lorin ever heard. [Lyman] also said that he knew the Book of Mormon was true, for he had seen an angel and he had made this known unto him.[24]

Once again, Lyman added his own visionary experience to that of Joseph Smith. It is possible that this encounter with the supernatural was a factor in his selection as an apostle. A revelation on priesthood to Joseph Smith in 1835 would explain that "the twelve traveling councilors are called to be the Twelve Apostles, or special witnesses of the name of Christ in all the world."[25] In later years, people would read into that sentence an assumption that an apostle was someone who had experienced one of these transcendent moments and had seen Jesus or an angel.[26] Whatever the meaning

---

23. Abby Maria Hemenway, ed., *The Vermont Historical Gazetteer, a History of Each Town: Civil, Ecclesiastical, Biographical and Military* (Claremont, NH: Claremont Manufacturing Co., 1877), 13:116.

24. Edward W. Tullidge, "Biographies," in *Tullidge's Histories: Containing the History of All the Northern, Eastern and Western Counties of Utah, also the Counties of Southern Idaho* (Salt Lake City: Juvenile Instructor, 1889), 2:174–75.

25. LDS D&C 107:23

26. Utah Apostle Boyd K. Packer said people sometimes ask an inappropriate "question about the qualifications to stand as a witness for Christ. The question

was, Lyman fulfilled the expectation beyond the average member's experience with spirits and revelation.

One of the families Orson and Lyman baptized in Charleston was the Jacob and Sarah Lang family. It included their seventeen-year-old daughter, Sarah, who was born on May 6, 1815, in a New Hampshire town fortuitously called Lyman. Perhaps interpreted as an omen, she accepted the invitation to marry the man of the same name two years later on September 4, 1834, in Kirtland. Her twenty-one-year-old sister, Susan, would herself marry Zerubbabel Snow on October 2, 1833, in Charleston. He would become a missionary of some fame and participate in Zion's Camp. Years later in 1869, he would become the elected attorney general of Utah Territory.

Like missionaries today, the Mormon evangelists of the 1830s were young men with a future on their minds, who were anxious to start a family even though they felt called to spread the word of the millennial return of Christ. Despite their belief that Jesus would reinvent society, they lived day-to-day as people who were planning for a normal future. The Second Coming was relegated, to some degree, to the abstract in the face of a world that was making its own immediate demands on them.

One of the famous Snow brothers from Charleston, Erastus was only fourteen years old in 1832. He chose not to be baptized at the time but wrote in his journal that he believed the missionaries: "Brother[s] O[rson] & L[yman] came into town preaching the Gospel of Christ ... & I believed it & two of my elder brothers which were of age obeyed it. From this time I beg[a]n to mend my ways and prayed to God to soften the hearts of my parents that

---

they ask is, 'Have you seen Him?" He confirmed that his colleagues in the quorum had at times answered the question "under the prompting of the Spirit, on sacred occasions, when 'the Spirit beareth record,'" giving the impression that such experiences are not unusual and perhaps a requirement. Boyd K. Packer, "The Spirit Beareth Record," April 1971, *The Church of Jesus Christ of Latter-day Saints*, www.lds.org/general conference.

I might have the privilege of obeying the Gospel: at length my prayers were answered & I was baptised by <my Bro. William> in the town of Charleston on the third day of February AD 1833."[27]

In the town of Mooers, New York, an individual by the name of Ira Ames, age twenty-seven, was baptized. He joined over the objection of his wife, Charity, after he attended a church conference on August 10 in Benson, Vermont, where he heard "Orson Pratt, Lyman, Sylvester and others [who] spoke to us." He said they "unfolded new principle after new principle, glory after glory, until my soul was fed with fatness and I wept many tears of joy. And not to this day (1858) have I ever attended a conference where I enjoyed myself and my religion more than I did there."[28] Simeon Carter recorded his impression of the same meeting: "We met in conference the tenth of August: There were fourteen elders and several priests and teachers present. Great union dwelt among us; two were ordained to the priesthood; two others were ordained, one an elder, and the other a priest. Brethren, O. Pratt and L. Johnson, were there; they have planted three or four churches since last February, and have baptized in all about seventy."[29]

In an autobiographical sketch in his journal, the convert recalled that Lyman Johnson and Orson Pratt stayed at his house for three days, while his wife, who felt bitter about this arrangement,

> suddenly seized her infant Son and left the house, determined never to live with me again. She knew that the Methodist circuit preacher was at John Shadin's house about a mile from my house. When she reached the house they were at breakfast, the Doors all open, and the Methodist preacher Sat in such a manner that he saw my wife as she approached the kitchen door. He called aloud to her as she approached. "Ah Mrs. Ames, how is that Mormon

---

27. Erastus Snow Journal, 1832-33, LDS Church History Library.

28. Ira Ames, "Journal and Record of the Life and Family of Ira Ames," Aug. 1832, LDS Church History Library.

29. Simeon Carter to "Brother Sidney" Gilbert, n.d., *The Evening and the Morning Star*, Nov. 1832, 6.

husband of yours? If I had been to your house when those two fellows were there I would have cracked their heads together." <Slapping his hands together up over his head.> All this was said in a sneering, jeering mocking tone and manner. It had a powerful effect on the mind of my wife, who turned instantly about without speaking, and returned home. She told me she was convinced I was right, told me of the preacher[']s words and that she saw that he was full of a devilish Spirit.[30]

Charity was baptized in Lake Champlain by Orson Pratt. Interesting that she would change her mind so quickly, but no doubt her interpretation of the minister's demeanor was different than what we might conclude today in thinking someone had a bad spirit. In the microcosm of nineteenth-century religious experience, people had been taught to anticipate evil spirits and miracles, so the missionaries reinforced, rather than challenged, preconceived expectations. Their gospel message made sense, in part, because it had not been diluted by ambiguity or metaphor, and it was reassuring to those who responded to it.

In the Finger Lakes district of New York, Lyman baptized eight more converts in a town called Spafford, to bring the total to eighty-nine people he and Orson had converted during a ten-month mission.[31] Lyman returned home with Elder Hazen Aldrich in December, but Orson stayed on until February 1833 with William Snow and baptized another fifteen converts. Orson summarized his mission by writing that he and his companions "traveled on foot near 4,000 miles, attended 207 meetings mostly in places where they had not heard the word; baptized 104 persons and organized several new branches of the church."[32] Among their converts,

---

30. Ames, "Journal and Record," Aug. 1832. Ames placed the event in early August 1832, but it was more likely in October. See Watson, *Orson Pratt Journals*, 14. Angle brackets indicate a later superlinear addition.

31. Watson, *Orson Pratt Journals*, 12-14.

32. Ibid., 16.

two middle-aged men, Hazen Aldrich and Daniel S. Miles, would become church-wide presidents of the Seventy in a few years.[33]

William Smith was no less diligent in spreading the gospel message. He found that he could use his certificate of ordination as a cleric to open doors where people assumed a priest was a professional minister. In retrospect, he wrote: "I accordingly made several circuits into the country round about in order to declare unto [people] the truths of the gospel." In the fall of 1832, he and Samuel, another brother of Joseph Smith, traveled "into an adjoining county," then he ventured out with brother Don Carlos Smith.[34] Enjoying the company of siblings, William then joined another brother, Hyrum, on a three-week mission to Erie County, Pennsylvania, in November-December 1832, during which time they baptized twenty-three people.[35] It must have been on this trip that William met his future wife, Caroline Amanda Grant, in Elk Creek Township in the far northwest corner of the state, sixty-five miles from Kirtland.[36] She was a sister of Jedediah Grant, who became the fiery counselor to Brigham Young in Utah.[37] Hyrum and William returned to Kirtland on December 16. Three days later Lyman Johnson ordained William an elder.[38]

---

33. Ibid., 12.

34. William Smith, *William Smith on Mormonism* (Lamoni, IA: Herald Steam Book and Job Office, 1882), 20-21.

35. "Extracts of Letters from the Elders Abroad," *Evening and the Morning Star*, Feb. 1833, 5-6.

36. Caroline Grant was born January 22, 1814, in Windsor, New York, one of four daughters of Joshua Grant and Athalia Howard Grant, who were married in 1804 in Sullivan County.

37. Jedediah Morgan Grant was one of eight sons of Joshua and Athalia Grant, born on February 21, 1816, in Windsor. He was baptized by John Boynton or Evan Greene in March 1833 at Sherman's Corners, Pennsylvania. His parents and siblings presumably were baptized in Erie County in 1832 or 1833, the year the family moved to Chagrin, Ohio, five miles from Kirtland.

38. Fred C. Collier and William S. Harwell, eds., *Kirtland Council Minute Book* (Salt Lake City: Colliers Publishing, 1996), 3. In between his mission assignments with his brothers, William mentioned that he served "several other" short preaching assignments "into different parts of the country."

A month after John Boynton's twenty-first birthday in 1832, he and Zebedee Coltrin departed on November 19 to the fruitful area of northwestern Pennsylvania. For a short mission, not quite two months in length.[39] But no sooner had they returned home on January 5, 1833, than they were sent back to Pennsylvania once again. Upon returning from the second jaunt to the neighboring state, Boynton was told to head out with Evan M. Greene to Maine,[40] stopping in Bradford, Massachusetts, along the way to see Boynton's parents.[41]

In January 1834, the Massachusetts-born missionary reported on his activities in *The Evening and the Morning Star*, the church newspaper that had been relocated to Kirtland, and gave evidence of his education and deep familiarity with the Bible, even if his prose was somewhat strained:

> I improve a few moments to inform you that I am well, that the Lord is present with me; his Spirit warms my heart; gives life to my soul; is my friend among enemies; my joy among friends; my comforter when alone; my companion in trouble; brings a hope like an anchor; makes the crown look near; and insures the victory by an endurance of faith unto the end. ... I have baptized about forty in this section, and there is more convinced of the truth, but are still lingering on the threshold of the church, and I think the Lord will gather some of them into his kingdom.
>
> Brother E. M. Green labored with me from the 16th of Jan. 1833, till the October following. While we were together we baptized about one hundred and thirty. ... Finally brethren, pray for me that I may have words of wisdom, and a door of utterance to declare the whole counsel of God, and rightly divide the word of truth; giving to every man his portion in due season. For my

---

39. Zebedee Coltrin journal, June 15, 1832-Mar. 23, 1833, LDS Church History Library.

40. "Brother John F Boynton & Ev[a]n Green[e] Started for the east to preach the gospel of Christ" (Coltrin journal, following the Jan. 15, 1833, entry).

41. Evan M. Greene journal, 1833-1835, July 13, 1833, Church History Library.

determination is, with the stick of Joseph in one hand, and the stick of Judah in the other, to labor diligently in this world that my skirts may be clear from the blood of all men, and I stand acquitted before the bar of God.[42]

The speed and ease with which the missionaries were able to create new branches where there had been no church members at all—converting hundreds in a few months—speaks to how much people longed for what they called primitive Christianity, devoid of pretense. It is interesting to see that a limited number of missionaries were reshuffled into various combinations from month to month. Like the others, Evan Greene would be on the road again by February 1833, serving his third mission since converting at age sixteen in 1831.[43]

Even though church officials in Kirtland had excommunicated McLellin (see chapter 1), he confidently left on another mission on January 28, 1833, this time with Parley P. Pratt. It was two months after his unexplained expulsion. If he repented and was reinstated, it was a quick turn-around. His temporary absence did not seem to affect his preaching because, stopping at several Missouri and Illinois towns, he and Pratt baptized fourteen people before returning to Independence in June 1833. Back home in Missouri, he would become an eyewitness to the mob violence that swept through Jackson County, as he and other leading men went into hiding to avoid arrest. When they re-emerged during a period of relative calm, they were apprehended but soon released on the promise they would leave Jackson County. The refugees crossed the Missouri River to the north into Clay County.[44]

---

42. John F. Boynton to "Brethren in the Lord," Jan. 20, 1834, *The Evening and the Morning Star*, Feb. 1834, 134.

43. Steven C. Harper, "Missionaries in the American Religious Marketplace: Mormon Proselyting in the 1830s," *Journal of Mormon History* 24, no. 2 (1998): 23. https://familysearch.org.

44. See Larry C. Porter, "The Odyssey of William Earl McLellin: Man of

Before the Missouri troubles, William Smith, John Boynton, Evan Greene, and others established small churches in nearby Erie County in northwest Pennsylvania. On Sunday, February 3, at a Springfield, Pennsylvania, service, William "spoke in tongues with much power" and was joined by Amos Hodges two weeks later. Amos was the son of Curtis Hodges Sr., who had joined the church and taken up preaching on his own, accompanied by his sons Ervine, Stephen, Amos, William, and Curtis Jr. While things were going so well in Erie County, William's thoughts—surprisingly by today's standards for missionaries—turned to courting Caroline Grant, whom he married on Valentine's Day, February 14. They traveled home to Kirtland for a honeymoon, but because of a shortage of funds were compelled to live temporarily with William's parents.[45] They enjoyed associating with other believers for a time in an environment where Mormons were considered normal and were nearly as numerous as non-Mormons. On June 21, 1833, William was ordained a high priest by Sidney Rigdon. William would reconnect with the Hodges family at Nauvoo in 1845.[46]

By now, Lyman Johnson was back in Kirtland for a three-month interlude. He and Orson Pratt left on March 26 for their second assignment to Vermont, this time to visit the churches they had previously founded. If Lyman kept a journal, it has not survived, but the records of his companions did. Pratt and John Murdock both wrote more about themselves than their companions.[47]

Diversity, 1806-83," in Shipps and Welch, *Journals of William E. McLellin*, 307-10.
    45. Kyle R. Walker, "William B. Smith," in *United by Faith: The Joseph Sr. and Lucy Mack Smith Family*, ed. Kyle R. Walker (American Fork: Covenant Communications, 2005), 255. Daughter Mary Jane was born in Kirtland on January 7, 1835, and daughter Caroline was born there in August 1836.
    46. Collier and Harwell, *Kirtland Council Minute Book*, 16. William's uncle John Smith was ordained a high priest at the same meeting.
    47. John Murdock, born July 15, 1792, in Kortwright, New York, was baptized in November 1830 in Kirtland, Ohio, by Parley P. Pratt. His missionary journal adds to the knowledge of Lyman Johnson's and Orson Pratt's activities. Murdock participated in Zion's Camp and was a high councilman, bishop at

Still, we know that in concert with the others, Johnson preached in homes and schoolhouses, baptized people, administered to the sick, attended branch conferences, and more generally defended members from the criticism of Protestant ministers.

On their way to Vermont, they visited Jamestown and Silver Creek near Buffalo, then turned eastward toward the Finger Lakes.[48] In Geneseo they found a hotbed of dissent that had developed in less than a year from the establishment of the branch. The point of contention was the vision of a multi-tiered heaven that Joseph Smith and Sidney Rigdon had recently announced. John Murdock and his companion joined the other elders to help discipline the president of the branch, Ezra Landen, a high priest who denied the validity of the vision.[49] It was only after Landen was threatened with expulsion that he acknowledged his fault and was allowed to retain his presiding office. As John Murdock recorded it:

> Bro. L. Johnson Came to me Said he & O Pratt had visited Ezra Land[en] in Geneseo who denied the vision & other Revelations & other members Joined him & they [Johnson and Pratt] wanted to get help. Br Rich & my Self went with him[.] We met in conference with Br Landing at 6 Oclock P.M 4 High Priests forming the council Viz O. Pratt. L. Johnson Leonard Rich & myself Presided in the meeting.

The hearing was held in May. Elder Pratt "laid the case before

---

Nauvoo and in Salt Lake City, mission president in Australia, and a patriarch in Utah. S. Reed Murdock, *John Murdock: His Life and His Legacy* (Layton, UT: Summerwood Publishers, 2000).

48. Zebedee Coltrin journal, Apr. 4, 12, 17, 1833, LDS Church History Library.

49. Landen's brief career as a Mormon was significant. He and Elder Daniel Bowen baptized John Young (Brigham's father) and sons Phineas and Joseph, along with 18-20 people in the Avon and Genesee area in the fall of 1832. See Lyman D. Platt, "Early Branches of the Church of Jesus Christ of Latter-day Saints, 1830-1850," *Nauvoo Journal*, 1991, 4, 12; Orson F. Whitney, *The Life of Heber C. Kimball*, 2nd ed. (Salt Lake City: Bookcraft, 1945), 24.

the conference [council] by stating that Br Landing [Landen] said the vision was of the Devil & he believed it no more than he believed the devil was crucified & many like things." Brother Landen spoke on his own behalf and mentioned the sacrifices and hardships he had endured as a Mormon. John Murdock responded that he and others had also made sacrifices but that everyone had to remain faithful. The next morning, "the church met according to appointment Br Orson led in expl[a]nation of the vision & other revelation[s] followed by my Self & Br Lyman."[50] Landen asked forgiveness, which was granted. A defection averted, the missionaries had, in a sense, performed a role that showed them to be following in the footsteps of the New Testament missionary St. Paul.

Johnson and Pratt arrived in New Hampshire in early June and worked together in the Bath area until mid-month, then went their separate ways to preach in different towns, occasionally holding meetings together. At Charleston, Pratt recorded that when the branch met in prayer, "the Lord heard their prayers & moved upon his servant Lyman by the power of the Holy Ghost to seal them up unto eternal life & after this the Brethren arose one by one & said that they knew that their names were sealed in the Lamb's Book of life & they all did bear this glorious testimony save two or three."[51]

The missionaries regrouped at summer's end in Utica to travel together to Kirtland. On September 16 they "took the stage until

---

50. John Murdock, "An Abridged Record of the Life of John Murdock, Taken from His Journal by Himself," 27-28, LDS Church History Library. The Vision of the Three Degrees of Glory (LDS and RLDS D&C 76) was published in the July 1832 issue of *The Evening and the Morning Star* as "A Vision." Murdock went to Warrensville and Orange and mentioned that the brethren "had Just received the Revilation [sic] called the vision." Lyndon Cook, *Revelations of the Prophet Joseph Smith*, 311n1: "Members of the Church during this period did not confuse 'The Vision' (section 76) with the 'First Vision' because the 1820 event was not generally known until after 1842."

51. Watson, *Orson Pratt Journals*, 24.

we came near to Geneseo. We then went to visit the church in that place and some of the brethren received not our teachings, among whom was Brother Landen, a high priest." History was repeating itself. It may seem odd that President Landen would slip into such an encore performance of backsliding, but this was a typical pattern that the missionaries themselves sometimes fell into: reform and recidivism, defensiveness and humility, re-assertion of rightness followed by a final conclusion. Often this would happen over the space of an hour in a single meeting, and other times it took place over several days or weeks. The record is littered with references to "unchristian conduct," a "rebellious spirit," followed by "meekness and humility" and finally a "satisfactory" reconciliation.

On September 22, Pratt "preached upon the gathering of the Jews" and explained the grandeur of the three degrees of glory. Six days later, he and Johnson were back in Kirtland, having this time traveled "about 2,000 miles, attended 125 Meetings, and baptized upwards of fifty persons."[52] They would stay for a half year to enjoy a well-deserved rest. By May 1834, the situation in Missouri and response from church headquarters in Ohio had progressed to the point that Joseph Smith decided to call up a church militia to march to Jackson County.

Simultaneously, John Boynton, Jared Carter, Thomas Marsh, and William McLellin were away preaching. Boynton wrote to Oliver Cowdery in August to describe the success he and Jared Carter were experiencing, sometimes together and sometimes working individually. Their approach was to visit existing branches and to contact the members' relatives and neighbors. "O that the cause might spread far and wide," Boynton wrote, "until Zion's borders shall be extended from the rivers to the ends of the earth; when the will of God shall be done on earth as it is in heaven, and Christ be crowned King of nations, as he now is King of Saints!"[53] In November, Boynton served

---

52. Ibid., 26.
53. Boynton to "Brother O. Cowdery," Aug. 31, 1834, *The Evening and the*

a short, weeklong assignment with McLellin to Painesville, Ohio. McLellin wrote that Boynton preached "a fine discourse" from Galatians 1:6-10 that lasted about an hour, but regretted that his companion "never mentioned the book of mormon once."[54]

Boynton's ceaseless travels reveal an unusual level of dedication, a characteristic that has not been traditionally associated with him. Cheryl Harmon Bean, in a study of early missionary activity, quoted a summary of Boynton's and Greene's 1833 mission to show Boynton's ability to attract converts: "On the 17th, they arrived in Springfield, Erie, Pennsylvania, in which vicinity there was already a branch of the Church; here they commenced a successful missionary labor, visited among the people, and held a number of meetings. On the 20, John F. Boynton baptized Rhoda Winegar, and on the 21, eight more were baptized: namely, Samuel T. Winegar, Alvin Hartshorn, Levi Allen, John Quincy, Horace Martin, John Winegar, Alvira Winegar, and Fanny Hall."[55]

After his initial success, Boynton set out alone on missions to Pennsylvania, Massachusetts, and Maine. He wrote from Saco in January 1834: "I have baptized about forty in this section, and there is more convinced of the truth."[56] It was this level of success that convinced the Three Witnesses—Oliver Cowdery, Martin Harris, and David Whitmer—to select him for the first Quorum of Twelve Apostles. This is significant because it confirms they were looking for men who had an ability to preach and convert people. For the apostles, the fire of adversity was not Zion's Camp, but rather the privations and persecution of the mission field. Selecting these seasoned missionaries also reinforced the importance to the church of

---

Morning Star, Sept. 1834, 192.

54. Shipps and Welch, *Journals of William E. McLellin*, 148.

55. Cheryl Harmon Bean, "LDS Baptisms in Erie County, PA 1831-1833," *Nauvoo Journal* 5 (Fall 1993): 61.

56. Boynton to "Brethren in the Lord," Jan. 20, 1834, in *The Evening and the Morning Star*, Feb. 1834, 134.

proselyting and the purpose of the Quorum of Twelve in spreading the gospel message.

Zeal can be a double-edged sword. The enthusiasm these men showed and their ability to work independently were winning traits in the mission field but led to their lack of success at church head-quarters. In the case of William Smith, he was overbearing enough to be an outstanding missionary, but this forcefulness was a handi-cap within an established Latter Day Saint community. On December 18, 1833, when Joseph Smith dedicated the church's printing press, he pronounced blessings on members of his family and Oliver Cowdery, and William received a blessing that, at face value, shows a person who must have had a severe character deficiency, a lack of humility, pointing to future problems. He was "the fi[e]rce Lion who devideth not the spoil because of his strength," he was told. "In the pride of his heart," the blessing read, "he will neglect the more weighty matters until his soul is bowed down in sorrow and then he shall return and call on the name of his God and shall find forgiveness and shall wax valiant."

Despite this warning to the recipient, the blessing concluded with the assurance that William would triumph in the end:

He shall be saved unto the utter most and as the roaring Lion of the forest in the midst of his prey so shall the hand of his gen-eration be lifted up against those who are set on high that fight against the God of Israel fearless and unda[u]nted shall they be in battle in avenging the rongs of the innocent and relieving the oppressed therfor the blessings of the God of Jacob shall be in the midst of his house notwithstanding his rebelious heart and <now> O God let the residue of my fathers house ever come up in remem-brance before thee that thou mayest save them from the hand of the oppressor and establish their feet upon the rock of ages that they may have place in thy house and be saved in thy Kingdom and let all these things be even as I have said for Christs sake Amen.[57]

---

57. Dean C. Jessee, Mark Ashurst-McGee, and Richard L. Jensen, *The*

On December 9, 1834, Joseph Smith Sr. pronounced an additional blessing on William. Known as a patriarchal blessing, it sanguinely informed him that "the Lord has chosen thee for a great work, and if thou art faithful he will send thee to distant lands, and in heathen countries thou shalt lift up thy voice and call men to repentance. The hand of the angel of God shall lift thee up. ... Yes, my son, this is the promise of the Lord unto thee—thou shalt be preserved."[58]

William's strength as a missionary was once again cited as his key talent, rather than his administrative ability. The apostles were not the kind of men who would sit behind desks or even, guru-like, contemplate the mysteries of the universe. That role was reserved for the prophet and president. They were organizationally inclined but impatient to get things done, more comfortable on a stage than in a library. They were good with words and metaphors and had strong personalities, and were driven to accomplish something tangible in terms of numbers and miles, with faith that imperceptible changes to the souls of their listeners would follow. Their job was to push people to Zion, to be fed spiritually by the prophet. In a sense, they were promoters outside a revival tent beckoning people inside, and not the main event.

Joseph Smith Papers: Journals, 1832-1842 (Salt Lake City: Church Historian's Press, 2008), 1:24. When the blessing was copied in September 1835, the words "notwithstanding his rebelious heart" were omitted. Joseph Smith Sr., "The Book of Patriarchal Blessings," 1:11, LDS Church History Library.

58. Ibid., 1:6.

3. SCHOOL OF THE PROPHETS

The world was changing in the 1830s. A surprising number of revolutionary inventions were altering everyday life, travel, communications, and manufacturing. The greatest impact of these inventions was on city life, outside the reach of Mormonism. Church members kept moving ever farther west, one step away from the modern world. The news they received from the cities sounded fantastical, and missionaries encountered some of the modern conveniences themselves, but in villages along the Mississippi and Missouri Rivers life continued on in quietude, devoid of much of the hustle-bustle and noise we now expect from tires on the road outside our window, the whir of computer hard drives, the hum of power lines, forced air from furnaces and air conditioners, the soft buzz of light bulbs.

In fact, the silence of the countryside would have been so complete, it would probably startle a modern visitor. Imagine what it was like if the man of the house had to travel into town and his wife might not see another human being for days. At night, absent a breeze, the whinnying of horses or the complete silence would have underscored a sense of isolation and sometimes loneliness. Thoreau commented that "the farmer can work alone in the field or the woods all day, hoeing or chopping, and not feel lonesome" but in the evening wanted his family around him. He was unaccustomed to being alone with his own thoughts.[1] As active and productive

---

1. Henry David Thoreau, *Walden* (London: Walter Scott, 1888), 134. "When he comes home at night he cannot sit down in a room alone, at the mercy of his

as a farmer was during the day, he probably would not reach for a book at night. Some would have. Mormons were self-selectively inquisitive, radical, and oriented toward self-improvement, so they may have spent more time reading than the average rural person.

The real barrier for such people was opportunity, being so far removed from the intellectual life of the cities. Travel was expensive and difficult. In 1835 there were still only about 700 miles of railroad tracks in the United States. By comparison, at the start of the Civil War the railroads would boast over 30,000 miles of track. Steam boats were newly present on the Great Lakes and some major rivers, but the cost of steam travel made it something people did on special occasions. The day's engineering marvel was the Erie Canal, where horses walked along adjacent berms and pulled packet boats by rope. With the canal came goods, including books, to the country's interior.

It is hard to envision how primitive and largely unexplored the American continent was. The Lewis and Clark Corps of Discovery Expedition took place thirty years earlier in 1804-06 when no one knew with certainty what the explorers might find. Even in the east, the roads were still unpaved and had deep ruts. Riders in stage coaches jostled and knocked into each other. Fellow passengers probably had a ripe smell about them because, due to the fact that there was not yet running water, people bathed infrequently. The stage coaches progressed at about nine miles per hour. If an axle broke, the driver might make up for lost time and run the horses too fast, tipping the carriage over at a turn. It happened so frequently that people expected to be upended somewhere along a distant journey.

The telegraph appeared a decade later. The mail was unpredictable. A mail carrier would only take the mail to houses near enough to be worth his time and money to travel to. Traveling missionaries

thoughts, but must be where he can 'see the folks,' and recreate, and, as he thinks, remunerate himself for his day's solitude."

did not know if they would receive letters from family and friends. Most of the time it didn't matter because letters were formulaic (How are you? We are fine.)[2] Spelling was phonetic and most writers were semi-literate, so one had to pick through the message as best one could. Nor was it customary to use an envelope. More often one wrote on a sheet of paper and then folded, sealed, and addressed it. Then the local postman added a note indicating that payment had been received in lieu of stamps, which were non-existent. Nor could anybody in the 1830s agree on what time it was. If a family owned a clock, it was set to the rising sun and gave a different time than the neighbor's clock. It would be fifty years before time zones were invented. The need to advertise the arrival time of trains in distant cities was the stimulus for standardizing time by zones.[3]

On average there were seven children in a family. One in five women died in childbirth, and about the same number of children died before adulthood. When winter came, people knew that a neighbor or family member who was in delicate health would die. Most ailments were allowed to run their course because there was no cure. The cholera epidemic of the early 1830s claimed 150,000 American lives. Doctors did not yet understand the transmission of disease by bacteria. There were no anesthetics. Indoor water closets were a thing of the future. Cuts and calluses were common and often festered. The family bathed in a common wooden tub.

Every morning women rose early to spend a Sisyphean day of sewing, cooking, cleaning, churning butter, feeding livestock, fetching water, and tending children. They cooked meals over an open hearth, and, if they were fortunate enough to afford a wood-burning stove, would wait one hour for the stove to heat up sufficiently to

---

2. Stephen E. Ambrose, *Undaunted Courage: Meriwether Lewis, Thomas Jefferson, and the Opening of the American West* (New York: Simon & Schuster, 1996), 22.

3. On November 18, 1883, "the Day of Two Noons," railroad clocks across the country were reset to match the new time zones.

begin baking bread. Food was preserved by cutting thin slices of fruits and vegetables and hanging them on pieces of string to dry. Before serving salted meat, a woman had to spend hours scrubbing the brine off and soaking and rinsing it. Meals were bland. For instance, cakes were made of cornmeal, sugar, and water.

The water was unclean, so everyone drank ale. Travelers who needed something to quench their thirst were offered a glass of whiskey. Mormon historian Gregory Prince has wryly observed that God should have told everyone to "boil your drinking water" as a commandment.[4] Tea and coffee were alternatives to alcohol and were safe because they were prepared from boiling water, but neither was yet consumed in large quantities.[5]

In the way of clothing, women owned two everyday home-made dresses and one dress that was set aside for special occasions. Shoes were difficult to make, so they were usually purchased, but children went without, as did some of the women. Men needed shoes for working in the fields. Men typically owned two pants, a couple shirts, and a few long nightshirts that served as both underwear and pajamas. There were no underpants in rural America.

People's homes were illuminated by oil lamps and consisted of one or two rooms where families slept together in common beds with straw mattresses. Tourists at historical sites are treated to a glimpse of large homes like the Johnson family residence or other similar structures that were deemed worth preserving because they were ostentatious, not because they were typical.

The Missouri Compromise of 1820 offered a respite from the racial tensions that had been building over the years. Ohio entered

---

4. Prepared response to Devery S. Anderson, "Willard Richards and Thompsonian Medicine" Mormon History Association Conference, Kirtland, 2003.

5. The average American in 1830 consumed 3 pounds of coffee and a half pound of tea in a year. Over the next hundred years, tea consumption would remain steady but coffee would constantly rise to 13 pounds and still not reach its upper limit. *Statistical Abstract of the United States* (Washington, D.C.: U.S. Bureau of the Census, 1950), 637.

the union in 1803 as part of the so-called Northwest Territory, a region that had never experienced slavery. People from the north and south were less like each other than New Yorkers and Londoners. The sectional differences in the eastern and western parts of the country were also immense.

Such was the environment when the Restoration Movement laid down its roots in Kirtland and Independence. From the perspective of modern observers, the 1830s frontier might as well have been a foreign country. There was little about Mormonism at the time that would seem familiar to today's Utah, Missouri, or Wisconsin Saints. Consider the fact that there were no regularly scheduled church services. If a meeting was anticipated, it was advertised by word of mouth. Often only the men attended and the women and children stayed home, and if the women did attend they sat on the opposite side of the room. It is difficult to comprehend all their daily habits or to reconstruct the rules that governed church protocol and etiquette at the time, but in reading the primary sources one can get a general sense of it.

Suffice it to say there were no prepared programs for church services, which proceeded much like Pentecostal meetings. People were allowed to share their ecstatic religious experiences with the congregation. At a series of meetings in Kirtland on January 22-23, 1833, Lyman Johnson and others, including a few women, joined Joseph Smith and Sidney Rigdon in speaking in tongues. "The gift was poured out in a miraculous manner, until all the Elders obtained the gift," the minutes read. The following day was even more spiritually gratifying. While fasting, and after preaching, singing, and praying, Joseph took up Jesus's example and washed the elders' feet, saying "through the power of the Holy Ghost that the Elders were all clean from the blood of this generation." The elders present understood that this blessing was a provisional one. On the other hand, by having their salvation sealed upon them, it meant that even if they lapsed into sin or rebellion they would be "given over unto the buffetings of Satan until the day of redemption" and then be saved. The elders followed Joseph's example in washing each other's feet.[6]

It was determined at these meetings that a class would be held for missionaries and others in need of theological instruction. The class would be called the School of the Prophets. It would be held for the first time on January 23.[7] The class had to be disbanded in April, but it left a lasting impact on the direction of the church. It was held in a room in the upper story of Newel Whitney's store next to some rooms that were, at the time, occupied by Joseph and Emma.[8] It fell to Emma to clean up after the classes, and she famously complained to her husband about discarded cigars and expectorated tobacco juice, prompting the revelation he received on February 27 known as the Word of Wisdom, advising members to cut back on their use of tobacco, alcohol, and hot drinks (tea and coffee).[9]

The Word of Wisdom is arguably a positive development, whether or not one sees it as a revelation, because of the effect it had on personal hygiene and health. It was also part of the national discussion

---

6. Fred C. Collier and William S. Harwell, eds., *Kirtland Council Minute Book* (Salt Lake City: Collier Publishing, 1996), 6-7. The concept of sealing people "up to eternal life" is discussed in Gregory A. Prince, *Power from on High: The Development of Mormon Priesthood* (Salt Lake City: Signature Books, 1995), 162-63.

7. The School of the Prophets would see later incarnations as late as 1884.

8. Lyndon W. Cook, *Revelations of the Prophet Joseph Smith: A Historical and Biographical Commentary of the Doctrine and Covenants* (Salt Lake City: Deseret Book, 1985), 186.

9. Linda King Newell and Valeen Tippets Avery, *Mormon Enigma: Emma Hale Smith*, 2nd ed. (Urbana: University of Illinois Press, 1994), 47; LDS D&C 89; RLDS D&C 86. On October 3, 1883, at the Salt Lake School of the Prophets, Zebedee Coltrin recalled that he was the only person still living who had been present when Joseph received the revelation on the Word of Wisdom. He said Lyman Johnson was one of the twenty-one elders present, twenty of whom used tobacco. "They all immediately threw their tobacco and pipes into the fire." Merle H. Graffam, ed., *Salt Lake School of the Prophets: Minute Book 1883* (Salt Lake City: Pioneer Press, 1992), 53.

about alcoholism, which was such a problem in America. Even people visiting from Europe commented on how much Americans drank—seven gallons of pure alcohol a year per person, meaning that each man, woman, and child would have to drink three bottles of beer per day to reach the average. The American Temperance Society was founded in 1826 to counter this alarming national habit.[10] Originally temperance meant only to moderate one's consumption of alcohol rather than to avoid it altogether. Church members continued to drink beer and wine but stopped consuming stronger distilled drinks and cut back on their use of tobacco.

Beyond dietary discussions, one of the topics of interest at the School of the Prophets was the prevalence of the Jerusalem temple in the Bible. Since Mormons intended to restore biblical beliefs and ritual, the centrality of a temple seemed clear. So, on March 23 the school's leaders appointed a committee to search for an appropriate site to construct such an edifice to qualify as a temple. Joseph Coe, Moses Daily, and Ezra Thayer found a location on the "crest of the bluff on the southern end of Kirtland Flats" owned by Peter French.[11] Coe met with French, and the purchase price for the 103 acres of $5,000 was agreed to. On June 17, 1833, Coe and wife conveyed the site for the "House of the Lord" to Newel Whitney and Company, Whitney being the bishop in Kirtland.[12]

Joseph Smith's brother William was one of the students at the School of the Prophets and no stranger to the acceptable means of demonstrating spiritual renewal such as speaking in tongues, which he did publicly at a church conference in Kirtland on January 22-23, 1833, along with washing the Saints' feet. His brother rewarded his

10. Daniel Okrent, *Last Call: The Rise and Fall of Prohibition* (New York: Simon and Schuster, 2010), 7-9.

11. Roger D. Launius, *The Kirtland Temple: A Historical Narrative* (Independence: Herald Publishing House, 1986), 39.

12. Kim L. Loving, "Ownership of the Kirtland Temple: Legends, Lies, and Misunderstandings," *Journal of Mormon History* 30 (Fall 2004): 3-4.

effort by sealing him up to eternal life.[13] These profound pentecostal experiences may have sustained William throughout his future missionary struggles.

Later in the year, in November 1833, Lyman Johnson and Orson Pratt attended a council of high priests in Kirtland to report on their missionary labors. What attracted the most attention from the council was their description of the doctrinal dispute about D&C Section 76 they had encountered in Geneseo, New York. The council concluded to write an epistle to the branch to assure them that "our brother Lyman Johnson" was "fully quailified" to arbitrate this controversy. "Brother Ezra Landin did not believe <all of> the revelations which had been delivered to this church by inspiration," the council noted. The high priests expressed dismay that President Landen went so far as to threaten to have Orson Pratt "turned out of at the door except he should desist" in speaking of the vision.

The branch president was in danger of being removed from office unless he would concede his error and profess allegiance to certain obligatory beliefs, they wrote.

> We want you to understand, that we hold no communion nor have no fellowship for those who do not believe the book of mormon, and the revelations which God has given to us in these last days. We are informed that our brother L[anden] endeavors to excuse himself for not believin[g] the Vision, saying, that it is not a revelation, but a Vision. We want you to understand from us that we pronounce such teachings the works of the devil, and one calculated to ensnare the souls of the saints. We plainly declare, and as men that expect to, and must be judged by the searcher of all hearts, that those who do not believe <all> the revelations and visions given to this church, that they do not believe the book of Mormon, and consequently have no fellowship with us.[14]

---

13. Collier and Harwell, *Kirtland Council Minute Book*, 6-7; Joseph Smith Jr., et al., *History of the Church of Jesus Christ of Latter-day Saints*, 2nd ed. rev., ed. B. H. Roberts, 7 vols., 1902–32 (Salt Lake City: Deseret Book, 1959): 1:323-24.

14. "An Epistle from a Counsel of High Priests of the Church of Christ,

The final chapter in the Geneseo drama awaited a visit from Johnson and Pratt during a third mission to the east. During this time, Lyman was trying to earn some money to support his family, working briefly at the Kirtland Temple site, for instance. He barely had time to become used to the normal routines of domestic life before his routine was again interrupted by a call from "a council of High Priests," and was instructed to accompany his now three-time companion Orson Pratt "to visit the Churches" that had been founded in the east. They left Kirtland on November 27 for what would prove to be an unsatisfying attempt to push back against the recriminations by Protestant ministers, mediate the disputes between members, and deal with the schismatic elements in the branches—all nevertheless again seemingly filling the role of Paul in the New Testament, foreshadowing their apostolic roles.

First they had the unpleasant task of confronting Ezra Landen, who had again decided he could not accept the vision of heaven that Joseph Smith and Sidney Rigdon had received. Many once-loyal Saints in and around Geneseo had experienced similar dissonance over the contradiction between the vision and the traditional Christian view of heaven and hell, both from the Bible and from the Book of Mormon.[15] As the presiding officer, Landen felt it his duty to denounce it as a false vision.[16]

Therefore, on December 31, Johnson presided over Landen's church trial, with Pratt acting as clerk. A jury was assembled consisting of Johnson, Pratt, John Murdock, and Amasa Lyman, all high priests, and four elders, as well as a priest and a teacher. Pratt wrote in his journal that "after his case was duly examined by the

---

Organized on the 6th of April, A.D. 1830, to Their Brethren of the Same Church, Residing at Geneseo, Livingston County, New York," Nov. 23, 1833, LDS Church History Library, Salt Lake City.

15. For a non-Mormon view, see "Changes of Mormonism," *Evangelical Magazine and Gospel Advocate* (Utica), Mar. 17, 1832, 87.

16. John Murdock, "An Abridged Record of the Life of John Murdock, Taken from His Journal by Himself," 27, LDS Church History Library.

conference & some points of the Revelations read & explained touching his situation[,] the conference were requested to give their decision & they una[n]i[m]ously gave their voices against him & he was cut off from the church."[17] Johnson and Pratt dutifully passed along the news to *The Evening and the Morning Star*:

> At a conference of elders of the church of Christ, convened at Geneseo, Livingston county, N. Y. on the 31st of December, 1833, EZRA LANDEN, formerly an elder in said church, was silenced by the voice of said conference for promulgating unscriptural principles, and refusing to give proper satisfaction for his conduct. His credentials were demanded by the conference, but they were denied. According to the rules and regulations of the church, he was then excommunicated from this body. LYMAN JOHNSON, *Moderator.* ORSON PRATT, *Clerk.*[18]

Two days later six other members resigned from the church in protest. On January 6, 1834, six relatives of these dissidents were removed from the church for "bad conduct." Five days later eight people were cut off from a neighboring congregation. When all was said and done, the only positive aspect of the trip was how far the elders traveled, about 1,000 miles, to visit the disparate branches and success they had in collecting money from easterners to support the members at church headquarters.[19] Johnson arrived back in Kirtland by stage about February 8, and Pratt arrived five days later.[20]

Following Landen's excommunication, Joseph Smith saw the need to create a standing high council to try cases too difficult for

---

17. Elden J. Watson, comp. and ed., *The Orson Pratt Journals* (Salt Lake City: Elden J. Watson, 1975), 29.

18. Lyman and Orson notified the church of Ezra's excommunication in "To Whom It May Concern," *The Evening and the Morning Star*, Feb. 1834, 134; see also Watson, *Orson Pratt Journals*, 29; Murdock, "Abridged Record," 25.

19. Watson, *Orson Pratt Journals*, 26–32.

20. Ibid., 31–32.

a bishop's court to resolve. He explained that, in New Testament times, Peter and two counselors had presided over a high council court at Jerusalem and it would be the model for the latter-day high council. It would serve as an appellate court. To validate the creation of this institution, Joseph invited three dozen men and women to his residence on February 17 to share their ideas about a church judiciary. He and his family had recently moved out of the Whitney store and purchased their own house near the temple site. The committee agreed to a twelve-man council that would consider evidence, with Joseph serving as president or judge, while others in the First Presidency would assist the president as needed. Before each case was deliberated, the council would draw lots to decide the number of councilmen needed for each case.

As it was envisioned, an equal number of counselors would be chosen to speak either for the church or to defend the accused. The more difficult cases might have six counselors speaking for the defendant and six speaking for the church, while cases of lesser importance would have fewer counselors speak. The trials were to proceed in six steps: the presentation of the evidence, the counselors speaking for and against the defendant, the accusers presenting their accusations, the accused conducting his or her defense, the president or presidents of the council rendering a decision, and the high counselors sanctioning "the same by their vote." In theory, the rights of the accused would be fairly represented whether he or she was even in attendance, chose to boycott, or remained silent during the trial. The president could "obtain the mind of the Lord by revelation" to settle disputes or clarify doctrines.

When the minutes were printed in the Doctrine and Covenants, additional remarks included reference to the functions of the future Quorum of the Twelve, explaining that the Twelve's decisions could not be appealed to the church presidency but that decisions by the high council could be. This autonomy, intended to limit the presidency's work load, would later be interpreted as an advancement of the Twelve above the high council, but it was not seen that way at the time.

The first men called to the Kirtland High Council were Luke Johnson, John Johnson Sr., Oliver Cowdery, Joseph Coe, Samuel H. Smith, John S. Carter, Sylvester Smith, Orson Hyde, Jared Carter, Joseph Smith Sr., John Smith, and Martin Harris.[21] Notice the future apostles among them. Lyman Johnson was also asked to stand as an alternate councilman. (Lyman, Luke, and John Johnson Sr. would themselves be disciplined by high councils in the future.) Two days after the meeting at the Smith home, John Johnson Sr. "laid his hands upon the head of his son Luke, and said, My Father in heaven, I ask Thee to bless this my son, according to the blessings of his forefathers; that he may be strengthened in his ministry, according to his holy calling. Amen."[22]

When the high council met to hear cases, one of the first items of business was a question that had arisen in Erie County, Pennsylvania, when Johnson and Pratt were there. Some of the members had refused or only reluctantly accepted the sacrament from someone who had been drinking or smoking. Pratt thought this was a harsh judgment of a fellow Saint, but Johnson thought otherwise. During the high council investigation, three of the counselors spoke for tolerance and three for strictness, but the final decision was for complete abstinence by the church council, at least from strong drinks and cigars: "No official member in this church is worthy to hold an office after having the Words of Wisdom

---

21. The corrected minutes were recorded in the Kirtland Council Minute Book, 32-35, LDS Church History Library. Two days later the minutes were accepted. Further revisions were made and canonized on August 17, 1835. LDS D&C 102; RLDS D&C 99. Luke Johnson and Orson Hyde served on the Kirtland High Council until January 13, 1836, and were replaced by Thomas Grover and Joseph Kingsbury. Dean C. Jessee, Mark Ashurst-McGee, and Richard L. Jensen, eds., *The Joseph Smith Papers: Journals* (Salt Lake City: Church Historian's Press, 2008), 1:149. See Collier and Harwell, *Kirtland Council Minute Book*, 147, 150, for other future apostles who served briefly on the high council.

22. Collier and Harwell, *Kirtland Council Minute Book*, 31.

properly taught to him, and he, the official member, neglecting to comply with, or obey them."[23]

In November 1833 church members were forced out of Jackson County, Missouri, into Clay County to the north. Joseph Smith's instructions, penned on December 5, 1833, from Kirtland said that the lands in Jackson County "should not be sold, but be held by the Saints, until the Lord in His wisdom shall open a way for your return."[24]

When the Kirtland High Council met on February 24, 1834, they took up the matter of William McLellin's intransigence. It was reported that the only property that had been legally lost in Jackson County was "owned by bro. Wm. E. McLellin," who had put thirty acres "into the hands of the enemy." He would have sold more "if a brother had not come forward & purchased it and paid him his money." The question on everyone's mind was "when, how and by what means Zion was to be redeemed from our enemies." Lyman Wight and Parley Pratt reported that the Saints who had relocated to Clay County were fine because of the generosity of the membership in other areas. Joseph Smith announced that he would offer armed resistance to the Missourians, that "he was going to Zion" as soon as he could gather supplies together "to assist in redeeming it." The high council approved of this, voting to endorse his determination to push back against the Missourians, which passed "without a dissenting voice."[25]

The men whose lives we are tracing were previously engaged. Lyman Johnson had been assigned to Upper Canada, later renamed Ontario, although he ultimately did not serve his mission. Others, including Jared Carter, Zebedee Coltrin, Brigham Young, and

---

23. Ibid., 33.

24. Joseph Smith to "Dear Brethren," Dec. 5, 1833, in *History of the Church*, 1:451.

25. Collier and Harwell, *Kirtland Council Minute Book*, 34–35. A revelation received the same day concerned the salvation and redemption of Zion and promised that the Mormons would prevail against their enemies "from this very hour" unless "they keep not" the commandments (LDS D&C 103; RLDS D&C 100).

Joseph Young, were preparing to leave for other destinations but were called back to participate in the assault on Missouri. Joseph Smith noted on May 9 that Lyman Johnson, Willard Snow, and others who had been headed north on proselytizing missions had returned to join the camp at Mansfield, Ohio.[26] This brought the number of future apostles participating in Zion's Camp to nine. Two more, McLellin and Marsh, were in Missouri awaiting assistance. John Boynton would have participated but was in the east on a mission. The issue is not whether they did their part, but whether, as the later explanation went, the march on Missouri was divinely designed as a boot camp for future apostles, testing their perseverance and faith. It does not seem to have been so.

The volunteers were gathered at a staging area near New Portage, Ohio, in the vicinity of present-day Akron, about fifty miles south of Kirtland. On May 5, 1834, over a hundred men arrived, and eventually the number would grow to over two hundred amateur soldiers, never achieving overwhelming numbers. The group was told God's presence "shall be with you even in avenging me of mine enemies."[27] The head count included women and children as well as men. Joseph Smith reportedly said on this date: "Having gathered and prepared clothing and other necessaries to carry to our brethren and sisters, who had been robbed and plundered of nearly all their effects; and having provided for ourselves horses, and wagons, and firearms, and all sorts of munitions of war of the most portable kind for self-defense—as our enemies are thick on every hand—I started with the remainder of the company from Kirtland for Missouri."[28]

They reached Clay County in June, assured that the state government would come to their aid when they saw the seriousness of their intent and would restore their fellow churchmen to the

---

26. *History of the Church*, 2:65.

27. LDS D&C 103:26; RLDS D&C 100:5.

28. *History of the Church*, 2:63.

property they had lost across the Missouri River in Jackson County. Instead, Missourians had amassed their own militia in Jackson County. A confrontation seemed inevitable until a violent storm arrived on June 19 that scattered the Missourians. The Mormons considered it a miracle, even though they were afflicted by cholera and lost thirteen men, one woman, and one child, and perceived spiritual victory in the otherwise unfulfilled march. After burying their dead southeast of Liberty in Clay County, they began a long walk home, forgetting the fierce disagreements they had experienced on their way down. Now they felt camaraderie. Even Joseph, who had treated subordinates harshly during the trip, would now nurture a strong sentimental spot in his heart for the men who had participated in this quixotic journey to Missouri.

In Luke Johnson's short life history, he mentioned only that he and others took the opportunity during the march to preach to curious onlookers as the infantry passed by or camped. Their forward progress halted by the Missouri River, the Johnson brothers rowed across and stepped foot in Jackson County as a testimony against the "Gentile oppressors":

> Having made a declaration before I started, that I would go into Jackson Co[unty], or die in the attempt, in company with my brother Lyman and others I procured a boat, and rowed over the Mo. River and landed in Jackson Co., where we discharged three rounds of our small arms, and immediately got into the boat, and with all our energies rowed back. Meanwhile the mob in Jackson Co. lined the shore, and commenced firing upon us, their balls skimming the waters near us: after landing, I returned fire and shot across the Mo. River.[29]

Joseph Smith may have accompanied Luke and Lyman in the boat. Willard Richards, writing in the name of Joseph Smith,

---

29. "The History of Luke Johnson by Himself," *Deseret News*, May 26, 1858, 57.

recorded: "On the first of July I crossed the Missouri River, in company with a few friends, into Jackson county, to set my feet once more on the 'goodly land.'"[30]

William Smith donated five dollars to the cause on April 30 for the "delivery of Zion,"[31] then responded to the call, submitting to the military regimen and walking 800 miles to Clay County along with the other militiamen. He contracted cholera but survived.[32] Unlike the Johnson brothers, he came to see the enterprise in a negative light. Biographer Kyle R. Walker writes that William could not "see the purpose of Zion's Camp" and was embarrassed by its failure.[33] As a result of missed work opportunities, he was "penniless once more" when he returned to Kirtland. Disgusted with his circumstances, he determined to turn his attention away from missionary work and try making a living by "farming, and Merchandizing."[34]

His reaction may have been influenced by the Fishing River revelation marking the end of Zion's Camp on June 22. It was a fresh directive that, instead of offering another strategy for success, assigned blame for the failure. According to the voice of God, it was "the transgressions of my people" and not any "individuals," meaning Joseph Smith, that had doomed the effort. God took note of the lack of military discipline. "My people must needs be chastened until they learn obedience," he declared. The "redemption of Zion" would have to wait "a little season" until the elders could be

---

30. Manuscript History Book A-1:509, written August 1843, original reading, LDS Church History Library; *History of the Church* 2:120.

31. Jessee, et al., *Joseph Smith Papers: Journals*, 1:43.

32. Lavina Fielding Anderson, *Lucy's Book: A Critical Edition of Lucy Mack Smith's Family Memoir* (Salt Lake City: Signature Books, 2001), 578.

33. Kyle R. Walker, "William B. Smith," in *United by Faith: The Joseph Sr. and Lucy Mack Smith Family*, ed. Kyle R. Walker (American Fork, UT: Covenant Communications, 2005), 255.

34. William Smith, *William Smith on Mormonism* (Lamoni, IA: Herald Steam Book and Job Office, 1883), 25.

"endowed with power from on high." This would be done at the temple that was still under construction in Kirtland, they were told.[35]

Upon their release from the camp on June 30, Luke and Lyman presumably returned to Ohio with Heber Kimball's company on July 26. In any case, they testified in August that charges brought against Joseph Smith of improper conduct in Missouri, filed by Sylvester Smith, were untrue. Luke told the council he had accompanied Joseph "most of the way to Missouri" and "did not see anything in [Joseph's] conduct to lessen his esteem of him as a man of God. But [Luke] said he heard brother Joseph reprove brother Sylvester concerning a certain something, respecting some bread. He did not hear the whole and thought at the time the reproofs were rather severe, but had learned since, they were not any more severe than were just." Brigham Young and others joined in upholding the prophet's character, contrary to Sylvester's testimony. Even if one accepted Sylvester's version of events, they entailed breaches of etiquette rather than military misconduct.[36]

About the time the call went out for volunteers, William McLellin and his wife had been getting settled in Liberty, Missouri, so she could give birth to their first child, Charles. The date was April 14.[37] Perhaps their angst over the approaching birth was what caused William to sell their land in Jackson County. Even so, he would eventually denounce Zion's Camp for its militarism, declaring that Joseph Smith had been "imbibing and encouraging

---

35. LDS D&C 105:2, 4-6, 9-11; RLDS D&C 102:2-3.

36. Collier and Harwell, *Kirtland Council Minute Book*, 45-58; "Dear Sir," *Latter Day Saints' Messenger and Advocate*, Oct. 1834, 10-11.

37. Larry Porter, "The Odyssey of William Earl McLellin: Man of Diversity, 1806-83," in *The Journals of William E. McLellin, 1831-1836*, eds. Jan Shipps and John W. Welch (Provo and Urbana: *BYU Studies* and University of Illinois Press, 1994), 303. The couple's subsequent travels can be traced through the births of their children in Ohio (Sarah Emeline, Jan. 1836), Missouri (James Martin, Feb. 1838), Illinois (Helen Rebecca, Feb. 1843), Iowa (Albert Eugene, June 1845), and Ohio (Marcus Nelson, Feb. 1848).

the spirit and practice of war."[38] From the perspective of the Missourians, he would argue, it was the last straw and the "reason why the church was ... never allowed to return again." The deaths from cholera were evidence of God's displeasure.[39]

Despite McLellin's unhappiness with events, he must have kept his criticisms to himself because he was appointed to the Missouri high council at a Clay County conference on July 3 and 7. Among other appointments to the council were Thomas Marsh, Orson Pratt, and Parley Pratt. In another development, Joseph decided that he could not be president of the church in Missouri while he was nearly 1,000 miles away in Ohio, so he appointed David Whitmer to stand in his stead in Missouri, along with William Phelps and John Whitmer as counselors. When Joseph visited Missouri, he explained, he would be president again as long as he was in the state. As confusing as this was, even more surprising to anyone who cared to take notice was that McLellin traveled back to Kirtland with Joseph Smith and stayed in Ohio rather than filling his position on the Missouri high council.[40] After disregarding the prophet's advice and selling his land in Missouri, he also disregarded his calling and chose instead to devote renewed energy to stabilizing the situation in Kirtland, which earned him the prophet's admiration and gratitude despite being contrary to the president's expressed intent for him.

38. William E. McLellin, "The Successor of Joseph, the Seer," *The Ensign of Liberty, of the Church of Christ*, Dec. 1847, 46.

39. William D. Russell, "Portrait of a 'True Believer' in Original Mormonism," *The William E. McLellin Papers, 1854-1880*, eds. Stan Larson and Samuel J. Passey (Salt Lake City: Signature Books, 2007), 123.

40. Donald Q. Cannon and Lyndon W. Cook, *Far West Record: Minutes of the Church of Jesus Christ of Latter-day Saints, 1830-1844* (Salt Lake City: Deseret Book, 1983), 70-73.

4. A QUORUM OF
TWELVE APOSTLES

Joseph Smith was not officially responsible for choosing the original Quorum of the Twelve, so he might be spared credit or blame for the selections except that he influenced at least one of them directly and others indirectly. Oliver Cowdery and David Whitmer were directed by revelation in June 1829, before the church had been founded, to search out twelve good men for this honor. The modern-day apostles would, like those in the Bible, take on Christ's errands "with full purpose of heart," preaching the gospel in "all the world."[1] It would take almost six years, but eventually the witnesses to the Book of Mormon completed their task, and in February 1835 Joseph Smith asked Brigham and Joseph Young to gather the Zion's Camp veterans together so he could bless them and, at the same gathering, make an announcement on who the apostles would be.

Joseph Smith told the Youngs that the "twelve Special Witnesses" would be ambassadors who would "open the door of the Gospel to foreign nations."[2] Accordingly, on February 14, a large number of Saints came together for what they had been assured would be a momentous occasion.[3] The veterans were seated together "in one part

---

1. LDS D&C 18:27-38; RLDS D&C 16:5-6.

2. Joseph Young Sr., *History of the Organization of Seventies* (1878; West Valley City, UT: Eborn Books, 1992), 3.

3. Roger D. Launius, *Zion's Camp: Expedition to Missouri, 1834* (Independence: Herald House, 1984), 163. Launius indicated that the meeting was held in "the unfinished temple," while Milton V. Backman Jr., *The Heavens Resound: A*

of the house by themselves" when Joseph announced that by inspiration from the Holy Spirit and a vision from God, he would be ordaining men, from among those who "went to Zion," to the new office in the priesthood, that of apostle. Twelve would be chosen to "go forth to prune the vineyard for the last time, or the coming of the Lord." The Second Coming was "nigh," he said, and would be realized in little more than half a century. "Even fifty six years, should wind up the scene," he confidently declared. The twelve would "feel the whisperings of the spirit" and would receive "power from on high," he explained.

Would the congregation accept the appointment of twelve apostles? he asked. He wanted to see confirmation from the men in the Zion's Camp group and asked them to stand if they were in agreement, which they did. He then asked the rest of the congregation to raise their hand if they agreed, which they also did.[4] After a one-hour intermission, the meeting resumed:

> President J[oseph] Smith Junr. arose and said: The first business of the meeting was for the three witnesses of the Book of Mormon to pray, each one, and then proceed to choose twelve men from the Church as Apostles to go to all nations, kindred, tongue[s] and people. The three Witnesses united in prayer (viz.) Oliver Cowdery, David Whitmer & Martin Harris. These three witnesses were then blessed by the laying on of the hands of the Presidency. They then according to a former commandment proceeded to make choice of the twelve.[5]

Joseph was personally impressed by the Zion's Camp participants

History of the Latter-day Saints in Ohio, 1830-1838 (Salt Lake City: Deseret Book, 1983), 198, countered that "members of the priesthood crowded into the new schoolhouse next to the rising temple." Fred C. Collier and William S. Harwell, eds., *Kirtland Council Minute Book* (Salt Lake City: Collier's Publishing, 1996), 70, indicated that both "brethren & sisters" attended this meeting.

4. Collier and Harwell, *Kirtland Council Minute Book*, 71.
5. Ibid., 72.

who had remained loyal to him through adversity. Yet despite the pressure to succumb to Joseph's influence, the three witnesses disregarded this display of militia zeal and drew instead upon missionary veterans, some of whom had not been in the militia. They gravitated toward men who were strong-willed and had independent spirits, who were forceful speakers. Off stage, the men they chose had less confidence than when preaching and had not found success in life generally in farming or business, for instance. In fact, it was a surprisingly diverse and ragtag group. But for all that, they were ready and willing to make whatever sacrifice was necessary in this instance. They knew that they would be accepting a lifetime missionary assignment.

The most surprising choice was that of William McLellin, who already had a checkered past in terms of devotion to church leaders. He had been a dynamic and effective missionary when he wasn't AWOL, but at the time of the February meeting, he was employed as a teacher at a Kirtland school. Historian Richard P. Howard postulated that McLellin's relationship with David Whitmer influenced the choice because Whitmer was impressed with McLellin's intellect and teaching experience.[6]

In the behind-the-scenes negotiations, Joseph Smith had rejected one nomination: Phineas Young, Brigham Young's brother, in favor of Joseph's own brother, William. Cowdery wrote to Brigham Young on February 27, 1848:

> At the time the Twelve were chosen in Kirtland, and I may say before, it had been manifested that brother Phineas was entitled to occupy the station as one of that number; but owing to brother Joseph's urgent request at the time, Brother David and myself yielded to his wishing and consented for William to be selected,

---

6. Richard P. Howard, "Mormonism's 'Stormy Petrel,'" in *The William E. McLellin Papers, 1854-1880*, eds. Stan Larson and Samuel J. Passey (Salt Lake City: Signature Books, 2007), 6.

contrary to our feelings and judgment, and to our deep mortification ever since.[7]

About two decades later in 1854, Phineas spoke to a group of church leaders in Salt Lake City about how his call to the quorum had been cancelled. According to Wilford Woodruff, "Phineas Young said that He was the first that was Chosen in the organization of the quorum of the Twelve Apostles but Brother Joseph said He wished I would let Wm. Smith have that place so I gave way to him."[8] Some fifty years after the formation of the quorum, in an interview that Zenas Gurley conducted with David Whitmer in January 1885, Whitmer corroborated Cowdery's and Young's recollections and confirmed that Phineas was the man who was originally selected for the position.[9]

On the same day their names were announced publicly, three of the men, Lyman Johnson, Heber Kimball, and Brigham Young, were ordained by the three witnesses in reverse order by age. Lyman Johnson was ordained first because he was the youngest. The following day John Boynton, Orson Hyde, Luke Johnson, William McLellin, David Patten, and William Smith were ordained. Of the remaining three, Parley Pratt was ordained on February 21, while Thomas Marsh and Orson Pratt did not

---

7. Oliver Cowdery to Brigham Young, Feb. 27, 1848, qtd. in Stanley R. Gunn, *Oliver Cowdery: Second Elder and Scribe* (Salt Lake City: Bookcraft, 1962), 268. See also Zenas H. Gurley Jr., interviewed by David Whitmer, Jan. 14, 1885, microfilm, LDS Church History Library; Lyndon W. Cook, ed., *David Whitmer Interviews: A Restoration Witness* (Orem, UT: Grandin Book. 1991), 157.

8. Scott G. Kenney, ed., *Wilford Woodruff's Journal, 1833-1898*, typescript, 9 vols. (Midvale, UT: Signature Books, 1983-85), 4:275. Woodruff added: "The above shows Phineas Young's feelings. There is not a word of truth in this Statement." The entry, including Woodruff's comments, was later crossed out in the journal, perhaps because Woodruff remembered that he attended a meeting on March 28, 1848, when Cowdery's letter was read. "We he[a]rd a letter read from Oliver Cowdery expressing his feelings Concerning some matters connected with the first calling of the Twelve," he wrote. Ibid., 3:335.

9. Cook, *David Whitmer Interviews*, 157.

receive their ordinations until April 26 (see Appendix B for transcripts of the ordinations).

Oliver Cowdery told the newly called apostles they had been chosen after years of prayerful search: "You have been ordained to the Holy Priesthood, you have received it from those who had their power and authority from an angel." He advised them to carry the "gospel to the ends of the earth" and testify to the Book of Mormon. He emphasized that this would necessitate "a long farewell to Kirtland," with compensating success in converts as long as they demonstrated faith, humility, and love. They would need to seek independent confirmation from heaven, he said, promising that if they did so they would see God "face to face"; if they honored their calling, they would also witness the second advent of Jesus Christ. First they would need to receive their "endowment of power" in the temple, then they could leave the shores of the United States for foreign climes. He admonished them to not forfeit their crowns of glory and, taking each by the hand, elicited from them a solemn pledge that they would devote themselves to the ministry, heart and soul.[10]

Nine of the apostles met with Joseph Smith on February 27. He told them to maintain good records. Two of them did. He also outlined their duties as enumerated, he said, words from heaven:

> They are the Twelve Apostles, who are called to the office of Traveling high council, who are to preside over all the churches of the Saints among the Gentiles, where there is no presidency established, and they are to travel and preach among the Gentiles, until the Lord shall command them to go to the Jews. They are to hold the keys of this ministry, to unlock the door of the kingdom of heaven unto all nations, and to preach the Gospel to every creature. This is the power, authority and virtue of their apostleship.[11]

---

10. Ibid., 80-84. Launius, *Zion's Camp*, 163, commented rightly that the majority of the apostles participated in Zion's Camp.

11. Collier and Harwell, *Kirtland Council Minute Book*, 86.

In short, they were to be missionaries, who would preside over all the loosely organized congregations outside Ohio and Missouri. They were not to be administrators within organized stakes, but rather ministers to spread the gospel throughout the world.

From the beginning, Joseph assumed a supervisory role over the Twelve. He informed them on March 12 that their first assignment would be to visit the branches ("churches") in the east beginning May 4, to speak in worship services and solicit money for the Saints in the west.[12] Prior to leaving the orbit of Kirtland, they were to accompany Joseph on a short speaking assignment to Huntsburg, about seventeen miles away, on March 28. While there, Elder McLellin baptized Jotham Gardner and his wife. The next day, "on Sunday, President J. Smith Jr. delivered a discourse in the same house of about three hour's length."[13]

The apostles were already familiar with missionary work, but their elevation as apostles caused no short amount of self-doubt. Meeting together on April 28, they asked God to forgive them their sins, which they acknowledged were "light minded and vain." In humility they asked Joseph for confirmation of the "mind and will" of God "concerning our duty the coming season."[14] Accordingly, Joseph received a revelation in their presence that has since been canonized. They were to function as a quorum of the priesthood under the prophet, as follows:

---

12. The apostles' schedule was published in "Bro. O. Cowdery," *Messenger and Advocate*, Mar. 1835, 90. Conferences were to be held in Westfield, Freedom, Lyonstown, and Pillow Point, New York, on May 9, 22, June 5, 19; West Loborough, Upper Canada, June 29; St. Johnsbury, Vermont, July 17; Bradford, Massachusetts, Aug. 7; Dover, New Hampshire, Sept. 4 (later canceled); Saco and Farmington, Maine, Sept. 18, Oct. 2 (Saco later changed to August 21 and Farmington changed to August 28).

13. William E. McLellin to Oliver Cowdery, Apr. 16, 1835, *Messenger and Advocate*, Apr. 1835, 102.

14. Collier and Harwell, *Kirtland Council Minute Book*, 111. These 1835 minutes were copied in 1836, and the Mar. 28, 1836, date should have been April 28, 1835, the same day the minutes of the Twelve give for asking forgiveness.

The twelve traveling counsellors are called to be twelve apostles, or special witnesses of the name of Christ, in all the world: thus differing from other officers in the church in the duties of their calling. ... The twelve are a traveling, presiding high council, to officiate in the name of the Lord, under the direction of the presidency of the church, agreeably to the institution of heaven; to build up the church, and regulate all the affairs of the same, in all nations: first unto the Gentiles, and secondly unto the Jews.[15]

There was another gathering of the Twelve with Joseph Smith on May 2 in what they called a "grand council." Joseph told them "it will be the duty of the twelve when in council to take their Seats together according to their ages. The oldest to be seated at the head, and preside in the first council, the next oldest in the Second, and so on until the youngest has presided."[16] Thomas Marsh was presumed to be the oldest apostle, although Marsh was unable to correctly remember his birth date, thinking it was 1799 when it was actually 1800.[17] David Patten was, in fact, the oldest. In any case, Marsh sat at the head of the table, with Patten next to him, followed by Brigham Young, Heber Kimball, Orson Hyde, William McLellin, and the rest. The prophet told them they were forbidden from entering any of the stakes of Zion, from serving in any stake capacities, and from regulating the affairs of the high councils. Conversely, he said, the standing high councils would have no authority over the Twelve outside of the stakes. He said:

The Twelve will have no right to go into Zion or any of its stakes and there undertake to regulate the affairs thereof where there is a

---

15. Doctrine and Covenants (1835) 3:11-12; see LDS D&C 107:23, 33; RLDS D&C 104:11-12, April 28-30, 1835.

16. "A Record of the Transactions of the Twelve apostles," May 2, 1835, in Patriarchal Blessing Book 2, LDS Church History Library.

17. "Acton Births, Deaths, Marriages, 1738-1844," 129, in Jay and Delene Holbrook, *Massachusetts Vital and Town Records* (Provo: Holbrook Research Institute, 1999), available online at www.ancestry.com.

standing High Council. But it is their duty to go abroad and regulate all matters relative to the different branches of the church. When the Twelve are together, or a quorum of them in any church, they will have to do business by the voice of the Church. No standing high council has authority to go into the churches abroad and regulate the matters thereof, for this belongs to the Twelve. No High Council will ever be established only in Zion or one of its stakes.[18]

The apostles were reminded that their ultimate duty was "to go abroad and regulate and Set in order all matters relative to the different branches of the church of the Latter Day Saints."[19] Interestingly, the first thing the Twelve did rather was to fill vacancies on the Kirtland High Council, the very thing they were advised against. On October 29, five of the apostles were temporarily placed on the high council to adjudicate a particular problem. In December seven of them were asked to serve on the council, and they accepted. Luke Johnson, who had been on the Kirtland High Council from the beginning, continued to function there until January 13, 1836, when he was replaced.[20] The apostles must have seen no harm in helping out where they could during this transitional period as they prepared to launch their careers abroad. It may also be significant that they shied away from any supervisory capacity on the high council in Kirtland, only as counselors.

At a general assembly in Kirtland on August 17, 1835, when Joseph Smith was in Michigan and the Twelve Apostles were in

18. Collier and Harwell, *Kirtland Council Minute Book*, 112.

19. "Record of the Transactions," May 2, 1835; Joseph Smith Jr., et al., *History of the Church of Jesus Christ of Latter-day Saints*, 2nd ed. rev., ed. B. H. Roberts, 7 vols., 1902-12, 1932 (Salt Lake City: Deseret Book, 1959), 2:220. See also Ronald K. Esplin and Sharon E. Neilsen, "The Record of the Twelve, 1835: The Quorum of the Twelve Apostles' Call and 1835 Mission," *BYU Studies Quarterly* 51, no. 1 (2012): 27.

20. Dean C. Jessee, Mark Ashurst-McGee, and Richard L. Jensen, eds., *The Joseph Smith Papers: Journals* (Salt Lake City: Church Historian's Press), 1:149.

the eastern states on their first mission, the Doctrine and Covenants, which included the Lectures on Faith, the Article on Marriage, and an Article on Governments and Laws in General, was
approved and recognized as church law. William Phelps read "the
written testimony of the Twelve," that the commandments given
by Joseph Smith were "verily true." Although the minutes of the
general assembly do not contain a signed statement by the apostles, Brigham H. Roberts, a church historian in Utah, presented
the "Testimony of the Twelve Apostles to the Truth of the Book of
Doctrine and Covenants" in his editing of the *History of the Church,*
volume two, published in 1904, as if it had been signed.[21] Based on
Roberts's claim, the LDS Church added this testimony to the book,
followed by the names of the apostles as though they signed the
document. It was added in 1921 and retained in additional print-
ings of the Doctrine and Covenants through 1981. The wording
came from an 1831 revelation given on November 1, 1831, about
the Book of Commandments.[22] Since no signed document has been
found linking the apostles with the 1835 testimony, the 1981 LDS
edition lists the names of the apostles without specifically claiming
that they endorsed the statement. It is probable that the Twelve did
not know that some of the revelations had been modified.

First Mission of the Twelve, May 4-September 26, 1835
McLellin recorded that the apostles departed from Kirtland by
wagon on Monday, May 4, in the early "morn[ing] at 2 O'clock."
Riding through the predawn darkness to Fairport, Ohio, they
boarded the steamboat *Sandusky* at 6:00 a.m. and sailed across Lake

---

21. *History of the Church,* 2:245n. Roberts thought it was "proper" to insert the
names and the word "signed" in parentheses to accompany the published testimony,
all based on his assumption that the 1835 testimony was signed by the Twelve.

22. Donald Q. Cannon and Lyndon W. Cook, *Far West Record: Minutes of
the Church of Jesus Christ of Latter-day Saints, 1830-1844* (Salt Lake City: Deseret
Book, 1983), 26-27. Also present at this meeting were future apostles Orson
Hyde, Luke and Lyman Johnson, and William E. McLellin.

Erie to reach Dunkirk, New York, at about 4:00 p.m. Then they paired up and went separate ways to different destinations.[23] Some of them left more evidence of their activities than others. The most interesting details come from the journals of William McLellin and Orson Pratt.

The missionaries continued on by pairs and converged at a common spot in the Westfield area for a conference beginning Saturday, May 9. On Sunday there was "a large assembly of peopl[e] ... in bro. Lewis' barn and Elder Marsh preached about two hours in the forenoon on the covenants of God ... The sacrament was administered by Elder Marsh." McLellin baptized five.[24] Following the conference, the pairs of apostles continued on, rendezvousing occasionally for branch conferences, baptisms, and to preach to non-Mormons in rented halls.

Examples of McLellin's experiences include staying on May 19 with a Mr. Drune, "a lame man who treated us with the best that he had," after which McLellin wrote in Taylor shorthand, "but his wife was a great slut, very nasty."[25] According to McLellin, in June they "attended an app[ointment] about six miles toward Watertown in a neighborhood of the Christian Order and J[ohn] F. Boynton preached to a small cong[regation]." His topic was "the plain simplicity of the Gospel, and I think," McLellin wrote, "that I never heard a better discourse for its length—it was forcible."[26] The next month in Dolton, New Hampshire, McLellin baptized Ethan Barrows and his mother, Amelia.[27]

Luke Johnson served alongside the others but left no known

---

23. Jan Shipps and John W. Welch, eds., *The Journals of William E. McLellin 1831-1836* (Provo and Urbana: *BYU Studies* and University of Illinois Press, 1994), 171; holograph in LDS Church History Library.

24. Ibid., 175.

25. Ibid., 178. LaJean Carruth identified and transcribed the Taylor shorthand after the book was published.

26. Ibid., 184.

27. Ibid., 191.

record of his labors. William Smith similarly left a light documentary footprint but was paired with Heber Kimball, so we know something of his general movements, if not his frame of mind or other activities beyond the fact that he occasionally delivered a sermon. In any case, some of the apostles traveled to Boston, where they "held forth to that people this important truth, that the Son of Man will appear in this generation, calling upon them to repent and prepare for the day, when the Lord shall cause the foundations of the earth to shake, and his glory eclipse all the bright luminaries of day and night."[28]

Also in June three of the apostles, Orson Hyde, William Smith, and Brigham Young, left their apostolic mission and traveled back to Ohio, to Chardon and Kirtland. A trial was scheduled to be held at the courthouse in Chardon before the Geauga County Court of Common Pleas. The case was the *State of Ohio vs. Joseph Smith Jr.* on a charge of assault and battery upon his brother-in-law Calvin Stoddard, which occurred on April 21.[29] The *Painesville Telegraph* explained that Stoddard "could not be obtained as a witness" at that time. On June 20, Joseph was tried and Calvin Stoddard said that Joseph "struck him on the forehead with his flat hand—the blow knocked him down, when Smith repeated the blow four or five times, very hard—made him blind—that Smith afterwards came to him and asked his forgiveness."

When William Smith was examined, he said he "saw Stoddard come along cursing and swearing—Joseph went out—Stoddard said he would whip him, and drew his cane upon Joseph—Joseph backed the cane off, and struck Stoddard with a flat hand—Stoddard fell down—Joseph struck him once or twice." Mother Lucy Smith testified that she heard "Stoddard talking loud—called Joseph 'a d—d

---

28. Orson Hyde and William E. McLellin to John Whitmer, *Messenger and Advocate*, Oct. 1835, 206.

29. Geauga County, Records, Common Pleas Court, Book Q:497-98, June 16, 1835, microfilm 20,278, Family History Library, Salt Lake City.

false Prophet, and a d—d one thing another." The court said the injured party was satisfied and "the assault might perhaps be justified on the principle of self-defence. The accused was then acquitted."[30]

After the court indicated that Joseph was not guilty as charged, William returned to his missionary work. Brigham Young was absent almost three weeks before catching up with the other apostles.[31]

Lyman Johnson and Orson Pratt walked long distances from conference to conference, preaching wherever they could find an audience in a home, schoolhouse, or public building. In some instances, when they arrived for a branch conference in Maine, New York, or Vermont, they were overjoyed to see the other apostles and to have the opportunity to resolve common issues, as well as to speak to a branch. Sometimes only a few of the apostles arrived at a given conference, but Johnson and Pratt, as examples, attended four gatherings in New York, two in Maine, and three in Massachusetts, Vermont, and Upper Canada over the space of four months, walking a total of over 1,500 miles.[32]

At the conferences the apostles presented a united front and drew upon each others' experiences to mediate disputes, enforce discipline, reinforce controversial doctrines, and perform church ordinances. They made a point of preaching about Joseph's and Sidney's vision of the three degrees of glory, as Orson Pratt recorded on May 17, 1835: "Elder Johnson preached in the forenoon & I in the afternoon upon the vision of Joseph & Sidney."[33] Following the Pillar Point conference, Johnson delivered a sermon on the same

---

30. *Painesville Telegraph*, June 26, 1835, emphasis omitted.

31. Brigham Young journal, June 8-28, 1835, LDS Church History Library.

32. "Record of the Transactions." It was about 300 miles north to York (Toronto); 500 miles from there to Farmington, Maine, to the east; another 200 miles south to Massachusetts; and 600 miles back home again. All of the Twelve were in attendance at Farmington; St. Johnsbury, Vermont; and Westfield and Freedom, New York.

33. Elden J. Watson, *The Orson Pratt Journals* (Salt Lake City: Eldon J. Watson, 1975), 62; holograph in LDS Church History Library.

topic.[34] When he preached in Dalton, Coos County, New Hampshire, in July, Ethan Barrows, an eighteen-year-old youth, listened carefully and later reported that Johnson, once again, recounted a personal visitation of an angel, which underscored his credentials as an apostle:

> I had the privilege of hearing a lecture from Elder Lyman E. Johnson, a Mormon elder, who preached in my father's house. From that time I was convinced that Mormonism was true. He reasoned from the Scriptures in a most powerful manner and showed the constituent parts of the church of Christ, and the errors of the world and its condition at the present time, together with the beauty of Christ's kingdom and of the gospel. In conclusion he testified to the truth of the Book of Mormon. He said that an holy angel had ministered with him and had shown him the plates from which the Book of Mormon was translated, and commanded him to testify to all the world that it was true.[35]

Perhaps the most significant event during the first apostolic mission occurred at a conference in St. Johnsbury, Vermont, in mid-summer. On Friday and Saturday, July 17-18, the apostles demonstrated their ability as administrators over the scattered branches when they tried Gladden Bishop, a schismatic elder whose divisiveness, argumentation, and refusal to submit to authority had created a significant problem in the eastern branches. The apostles considered his case, and even though they did not have all the evidence they wanted, decided to withdraw his preaching license in order to keep peace and maintain the authority of the branch presidents.[36]

---

34. Shipps and Welch, *Journals of William E. McLellin*, 185. This meeting was also called the Pillow Point Conference.

35. "Journal of Ethan Barrows," *Journal of History* 15 (Jan. 1922): 36, written ca. 1892.

36. "The Twelve Write," *Messenger and Advocate*, Aug. 1835, 167. The best accounts of this mission are "Dear Brother," ibid., Oct. 1835, 204-7; Watson, *Orson Pratt Journals*, 60-72; Orson F. Whitney, *The Life of Heber C. Kimball*, 2nd ed. (Salt Lake City: Bookcraft, 1945), 79-84; Shipps and Welch, *Journals of*

Following this, the Twelve were invited to preach to a large audience, after which they baptized several people. Orson Pratt wrote: "The 12 set in council & transacted such business as came before us. Publick meetings were held in the same <place> on the 2 days following. 9 came forward & were baptized."[37] McLellin recorded that "on Saturday Elder O. Hyde & Ly[man] Johnson preached to quite a large congregation. Sunday I preached in the forenoon to about 1500 persons on the rise and government of the church of christ & P[arley] Pratt preached in the afternoon on the Kingdom of christ, 9 were baptized during the meeting."[38] Brigham Young, although not the easiest diarist to understand, thought the congregation was larger than his colleagues had estimated: "[July] 19 Sunday the barn and yard was crow[d]ed it was thought their ware betwene 2 and 3 thousand People their was 144 cariges that was counted by the Brotherin."[39]

One gentleman in attendance wrote to describe the atmosphere on July 20 and documented the two interesting discourses he was privileged to hear:

An Old barn, standing by the road-side, has been fitted up as a temporary place for assemblage, and on entering it, we found quite a numerous audience collected, the majority of which were females. On the scaffold of the barn were seated the twelve Mormon Apostles, so called by believers, from Ohio. They looked

William E. McLellin, 171-210; and Esplin and Neilsen, "Record of the Twelve," 4-52. For information about Gladden Bishop, see Richard L. Saunders, "The Fruit of the Branch: Francis Gladden Bishop and His Culture of Dissent," in Roger D. Launius and Linda Thatcher, eds., *Differing Visions: Dissenters in Mormon History* (Urbana: University of Illinois Press, 1994), 102-19.

37. Watson, *Orson Pratt Journals*, 67. Terminal punctuation and capitalization added.

38. Shipps and Welch, *Journals of William E. McLellin*, 190.

39. Brigham Young journal, July 19, 1835, LDS Church History Library. McLellin thought there were about 1,500 people in attendance, while the minutes mentioned over 1,000. Orson Hyde to *Messenger and Advocate*, Aug. 1835, 167, similarly estimated 1,000-1,500.

fresh from the back-woods. A brother [William] of Joe Smith, the chief prophet, composed one of the number.[40]

Though the observer wrote with a dismissive tone about some of the content of the sermons, his candidness allows us to gauge the reaction of the audience and provides an excellent summary of the content of what William McLellin and Parley Pratt conveyed. It is a rare, and we think essential, glimpse into the major concerns of the apostles and their preaching style.

After singing two or three hymns, one of the Apostles arose and commenced murdering the King's English, in an address on the abuse of gifts. He said that God in his mercy, had vouchsafed "to the church of the latter-day saints," i.e. the Mormons, certain peculiar gifts—and among these were "the gift of tongues," and "the gift of healing." It was considering the abuse of these two gifts, especially, that he wished to address the audience, at the present time; inasmuch, as that through the abuse of them, by the saints, great harm had resulted to the church.

For instance, "if a saint had the gift of tongues come upon him," he would at once speak out, without regarding the time or place; sometimes half a dozen saints would be moved by the gift at one time, and all would speak out together. This, said the Apostle, is wrong; it creates confusion, and affords the ungodly an opportunity to taunt the church with speaking "unmeaning gibberish." No saint, he continued, however strongly moved by the gift of tongues, should speak out, unless the occasion warranted it, and not even then, if an interpreter were not present.

After having lectured the church sufficiently on the abuse of the gift of tongues, the Apostle proceeded to speak concerning the gift of healing, which he said had been abused by the church to as great an extent as the first mentioned gift—even some of the

---

40. "Mormonism in New England," *Maine Farmer and Journal of the Useful Arts,* Oct. 9, 1835, 288; reproduced in appendix 3. Local residents remembered that the "Snow barn" was used as a meeting house. See Edward T. Fairbanks, *The Town of St. Johnsbury, Vermont* (St. Johnsbury: Cowles Press, 1914), 218-19.

Apostles were deserving of reprehension for their abuse of this gift. They had attempted to exercise it on "adulterous people"—on persons devoid of faith, and therefore had failed—thus bringing disgrace upon themselves and subjecting the whole church to the derision of the unrighteous.

The speaker gave caution about over-using this gift, then the second apostle, Parley Pratt, proceeded to defend the Latter-day Saint faith:

He said the latter-day saints believed the bible to be a divine revelation, and that so far as its precepts extended, it was sufficient and worthy of all observance. But the old revelations were not suited to the present condition of mankind. The state of society had [been] altered—manners and customs had changed—mankind had become more enlightened, and had new wants. To meet the wants engendered by a more civilized state of society, said the speaker, fresh revelations were needed, and these in mercy to man had been gracefully supplied. In doing this, continued the speaker, the Almighty had but granted us the same which he had bestowed on mankind in former ages. Every successive generation, said he, from the creation of the world to the time of Christ, has had its prophet, its revealer, to make revelations suited to the condition, or conditions of mankind at these periods. He would urge this fact as argument against those who said that the old revelations were sufficient, and that it was contrary to the designs of Providence to give new revelations for the instruction of the people.

The speaker then proceeded to read from the Book of Mormon various passages, the purport of all which was, that the Almighty had set apart a tract of country in the "westward bounds of Missouri," for the inheritance of the latter-day saints; that it was to be called "the New Jerusalem"—that although it belonged to the saints by right, yet they were to obtain the lands by purchase, in order that they might rest in quiet. Here, said he, the latter-day saints are to be gathered from all quarters, and they are commanded to dispose of their flocks and herds, purchase land, and take up their abode in the New Jerusalem. These revelations, said the speaker, were made in the year 1831, "and I am witness that they were made."[41]

The dedication and talent demonstrated by these men on their first mission together as a quorum are altogether impressive. Each man had individual shortcomings, as noted by the critical commentator, but collectively communicated sincerity of message and gravity of mission. It was a good start, although conflicts would soon arise, resulting in mutual charges, counter-charges, suspicions, investigations, and trials, both metaphorical and literal.

---

41. "Mormonism in New England," 288.

5. JOSTLING FOR POSITION

The creation of a new, prestigious leadership quorum spawned, perhaps unsurprisingly, jealousy outside the Quorum of the Twelve Apostles and tension within. Over the next few months, the quorum would find itself faced with an assortment of challenges, individually and collectively. Accusations of impropriety would arise before the apostles had even returned from their first mission, and finger-pointing among themselves would ensue as a result of the outside criticisms and influences.

A gathering of the high council in Kirtland on August 4, 1835, was overseen by members of both the Kirtland and Missouri presidencies. The combined membership included Joseph Smith, Oliver Cowdery, Sidney Rigdon, and Hyrum Smith (evidently filling in for Frederick G. Williams), and the Missouri presidency consisting of David Whitmer, John Whitmer, and William W. Phelps. There were two matters of business before the council. First, it was announced that the council would withdraw fellowship from William McLellin and Orson Hyde unless they appeared and told why they had spoken disparagingly of Sidney Rigdon's school. The council considered, as evidence in the case, an excerpt from a letter McLellin had written to his wife, Emeline, saying it was good she was not attending Rigdon's school in Kirtland "since Elder Hyde has returned and given me a description of the manner in which it is conducted."[1]

---

1. Jan Shipps and John W. Welch, eds., *The Journals of William E. McLellin, 1831-1836* (Provo and Urbana: *BYU Studies* and University of Illinois Press, 1994), 207n65.

"We hereby inform Elders M'Lellin and Hyde," the council announced, "that we withdraw our fellowship from them until they return and make satisfaction face to face."[2] As final as this decision sounded, the apostles were about to return home anyway.[3] When the quorum arrived, the apostles in question appeared before the council and asked forgiveness. Oliver Cowdery recorded in Joseph Smith's journal for September 26: "This evening, the twelve having returned from the east this morning, we met them, and conversed upon some matters of difficulty which ~~was~~ <ware> existing between some of them, and president [Sidney] Rigdon, and all things were settled satisfactorily."[4]

The second issue before the council was a July 29 letter by Warren A. Cowdery, Oliver's brother and presiding high priest in Freedom, New York. Warren accused the apostles of neglecting their duty to recommend that people gather to Missouri and to solicit donations for the Kirtland Temple. They were "a kind of outlaws," he suggested. The council took this up, along with other "reports derogatory to the character and teaching of the Twelve," and concluded that the accusers' "minds were darkened in consequence of covetousness or some other cause other than the Spirit of Truth."[5] Warren's brother Oliver recorded, somewhat sanguinely, that "all things were settled satisfactorily."[6]

---

2. Joseph Smith Jr., et al., *History of the Church of Jesus Christ of Latter-day Saints*, 2nd ed. rev., ed. B. H. Roberts, 7 vols., 1902–32 (Salt Lake City: Deseret Book, 1959), 2:240.

3. Minutes, Aug. 4, 1835, in Joseph Smith Letterbook 1:90-93, LDS Church History Library, Salt Lake City.

4. Dean C. Jessee, Mark Ashurst-McGee, and Richard L. Jensen, eds., *The Joseph Smith Papers: Journals* (Salt Lake City: Church Historian's Press 2008), 1:64, 66; also Fred S. Collier and William S. Harwell, *Kirtland Council Minute Book* (Salt Lake City: Collier Publishing, 1996), 140. According to Heber Kimball, false information had been channeled to Oliver Cowdery by Warren Cowdery and Jared Carter, who knowingly used it to damage the apostles' reputations. Orson F. Whitney, *The Life of Heber C. Kimball*, 2nd ed. (Salt Lake City: Bookcraft, 1945), 86-87.

5. Collier and Harwell, *Kirtland Council Minute Book*, 140.

6. Jessee, et al., *Joseph Smith Papers: Journals*, 1:66.

Showing the relative instability of the Kirtland leadership at the time, another high council meeting was held two days later on September 28, with another roster of participants, Joseph Smith, Sidney Rigdon, and Thomas Marsh serving as high councilmen and Oliver Cowdery, Hyrum Smith, and John Whitmer as the presiding officials. The hearing was to consider whether the apostles had overstepped their bounds in disciplining Gladden Bishop, who had traveled ahead of the apostles to complain of his treatment. For their part, the Twelve felt imposed upon to have to explain themselves. They added that Bishop claimed to be "one of the two witnesses" mentioned in the Book of Revelation and believed he was possessed of a spiritual magnetism that drew men to him and made women instantly fall "in love with him." The high council concluded that the traveling twelve had been correct in their decision and had acted "in righteousness." Bishop made a "humble confession ... and asked forgiveness of the High Council and all the Church," which was granted, and his confession was published in the *Messenger and Advocate*. He was then re-ordained an elder and given a new preaching license.[7]

The first sign of cracks within the quorum appeared on October 29, 1835, beginning with an argument between Joseph Smith and William Smith that left the other apostles shocked at Joseph's patience with his brother's insubordination. Their revulsion quickly turned to expressions of dissatisfaction over nepotism, especially considering how harshly Joseph had reacted to minor missteps by Hyde and McLellin, compared to William's more egregious misbehavior. The outburst occurred during the church trial of David Elliot and his wife, who had allegedly beaten their fifteen-year-old daughter. Joseph and William disagreed about this, and tempers on both sides escalated into insults, after which William refused to

---

7. Ibid., 141-43. See also "Extracts of Conference Minutes," *Messenger and Advocate*, Sept. 1835, 186.

apologize.[8] Two days later he insulted Joseph again, then returned his minister's license in further defiance.[9]

Orson Hyde hand-delivered a letter on December 15 outlining his concerns to Joseph Smith about how the prophet had pampered his brother William. Rather than talk it over, Hyde felt uncertain enough about how Joseph would receive his criticism that he turned to written communication, providing him with "greater liberty" to vent his inner feelings. He reminded Joseph that although he, Orson, had contributed a substantial amount to a store in Kirtland which they both had an interest in, when he visited the store he was offered no credit. Because he had attended to his mission assignments, he had been "reduced ... to nothing in a pecuniary" way. William, on the other hand, "could go to the Store and get whatever he pleased."[10] Hyde continued:

> While we were abroad this last season we strain[e]d every nerve to obtain a little something for our families and regularly divided the monies equally for ought that I know, not knowing that William had such a fountain at home from whence he drew his support. I then called to mind the revelation in which myself, McLellen and Patten where chastened and also the quotation in that revelation of the parable of the twelve sons ... I would now ask if each of the twelve have not an equal right to the same accommodations from that Store provided they are alike faithful.[11]

Hyde said he had received offers to go into business and had turned them down. Now he wondered if he had been wise to say no.

---

8. *History of the Church*, 2:294-95.

9. Jessee, et al., *Joseph Smith Papers: Journals*, 1:80.

10. The purpose of the store is explained in *History of the Church*, 2:333.

11. Orson Hyde to Joseph Smith, Dec. 15, 1835, ibid., 2:107-10, complained further that William could "get whatever he pleased" and there was "no one to say, why do ye so?" He had run up an account of about $700. "If each one [of the Twelve] has the same right, take the baskets from off our noses, and put one to William's nose," he suggested. Hyde was upset and threatened to resign his position as an apostle over this.

Joseph suggested that they meet and talk, which they did, and Hyde later confirmed that his concerns had been taken seriously. He came away feeling "more than satisfyed."[12]

That evening, Joseph attended a debate at William's home where he became entangled in an even greater altercation with William, who physically assaulted him and "some others," including Jared Carter.[13] Two days later William begged for forgiveness, writing to Joseph: "Do not cast me off for what I have done, but strive to save me in the Church as a member. I do repent of what I have done to you and ask your forgiveness."[14] He had been "called to an account by the 12," he wrote, and had offered to resign for the disgrace he had brought upon the quorum.[15]

A member of the high council, Orson Johnson, filed a formal charge against William on December 29 for disrespecting the church president and "attempting to inflict" injury on him. The case came to trial on January 2, 1836, and William again assumed "a spirit of meekness and humility." For admitting his wrong and apologizing, he was forgiven. Things seemed resolved for the moment.[16]

In the middle of the ongoing conflict, the apostles were stunned on November 3 when Joseph received "the word of the Lord" saying that the Twelve were "under condemnation" for having dealt "with each other" unequally—for favoring some over others "in

---

12. Jessee, et al., *Joseph Smith Papers: Journals*, 1:124-28. The December 15 letter is copied under December 17.

13. Ibid., 2:106-7. Joseph Smith's injuries were apparently substantial. On December 18 he accused William of attacking him while he was removing his coat. "Having once fallen into the hands of a mob, and been wounded in my side, and now into the hands of a brother, my side gave way, and after having been rescued, from your grasp, I left your house." He said that for a time he was "not able to sit down, or rise up, without help, but through the blessings of God I am now better." Ibid., 2:116.

14. Ibid., 2:111-13.

15. Jessee, et al., *Joseph Smith Papers: Journals*, 1:129-130.

16. Collier and Harwell, *Kirtland Council Minute Book*, 153-54.

the division of the moneys which came into their hands." This was, of course, the very complaint Orson Hyde had lodged against Joseph Smith in his treatment of his family. It was Joseph who had introduced inequality among the quorum. But now the tables were turned and the accusation had come back in the name of "the Lord your God," removing from Joseph Smith the onus of having to cite a specific offense. Apostles Patten, Hyde, and McLellin were singled out for chastisement for not having been "sufficiently humble." "I appointed these twelve," the voice of God declared, "that they should be equal in their ministry and in their portion and in their evangelical rights, wherefore they have sined a verry grievous sin, inasmuch as they have made themselves unequal and have not hearkened unto my voice therfor let them repent speedily and prepare their hearts for the solem assembly and for the great day which is to come Verely thus saith the Lord Amen."[17]

Warren Parrish, who recorded the revelation, read it to Hyde and McLellin two days later. Initially taken aback, they soon concluded, "after examining their own hearts," that it was true and "accknowledged it to be the word of the Lord and said they were satisfied."[18] Despite the profession of humility, it was clear there were, in fact, ongoing tensions between the apostles and the first presidency. Most of the apostles felt they had been abused in one way or another by the presidency, and the issue came to a head on January 16, 1836, when the presidency asked the Twelve if it had any concerns. Yes, Thomas Marsh said, the apostles were unhappy over having been accused of wrongdoing during their recent mission and for being held suspect by the high council, which took it upon itself to review their case even though it lacked jurisdiction. In addition, the apostles had been seated below the high council at a recent function, as if the apostles were subordinate to them rather

---

17. Jessee, et al., *Joseph Smith Papers: Journals*, 1:83. This revelation is not in the Doctrine and Covenants.

18. Ibid., 2:65-66.

than equal in authority. Considering that the Twelve had "passed through many trials," Marsh continued, "the presidency ought not to suspect their fidelity nor lose confidence in them, neither [should the presidency] have chastened them upon such testimony as was lying before them." The First Presidency had believed Warren Cowdery over them and had failed to hold Warren accountable for slander after it was determined that he had misrepresented the facts.[19] Oliver Cowdery, too, had abused them, and "on a certain occasion had made use of language to one of the twelve that was unchristian and unbecoming any man." In the future, "they would not submit to such treatment," they announced.

Joseph asked if they were "determined to persevere in the work of the Lord." After receiving an affirmative answer, he reassured them that he had the utmost confidence in them. He asked forgiveness for his insensitivity, pleading that mistakes had been made on all sides. "The 12, are not subject to any other than the first presidency; viz. myself S. Rigdon and F G. Williams," he intoned. "I do place unlimited confidence in your word for I believe you to be men of truth, and I ask the same of you," he said. Elder Rigdon apologized, saying he should have investigated the claim made by Warren Cowdery before assuming it was true. The apostles said they found these explanations to be adequate.[20]

There followed a brief period of unity and spiritual manifestations, although the inequality that had been complained of would be reinforced through the imposition of seniority by age, the oldest apostle being singled out as the president of the quorum. On January 22, Joseph wrote about the presidency's preference for Marsh:

---

19. Warren A. Cowdery issued an apology for the "wounding ... of feelings," which he said he "most deeply regrets," although it was not something he had intended, he wrote to the *Messenger and Advocate*, Feb. 1836, 263.

20. Jessee, et al., *Joseph Smith Papers: Journals*, 1:158-59. In 1845 the words "where I am not, there is no first presidency; over the twelve" were added to the journal entry as recorded in Manuscript History B-1:691. See *History of the Church*, 2:374.

We then laid our hands upon Elder Thomas B. Marsh who is the president of the 12 and ordained him to the authority of anointing his brethren, I then poured the consecrated oil upon his head in the name of Jesus Christ and sealed such blessings upon him as the Lord put into my heart; the rest of the presidency then laid their hands upon him and blessed him each in their turn beginning at the eldest; he then anointed <and blessed> his brethren from the oldest to the youngest, I also laid my hands upon them and pronounced many great and glorious [blessings] upon their heads; the heavens were opened and angels ministered unto us.[21]

The special status enjoyed by Marsh was noted in a report by Oliver Cowdery after he and Marsh met on January 23: "In the evening Elder Marsh called at my house: we talked much upon the subject of visions: He greatly desired to see the Lord. Brother Marsh is a good man, and I pray that his faith may be strengthen[ed] to behold the heavens open."[22] The former tension between Marsh and Cowdery had dissipated, and the quorum president was being treated with special attention as one of an inner circle of top church leaders. This would pay dividends in the near future as other apostles would rediscover sharp elbows and would fall into a pattern of publicly clashing with the presidency and then reconciling. However, some of the challenges that loomed ahead would prove difficult to so blithely overcome.

Many of the apostles participated during the winter of 1835-36 in studying Hebrew at the School of the Prophets. On December 2, after conducting a funeral together, Orson Pratt and Lyman Johnson mentioned that they "studied the Hebrew language" in the latter part of the day. Orson was still renting a room with Lyman and Sarah Johnson for $5 a month.[23] Their other classmates at the

---

21. Jessee, et al., *Joseph Smith Papers: Journals*, 1:171.
22. "Oliver Cowdery's Sketch Book," Jan. 23, 1836, LDS Church History Library.
23. Elden J. Watson, comp. and ed., *The Orson Pratt Journals* (Salt Lake City:

Hebrew school included John Boynton, Luke Johnson, William McLellin, and William Smith. Some of these erstwhile scholars continued to serve as *ad hoc* high councilmen despite the divine injunction against being involved in stake business. There were apostles on the high council when it heard a dispute between Joseph Smith and Almon Babbitt, for example.[24] Perhaps it was one way they were able to pay their way while they were at home between assignments, since they did not seem to be involved to any great extent in secular pursuits. They seemed to be professional ministers now, at home and abroad.[25]

Lyman Johnson felt lucky to be in Kirtland when Sarah delivered her first child in February 1836.[26] Meanwhile, his father's tavern was doing well. It was suggested as a place where four Egyptian mummies could be displayed after they were purchased in 1835 by Joseph Smith and others from a traveling curiosity peddler. Joseph would transcribe the writing on the associated papyri into what he would call the Book of Abraham.[27]

William Smith had no sooner returned home from his mission than he moved his wife, Caroline, into a new home. After the dramatic events involving his assault on his brother and his narrow escape from a church trial, the record is silent about his activities except for a sudden, unexpected entry in his brother's journal

---

By the compiler, 1975), 74; Andrew Jenson, "Lyman Eugene Johnson," *Latter-day Saint Biographical Encyclopedia*, 4 vols. (Salt Lake City: Andrew Jenson History Company, 1901–30), 1:92.

24. Collier and Harwell, *Kirtland Council Minute Book*, 150-53.

25. Stanley B. Kimball, in his biography, *Heber C. Kimball: Mormon Patriarch and Pioneer* (Urbana: University of Illinois Press, 1981), 28, wondered how Heber could give $200 toward the temple when the average wage was less than a dollar a day. In fact, the apostles were allowed a percentage of the tithing they collected. D. Michael Quinn, *The Mormon Hierarchy: Extensions of Power* (Salt Lake City: Signature Books and Smith Research Associates, 1997), 204-05.

26. "Sarah M. Johnson," *Genealogies*, https://familysearch.org.

27. For more on the Book of Abraham, see Robert K. Ritner, ed., *The Joseph Smith Papyri: A Complete Edition* (Salt Lake City: Signature Books, 2013).

for January 28, 1836, reporting that William saw "the h[e]avens op[e]ned & the Lords host protecting the Lords anointed."[28] In February, William got into trouble again when he lost his temper with the Hebrew teacher Joshua Seixas.[29] Surprisingly, it did not prevent William from receiving yet another vision, this time a glimpse of the future of "the Twelve … in old England." He "prophesied that a great work would be done by them in the old countries, and God was beginning to work in the hearts of the people."[30]

On January 20, 1836, John Boynton married nineteen-year-old Susannah (Susan) Lowell at the home of John and Elsa Johnson in Kirtland. Joseph Smith performed the ceremony using wording from the new Article on Marriage, part of the Doctrine and Covenants, which outlawed polygamy, among other things. Joseph's journal reads, "I then envited them to join hands and I pronounced the ceremony according to the rules and regulations of the church of the Latter-day Saints, in the name of God, and in the name of Jesus Christ I pronounced upon them the blessings of Abraham Isaac and Jacob and such other blessings as the Lord put into my heart."[31]

Heber Kimball's daughter Helen remembered how, at the time, it was common to see apostles in and around Newel Whitney's store. She had her eye on the owner's son Horace, whom she would eventually marry as her second husband. Elder Boynton gave her future husband a flute, she remembered, and everyone was grateful for this because prior to that, Horace had engaged in "incessant practice" on a fife, testing the limits of everyone's patience. The flute was more soothing. Boynton gave the young man his first lessons, after which Newel supervised his son's progress. The flautist came into demand

---

28. Jessee, et al., *Joseph Smith Papers: Journals*, 1:174.

29. William Smith, *William Smith on Mormonism* (Lamoni, IA: Herald Steam Book and Job Office, 1882), 23.

30. Kyle R. Walker, ed., *United by Faith: The Joseph Sr. and Lucy Mack Smith Family* (American Fork, UT: Covenant Communications, 2005), 261-62.

31. Jessee, et al., *Joseph Smith Papers: Journals,* 1:165.

at young people's parties, producing "sweet strains that flowed soft and mellow from his instrument."[32]

Thomas Marsh wrote an 1835 opinion piece for the *Messenger and Advocate*, deducing that the current "tribulations and afflictions" in the church were signs of the end of times.[33] He assured readers that they had "great reason to rejoice, seeing you have already been brought to pass through many tribulations because of your faith." They had been sustained in the church through the "opening of the heavens, the ministering of angels, and by the raising up a prophet in these last days." It was true that even more "perilous times" lay ahead, he wrote, which would require "great faith and diligence, that Zion may be redeemed." Their destiny was to return to Missouri, he intimated.[34]

The leadership continued to prepare people for the pentecostal experience Joseph Smith had predicted for the Kirtland Temple dedication in March 1836. Church members had already participated in enough highly emotional worship services that the expectation of a spiritual outpouring would not have been unusual. Still, the construction and dedication of the temple were shrouded in some mystery. For example, historian Mark Staker attempted to document one of the most cherished stories surrounding the temple, that members allowed their best china to be ground up into the stucco to make it sparkle. Staker ultimately concluded that the story was not true.[35] It is difficult for people today to imagine how members in the 1830s could have denied the faith after attending the temple dedication, where it was later said that an angel flew

---

32. Jeni Broberg Holzapfel and Richard Neitzel Holzapfel, eds., *A Woman's View: Helen Mar Whitney's Reminiscences of Early Church History* (Provo: BYU Religious Studies Center, 1997), 387.

33. He cited Acts 14:22, that it is only through "much tribulation" that we "enter into the kingdom of God."

34. "To the Saints," *Messenger and Advocate*, Nov. 1835, 219-20.

35. Mark Lyman Staker, *Hearken, O Ye People: The Historical Setting of Joseph Smith's Ohio Revelations* (Salt Lake City: Greg Kofford Books, 2009), 437.

through the window and sat down next to Joseph Smith Sr. These events were, as always, discerned by spiritual eyes and were not apparent to everyone, nor were they reported immediately.

However, some of those who attended the dedication on March 27 did report seeing angels or hearing people speak in tongues. At a later worship service on April 3, featuring Thomas Marsh and David Patten as speakers, Joseph Smith recorded privately that when he and Oliver Cowdery retired behind a curtain, they received astonishing visitations, one after another, from Jesus, Moses, Elias, and Elijah.[36] For all the anticipation the apostles invested in the promise of a spiritual endowment, all William McLellin could "in all candor say" was that he was "most egregiously mistaken or disappointed!"[37] He was probably not so much disillusioned at the time as driven to further self-purification in the hope that the promised event would yet occur in his life. Still, their anticipation created a bond among them as they fasted and prayed and met together prior to the dedication, and for the moment the future looked bright.

Three days after the event when Joseph saw Jesus behind the veil, Lyman Johnson left Kirtland for another tour of the eastern branches, with Milton Holmes and John Herrit as mission companions. Their itinerary took in New York, Massachusetts, Maine, and New Brunswick of Lower Canada. The *Messenger and Advocate* summarized their progress:

> The Elder [Johnson] gives us to understand that he has met with little opposition, except from those whose craft was in danger; but that God had in every instance thus far given him wisdom that his adversaries had not been able to gainsay nor resist. He f[u]rther

---

36. *History of the Church*, 2:382-83, 386, 391, 411, 430; Leonard J. Arrington, *Brigham Young: American Moses* (New York: Knopf, 1985), 53; Shipps and Welch, *Journals of William E. McLellin*, 319-20; and Watson, *Orson Pratt Journals*, 75. Elias and Elijah are the same biblical name in two different languages.

37. William E. McLellin to Elder D. H. Bays, May 24, 1870, *Saints' Herald*, Sept. 15, 1870, 554.

adds, although this mission has not been as successful as some others in bringing souls into the kingdom, yet through the assistance of God he had been instrumental in establishing a small branch of a church of eighteen members in the town of Sackville [Maine].[38]

Brigham Young joined the three at Newry, Maine, on August 12-14.[39] He wrote that on Sunday he "preached in forenoon, Elder L. E. Johnson in afternoon."[40] Afterward they traveled to Boston. When Lyman returned to Kirtland in September, the newspaper reported that he had "baptized five since he wrote us, making 27 in all since he left home in April last."[41]

John Boynton baptized twenty-two-year-old Lorenzo Snow in the summer, bringing the future president of the Utah church into the fold from a small town thirty miles south of Kirtland. Lorenzo's sister had preceded him into the church and was living in Kirtland, where she offered to put him up while he attended Hebrew class. The fact that Boynton would take on the conversion of the Snow boy shows the laxity with which the apostles took the demarcation between stake and mission jurisdictions. In July, Boynton was overjoyed to be able to receive his parents, two sisters, and two brothers-in-law into the city after their emigration from Boston and that circumstances allowed him and his wife Susan to be together without interruption for several months.[42] As a result, their first son, John Lowell, would be born nine months later in April 1837.

---

38. "From the Elders Abroad," *Messenger and Advocate*, July 1836, 352. See Richard E. Bennett, "Plucking Not Planting," in *The Mormon Presence in Canada*, ed. Brigham Y. Card, et al. (Logan: Utah State University Press, 1990), 23.

39. Brigham Young to Oliver Cowdery, Sept. 15, 1836, *Messenger and Advocate*, Nov. 1836, 408. See also "From the Elders Abroad," ibid., Sept. 1836, 381-82.

40. Brigham Young diary, Aug. 14, 1836, typescript in authors' possession.

41. "From the Elders Abroad," 381.

42. Caroline Barnes Crosby, Memoirs, ca. 1851, microfilm, Church History Library; also in Edward Leo Lyman, Susan Ward Payne, and S. George Ellsworth, eds., *No Place to Call Home: The 1807-1857 Life Writings of Caroline Barnes Crosby, Chronicler of Outlying Mormon Communities* (Logan: Utah State University Press, 2005), 45.

The summer also saw Luke Johnson retracing his brother's steps through New York and Upper Canada. He went to Jefferson County to allow his lovesick companion, Orson Pratt, to see one particular former convert.[43] The year previously Orson had baptized eighteen-year-old Sarah Marinda Bates. Now he was intent on marrying her. On their arrival, Luke performed the marriage on the Fourth of July, giving the couple three days for a honeymoon. Then they left Sarah with her parents while they continued on to Upper Canada. At the end of their mission, they met at Sackets Harbor to arrange and lead a delegation of emigrants, including Sarah, to a new home in Kirtland.[44]

The other apostles were just leaving on new mission assignments in mid-summer when William McLellin was returning from a mission to Kentucky. When he arrived in Kirtland, he found that a lot had happened in a short time, and what he saw shocked him. Joseph Smith and others had become involved in commercial activities in a large way, which seemed to be a manifestation of so much "pride and folly." He was so upset that in August he resigned his apostolic commission and turned in his preaching license.[45] He and Emeline and their two children quietly moved to Illinois.[46] However, the McLellin odyssey was not yet over.

His colleagues in the quorum appealed to him on December 18

---

43. "History of Luke Johnson (by Himself)," *Deseret News*, May 26, 1858, 57.

44. "History of the Life of Oliver B. Huntington: Also His Travels and Troubles," L. Tom Perry Special Collections, Harold B. Lee Library, Brigham Young University, Provo, 27; typescript available on the *New Mormon Studies CD-ROM: A Comprehensive Resource Library* (Salt Lake City: Smith Research Associates, 2009).

45. William E. McLellin to John L. Traughber, Dec. 14, 1878, in *The William E. McLellin Papers, 1854-1880*, eds. Stan Larson and Samuel J. Passey (Salt Lake City: Signature Books, 2007), 513.

46. Larry C. Porter, "The Odyssey of William Earl McLellin: Man of Diversity, 1806-83," in Shipps and Welch, *Journals of William E. McLellin*, 321. William wrote to James Cobb on August 14, 1880: "I left the church in Aug. 1836, not because I disbelieved the Book [of Mormon] or the (then) doctrine preached or held by the Church, but because the Leading men to a great extent

to return home: "When you left Kirtland, You left home. Come home, Come home." "If you will not come otherwise" they wrote, "one or all of us will go after you. Your place is yet vacant." Their appeals struck McLellin right in the heart. His response in January 1837 was: "My course I know has been novel in the history of the transactions of the anointed. The reasons of my conduct are few and I deem it unnecessary to make an attempt to as[s]ign them in this place. Suffice it to say, I am sorry for the course that I have pursued. Can You, Will you forgive me? Will Brother Joseph forgive me? And will the Church forgive me?"[47] They said they would. He rejoined his quorum in Kirtland for a time.

During this period Thomas Marsh was in Missouri helping church members in Clay County move to Caldwell County, a political designation that was created for Mormons. In a short time, the newly founded town of Far West, established in August 1836, would become the county seat and headquarters of the church in Missouri. Marsh served a short mission to Tennessee and Kentucky, afterward purchasing a lot for his own family in Caldwell County.

All the while Joseph Smith was formulating plans for expansion beyond the boundaries of the United States and Canada. In his enthusiasm, and in the chaos of Kirtland in 1837-38, he neglected to inform the quorum president, Thomas Marsh, that he wanted to send some apostles to England. The fact that Marsh was still in Missouri played a role in this oversight. However, on May 10, 1837, Marsh and the second-highest-ranking apostle, David Patten, wrote to Parley Pratt in Canada, "We have heard that you have left Kirtland for Toronto Upper Canada, and that you [have] intended to leave there soon for England." If that was the case, they needed to be informed. Things should proceed in an orderly way, Marsh advocated.

---

left their religion and run into and after speculation, pride, and popularity!" Larson and Passey, *William E. McLellin Papers*, 523.

47. William E. McLellin to "My dear old Friends [apostles]," Jan. 24, 1837, in Shipps and Welch, *Journals of William E. McLellin*, 229-30.

Dear Brother—are we not fellow labourers & fellow sufferers in the same cause? ... Much depends, very much on the way and manner in which the glorious gospel is first introduced into that country[,] then be not hasty, but grant us, or unto me Thomas [Marsh] at least to council you upon this subject, for unto this was I anointed & unto the 12 it belongs to know within themselves, or within their own quorum when and how to go to the nations, and to spread the light of the Everlasting truth to the ends of the earth.

They urged Pratt "not [to] go till we see you!!!" They also argued that before launching a new missionary effort, they needed to smooth out the difficulties that had sprung up among the apostles. "You cannot leave here, in the present unsettled state of things & prosper as you otherwise would." They neglected, in their letter, to mention the recent death of Pratt's wife, Thankful Halsey, who passed away at the end of March after giving birth, probably indicating that they had not heard. Pratt was in Toronto converting future Utah church president John Taylor, among others, and had made occasional trips back to Kirtland to refresh his supply of tracts, transporting his pregnant wife there for her delivery.[48] After her death, and leaving his newborn son, Parley Jr., with a wet nurse, he returned to Canada to complete his mission assignment.

Marsh and Patten informed him that they were calling everyone "together as soon as circumstances will admit" to "obtain wisdom and council from God." The meeting would be confidential and would be held in Kirtland on July 24, 1837, at 9:00 a.m. Only the apostles would be in attendance.[49] Even eliminating the trauma of Pratt's recent tragedy, the timing was not good to expect him to

48. Janet Lisonbee, *In Memory of the Early Saints Who Lived and Died in the Kirtland, Ohio, Area* (N.p., by the author, 2003), 11-12; Terryl L. Givens and Matthew J. Grow, *Parley P. Pratt: The Apostle Paul of Mormonism* (New York: Oxford University Press, 2011), 83-86, 91-92. The tracts were sold to investigators at a profit for Pratt (90).

49. Thomas Marsh and David Patten to Parley P. Pratt, May 10, 1837, copied into the Joseph Smith Letterbook, 2:62-63, LDS Church History Library.

attend a secret meeting in Kirtland, where rumors were circulating that some of the leading brethren wanted to depose President Smith. It is unclear whether Marsh understood the depth of trouble he was stepping into. However, Pratt responded that during his brief stay in Kirtland he had seen "many" stalwarts fall away to become "enemies and apostates," then added the unfathomable, that he himself had been "overcome by the same spirit in a great measure, and it seemed as if the very powers of darkness which war against the Saints were let loose upon me."[50]

Pondering the meaning of this confession, Marsh started for Kirtland on June 13, accompanied by Patten, William Smith, and others, and ran into Pratt "about five miles west of Columbus." Pratt was moving his things to Far West. Marsh "prevailed on him to return with us to Kirtland," and they continued north together.[51] No sooner had the group arrived in Kirtland about July 8, however, than Patten confronted Joseph Smith. Many years later Brigham Young remembered that Patten insulted Smith, and "Joseph slap[p]ed him in the face & kicked him out of the yard. This done David good."[52] Whether or not it did, and whether or not they reconciled, Parley Pratt found a way to get over his disillusionments and "went to brother Joseph Smith in tears." He said that, "with a broken heart and contrite spirit," he "confessed wherein [he] had erred murmured, or done or said amiss."[53]

Marsh followed suit and did what he could to alleviate the tension he had felt between himself and Joseph over not being kept informed. A convert from Canada, Mary Fielding, said Marsh interjected a spirit of calm at a time when it was most needed, writing

---

50. Scot Facer Proctor and Maurine Jensen Proctor, eds., *Autobiography of Parley P. Pratt*, rev. ed. (Salt Lake City: Deseret Book, 2000), 209-10. Parley's level of dissent against Joseph Smith was demonstrated in his May 23, 1837, letter to Smith published in *Zion's Watchman*, Mar. 24, 1838.

51. "History of Thos. Baldwin Marsh," *Deseret News*, Mar. 24, 1858, 18.

52. Brigham Young, qtd. in Scott G. Kenney, ed., *Wilford Woodruff's Journal*, 9 vols. (Midvale, UT: Signature Books, 1983-85), 5:63.

53. Proctor and Proctor, *Autobiography of Parley P. Pratt*, 210-11.

that "Elder Marsh is a most excelent Man. He seems to be a Man of great faith. He says he believs the difficult[ie]s between the Presidency & the twelve will very shortly be settled."[54]

Marsh moved in with Joseph and Emma Smith while Elizabeth and the children were still out of state. Meeting at the Smith home, where "several of the brethren who were disaffected were invited," Marsh acted as the "moderator" and declared the meeting a success. A "reconciliation was effected between all parties," he wrote.[55] On July 23, Joseph received a revelation declaring that Marsh's sins were forgiven. Such a declaration was a two-edged sword that both condemned him for unnamed bad behavior and offered absolution. "Be thou humble," Marsh was commanded, "and the Lord thy God shall lead thee by the hand and give thee answer to thy prayers. ... [P]ray for your brethren of the twelve. Admonish them sharply for my name's sake, and let them be admonished for all their sins, and be ye faithful before me unto my name." However much the reminder that he had sinned to the extent that he deserved removal from office may have stung, Marsh took it well and was comforted.

The revelation included a warning to the Twelve: "Exalt not yourselves; rebel not against my servant Joseph for Verily I say unto you I am with him and my hand shall be over him; and the keys which I have given him, and also to youward shall not be taken from him untill I come."[56] According to the revelation, Thomas held the keys of discipleship among all nations. In this capacity, he was to "unlock the door of the kingdom in all places" where the church presidency had not established a stake. "Vengeance" would speedily come upon the earth, the revelation continued, as humankind

---

54. Mary Fielding to Mercy Fielding Thompson, July 8, 1837, LDS Church History Library.

55. "History of Thos. Baldwin Marsh," 18.

56. "Youward" is a biblical term that fell into the same category of archaic nonuse in America as "froward" and "thitherward."

had become so corrupt. This would begin and go forth, not from the ends of the earth, but from the mother church, "my house" in Kirtland, until darkness would cover the whole earth "and gross darkness the ~~people~~ minds of the people."

> Behold vengeance cometh speedily upon the inhabitants of the earth. A day of wrath! A day of burning! A day of desolation! Of weeping! Of mourning and of lamentation! And as a whirlwind it shall come upon all the face of the earth saith the Lord. And upon my house shall it begin and from my house shall it go forth saith the Lord.[57]

Heber Kimball's wife, Vilate, copied the revelation "from Elder Marsh[']s book as he wrote it from Joseph[']s mouth" and sent it to her husband in a letter.[58] Dark and ominous, the intent was to rally disaffected members whose corruption had placed a target on their backs. They would not read about the pre-millennial destruction in the newspapers, they were informed, but would experience it firsthand as the chosen ones who had failed to meet God's expectations for them.

In a twist of irony that would reveal itself later, Marsh became the staunchest supporter of Joseph Smith during the Kirtland revolt. Three of the apostles, who sided with the dissenters, were disfellowshipped on Sunday, September 3. Marsh convinced the wavering Johnson brothers to reconsider and reconcile themselves to the church and arranged a meeting at Joseph's house with John Boynton and others to work out their differences. Vilate confirmed to her husband, Heber, that a period of good feelings ensued, Marsh having convinced Boynton and Lyman Johnson to "make their confession." According to Marsh's confidant, "he thought there would be

---

57. Jessee, et al., *Joseph Smith Papers: Journals*, 1:307–08; LDS D&C 112; RLDS D&C 105.

58. Vilate Kimball to Heber C. Kimball, Sept. 6–11, 1837, LDS Church History Library.

no difficulty" with the other Johnson brother when Luke came "to find the rest all united."[59]

On September 10 an "assembly" at the temple included confessions by John Boynton and the Johnsons, after which the remaining congregation of loyal members indicated that it was satisfied. By this means, the apostles were "received into the fellowship of the Saints and [would] retain their Apostleship." On paper it looked like the ship of latter-day saints was righting itself. However, things were unstable enough that Marsh felt he needed to leave immediately for Missouri and left a letter for someone else to read out loud giving his endorsement of the three apostles. "Elder Young also stated the same to the congregation." The reinstated apostles then administered the sacrament.[60]

Marsh arrived in Far West sometime before October 10 and was there on November 12 when his wife gave birth to Mary Elizabeth. Two months later, Joseph Smith and Sidney Rigdon were forced to leave Kirtland in the middle of the night. As they began their mid-winter trek to Far West, Marsh and Patten took control of the church in Missouri, where they had become angered by the accusations and threats they had heard from men in the leadership.[61] Their mission experiences had made the apostles accustomed to taking charge wherever they saw the need to put the church in order.[62]

---

59. Ibid.

60. Collier and Harwell, *Kirtland Council Minute Book*, 188–89.

61. Leland Homer Gentry, "A History of the Latter-day Saints in Northern Missouri from 1836 to 1839," PhD. diss. (Provo: Brigham Young University, 1965), 119, 131, explained that the dissenters in Missouri maintained "a continual correspondence" with "the gang of marauders in Kirtland." Oliver Cowdery and Lyman Johnson brought unpaid notes with them from Kirtland and demanded payment on them.

62. Historian Lyndon Cook found Marsh "jealous to win greater recognition and influence." While "evidence shows that Oliver and his cohorts were embittered, the means Thomas used did not justify the end," in Cook's estimation. Lyndon W. Cook, "'I Have Sinned against Heaven ...' Thomas B. Marsh Returns to the Church," *BYU Studies* 20 (Summer 1980): 393–94.

Despite being outside their jurisdiction, Marsh and Patten determined to do the very thing in Missouri that the dissidents had done in Kirtland and topple the leaders. At a meeting at Marsh's house on January 20, 1838, euphemistically referred to as a "social gathering," he and Patten conferred with seven of the high councilmen about taking action against "the Presidents in this place ... being grieved at their doings." After agreeing to act, they "appointed a committee to visit" the stake presidency and "e[n]quire into their feelings and determinations."[63] If this soirée was indeed a party, it had acquired a more serious agenda than small talk.

Marsh called the high council together as a "Committee of the whole church in Zion" and opened a three-day trial on alternate days, February 5-9, at different locations throughout Missouri. The committee charged David Whitmer, William Phelps, John Whitmer, and Oliver Cowdery with selling their lands in Jackson County, misuse of funds, and violating the Word of Wisdom. The council voted to remove the Whitmers and Phelps from office.[64] The next day the committee met with the bishop of the Missouri churches and, at the request of the intervening apostles, appointed Marsh and Patten as "presidents, pro. tempor. of the Church of the Latter Day Saints in Missouri, or until Presidents Joseph Smith jr and Sidney Rigdon arrives in the Land of Zion."[65] LDS historian Ronald K. Esplin found this an acceptable development, explaining that "though the apostles had no jurisdiction in an organized

---

63. Donald Q. Cannon and Lyndon W. Cook, eds., *Far West Record: Minutes of the Church of Jesus Christ of Latter-day Saints, 1830-1844* (Salt Lake City: Deseret Book, 1983), 135.

64. Ibid., 137-41. "I told them," wrote Oliver Cowdery, "that if I had property; while I live and was sane, I would not be dictated" in how to dispense with it. "And when I or my family were sick or any other time, I would eat and drink what I thought would do me the most good: this was about the substance of what the others told them." Oliver Cowdery to Warren and Lyman Cowdery, Feb. 4, 1838, Oliver Cowdery Letterbook, 83-84, Henry E. Huntington Library, San Marino, California.

65. Cannon and Cook, *Far West Record*, 141.

stake, members expected Marsh and Patten, prominent residents who shared their concerns, to provide leadership."[66]

A month later Marsh and Patten would call the high council together again, this time to excommunicate William Phelps and John Whitmer on March 10, making the takeover complete.[67] Joseph arrived four days later and "approved of the proceedings of the High Council, after hearing the minutes."[68] A few days later, the prophet composed what was called the "Motto of the Church of Christ of Latterday Saints" and asked Marsh, Patten, Young, and three other men to endorse it. It represented a doubling-down on Joseph's part in his contest with the dissenters—a poker game of sorts in which he refused to fold:

> The Constitution of our country formed by the Fathers of Liberty.
> Peace and good order in society. Love to God and good will to man.
> All good and wholesome Law's; And virtue and truth above all things.
> And Aristarchy live forever!!!
> But Wo, to tyrants, Mobs, Aristocracy, Anarchy and Toryism: And all those who invent or seek out unrighteous and vexatious lawsuits under the pretext or color of law or office, either religious or political.
> Exalt the standard of Democracy! Down with that of Priestcraft, and let all the people say Amen! that the blood of our Fathers may not cry from the ground against us.
> Sacred is the Memory of that Blood which baught for us our liberty.[69]

---

66. Ronald K. Esplin, "Thomas B. Marsh as President of the First Quorum of the Twelve, 1835-1838," in *Hearken, O Ye People: Discourses on the Doctrine and Covenants* (Sandy, UT: Randall Book Company, 1984), 181-82.

67. Cannon and Cook, *Far West Record*, 149.

68. Ibid., 151.

69. This was copied into Joseph Smith's Scriptory Book and signed by "Joseph

One can see Joseph working through a solution to the dilemma of needing or wanting to break the laws and procedures that were put in place to prevent anarchy. At what point, he wonders, does one break the rules in order to preserve them? Right before he left Kirtland, he and Rigdon presented for consideration a set of "rules & regulations governing the House of the Lord" after John Boynton had, a month prior, drawn a sword from his cane and threatened William Smith.[70] In December the dissenters armed themselves and followed Boynton's example by bringing their weapons into the temple and, in this case, taking it by force. Now the apostles in Missouri had exacted their own coup. Everything seemed to be coming unraveled.

On April 12 the Missouri high council heard a complaint that Oliver Cowdery had spoken against Joseph Smith's character by mentioning the prophet's relationship with Fanny Alger. Cowdery, according to the complaint, had missed some Sunday services. After deliberation, the verdict was that Cowdery should be excommunicated.[71] The next day Lyman Johnson and David Whitmer were excommunicated.[72] With that accomplished, Marsh went north with Smith and Rigdon to explore sites in Daviess County for the remaining refugees, which would now include members escaping from Ohio.[73]

The next month James Marsh, the fourteen-year-old son of Thomas and Elizabeth, died after a four-day illness. One can imagine the grief they felt and the comfort they received in remembering

---

Smith Jr, Geo. W. Robinson, Thomas B. Marsh, D. W. Patten, Brigham Young, Samuel H. Smith, George M. Hinkle, and John Corrill" (Jessee, et al., *Joseph Smith Papers: Journals*, 1:237-38, emphasis omitted). Aristarchy is government by a "body of good men in power." Noah Webster, *American Dictionary of the English Language*, 1828.

70. Lavina Fielding Anderson, ed., *Lucy's Book: A Critical Edition of Lucy Mack Smith's Family Memoir* (Salt Lake City: Signature Books, 2001), 598.

71. Cannon and Cook, *Far West Record*, 163, 167-69.

72. Ibid., 176, 178.

73. "History of Thos. Baldwin Marsh," 18.

their son's account of his vision of God the Father. This was recounted in the obituary in the *Elders' Journal*:

> DIED on the 7th of May last, James G. Marsh, second son of Thomas B. Marsh, aged 14 years, 11 months and seven days. ... It seems that the Lord had respect unto this lover of righteousness, for when he was but about nine years of age, he had a remarkable vision, in which he talked with the Father and many of the ancient prophets face to face, and beheld the Son of God coming in his glory. ...
>
> A few minutes before he died, a number of boys who had been his playmates came in to see him; he seemed glad to see them and said to them, "Good evening, boys, I shall never see you again in time, so farewell, be good boys and serve the Lord." When his father saw that he prayed the Lord to take him, he said, "My son, are you confident that if you die now your spirit will rest in the celestial paradise?" He answered, "Yes, sir." "Then," said his father, "my son, go in peace and expect to come forth at the resurrection of the just where you and I will again strike hands." He again answered, "Yes, sir, I will," and immediately he fell asleep without a struggle or a groan.[74]

Amid the turmoil accompanying the banishment of once-favored associates, and in the process of doing what he thought he needed to do to stabilize the church, balanced on the edge of survival, Marsh turned his attention to the foreign mission Joseph Smith had spoken of. On July 8, 1838, Joseph received another revelation, this one directing Marsh to stay in Missouri for another year and then to gather the apostles together in Far West in April 1839 at the start of their great mission, when they would "go over the great waters, and there promulgate my [Christ's] gospel."[75] As president of the Quorum of the Twelve, Marsh had been the leader of the first major

---

74. "Obituary," *Elders' Journal*, July 1838, 48.
75. LDS D&C 118; not in RLDS D&C.

mission of the Twelve, and he was ready to lead them again in this venture into truly uncharted territory.

William Smith went to Missouri at the same time his brother traveled there, but then he returned, reaching Kirtland on December 10, 1837. Little is known about what William did, only that he retraced his steps to Missouri in the spring of 1838. He appears to have deliberately kept his distance from the other Saints in Missouri as he, Caroline, and the children established themselves some thirty miles away from Far West.[76] At a conference held on April 7, 1838, David Patten said he could not recommend William due to a report he had "heard respecting his faith in the work."[77] It is a vague accusation, and nothing more is known about it. During the summer William and Caroline fell ill, and when they recovered they found the Mormon War heating up around them. Church members organized militias to battle the state's troops and militias in several counties. On November 1, Joseph Smith, his brother Hyrum, Sidney Rigdon, Parley Pratt, and others were taken prisoner. According to Mother Smith:

> As soon as William was able to stir about a little he besought his father [Joseph Sr.] to move to Illinois, but Mr. Smith would not consent to this, for he was in hopes that our sons [Joseph and Hyrum] would be liberated, and peace again be restored. William continued to expostulate with him, but to no effect, as Mr. Smith declared that he would not leave Far West, except by revelation. William said that he had [a] revelation [that they should depart]; that he himself knew that we would have to leave Far West. Mr. Smith finally said that the family might get ready to move, and then, if we were obliged to go, there would be nothing to hinder us.[78]

---

76. Anderson, *Lucy's Book*, 630.

77. Cannon and Cook, *Far West Record*, 160.

78. Anderson, *Lucy's Book*, 636-37, 674-75. Brigham Young was critical of William's "revelation" (128, 213). He and his counselors and the twelve apostles in Utah signed an epistle on August 23, 1865, alleging that at the time of the Missouri War, William had proven himself to be "a wicked man" who had said

The Saints were, in fact, forced to evacuate, and Joseph sent instructions to his family that they needed to "leave the state." William sent a team and wagon for his mother and sisters and, while his brother Don Carlos moved them, he looked to his own immediate family, moving his wife and daughters to Quincy, Illinois, in February 1839.[79] After a short stay, William relocated to a satellite town, Plymouth, which Don Carlos Smith reported to Joseph and Hyrum from Quincy in March was "forty miles from here." Don Carlos wrote that William was "anxious to have you liberated, and see you enjoy liberty once more."[80] The letter included a postscript from William saying he would have visited them in jail if it had "not been for the multiplicity of business that was on my hands; and again, I thought that perhaps the people might think that the 'Mormons' would rise up to liberate you," that "too many going to see you might make it worse for you." He longed to see them and to have them "come out of that lonesome place. I hope you will be permitted to come to your families before long. Do not worry about them, for they will be taken care of. All we can do will be done; further than this, we can only wish, hope, desire, and pray for your deliverance."[81]

Most of the other apostles stayed to help the impoverished church members relocate to Illinois. Then, absent William, they slipped back into Far West in the middle of the night on April 26, 1839, to fulfill their prior instruction to launch their mission from Far West. Taking advantage of the chance to act officially as a quorum, they summarily excommunicated the schismatic leader Isaac

that if it were up to him, "his brother Joseph would never get out of the hands of his enemies alive," that "he would have hung him years before." James R. Clark, ed., *Messages of the First Presidency of the Church of Jesus Christ of Latter-day Saints, 1833-1964* (Salt Lake City: Bookcraft, 1965), 2:230.

79. Anderson, *Lucy's Book*, 677–80.

80. *History of the Church*, 3:273.

81. Ibid., 3:274. The letter was copied into Joseph Smith's Letterbook, 2:38–39, Church History Library.

Russell and adherents. They had also brought with them a high councilman, Alpheus Cutler, who was said to be as rugged as his name and was an expert stone mason. He would famously split with the apostles, but for now he was willing to risk physical safety for a literal reading of the revelation calling the apostles to England.[82] Now that Cutler was there, he supervised the choice and burial of a memorial cornerstone for the future temple—a temple the church was commanded to build before it became obvious that it would not be possible to do so. Sometime in the future, they assumed, it would be done. There was one other matter of business. Thomas Marsh had since shown disloyalty by expressing pacifistic criticisms of the church, which left a vacancy in the quorum. The death of David Patten at Crooked River, where he had led an ill-fated charge against state troops, had left another vacancy to be filled. Joseph Smith sent word to ordain Wilford Woodruff and George A. Smith. The apostles did so in whispers under the moonlight. The ordinations were voiced by Brigham Young and Heber Kimball, now ranking apostles according to age.[83]

At a general conference the next month in Quincy, the escaped prisoner Joseph Smith announced that William Smith and fellow apostle Orson Hyde would have to appear at "the next general conference of the Church, to give an account of their conduct," and that until that time they were suspended from office.[84] LDS Assistant Church Historian Andrew Jenson later reported that William had

82. *History of the Church* 3:336-39; Cutler became one of Joseph Smith's bodyguards in Illinois. D. Michael Quinn, "The Culture of Violence in Joseph Smith's Mormonism," *Sunstone*, online at www.sunstonemagazine.com.

83. LDS D&C 118:5 (not in RLDS D&C) specified that the apostles were to begin their mission to Great Britain at the Far West temple site on April 26, 1839. Even though the Mormons were evacuating the state, Joseph Smith instructed Young and Kimball on January 16, 1839, that the revelatory instructions were still in place. George C. Lambert, comp., *President Heber C. Kimball's Journal: Seventh Book of the Faith-Promoting Series* (Salt Lake City: Juvenile Instructor Office, 1882), 76.

84. Minutes, May 4-6, 1839, *History of the Church*, 3:345.

"expressed himself in such a vindictive manner against Joseph that the Church suspended him from fellowship, May 4, 1839." If that were true, he quickly repented because he was acting in his office as an apostle three weeks later and was confirmed, along with Hyde, by a vote of the October conference in Commerce (Nauvoo).[85]

That William was not in full harmony with his quorum was nevertheless evident by the fact that he was still in Illinois and the others were in England. He apologized for this negligence in 1840 in the *Times and Seasons*, saying it was "because of my impoverished situation" which had "rendered it necessary for me to use every exertion to support my family." He hoped to still "lift up my voice on the shores of Europe, or wherever the Lord may direct."[86] Forty-five years later, in his *Historical Record*, Andrew Jenson took another aim at William, saying the apology sounded hollow and "came with an ill grace" because William, of any of the apostles, "was better situated to leave his family" at that time.[87] Even though this criticism came nearly half a century after the fact, William bristled at it, insisting that "at the time of the English mission" his "wife was under treatment for dropsy [kidney failure], of which she finally died in the spring of 1845."[88] Caroline died of kidney problems but was not seriously ill until 1842, so William may have conflated events to about the same degree Jenson expanded them.

In any case, William was on hand in September 1840 to receive

---

85. Jenson, "William Smith," *Latter-day Saint Biographical Encyclopedia*, 1:87; *History of the Church*, 4:12. Wilford Woodruff wrote: "Brother Wm. Smith was restored to his Quorum." Scott G. Kenney, ed., *Wilford Woodruff's Journal, 1833–1898*, typescript, 9 vols. (Midvale, UT: Signature Books, 1983–85), 1:334. James Mulholland recorded for June 27, 1839, that Joseph "attended a conference of the Twelve—at which time Br Orson Hyde, made his confession and was restored to the Priesthood again." Jessee, et al., *Joseph Smith Papers: Journals*, 1:343.

86. William Smith to D. C. Smith, *Times and Seasons*, Dec. 15, 1840, 252–53.

87. Jenson, "The Twelve Apostles," *Historical Record*, Mar. 1886, 44; rpt. in *Latter-day Saint Biographical Encyclopedia*, 1:87.

88. "William B. Smith," *The Expositor*, Aug. 1886, 399. The *Expositor* was an RLDS publication.

a deathbed final blessing from his father, in which William was promised that his "voice shall be heard in distant lands, from place to place, and they shall regard thy teachings." It was prophesied that "thy days shall be many, thou shalt do a great work, and live as long as thou desirest life."[89]

He took a short mission in 1841 to Ohio, New Jersey, and Pennsylvania to collect money for the temple and church-owned hotel in Nauvoo. Once again, unable to perceive any virtue in this sunshine soldier, Assistant Church Historian Andrew Jenson accused him of "collect[ing] means for his own benefit" but without giving any evidence of this.[90] In fact, while William was traveling on an Ohio riverboat in April 1841, he was documented promoting the Book of Mormon. The Rev. James Murdock left an account of the apostle telling him the book traced "a company of Jewish Christians" from Israel to America "under the guidance of Lehi their priest and prophet." They "planted themselves in the western part of the present State of New York," Murdock said. "So long as their Christian" values "remained unsullied, they were prosperous," William had explained. "But when their piety degenerated, they became split into parties" and were "assailed by their heathen neighbors, conquered and either exterminated or enslaved, and thus ceased to be a Christian people."[91]

In a letter to brother Don Carlos Smith from Pennsylvania, dated May 8 but apparently not mailed until after May 17, William explained how a man he met had paid for his boat fare to St. Louis and loaned him money for his missionary journey, an act of kindness that moved William to pray that the man would be rewarded "for his kindness, even a hundred fold." He "had little or no money,"

---

89. Anderson, *Lucy's Book*, 719.

90. Jenson, "The Twelve Apostles," *Historical Record*, Mar. 1886, 44; Jenson, *Latter-day Saint Biographical Encyclopedia*, 1:87.

91. James Murdock, June 19, 1841, in *Congregational Observer*, July 3, 1841, 1. See appendix 3 for more of the interview.

William wrote, but he had experienced some successes. He gave every indication that he was a dedicated apostle and missionary.[92]

In April the next year, William founded a Nauvoo newspaper called the *Wasp* to counter the mockery of the nearby *Warsaw Signal*, edited by Thomas Sharp. Feeling that he could match the anti-Mormon editor wit for wit, insult for insult, William engaged in rhetorical volleys with this rival, marked by character assassination. Smith called Sharp "Thom-ASS" and the "long-nosed Sharp," while Sharp called Smith a "polecat" (skunk) and an "infernal devil." As clever as William may have thought he was, the net effect was to increase anti-Mormon sentiment in the towns surrounding Nauvoo.[93]

In the headquarters itself, William was a respected member of the Nauvoo City Council from May 1842 on and was elected to the Illinois legislature in August 1842, upon which he reluctantly resigned his editorship of the *Wasp*. He was told it would not be advantageous for him to appear to be so volatile.[94] Apparently no one saw the harm in his retention of the rank of major in the Nauvoo Legion. In December, John Taylor took over the editorship of the newspaper and immediately changed the name to the friendlier *Nauvoo Neighbor*.

Kyle R. Walker indicates that in the legislature in Springfield on December 9, William "defended the Nauvoo Charter" by pointing out "that it granted privileges no different from those of five other cities in the state and that Nauvoo's charter was singled out because of religious intolerance." His reasoning convinced the House to reject the proposal to repeal the city's expansive charter.[95]

---

92. William Smith to D. C. Smith, May 8, 1841, *Times and Seasons*, June 15, 1841, 444-45.

93. Jerry C. Jolley, "The Sting of the *Wasp*: Early Nauvoo Newspaper, April 1842 to April 1843," *BYU Studies* 22 (Fall 1982): 487-96.

94. T. Edgar Lyon, "Nauvoo and the Council of Twelve," in *The Restoration Movement: Essays in Mormon History*, eds. F. Mark McKiernan, Alma R. Blair, and Paul M. Edwards (Independence: Herald House, 1979), 184.

95. Walker, "William B. Smith," 268-69.

William served in the legislature through the spring of 1843 with social skills that were said to be an asset, in accord with the profile of William painted by a young Mormon woman in Nauvoo, who found him to be "genteel, good looking and capable of appearing in the most refined modern society."[96]

During the summer of 1843, William served another mission in the eastern states, taking with him his seriously ill wife Caroline. During the mission he wrote two pamphlets defending his ministry. In one case, he had become embroiled in a standoff with Abraham Burtis, the presiding elder of a branch in New Egypt, New Jersey, about forty miles northeast of Philadelphia. He had criticized Elder Burtis's handling of the branch, and Burtis had retaliated with unfavorable comments about Smith. In October nine elders supervised by William's brother-in-law Jedediah M. Grant ruled that Burtis's license should be "demanded, and he be suspended until he makes satisfaction." William felt the punishment light and "offered an amendment that he be cut off from the Church." A vote was taken, and Burtis was excommunicated by a vote of seven to two.[97] Smith left his ailing wife in Philadelphia and returned to Nauvoo in April 1844 to receive his endowment at the Red Brick Store on May 12.[98]

The *Nauvoo Neighbor* announced on May 15, 1844, that "in consequence of the sickness of his family," with his wife being still "in the hands of a doctor in the city of Philadelphia," William would not run for re-election.[99] He was not in Nauvoo on June 27 when his two brothers were killed. Into this void, Andrew Jenson

96. Holzapfel and Holzapfel, quoting Helen Mar Kimball, in *A Woman's View*, 260.

97. William Smith, *Defence of Elder William Smith, against the Slanders of Abraham Burtis, and Others* (Philadelphia: Brown, Bicking & Gilbert Printers, 1844), 18.

98. Devery S. Anderson and Gary James Bergera, eds., *Joseph Smith's Quorum of the Anointed, 1842-1845: A Documentary History* (Salt Lake City: Signature Books, 2005), 76.

99. "For the Neighbor," *Nauvoo Neighbor*, May 15, 1844, 2.

imagined another yarn about William being in rebellion against his brother and the church, saying they had quarreled over some property and that "William left on a steamboat for the East accompanied by his family."[100]

In contradiction, William was accompanied by Brigham Young, Heber Kimball, and Lyman Wight; or at least they met each other in St. Louis and boarded the riverboat *Louis Phillipe* together to travel to distant cities to promote Joseph Smith's candidacy for the U.S. presidency. Kimball and Wight wrote on June 23 to tell Joseph about "the power and demonstration of the spirit" William had shown in preaching to the passengers one night.[101] Joseph would never receive the letter. In four days he would be dead. Unaware of the prophet's assassination, Brigham Young wrote to Willard Richards on July 8 about how "the Twelve have been faithful in all things. William Smith," he singled out for special commendation, "is a great man in his calling in this country."[102]

On June 30, George Adams hand-carried a letter from Willard Richards to the apostles in Massachusetts to tell them about the martyrdom of Joseph and Hyrum and to suggest that Brigham Young, Heber Kimball, George Smith, Wilford Woodruff, and Orson Pratt return immediately to Nauvoo, but that "William Smith, whose life is threatened, with all the Smiths," remain in the east along with "John E. Page, Lyman Wight, Parley P. Pratt and Orson Hyde" so they could assist in "publishing the news in the eastern cities" to "as many in the church as possible." This was "for you to decide," Richards added.[103] The letter influenced William

100. Jenson, "The Twelve Apostles," *Historical Record*, Mar. 1886, 45; Jenson, *Latter-day Saint Biographical Encyclopedia*, 1:87.

101. Lyman Wight and Heber C. Kimball to Joseph Smith, June 19, 1844, in *History of the Church*, 7:136.

102. Brigham Young to Willard Richards, July 8, 1844, Journal History of the Church, 1830-present, microfilm, LDS Church History Library.

103. Willard Richards to Brigham Young, June 30, 1844, in *History of the Church*, 7:148.

Smith, who wrote that, with his wife declining, he determined "to remain still a while longer in the east."[104]

The seeds for future confrontation between William Smith and Brigham Young may have been sown shortly afterward when Brigham and others returned and William Marks, the Nauvoo stake president, called a meeting on August 8 "to choose a guardian or President and Trustee" for the church. Brigham acknowledged the right of the Smith family to claim the patriarchal office but not the presidency. "Do you want a patriarch?" he asked. "Here is brother William [Smith] ... here is Uncle John Smith ... The right of patriarchal blessings belongs to Joseph's family." The general guardianship belonged to the Twelve, whom Joseph had given the "keys of the kingdom" before his death.[105]

William wrote from Bordentown, New Jersey, that he wanted to be remembered "in the clames [claims] of the Smith family" but thought Young was the right one, as president of the Quorum of the Twelve, "to receive revelations from Joseph for the government of the church." So far, so good. Everyone was conciliatory. William added that he would choose Rigdon as patriarch. "He would be my choice," he wrote, after determining "first that the office does not belong to me at present."[106] As magnanimous as this appeared, William had broached a sensitive topic in the wake of Rigdon's claim to be the rightful heir as surviving member of the presidency of the church. It is perhaps important to keep in mind that to this point, although William was short-tempered and temperamental,

---

104. William Smith, *A Proclamation and Faithful Warning to All the Saints Scattered about in Boston, Philadelphia, ... and Elsewhere in the United States.* Apparently no copy of this pamphlet, written in early October 1845, has survived. Sharp reprinted it in the *Warsaw Signal*, Oct. 29, 1845, 1, 4.

105. "At a Special Meeting ... Held in Nauvoo, at 10 a.m. on Thursday, August 8, 1844," in *History of the Church*, 7:234.

106. William Smith to Brigham Young, Aug. 27, 1844, qtd. in Calvin P. Rudd, "William Smith: Brother of the Prophet Joseph," M. A. thesis (Provo: Brigham Young University, 1973), 183-84.

other members of the church leadership were equally so. He failed to stand out in a field of men whose status seemed to rise and fall like a stock market report from one day to the next. But it was Brigham Young, not William Smith, who was the first to take offense and strategize about how to move the other out of the way. All of the apostles were under extreme emotional strain. Despite assassinations, threats, financial loss, theological conundrums, and intra-hierarchical disputes, they all more or less carried on, true to the inner commitment they felt. In the next few chapters, we will explore their individual paths in more detail.

6. COLLAPSE OF KIRTLAND

When the church moved from New York to Ohio in 1830-31, the members expected a utopian existence in the quiet town of Kirtland, which had "a few stores and shops, a grist mill, a post office, one hotel, and a few" churches and other "community buildings."[1] A significant number of the residents in town and in the outlying areas had been baptized into the church. It appeared that the immigrants could just settle in and enjoy the hospitality, begin to contribute to the prosperity of the small farming community, and enjoy the doctrines of the Restoration preached from the pulpit on Sundays by the converted minister Sidney Rigdon. Instead, problems arose from the beginning that would dog the church for the next decade.

Consider the spiritual hysteria that infected the worship services shortly after the first missionaries arrived. Max H. Parkin, in his thesis on the Kirtland period of Mormon history, indicated that the new converts suffered from the kinds of extremes that were characteristic of "religious revivals, as well as from outlandish expressions peculiar to Mormonism itself." People exhibited strange manifestations of spirituality, in part because the first missionaries moved on to other areas farther west after baptizing throngs of people in Ohio. There was an "absence of Mormon leadership" even after the immigrants from New York arrived, due to their interest in

---

1. The Mormons nevertheless added roads, houses, "a printing office, a church store, a bank, several ancillary buildings," and a temple. Roger D. Launius, *Joseph Smith III: Pragmatic Prophet* (Urbana: University of Illinois Press, 1988), 4.

Missouri as an alternative gathering place and their emphasis on missionary efforts in other states. In addition to that, the leaders themselves sometimes indulged in spiritualism.[2]

The *Painesville Telegraph*, edited by Eber D. Howe, printed a significant number of articles on the new religion. Painesville was located ten miles north of Kirtland, near Lake Erie. The newspaper described some of the practices among the so-called "Mormonites" already in 1830 before Joseph Smith arrived:

> They would fall, as without strength, roll upon the floor, and, so mad were they that even the females were seen on a cold winter day, lying under the bare canopy of heaven, with no couch or pillow but the fleecy snow. At other times they exhibited all the apish actions imaginable, making grimaces both horrid and ridiculous, creeping upon their hands and feet, &c. Sometimes, in these exercises the young men would rise and play before the people, going through all the Indian maneuvers of knocking down, scalping, ripping open, and taking out the bowels. At other times, they would start and run several furlongs, then get upon stumps and preach to imagined congregations, baptize ghosts, &c. At other times, they are taken with a fit of jabbering after which they neither understood themselves nor anybody else, and this they call speaking foreign languages by divine inspiration.[3]

John Corrill, writing in 1839 when he was no longer a Mormon, remembered converts preaching from stumps to no one in particular and "all the while so completely absorbed in visions as to be apparently insensible to all that was passing around them."[4] John Whitmer mentioned similar expressions of religious enthusiasm and concluded: "Thus the devil blinded the eyes of some

---

2. Max H. Parkin, "Conflict at Kirtland" (master's thesis, Brigham Young University, 1966), 66.

3. "Mormonism," *The [Painesville] Telegraph*, Feb. 15, 1831, 1.

4. John Corrill, *A Brief History of the Church of Christ of Latter Day Saints* (St. Louis: By the author, 1839), 7.

good and honest disciples."[5] Parley Pratt observed this behavior on returning from his mission to the far side of the Missouri River and thought an evil spirit had infected the membership, "a false and lying spirit."[6]

After Joseph Smith arrived in Kirtland about February 1, 1831, he was alerted to the "many false spirits" at work in that area. Three months later a revelation addressed the problem of mischievous spirits that had "gone forth in the earth, deceiving the world: and also satan hath sought to deceive you, that he might overthrow you."[7] Assault by evil spirits was only one of the threats to the infant church and was not as serious as the rival claims to prophesy that were dividing the members.

For instance, in September 1830 in New York, one of the eight witnesses, Hiram Page, claimed he was receiving God's word through a seer stone, the same as Joseph Smith. When Oliver Cowdery and others accepted Page's pronouncements as true messages from God, Joseph received a competing message explaining that "no one shall be appointed to receive commandments and revelations in this church, excepting my servant Joseph Smith, Jr. for he receiveth them even as Moses."[8]

An even greater threat to Smith's revelatory role occurred in Kirtland in 1831 when a woman named Hubble claimed to be a prophetess. According to John Whitmer, Mrs. Hubble maintained that the Book of Mormon was true and that "she should become a teacher in the Church of Christ." She "appear[ed] very sanctimonious and deceived some, who were not able to detect her in her hypocrisy."[9] This was again resolved by another revelation in

---

5. Bruce N. Westergren, ed., *From Historian to Dissident: The Book of John Whitmer* (Salt Lake City: Signature Books, 1995), 57.

6. Scot Facer Proctor and Maurine Jensen Proctor, eds., *Autobiography of Parley P. Pratt,* rev. ed. (Salt Lake City: Deseret Book, 2000), 72.

7. 1835 D&C 17:1; LDS D&C 50:2-3; RLDS D&C 50:1.

8. 1835 D&C 51:2; LDS D&C 28:2; RLDS D&C 27:2.

9. Westergren, *From Historian to Dissident,* 37.

February 1831, through which God established that only Joseph could receive revelations for the entire church.[10]

A problem with the revelations was that they supported the prophet's immediate needs rather than expressing universally applicable principles. For instance, no sooner had Joseph arrived in Kirtland than he was directed by revelation from God announcing that the members were to pool their resources and forfeit private ownership in favor of a collective control of all the members' assets.[11] Not everyone accepted this as the word of God, as opposed to human initiative, and those who were most enthusiastic had little to contribute or thought they would "glut themselves upon the labors of others," as John Whitmer put it. They became less enthusiastic after learning that they would be the workers and others would be exempt from manual labor.[12]

In 1833 when Mormons in Jackson County, Missouri, were expelled from their land after the revelations had promised them the area as an eschatological gathering place, it was too much for some of the converts to bear. God had also seemed to assure that Zion's Camp would be a success in reclaiming their homes, and the subsequent failure of the maneuver was a blow to everyone. Some of the members objected to the militancy itself, including William McLellin, who left the church but then had a change of heart and requested in January 1837 that his ministerial license be returned to him, hoping it would make him feel like preaching again.[13] After his 1838 separation from the church, he maintained

---

10. 1835 D&C 14:1-2; LDS D&C 43:2-7; RLDS D&C 43:1-2.

11. 1835 D&C 13:8-12; LDS D&C 42:30-42; RLDS D&C 42:8-12.

12. Westergren, *From Historian to Dissident*, 37. For instance, a revelation of February 1831 informed members that "it is meet that my servant Joseph Smith, jr. should have a house built, in which to live and translate." Although he was constructing a commune, it was not one where he or his advisors would have to do physical work. 1835 D&C 61:3; LDS D&C 41:7; RLDS D&C 41:3.

13. William E. McLellin to "My dear old Friends," Jan. 24, 1837, qtd. in Jan Shipps and John W. Welch, eds., *The Journals of William E. McLellin 1831-1836* (Provo and Urbana: *BYU Studies* and University of Illinois Press, 1994), 229-30.

that the atrocities committed by Mormons during the war in Missouri proved that Smith was a "fallen prophet and the church ... rejected by God."[14]

For all of this, the "great apostasy" of 1837 constituted the greatest threat to the church's progress and led to the excommunication in December of Luke Johnson, Martin Harris, and Warren Parrish, and over the next several months in Missouri of Lyman Johnson, William McLellin, Oliver Cowdery, David Whitmer, John Whitmer, and many more. The general complaint was that Joseph Smith had succumbed to vanity by improving the revelations prior to publication to make God sound more polished; also for amassing real estate and chattel in the run-up to the Kirtland bank failure.[15] George A. Smith, an eyewitness to the conflicts of 1837, told an audience thirty years later that the dissenters were guilty of "adultery or covetousness" and had "gone to hell." There they would "lift up their eyes, asking for some relief or benefit from those they once tried to destroy."[16] It is interesting that in casting about for a reason to dismiss the dissenters, he would land on the same charges they brought against Joseph Smith. It is also interesting he would fail to acknowledge that the reason these men were called to high office was because they were individuals

---

14. William E. McLellin to "Elder D[avis] H. Bays," May 24, 1870, in *The William E. McLellin Papers, 1854–1880*, eds. Stan Larson and Samuel J. Passey (Salt Lake City: Signature Books, 2007), 460; and Shipps and Welch, *Journals of William E. McLellin*, 311. John E. Page reached a similar conclusion in the 1860s. See William Shepard, "Shadows on the Sun Dial: John E. Page and the Strangites," *Dialogue: A Journal of Mormon Thought* 41 (Spring 2008): 54. Granville Hedrick was presumably influenced by Page or McLellin. Shepard, "The Concept of a 'Rejected Gospel' in Mormon History," *Journal of Mormon History* 34 (Summer 2008): 162–63.

15. For an examination of causes of dissent in Kirtland, see Marvin S. Hill, "Cultural Crisis in the Mormon Kingdom: A Reconsideration of the Causes of Kirtland Dissent," *Church History* 49 (Sept. 1980): 286–97.

16. George A. Smith, Jan. 10, 1858, *Journal of Discourses*, 26 vols. (London: Latter-day Saints Book Depot, 1854–86), 7:115.

of sound judgment and moral consistency. They had remained loyal to Joseph Smith through thick and thin, when most other people would have long since abandoned him. When some of them decided to break off their association with the church, it was not a decision they took lightly.

The Kirtland Safety Society

The church leadership decided to create a bank to help the Kirtland economy.[17] The neighboring communities that had banks were experiencing growth, so it was assumed to be a necessary step toward the town's future.[18] In November 1836 articles of agreement were drafted for an institution called the Kirtland Safety Society Bank, a name that would soon prove to be ironic. The Ohio legislature rejected the bank's application for a charter in December, but the founders blithely added "Anti-Banking Company" to the name. Some of the people of Kirtland were wary of this. Lyman Johnson attended an organizational meeting in January 1837 but decided against investing; nor did John Boynton participate. Most of the Smith family did, but William withheld funds, or at least his name was not included in the index of investors.[19] John Johnson and son Luke enthusiastically contributed $600 (about $12,000 in today's currency) and $47 respectively.[20] As everyone would soon learn, it didn't necessarily matter who

---

17. Milton V. Backman Jr., *The Heavens Resound: A History of the Latter-day Saints in Ohio, 1830-1838* (Salt Lake City: Deseret Book, 1983), 314, found evidence that Mormons thought a bank would allow "a means to transform into cash some of the assets they and other members possessed in land."

18. Roger D. Launius, *The Kirtland Temple: A Historical Narrative* (Independence: Herald Publishing House, 1986), 78-79, explained: "The optimism expressed by the Kirtland Saints for the development of the local economy prompted Joseph Smith and other church leaders to sponsor a bank, an effort designed to capitalize on an already favorable business climate."

19. Marvin S. Hill, C. Keith Rooker, and Larry T. Wimmer. "The Kirtland Economy Revisited," *BYU Studies* 17 (Summer 1977): 469.

20. Ibid., 466-68.

contributed and who did not because when a community's financial institution collapses, everyone loses.

The Latter-day Saints were hardly alone in placing their faith in their "anti-bank." Without a national currency, it was common in the nineteenth century for non-banking institutions to issue notes that served as the means of exchange. Paper money bore the name of a mill or some other institution emblazoned across the front. As historian Mark Staker wrote in his history of Ohio, "businesses of all kinds commonly lent money in the form of banknotes that they printed individually and which were used much like promissory notes. ... These banknotes were backed by very small amounts of specie and large amounts of less liquid forms of capital such as land, grain, cotton, canals, industries, books, or even sandstone."[21] It is easy today to think of the notes issued by the Safety Society as currency, but they were really just I.O.U.s without collateral.

The growth of banks was partly the result of land speculation. In unsettled areas of the country, cash-poor pioneers wanted to purchase as much land as possible and borrowed money on credit to do so, with the land serving as collateral. As banks accommodated this demand, market forces pushed prices higher. Land speculators didn't mind paying higher prices because they could borrow the money they needed to make the purchase. The result was that everyone felt like they were participating in a prosperous windfall and no one imagined the bottom would fall out, but it did and about one-third of the banks failed.

Some people lost everything. As banks tried to save themselves, they exacerbated the problem by selling stock. As Staker explained, nineteenth-century banks did not generate funds by

---

21. Mark Lyman Staker, *Hearken, O Ye People: The Historical Setting of Joseph Smith's Ohio Revelations* (Salt Lake City: Greg Kofford Books, 2009), 447. See also George Alter, et al., "The Savings of Ordinary Americans: The Philadelphia Saving Fund Society in the mid-Nineteenth Century," *Journal of Economic History*, Dec. 1994, online at the *National Bureau of Economic Research*, www.nber.org.

inviting common people to invest in savings accounts. "Banks usually solicited only the affluent to invest as stockholders, and they shaped the price of their stock to exclude ordinary citizens."[22] In Kirtland, with its more egalitarian intent, people could purchase stock in installments. That proved to be a double-edged sword because the greater numbers of people who participated, the greater number were susceptible to loss.

In a related development, Lyman Johnson is representative of the changing circumstances one can find oneself in as one grows older and has greater financial needs. One feels more anxious about the state of one's finances after marrying and starting a family, and in his case he borrowed an excessive amount of money for a mercantile venture to support his family while he was away on apostolic errands. Others were thinking along the same lines, making Kirtland a boom town. Heber Kimball recorded what he found when he returned from a mission in October 1836:

> On our arrival in Kirtland we were much grieved to see the spirit of speculation that was prevailing in the church; trade and traffic seemed to engross the time and attention of the Saints: when we left Kirtland a City lot was worth about 150 dollars, but on our return to our astonishment the same lot was said to be worth from 500 to 1000 dollars according to location; and some men who when I left could hardly get food to eat, I found on my return to be men of supposed great wealth; in fact every thing in the place seemed to be moving in great prosperity, and all seemed determined to become rich; in my feelings they were artificial or imaginary riches.[23]

He said that he and "most of the Twelve were appointed directors" of the bank, which "issued paper to a considerable extent."

This appearance of prosperity led many of the Saints to believe

---

22. Staker, *Hearken, O Ye People*, 464.

23. "History of Heber Chase Kimball by His Own Dictation," 47–48, handwriting of Thomas Bullock, Heber C. Kimball Papers, LDS Church History Library, Salt Lake City.

that the time had arrived for the Lord to enrich them with the treasures of the earth and believing so, it stimulated them to great exertions, so much so, that two of the Twelve Lyman E. Johnson and John F. Boynton went to New York and purchased to the amount of twenty thousand dollars worth of goods and entered into the Mercantile business, borrowing considerable money from Polly Voce and other Saints in Boston and the regions round about, and which they have never repaid.[24]

What surprised Johnson and Boynton, as they looked forward to an expectation that they could repay their loans and live comfortably, was that they had to continually adjust their prices to keep pace with inflation. According to Warren Cowdery, older brother of Oliver and editor of the *Messenger and Advocate*, the Kirtland economy had been doing so well that many people came to believe they were set for life as they accrued notes and deeds and increased their standard of living by making purchases on credit. He categorized the Saints into three groups: those who were self-disciplined and did not make investments, those who lost their investments and moved on, and those who "rushed blindly on, till ruin stared them in the face," and now found themselves unable to recover from their losses.[25]

In the spring of 1837, the Safety Society closed its doors and stopped redeeming banknotes with specie.[26] Wilford Woodruff

---

24. Mary ("Polly") Vose was born in 1780 and resided in Boston. She was converted through Orson Hyde and Samuel Smith, being baptized on July 29, 1832. Unmarried, she provided John Boynton and Lyman Johnson with funds. She remained a faithful member and, with her niece Ruth Vose Sayers, gathered to Salt Lake City in 1857. She died in 1866.

25. "The Change of Times," *Messenger and Advocate*, June 1837, 520-21.

26. According to Backman, *Heavens Resound*, 320, a total of 200 Mormons invested in the society and lost "nearly everything." He summarized that "it has been estimated that the financial loss approached $40,000, almost the total cost of building the Kirtland Temple. The loss was sustained by persons whose income averaged about $400 annually." For Joseph Smith's activities with the Safety Society, see Hill, et al., "Kirtland Economy Revisited"; Staker, *Hearken, O Ye People*, 463-501.

recorded that on April 9 in the Kirtland Temple, Joseph Smith blamed the bank's failure on "characters that professed to be his friends & friends to humanity" but had "turned tr[a]itors & opposed the Currency."[27] A convert who had been enthralled by Lyman Johnson's preaching in New York, Ira Ames, wrote that Lyman and Boynton had purchased a farm in Kirtland by making a down payment and borrowing the balance, then subdivided the land to sell at inflated prices. Ames bought eighteen acres at $100 per acre. After paying the apostles $1,500, he signed a mortgage. In the crisis following the bank failure, Boynton and Johnson were unable to meet their payments on the farm and the land reverted back to the original owner. Ames lost his land, along with his $1,500 and his improvements. He bitterly lamented: "Boyington and Johnson tried to get my horses from me on the $300."[28]

Historian Ronald K. Esplin explained that "it was in this atmosphere that some of the Saints—especially certain leaders—began to differ publicly with the Prophet over fundamental issues of leadership." They wondered "whether Joseph Smith should confine his leadership to matters narrowly religious or whether it was appropriate for him to also advise the Saints in economic and other 'temporal' affairs." Boynton and Johnson were roundly criticized for being "merchant apostles," Esplin wrote, and they, in turn, blamed Joseph Smith for their predicament. Luke Johnson was "more quietly critical" but felt disheartened and "moved to the fringes of Kirtland Mormon society."[29] Warren Parrish, an officer in the Kirtland Safety Society and Joseph Smith's former respected secretary, emerged in the spotlight as a leading critical voice and opponent of Joseph throughout most of 1837.

---

27. Scott G. Kenney, *Wilford Woodruff's Journal, 1833-1898*, 9 vols. (Midvale, UT: Signature Books, 1983-85), 1:138.

28. Ira Ames Journal, first entry in 1837, LDS Church History Library.

29. Ronald K. Esplin, "Thomas B. Marsh as President of the First Quorum of the Twelve, 1835-1838," in *Hearken, O Ye People: Discourses on the Doctrine and Covenants* (Sandy, UT: Randall Book, 1984), 178.

When Parley Pratt returned to Kirtland in the spring during a pause in his Canadian mission, he became caught up in the whirlwind of accusations and counter-accusations. His tale is illustrative of the real pain that otherwise devout members of the church were experiencing. While in Kirtland, Pratt's first son was born, but the joy he felt was short-lived with the death of his wife Thankful about three hours afterward. He soon remarried, and in the midst of personal turmoil was suddenly ordered to relinquish his home due to the economic crash, for which he blamed the "powers of darkness." It was these dark forces, he said, that drew him into the ranks of the discontented so that he found himself denouncing Joseph Smith over his secular ventures.[30] During this period of rebellion, he wrote to Joseph that, as later published in *Zion's Watchman*, the "speculating spirit" in Kirtland had persuaded leaders to indulge in "*lying, deceiving* and *taking* advantage" of neighbors. Joseph had sold him three lots for $2,000 when they had been valued at $100, he complained.[31] A postscript not included in *Zion's Watchman* read, "Do not suppose for a moment that I lack any Confidence in the Book of Mormons or Doctrine and Covenants. Nay it is my firm belief in those Records that hinders my Belief in the course we have Been Led of Late."[32]

More than half of the apostles and other leading men called for Joseph Smith to step down, but even so, Joseph spoke in the temple on May 28, defiantly prophesying that "he would stand & his enemies fall."[33] Some of the members rallied by him, some stood

---

30. Terryl L. Givens and Matthew J. Grow, *Parley P. Pratt: The Apostle Paul of Mormonism* (New York: Oxford University Press, 2011), 90–92; Proctor and Proctor, *Autobiography of Parley P. Pratt*, 209–10.

31. Parley P. Pratt to Joseph Smith, May 23, 1837, *Zion's Watchman*, Mar. 24, 1838, emphasis retained. Warren Parrish came into possession of this letter and forwarded it to the Methodist newspaper in New York City edited by La Roy Sunderland.

32. Parley P. Pratt to Joseph Smith, May 23, 1837, rpt. in Arthur H. Deming, ed., *Naked Truths about Mormonism*, Apr. 1888, 4. The present location of the letter is unknown.

33. Kenney, *Wilford Woodruff's Journal*, 1:147.

in opposition to him, and others remained neutral. Four loyalists, Able Lamb, Artemus Millet, Marlow Redfield, and Israel Rogers, asked the high council to launch an investigation of Lyman Johnson, Warren Parrish, Parley Pratt, David Whitmer, and Frederick Williams for statements "unworthy of their high calling" and "injurious to the Church of God in which they are high officers."

Johnson and Pratt, filing their own charges with Bishop Whitney and counselors, counter-charged Joseph Smith, as follows:

To the Bishop & his council in Kirtland the Stake of Zion
We prefer the following charges against Pres. Joseph Smith, Jr. viz. for lying & misrepresentation—also for extortion—and for speaking disrespectfully against his brethren behind their backs.
Lyman E. Johnson
Orson Pratt
Kirtland May 29th 1837

This was followed by a complaint against Father Smith by Luke Johnson:

To the Bishop & his council in Kirtland the Stake of Zion
I prefer the following charges against Pres. Joseph Smith Sen viz. closing the doors of the House of the Lord against the high council & refusing to admit them into the same to transact the business of the church
Also for speaking reproachfully against his brethren
Luke Johnson
Kirtland 29th May 1837

Also on the same day, Warren Parrish accused Sidney Rigdon of doctrinal error and laxity of faith:

To the Bishop & his council in Kirtland the Stake of Zion
I prefer the following charges against Pres. Sidney Rigdon viz. expressing an unbelief in the revelations of God, both old and new. also an unbelief in the agency of man and his accountability

to God, or that there is such a principle existing as Sin—and also, for lying & declaring that God required it at his hands

Kirtland 29th May 1837

W. Parrish[34]

The bishopric turned the complaints over to the high council, which ignored them, although Rigdon had no trouble getting his own complaint against the dissenters heard. Rigdon wanted Lyman Johnson, Warren Parrish, Whitmer, Williams, Lyman Johnson, and Parley Pratt tried for their memberships, but the results turned out to be disastrous for Rigdon. The defendants raised procedural objections that he could not give satisfactory answers to regarding conflicting areas of responsibility. Pratt "objected to being tried by President Rigdon or Joseph Smith Jr. in consequence of their having previously expressed their opinion against" him, he said, "stating also that he could bring evidence to prove" it. Rigdon decided that "under the present circumstances," they "could not conscientiously proceed to try the case," and he "left the stand." The clerk, Marcellus F. Cowdery, son of Warren Cowdery, noted that "the Council and assembly then dispersed in confusion."[35] Nothing had been resolved, and it seemed that things were significantly worse than before.

While disaster and suspicion spread throughout Kirtland, Thomas Marsh, president of the quorum, was in Missouri tending to the church's needs there. He was one of four in the quorum who stayed loyal to Joseph Smith, along with Kimball, Patten, and Young. Some of the other leading members were wavering, expressing their confidence in Joseph Smith one day and disgust the

---

34. "To the Bishop & his council," Newel K. Whitney Collection, L. Tom Perry Special Collections, Harold B. Lee Library, Brigham Young University, Provo, Utah.

35. Fred C. Collier and William S. Harwell, eds., *Kirtland Council Minute Book* (Salt Lake City: Collier's Publishing Co., 1996), 181-84, 186. One-third of the high councilors were apparently sympathetic to the dissenters.

next, but the fissure was becoming too wide for some of them to cross back over again.

Marsh was preparing to journey to Kirtland for the quorum meeting there when Joseph Smith received the revelation on June 4, 1837, instructing some of the apostles to leave the United States and cross the Atlantic Ocean. Heber Kimball recorded: "The word of the Lord to me [Kimball] through Joseph the prophet [was] that I should gow to England to open the dore of procklamation to that nation and to he[a]d the same."[36] On June 9, Marsh and Patten began their journey to Kirtland. Marsh explained in his 1858 autobiography that his intent was to "try and reconcile some of the Twelve and others of high standing who had come out in opposition to the Prophet."[37]

Kimball was set apart for his mission by the First Presidency on June 11. Suddenly, Orson Hyde "entered the room, begged forgiveness, and asked if he could accompany Heber to England," and was told he could.[38] Two days later when Kimball encountered John Boynton and Lyman Johnson, Boynton said he thought Kimball was a "damn fool" for undertaking an errand "for the fallen Prophet," adding that he would not lift a finger to help Joseph if he were "shipwrecked on Van Dieman's Land," the nineteenth-century term for Tasmania. Lyman, responding more kindly, said he was sorry Kimball would no doubt endure hardships on such a venture, and in a touching gesture "took from his shoulders a good, nice camlet cloak and put it" on Kimball, who said it was the first overcoat he had ever owned.[39]

Kimball arrived in New York City on June 22 with Joseph

---

36. Heber C. Kimball Journal, June 4, 1837, LDS Church History Library.

37. Thomas B. Marsh, "History of Thos. Baldwin Marsh," *Deseret News*, Mar. 24, 1858, 18.

38. James B. Allen, Ronald K. Esplin, and David J. Whittaker, *Men with a Mission, 1837-1841: The Quorum of the Twelve Apostles in the British Isles* (Salt Lake City: Deseret Book, 1992), 25.

39. Heber C. Kimball, Nov. 22, 1857, *Journal of Discourses*, 6:65.

Fielding, Orson Hyde, and Willard Richards and sailed for England on July 1 to become the first missionaries to that land.[40] Joseph Smith had not consulted with Marsh about this, an oversight that threatened to disturb what little rapport was left between them. In Dayton, Ohio, Marsh and Patten encountered Parley Pratt on his way to Far West, but talked him into returning with them.[41] They reached Kirtland in mid-July, at a time when their colleagues in England, Kimball and Hyde, were already conducting meetings in Preston. Learning of this, Marsh and Patten were angered by such a breach in protocol.[42] Brigham Young encouraged Patten "to go to Joseph," but before he did he spoke with his brother-in-law War-ren Parish and "got his mind prejudiced," as Young expressed it, so that when David saw Joseph he ended up insulting him, and Joseph responded by slapping and kicking him. Far from being scandalized by this treatment of a fellow apostle, Young thought it was good medicine and "done David good."[43]

The Pratts decided to put their differences with Joseph behind them. After demonstrating a healthy dose of contriteness, they were restored to fellowship sometime before the end of July, while Joseph looked for an escape from the mounting unrest in Kirtland and took Marsh and Young with him on an assignment to Upper Canada on July 27, on a trip that began badly when they were detained by mar-shals. They extricated themselves from the legal issues impeding their progress and were allowed to cross the border, where they experienced a refreshing interlude. They enjoyed spending their time "preaching,

---

40. Allen, et al., *Men with a Mission*, 25.

41. Marsh, "History of Thos. Baldwin Marsh," 18.

42. Lyndon W. Cook, "'I Have Sinned against Heaven ...' Thomas B. Marsh Returns to the Church," *BYU Studies* 20 (Summer 1980): 393. Marsh arrived about the third week of July. Any friction between him and Joseph Smith quickly faded. He lived at Joseph's home, traveled with him, and consulted with him in editing the *Elders' Journal*.

43. Brigham Young, qtd. in Kenney, *Wilford Woodruff's Journal*, 5:63.

baptizing, blessing the Saints and strengthening the branches" without having to think about finances, they said.[44]

Back home in Kirtland, Joseph Smith Sr. delivered a lively sermon in which he defended his son and excoriated his critics. Warren Parrish stood up and objected to the tone of Father Smith's remarks, at which William came to his father's aid and tried to physically remove Parrish from the temple. At that point John Boynton blocked the way and threatened William with a sword if he did not withdraw. According to Mother Smith, her husband had "reflected somewhat sharply upon Warren Parrish" but did not deserve to be cast out of the temple. Parrish was "highly incensed" and dragged her husband along the floor. "My husband appealed to Oliver Cowdery," a justice of the peace, she wrote, "but Oliver never moved from his seat."

> William, seeing the abuse which his father was receiving, sprang forward and caught Parrish, and carried him in his arms nearly out of the house. At this John Boynton stepped forward, and drawing a sword from his cane, presented it to William's breast, and said, "if you advance one step further, I will run you through." Before William had time to turn himself, several gathered around him, threatening to handle him severely, if he should lay the weight of his finger upon Parrish again. At this juncture of affairs, I left the house, not only terrified at the scene, but likewise sick at heart, to see that the apostasy of which Joseph had prophe[s]ied was so near at hand.[45]

Lucy said that a young woman who lived in David Whitmer's

---

44. Joseph Smith Jr., et al., *History of the Church of Jesus Christ of Latter-day Saints*, ed. B. H. Roberts, 2nd ed. rev., 7 vols. (Salt Lake City: Deseret Book, 1959), 2:502-3, 508.

45. Lavina Fielding Anderson, ed., *Lucy's Book: A Critical Edition of Lucy Mack Smith's Family Memoir* (Salt Lake City: Signature Books, 2001), 597-98. According to Lucy, Joseph "went to Cleveland" rather than Canada. J. Christopher Conkling, *A Joseph Smith Chronology* (Salt Lake City: Deseret Book, 1979), 103, dates the altercation to the period of Joseph's Canadian mission.

home who was believed to be able to detect "certain things and to prophecy by looking through a certain black stone" told David that he or Martin Harris "would fill Joseph's place; and that the one who did not succeed him, would be the Counsellor to the one that did."[46] Such was the precarious state of things—that predictions were being made about Joseph's successor. When Joseph returned in late August, he reasserted his authority in a published warning against "speculators, renegadoes and gamblers, who are duping the unsuspecting and the unwary, by palming upon them, those bills, which are of no worth here."[47] The problem, he wrote, was not with himself or the bank directors for issuing unsecured notes but rather, like his father had said, with those who expected to be paid in cash for the notes they held. Probably everyone involved with the bank was mystified by its failure, just as they had probably been by its early success when they discovered how easy it was to create money out of thin air.

Luke and Lyman Johnson retained some resources with which they purchased forty acres each in Missouri on August 8, indicating among other things their intent to stay with the church. They also served together on the Far West High Council on a case brought before the council the week before.[48] In their absence, and unknown to them, Oliver Cowdery had rendered a judgment against them in Kirtland on August 7 for failure to pay a promissory note of $26.27.[49] In later reconstructions of events, this looked like a hasty departure and attempt to evade obligations, but it was neither.

---

46. Anderson, *Lucy's Book*, 600. For a sensitive account of David Whitmer, see Ronald E. Romig, "David Whitmer: Faithful Dissenter, Witness Apart," in Roger D. Launius and Linda Thatcher, eds., *Differing Visions: Dissenters in Mormon History* (Urbana: University of Illinois Press, 1994), 23-44.

47. "Caution," *Messenger and Advocate*, Aug. 1837, 560.

48. John Hamer, *Northeast of Eden: A Historical Atlas of Missouri's Mormon County* (Ann Arbor: Far West Cultural Center, 2004), 18, 26; Donald Q. Cannon and Lyndon W. Cook, eds., *Far West Record: Minutes of the Church of Jesus Christ of Latter-day Saints, 1830-1844* (Salt Lake City: Deseret Book, 1983), 115-16.

49. Oliver Cowdery's Docket, Kirtland, Geauga County, Ohio, June 14,

Joseph Smith moved against discontented church members on September 3 in a meeting in the temple orchestrated by him. Brigham Young helped out by packing the gallery with loyalists. "Owing to the disaffection existing in the hearts of many," Brigham later recalled, "I went to the brethren whose votes could be relied on, early in the morning, and had them occupy the stand and prominent seats."[50] It began with a vote about whether Joseph Smith should "still act as ... the presiding officer of the Church," which received a unanimous vote in the affirmative. Sidney Rigdon and Frederick Williams were presented as alternate presidents to serve with Joseph Smith as the "three First Presidents of the Church," which was approved unanimously. Oliver Cowdery, Joseph Smith Sr., and Uncle John Smith were sustained as assistants to the presidency. Newel Whitney was sustained as bishop, along with counselors Reynolds Cahoon and Vincent Knight.

The names of the Twelve were presented individually to enthusiastic receptions until John Boynton's name was read, and it was suggested that he needed to explain himself. Not one to shy away from a challenge, he delivered a spirited defense, pointing out the inherent fraud in the management of the Safety Society bank. George Robinson, clerk of the conference, wrote that his confession was deemed unsatisfactory. Apostles Marsh and Young countered that they were looking for evidence of "hearty repentance." So, Boynton continued to talk about the bank, which he had been told was "instituted by the will & revelations of God, & he had been told that it never would fail, let men do what they pleased." Joseph Smith countered by asserting that he had

1837, to Sept. 15, 1837, Henry E. Huntington Library, San Marino, California. According to D. Michael Quinn, *The Mormon Hierarchy: Origins of Power* (Salt Lake City: Signature Books, 1994), 556, Lyman Johnson was "found guilty 1837 and 1838 for defaulted debts."

50. Leonard J. Arrington, *Brigham Young: American Moses* (New York: Knopf, 1985), 61. See also John G. Turner, *Brigham Young, Pioneer Prophet* (Cambridge, MA: Belknap Press of Harvard University Press, 2012), 53.

implicitly warned people by telling them that "unless the institution was conducted upon righteous principles it could not stand." The clerk recorded that "the Church was then called upon to know whether they were satisfied with the confession of Elder Boynton. Voted in the negative."[51]

The congregation reached the same conclusion about Luke and Lyman Johnson even though the brothers were not available to defend themselves. Sidney Rigdon delivered a long denunciation of them for "leaving their calling to pursue" money, which he found to be "derogatory to [their] calling." Those in attendance were asked whether they accepted Father Johnson as a high councilor, but they declined to endorse him, marking the end of his affiliation with the church. Three other high councilmen were removed from office: Joseph Coe, Joseph Kingsbury, and Martin Harris. This would guarantee, they thought, that future judicial decisions would go the way of the loyalists. Writing in qualified sympathy for John Johnson, historian Susan Easton Black explained that

> financial difficulties plagued him in 1836. He was a defendant in a number of lawsuits for various sums of money owed on unpaid notes. Five of the suits were for nonpayment of private loans. According to family tradition, one lawsuit was for selling "spirituous liquors" contrary to existing laws. The prosecution discontinued this suit when Father Johnson agreed to mend his ways. The failure of the Kirtland Safety Society, of which he was a charter member, added to his problems.[52]

---

51. Collier and Harwell, *Kirtland Council Minute Book*, 184–87. On January 5, 1837, Wilford Woodruff recorded Joseph Smith's words concerning the Kirtland Safety Society: "He was alone in a room by himself & he had not ownly the voice of the Spirit upon the Subject but even an audable voice. He did not tell us at that time what the LORD said upon the subject but remarked that if we would give heed to the Commandments the Lord had given this morning all would be well." Kenney, *Wilford Woodruff's Journal*, 1:120.

52. Susan Easton Black, *Who's Who in the Doctrine & Covenants* (Salt Lake City: Deseret Book, 1997), 153.

It may be difficult now to look back and understand how, at the time, men of devotion to their faith could be split on whether the church's founder had faltered, but from the perspective of the critics, they were devout believers who had been repeatedly asked to show contrition for their mistakes, whereas they believed Joseph had shown no remorse for his sins. In fact, he was doing everything he could to consolidate his authority at the expense of those below him. Joseph condemned Cowdery and Whitmer on September 4 in a letter in a communication that was to be delivered to "the whole Church in Zion," in other words, Missouri. He put John Corrill and other leaders on notice that the status of the Far West presidency was precarious:

> Oliver Cowdery has been in transgression, but as he is now chosen as one of the Presidents or Councilors I trust that he will yet humble himself & magnify his calling but if he should not, the Church will soon be under the necessaty of raising their hands against him[.] Therefore pray for him, David Whitmer[,] Leonard Rich & others[.] [They] have been in transgression but we hope that they may be humble & ere long make satisfaction to the Church otherwise they cannot retain their standing, Therefore we say unto you beware of all disaffected Characters[.]

John Whitmer and William Phelps, David Whitmer's counselors in Missouri, were added to the watch list as an addendum, in the form of a revelation Joseph received between writing and sending the letter. In it, God decreed that the counselors "have done those things which are not pleasing in my [God's] sight[.] Therefore if they repent not they shall be removed out of their places."[53]

An interesting wrinkle in the story is that John Boynton and the Johnsons appeared in Kirtland a week after they were removed

---

53. Dean C. Jessee, Mark Ashurst-McGee, and Richard L. Jensen, eds., *The Joseph Smith Papers: Journals* (Salt Lake City: Church Historian's Press, 2008), 1:245. This revelation is not found in the Doctrine and Covenants.

from the quorum, only to be reinstated as if nothing had happened. This occurred at an assembly held September 10, at which they "made confession to the Church" and were voted to "retain their office of Apostleship." Having been restored to office, they administered "the Lord's Supper," Elder Boynton giving the closing prayer, according to the Kirtland Council Minute Book.[54] The minutes indicate that Joseph coached the congregation by reading a letter from Thomas Marsh stating that "before he left for Missouri, [he] had received satisfaction from these Elders. Elder Young also stated the same to the congregation." Why Young would remember this now and not a week earlier is odd, and it was probably nothing more than an embellishment to the minutes intended to smooth over a previous error. Probably Joseph had mistakenly assumed that the absent apostles were in apostasy. In any case, Joseph Smith, Sidney Rigdon, William Smith, and Vinson Knight decided to travel to Missouri, leaving on September 27, to see what the situation was.[55]

Vilate Kimball wrote to her husband to explain how the September 3 meeting had gone, how they had "proceeded to call a vote upon the heads of the twelve, commencing at the oldest." She said "they were all received in their apostleship by a unanim[o]us [consent] except Luke and Limon Joh[n]son and Jo[h]n Boynton" and that "the vote went against them." Martin Harris was "so angry" about being dropped from the high council that he stormed out of the meeting.[56] In a twist that caught Vilate by surprise, Warren Parrish was accepted back into fellowship. "Elder [Warren] Parrish (who has been the most rebel[li]ous), is again restored to the

---

54. Collier and Harwell, *Kirtland Council Minute Book*, 188-89.

55. *History of the Church*, 2:518.

56. Vilate Kimball to Heber C. Kimball, Sept. 6-11, 1837, LDS Church History Library. Harris was received back into the church by July 18, 1840. H. Michael Marquardt, "Martin Harris: The Kirtland Years, 1831-1870," *Dialogue: A Journal of Mormon Thought* 35, no. 3 (Fall 2002): 16.

fellowship of the church. I have never saw him so humble as he is now," she continued.

> Br Luke got home last thursday [September 7] and let me tell you, he was the first one to come forward yesterday and make a humble confession to the church. He was received into their full fellowship by a unanimous vote. He was succeeded by Br Liman and John [Boynton] who also gave ample satisfaction, and was joyfully received by the unanimous vote of the church. They was then called upon to administer the holy sacrament of the Lord. Yo'uld be sure this was a pleasing sight. I think I could realize some of the feelings of the Prodigal, when his rebellious son returned home. I have before mentioned that Br Luke went to see Br Mclelin, but as good luck would have it, he did not see him; he had gone with his Family to Missouri; no doubt the hand of the Lord was in it. If he had seen him with the feelings that [McLellin] then possessed, he would [have] undoubtedly prejudiced his mind against the church.[57]

Shortly after the September 10 meeting, Lyman Johnson moved his family, consisting of his wife, Sarah, and one-year-old daughter of the same name, to Far West. Leland Gentry explained that some church members left Kirtland to "avoid the numerous court actions pending against them."[58] One wonders about Lyman's assets because

---

57. Vilate Kimball to Heber C. Kimball, Sept. 6-11, 1837. At a church conference in the tabernacle in Salt Lake City on April 7, 1895, Wilford Woodruff, while speaking on the "Power of Evil," recalled Lyman Johnson's rebellion in Kirtland: "I saw one of these Apostles in the Kirtland Temple, when the Sacrament was being passed, stand in the aisle and curse the Prophet of God to his face while he was in the stand, and when the bread was passed he reached out his hand for a piece of bread and flung it into his mouth like a mad dog. He turned as black in the face almost as an African with rage and with the power of the devil. What did he do? He ate and drank damnation to himself. He did not go and hang himself, but he did go and drown himself, and the river went over his body while his spirit was cast into the pit, where he ceased to have the power to curse either God or His Prophet in time or in eternity." "Discourse by President Wilford Woodruff," *Millennial Star*, May 30, 1895, 340.

58. Leland Homer Gentry, "A History of the Latter-day Saints in Northern Missouri from 1836 to 1839" (PhD., diss., Brigham Young University, 1965),

reading between the lines of a letter from Kirtland dissenter Stephen Burnett to Johnson in Far West, one gets the impression that Lyman had adequate funds:

> You state in your letter that you have lost six thousand dollars Kirtland paper—now I will tell you what Joseph Smith Jr told me when he was here on his [trip] West last Sept, I asked him about you, he said you has [a] bagg of money & could pay all of your debts if you would, I asked him if you did not loose by the bank & he said no—not a cent, He said you never took it [scrip] for goods any longer tha[n] it would pay your debts. And after that you refused to take it, besides you [were] loaned two thousand out of the bank which you never paid but exchanged a large amount with a broker in St Louis at 5 per cent for specie when you and Luke went west last fall and you bought land, hired a house built &c, this however I believe to be a lie amongst the rest.[59]

The reconciliation with the three apostles was short-lived. At the same time Lyman was attempting to settle into the community in Far West, his brother Luke and fellow apostle John Boynton sponsored a dance in Kirtland and were excoriated for "mingling with the world" in merriment. At an assembly in the temple on

---

118. He assumed that some of those who moved to Missouri did so looking for additional audiences "for their work of dissent."

59. Stephen Burnett to Lyman E. Johnson, Apr. 15, 1838. This letter was copied on May 24, 1838, and recopied by James Mulholland in June 1839 into the Joseph Smith Letterbook, 2:64-66, LDS Church History Library. Burnett converted in 1830 and served several missions before defecting from the church. He had several theological articles published in the *Messenger and Advocate*. Johnson's Far West real estate purchases were mentioned by Vilate Kimball: "I saw Br. Limon Johson to day. He said I must tell you he had bought for himself and Br Boynton one hundred acres of land apiece lying within three miles of Far West City. He has also bought each of them a lot in the city. He has a corner lot lying between Br. Pattens and the one resurved for you. He wished you to tell Br Hyde if he could not find a lot to send him that he would divide with him. He has got a house now building upon it 18 X 28." Vilate Kimball to Heber C. Kimball, Sept. 12, 1837.

October 22, the clerk listed those who "had been guilty of meeting with the world on Thursday last and some of them guilty of dancing." The Johnsons (Luke and Susan) and Boyntons (John and Susan) were among twenty-five men and women who were given the harsh penalty of disfellowshipment for their dancing. Luke and ten others acknowledged this on October 29 and were forgiven, but the others were referred to the high council "for attending a ball at the store of Johnson & Boynton" and dancing. At the November 1 high council hearing, John and Susan Boynton were told to appear in a week to "make satisfaction or be excluded from fellowship of the Church."[60] Given their prior history of repentance over such minor issues, it is assumed that they confessed to having engaged in such frivolities.

In another development a week earlier, the high council equivocated on whether to grant a tavern license to John Johnson Jr., who had decided to follow in the footsteps of his father. The council appointed Reynolds Cahoon, John Gould, and Luke Johnson to determine if John Jr. might agree to "desist from selling spirituous liquors to those who are in the habit of getting intoxicated, and request him [that] if Mormons drink spirits there, he would report them to the authorities of the Church."[61] It is not known whether the young man agreed to this, or even if the tavern was his or his father's, but it is known that his father's tradition had been to sell brandy, gin, rum, whiskey, wine, and other alcoholic drinks.[62]

Joseph Smith asked that a general assembly be convened in Far West, on November 6-7. Joining him on the stand were his loyal followers Sidney Rigdon, Hyrum Smith, and Thomas Marsh, next to recently turned critics Oliver Cowdery, Lyman Johnson, William McLellin, William Phelps, David Whitmer, and John

---

60. Collier and Harwell, *Kirtland Council Minute Book*, 196–201.
61. Ibid., 197.
62. Staker, *Hearken, O Ye People*, 416.

Whitmer.[63] Like Parley Pratt, who clarified that his disappointment in Joseph Smith did not imply disbelief or disloyalty to the faith, these were all stalwarts, Sidney Rigdon proposed that they endorse Joseph as "the first President of the whole Church, to preside over the same," and everyone agreed to this. However, Frederick Williams was rejected as one of his counselors and was replaced by Hyrum Smith. All the twelve apostles were sustained by the congregation, and even David Whitmer was supported as the president of the church in Missouri, although only after considerable discussion and a less-than-unanimous vote. His counselors John Whitmer and William Phelps were also accepted.[64]

In essence, everyone agreed to a shaky armistice. It was different in Kirtland, as Smith and Rigdon would discover in December when they returned to find John Boynton and Luke Johnson once again associating with Joseph Coe, Martin Harris, and Warren Parrish. As John Smith informed his son George A. Smith, though without a complete grasp of the church structure, "John E. Page and John Taylor are appointed to fill [vacancies in the] Bishoprick in the place [of] Luke Johnson & John Boynton."[65]

Hepzibah Richards, a sister of Willard who went by "Hepsy," wrote to her brother in mid-January 1838 to report that "Luke Johnson and John Boynton are no lo[nger] of the number of the 12. Elders John Taylor and John Page are chosen to fill their places."[66]

---

63. By this time, McLellin had already been restored to his apostleship, since he is listed with other licensed "ministers of the gospel" in the *Messenger and Advocate*, Mar. 1837, 472. See his letter to "My dear old Friends," Jan. 24, 1837, in Shipps and Welch, *Journals of William E. McLellin*, 229-30, in which he requests their forgiveness.

64. Cannon and Cook, *Far West Record*, 121-23.

65. John and Clarissa Smith to George A. Smith, Jan. 1, 1838, George A. Smith Papers, LDS Church History Library. George A. Smith would later become a Utah apostle.

66. Hepzibah Richards to Willard Richards, Jan. 18-19, 1838, in Kenneth W. Godfrey, Audrey M. Godfrey, and Jill Mulvay Derr, eds., *Women's Voices: An Untold History of the Latter-day Saints, 1830-1900* (Salt Lake City: Deseret Book, 2000), 73.

This was slightly inaccurate because Taylor and Page were chosen as replacements but not ordained until the end of the year, perhaps allowing a suitable delay to give the former apostles a chance to change their minds. Luke would later regret that he retained his determination to go his own way, but he had bent his will to Joseph's one too many times, he believed. He later blamed his waywardness on the "spirit of speculation, which at that time was possessed by many of the Saints and elders." It had distracted him from his spiritual calling. "My mind became darkened, and I was left to pursue my own course," he wrote.[67]

The once-united Saints were now bitterly divided, old friendships wrenched apart.[68] The dissenters called supporters "lick skillets," akin to calling someone a boot licker. The loyalists called the dissatisfied members apostates. Before long, the dissenters went their own way and established their own Church of Christ, the original name given to the Latter-day Saints before Joseph changed it. It was to be the "old standard Church of Christ," they insisted. Historian Dean Jessee summarized the beginning of 1838 by noting that "under the leadership of Warren Parrish, who had been Joseph Smith's secretary, approximately thirty prominent men of the Church, including a member of the First Presidency, several of the Twelve, high council, First Council of Seventy, and witnesses of the Book of Mormon, had renounced Joseph Smith and the Church and had established a new organization—the Church of Christ. During this time of apostasy, approximately three hundred left the Church, representing about 15 percent of the Kirtland membership."[69]

---

67. "History of Luke Johnson," 57.

68. An example of relationships shattered by the divisive forces in Kirtland comes from Caroline Barnes Crosby, who listed John Boynton, Luke and Lyman Johnson, and Warren Parrish as "some of our nighest neighbors and friends. We had taken sweet counsel together, and walked to the house of God as friends," in Godfrey, et al., *Women's Voices*, 56.

69. Dean C. Jessee, *The Papers of Joseph Smith* (Salt Lake City: Deseret Book, 1992), 2:217n2.

Benjamin Johnson recalled the heart-wrenching separation of friends, missionary companions, and family members and how "notes became due for lands bought at great prices," resulting in disappointment and bad feelings so that "brotherly love was found smothered by the love of the world." He lamented that "brethren who had traveled, ministered and suffered together, and even placed their lives upon the same altar, now were governed by a feeling of hate and a spirit to accuse each other, and all for the love of Accursed Mammon." He added with some eloquence:

> All their former companionship in the holy anointing in the Temple of the Lord, where filled with the Holy Ghost, the heavens were opened, and in view of the glories before them they had together shouted "Hosanna to God and the Lamb," all was now forgotten by many, who were like Judas, ready to sell or destroy the Prophet Joseph and his followers. And it almost seemed to me that the brightest stars in our firmament had fallen. Many to whom I had in the past most loved to listen, their voices seemed now the most discordant and hateful to me. From the Quorum of the Twelve fell four of the brightest: Wm. E. McLellin, Luke and Lyman Johnson and John Boyington; of the First Presidency, F. G. Williams; the three Witnesses to the Book of Mormon, Oliver Cowdery, David Whitmer and Martin Harris. Of other very prominent elders were Sylvester Smith, Warren Cowdery, Warren Parrish, Joseph Coe and many others who apostatized or became enemies to the Prophet. I was then nineteen years of age, and as I now look back through more than fifty years of subsequent experience, to that first great Apostasy, I regard it as the greatest sorrow, disappointment and test through which I have ever passed.[70]

Developments in Kirtland between mid-December 1837 and mid-January 1838 are sparsely documented, but we know that Uncle John Smith, president of the high council, gathered a fiercely

---

70. Benjamin F. Johnson, *My Life's Review* (Mesa: Twenty-first Century Printing, 1992), 27-29.

loyal group of men together on the high council to excommunicate some fifty dissenters before the end of the year. In a letter to
his son, he explained:

> The spiritual condition at this time is gloomy also. I called the
> High Council together last week and laid Before <them> the case
> of a compan<y> of Decenters 28 persons[,] where upon mature
> Discussion [we] proceeded to cut them off from the ch[urc]h; the
> Leaders were Cyrus Smalling Joseph Coe Martin Harris Luke
> Johnson John Boynton and W[arren] W Parrish. We have cut off
> Between 40 & 50 from the Chh Since you Left ... Joseph and
> Hyrum & Pres Rigdon ... mean to go to the west [to Missouri] as
> soon as they can settle their affairs here. ... R[eynolds] Cahoon &
> myself are to presid[e] over the stake of Kirtland[.][71]

Historian Leonard Arrington hypothesized that Brigham
Young doubtlessly "testified against many of these excommuni-
cants" before he was driven from Kirtland on December 22. He
told the agitators that Joseph Smith "had not transgressed and
fallen," despite what the "apostates declared."[72] Joseph's revelation
of January 12 directed the "presidency of my Church" to take their
families west as "soon as it is practicable," sealing Kirtland's fate as
a one-time church headquarters. "Your labors are finished in this
place for a season," it read. "Let all your faithful friends arise with
their families also, and get out of this place, and gather themselves
together unto Zion and be at peace among yourselves, O ye inhabitants of Zion, or their shall be no saf[e]ty for you. Even so Amen."[73]

In her letter to her brother in England, Hepsy Richards wrote
of "a large number" of former members who had become aggressive and were trying to take over the temple. They had acquired

---

71. John and Clarissa to George A. Smith, Jan. 1, 1838. Material added to
letter by Andrew Jenson not included.
72. Arrington, *Brigham Young*, 61.
73. Jessee, et al., *Joseph Smith Papers: Journals*, 1:283-84.

keys to the two front doors, and a judge had delivered the printing press into their hands on January 15, selling it at auction as compensation for losses they had suffered with the demise of the Safety Society Bank. However, in retaliation against the dissenters for having prevailed in court, the loyalists torched the press building one evening and burned it to the ground:

> The printing-office has been attached on a judgment that [Grandison] Newell held against the Presidents of K[irtland] money. Last monday it was sold at auction into the hands of Mr. [Nathaniel] Millican, one of the dissenters. At one o[']clock the night following cousin Mary waked me, and said that Kirtland was all in flames. It proved to be the Printing-office—the fire was then in its height and in one hour it was consumed with all its contents. The Temple and other buildings badly scorched. Tuesday eve a meeting was held and a patrol consisting of 21 men, 3 for each night in the week, chosen to guard the city to prevent further destruction by fire. A part of these men are members of the church—a part dissenters.[74]

Benjamin Johnson expressed shock that the *Elders' Journal* building "was set on fire by Bro Lyman R. Sherman and destroyed."[75] Sherman, one of the presidents of the Seventy, was summoned to court, with his accomplices, to answer to Justice of the Peace Warren Cowdery, a dissenter. Cowdery was unable to find any material evidence or eyewitness testimony of arson, so he discharged the defendants.[76]

After Joseph and Sidney fled Kirtland, many of the loyalists feared that their lives were in danger. As Hepsy wrote in January,

---

74. Hepzibah Richards to Willard Richards, Jan. 18-19, 1838, qtd. in Godfrey, et al., *Women's Voices*, 71.

75. Benjamin Franklin Johnson, "A Life Review," ca. 1894, 24, in Benjamin Franklin Johnson Papers, LDS Church History Library. At the top of this page, Johnson wrote: "Printing office burned by L R Sherman"; also in Johnson, *My Life's Review*, 29-30.

76. Oliver Cowdery's Docket Book, Jan. 17-19, 1838, Henry E. Huntington Library.

"All our friends design leaving this place as soon as possible." She added that "the feeling seems to be that Kirtland must be trodden down by the wicked for a season ... Probably several hundred families will leave within a few weeks."[77] The *Painesville Republican* printed a letter from Warren Parrish proposing that Joseph and Sidney had been less than honest in their statements and had engaged in financial fraud. They "lie by revelation," Parrish wrote, "swindle by revelation, cheat and defraud by revelation, run away by revelation; and if they do not mend their ways, I fear they will at last be damned by revelation." An accompanying note signed by Luke Johnson, John Boynton, Sylvester Smith, and Leonard Rich affirmed the facts related by Parrish "according to our best recollections," as well as the sentiment.[78] In March, Parrish and Boynton had letters published in Belfast, Maine, relating events from the past few years, expressing the opinion that Joseph and Sidney had defrauded many people. Boynton dwelt on his sacrifice for the church:

> It has been my lot to be called and chosen one of the twelve Latter Day Apostles. I have held important stations in the church for about five years, and have travelled much and preached much in the Eastern States, and built up many churches; and indeed I have baptized hundreds in your own State, and did it in all honesty and good faith; but after becoming acquainted with the above facts, and many others of the like character, I have, with the same principles of honesty and good faith, withdrawn from them.[79]

Historians James B. Allen and Glen M. Leonard summarized the exodus from Kirtland in this way:

With the Prophet now living in Missouri, many of the faithful

---

77. Hepzibah Richards to Willard Richards, Jan. 22, 1838, LDS Church History Library.

78. Warren Parrish to the *Painesville Republican*, Feb. 15, 1838, 3.

79. "Mormonism," *Waldo Patriot*, May 4, 1838, 1. For the full text of the letter, see appendix 3.

who remained in Kirtland wanted to follow him. On March 6, 1838, the seventies met in the temple to plan the migration. They extended the privilege of joining the exodus to all members of the Church. The result was the pioneer party known as Kirtland Camp, which left the city on July 6 with 515 people, 27 tents, 59 wagons, 97 horses, 22 oxen, 69 cows, and 1 bull. ... As they traveled westward, the Saints were frequently hampered by muddy roads and by the need to work at odd jobs along the way in order to earn enough money to continue. Discouragement was great, and before reaching Springfield, Illinois, the group had been reduced to about 260 persons. On October 2, after traveling 866 miles, Kirtland Camp was met by Joseph Smith, Sidney Rigdon, and others and happily escorted into Far West. Two days later this group of Saints began to settle at Adam-ondi-Ahman.[80]

Seven years after Kirtland was designated as the church's headquarters, and after seeing the impressive temple that still stands today as an architectural showpiece, the town was abandoned as quickly as it had been built up. From then on it fell back into its former, slower pace of sustainable development along the path it had been on before the arrival of the Mormons. The loyalists anticipated better times in Missouri but were sorely mistaken. The Quorum of the Twelve Apostles had its first casualties, but only after the apostles had endured more physical and emotional strain than anyone could reasonably be expected to endure. These men had signed up for a church and had inherited a military camp. They had not expected to be required to follow orders, and their consciences, after leading them to the church, led them away from it. One of them chose to stay away for a period of time and then returned, while the other two would go in other directions, receiving secular acclaim and not looking back again.

---

80. James B. Allen and Glen M. Leonard, *The Story of the Latter-day Saints*, rev. ed. (Salt Lake City: Deseret Book, 1992), 124–25.

7. THE END OF ZION

While Joseph Smith and his supporters in Kirtland struggled with former and dissenting Mormons to retain leadership of the church in 1837, seeds for a similar struggle were germinating 800 miles to the southwest in Missouri. David and John Whitmer and William Phelps, the Missouri presidency, operated independently because of the distance, which created a communication barrier with the presidency of the church in Kirtland. Because President Whitmer resided in Kirtland during the formative settlement of Far West, his two counselors acted as the presidency during that time. Historian Leland H. Gentry documented that Phelps and John Whitmer used money donated by other church members to purchase Missouri lands in their own names and resold it to impoverished Saints. A furor arose when others discovered that the two officials retained a small part of the profits. Gentry explained that "such actions, so completely at variance with the spirit of the law of Consecration, brought immediate protest from several quarters. Inasmuch as the two men were merely the agents of the Church, it was never contemplated that they would use their positions for personal advantage."[1]

Seven high councilors held a meeting in Far West on April 3, 1837, and resolved to have Missouri presidency members Phelps and John Whitmer appear before them to explain their authority for

---

1. Leland Homer Gentry, "A History of the Latter-day Saints in Northern Missouri from 1836-1839," (PhD. Diss. Brigham Young University, 1965), 103-04.

platting Far West as a city and selecting the site for the Far West temple without input from the high council and the bishop, among other charges. The most emotional issue was the claim that Phelps and Whitmer had profited from the sale of lands. The high council chaired several hearings from April 5-7 that Presidents Phelps and Whitmer, Bishop Partridge and his counselors, and Apostles Marsh and Patten attended.[2] Phelps threatened to adjourn the hearings if the apostles and bishopric were not removed, but Marsh threatened counter-charges if they were excluded. Patten spoke against Phelps and Whitmer "with apparent indignation," stating that their actions had been "iniquitous & fraudulent in the extreme, in the unrighteously appropriating Church funds to their own emolument which had been plainly proven."[3] The presidency had no choice but to "transfer the Town Plott" to Far West "into the hands of the Bishop of Zion."[4] Marsh later explained what had occurred, saying that the Missouri presidency had conducted transactions "independently of the aid, or council of either the bishop or High Council" or the First Presidency.[5]

Marsh, convinced of the corruption of the local presidency and willing to be Joseph Smith's accomplice in Missouri, led the attack against the Missouri presidency, apostle Lyman Johnson, and others thought to be disloyal to Joseph Smith. He stood by the prophet when almost no one else did. Historian Lyndon W. Cook evaluated Marsh's motives: "Jealous to win greater recognition and influence, Thomas indulged in excessive behavior, all in the name

---

2. Marsh had a vested interest in how Phelps and Whitmer used the money because he and Elisha Groves had collected $1,450 during a recent mission to Kentucky and Tennesee "to assist the destitute Saints." Donald Q. Cannon and Lyndon W. Cook, *Far West Record: Minutes of the Church of Jesus Christ of Latter-day Saints, 1830-1844* (Salt Lake City: Deseret Book, 1983), 108n3.

3. Ibid., 107-10.

4. Ibid, 110.

5. Thomas B. Marsh to Wilford Woodruff, Apr. 30, 1838, qtd. in Cannon and Cook, *Far West Record*, 109n3.

of Joseph Smith. While evidence shows that Oliver [Cowdery] and his cohorts were embittered, the means Thomas used did not justify the end."[6]

Joseph Smith had learned in Ohio that there was a danger in allowing dissent in any form. As soon as he arrived in Missouri in March 1838, he approved the disciplinary actions of senior members of the Twelve Apostles and the Far West High Council against the men he had trusted with positions of responsibility from an early date. The first step in this retaliation had been the reigning in of William Phelps and John Whitmer in April 1837. On January 20, 1838, at the social meeting held in Far West at Marsh's home, he and David Patten and seven Far West high councilors chose from among themselves a committee of three high councilmen, George Hinkle, Thomas Grover, and George Morey, to investigate "the proceeding[s] of the Presidents in this place viz David Whitmer W. W. Phelps John Whitmer and Oliver Cowdery." Six days later the committee condemned the local presidency for not having strictly followed the church dietary code, the Word of Wisdom, and for disregarding the directive against selling their land in Jackson County to those not of their faith,[7] as well as for asserting that they would not be governed by ecclesiastical intimidation or self-serving prophecy, which the Missouri presidency had

6. Lyndon W. Cook, "'I Have Sinned against Heaven, and Am Unworthy to Your Confidence, But I Cannot Live without a Reconciliation': Thomas B. Marsh Returns to the Church," *BYU Studies* 20 (Summer 1980): 393–94.

7. Ironically, in "An Appeal," *The Evening and the Morning Star*, Aug. 1834, 183, William W. Phelps and David and John Whitmer joined Edward Partridge and others, explaining that "to sell our land would amount to a denial of our faith, as that land is the place where the Zion of God, shall stand, according to our faith and belief in the revelations of God." This may have been based on a letter Joseph Smith sent to Phelps and others in August 1833: "It is the will of the Lord that the Store shou[l]d be kept and that <not> one foot of <land> perchased should <be> given to the enemies of god or sold to them." Dean C. Jessee, comp. and ed., *Personal Writings of Joseph Smith*, 2nd ed. rev. ed. (Salt Lake City and Provo: Deseret Book and Brigham Young University Press, 2002), 311.

characterized as inappropriate "ecclesiastical power"—ecclesiastical abuse in today's parlance.[8]

Upon the recommendation of the committee, the high council, consisting of the two visiting apostles and seven high councilmen, resolved in part "that under existing circumstances" they would no longer receive the existing Missouri leaders "as Presidents" of the church. Marsh prepared a written notice informing David Whitmer and his counselors John Whitmer and William Phelps that their services would no longer be required, pending endorsement from the general membership of the council's proposal.[9]

In response, President Whitmer and his counselors, along with others who had fallen out of favor with the loyalists, met in Far West on January 30. The minutes of their deliberations are in Oliver Cowdery's letterbook:

> At a meeting the following members of the Church of Latter Day Saints, viz: F. G. Williams, D. Whitmer, W. W. Phelps, John Whitmer, Jacob Whitmer, Lyman E. Johnson and O. Cowdery convened at the house of Oliver Cowdery in Far West, Caldwell Co., Mo. by common consent, to take into consideration the state of said church and the manner in which some of the authorities of the same have [attempted] for a time past, and are still endeavoring[,] to unite ecclesiastical and civil authority, and force men under pretense of incurring the displeasure of heaven to use their earthly substance contrary to their own interest and privilege; and also how said authorities are endeavoring to make it a rule of faith for said church to uphold a certain man or men *right* or wrong, when Frederick G. Williams was called to the chair and Oliver Cowdery was appointed clerk.
>
> After consultation, Oliver Cowdery, David Whitmer, [and] Frederick G. Williams were appointed a committee to draft a declaration and resolutions, to present to the next meeting; and W. W. Phelps, John Whitmer and Lyman E. Johnson, were appointed

---

8. Cannon and Cook, *Far West Record*, 135.
9. Ibid., 135-36.

a committee to look for a place for the above named individuals in which to settle, where they may live in peace, and also report to the said meeting.[10]

When the church membership convened in Far West on February 5, Thomas Marsh read aloud a revelation of September 4, 1837, declaring that William Phelps and John Whitmer were in transgression, that they would be "removed out of their places" if they failed to repent. Apostle David Patten and other loyalists on the high council condemned the presidency for selling their land in Jackson County. Bishop Partridge protested that the meeting was "hasty and illegal," as did John Corrill, who likewise spoke "against the High Council in regard to their proceedings, and labored hard to show that the meeting was illegal, and that the Presidency ought to be had before a proper tribunal," but Marsh countered that they were meeting "according to the directions of Br Joseph." Marsh "considered it legal" because Joseph had requested it.[11]

Corrill and Partridge were overwhelmed by the insistence of Marsh and Patten, who quickly gained the support of other prominent men. Lyman Wight thought that by "selling their lands in Jackson County," Whitmer, Phelps, and Cowdery had "flatly denied the faith," to which Moses Martin added that the situation in Missouri was due "to the wickedness and mismanagement" of the Missouri presidency.

When a vote was called, it was unanimously in opposition to the presidency, "excepting eight or ten" men who wanted to wait until Joseph Smith could come to supervise the inquest.[12] No action was taken against the presidency's memberships.

---

10. Oliver Cowdery Letterbook, 85, Henry E. Huntington Library, San Marino, California; emphasis retained. On May 18, traveling with Smith and Rigdon, Marsh ran into Oliver Cowdery, Lyman Johnson, and others "encamped, who were also exploring northward on Grand River." "History of Thos. Baldwin Marsh," *Deseret News*, Mar. 24, 1858, 18.

11. Cannon and Cook, *Far West Record*, 137-39; cf. josephsmithpapers.org.

12. Ibid., 137-40.

Inexplicably, in the fervently emotional atmosphere of charges, countercharges, and the wrenching apart of friendships, the Far West High Council essentially ceased to be the ruling authority within the stake. On February 10, Thomas Marsh and David W. Patten were voted "Presidents, pro. tempor. of the Church of Latter Day Saints in Missouri, or until Presidents Joseph Smith jr. and Sidney Rigdon arrives in the Land of Zion."[13] Even during a hearing on March 10 when William Phelps and John Whitmer were excommunicated, Thomas Marsh and David Patten were acknowledged as the church's Missouri presidency.[14]

When Cowdery was notified on April 12 that Bishop Edward Partridge and his counselors would preside over a high council trial to investigate his alleged disloyalty, he decided to not cooperate in the staged event, instead sending a letter that eloquently objected to an impromptu council presuming to judge his handling of "temporal interests." He wrote that under the circumstances, faced with the prospect of being confronted by individuals who were predisposed to deprive him of his "Constitutional privileges and inherent rights," he "respectfully ask[ed] leave" to "withdraw from" the society he had once promoted.[15]

It proved to be a lengthy trial. Joseph Smith and others testified against Cowdery based on what they considered to be character flaws. In judging the case, Bishop Partridge decided that there was substance to six of the nine charges and that Cowdery was unworthy to be a member of the church. The high council agreed; Cowdery was excommunicated.[16]

Throughout the hearing, the concern had been Cowdery's criticism of what he termed Joseph Smith's "dirty, nasty, filthy affair"

---

13. Ibid., 141. Joseph Smith arrived at Far West with his family on March 14, 1838, and Sidney Rigdon on April 4.

14. Ibid., 141, 145–49.

15. Ibid., 164–66.

16. Ibid., 163, 168–69.

with Fanny Alger,[17] something historians are of different opinions about, whether she was the first of Joseph's plural wives or an extramarital interest; there is not much disagreement about the fact that there was a relationship of some sort.[18] Whatever the nature of the relationship was, Cowdery could not accept it and refused to retreat from his position that the prophet had strayed from the church's teachings on marriage. It was nine years, almost to the day, since he first met Joseph and became a scribe for the Book of Mormon. Cowdery had been the second person to receive a preaching commission in the nascent church. The trial represented a complete severing of ties, as well as a warning to other malcontents.

The cleansing process picked up the next day when Marsh, Patten, Brigham Young, and the high council took up seven charges against Lyman Johnson by Alanson Ripley.[19] They were (1) "stirring up people to prosecute … lawsuits" against the innocent; (2) "virtually denying the faith" by "vindicating the cause of the enemies of this Church, who are dissenters from us," when Lyman claimed certain proceedings were illegal, as well as missing some of his Sabbath meetings, "not observing his prayers," and "not observing the word of wisdom"; (3) by saying that Joseph Smith owed him $1,000; (4) "for laying violent hands on our Brother Phineas Young, and by

17. Oliver Cowdery to Warren A. Cowdery, Jan. 21, 1838, Oliver Cowdery Letterbook, 81, Huntington Library. Concerning the relationship, see Richard L. Bushman, *Joseph Smith: Rough Stone Rolling* (New York: Knopf, 2005), 323-27.

18. Don Bradley, "Mormon Polygamy Before Nauvoo? The Relationship of Joseph Smith and Fanny Alger," in *The Persistence of Polygamy: Joseph Smith and the Origins of Mormon Polygamy*, eds. Newell G. Bringhurst and Craig L. Foster (Independence, MO: John Whitmer Books, 2010), 14-58; Bushman, *Rough Stone Rolling*, 323-27; Todd Compton, *In Sacred Loneliness: The Plural Wives of Joseph Smith* (Salt Lake City: Signature Books, 1997), 25-42; Brian D. Hales, *Joseph Smith's Polygamy*, 3 vols. (Draper, UT: Greg Kofford Books, 2013), 1:85-152; George D. Smith, *Nauvoo Polygamy: "… But We Called It Celestial Marriage,"* rev. ed. (Salt Lake City: Signature Books, 2011), 38-43.

19. Alanson Ripley joined the church in Ohio and served in Zion's Camp in 1834. In May 1838 he traveled to northern Missouri and surveyed Adam-ondi-Ahman. He was a bishop for a time in Iowa Territory.

kicking and beating him";[20] (5) for threatening to go to a secular court; (6) for telling a falsehood in another context; and (7) for giving someone whiskey during business negotiations.

Johnson took the same path as Cowdery and refused to take part in the proceedings, instead sending a letter of protest:

Far West, Mo April 12th 1838

Sir Yours of the 9th inst. containing a copy of six [seven] charges, preferred, before the Council by A. Ripley, against me has been received, and it appears to me to be a novel document, assuming a right to compel me under pain of religious [c]ensure and excommunication not to appeal a [civil] lawsuit or change the venue of the same in which I am deeply interested, without the consent of a religious body.

This assumption of power being manifest in the fifth Charge, I should not condescend to put my constitutional rights at issue upon so disrespectful a point as to answer any other of those charges until that is withdrawn & untill then shall withdraw my self from your society and fellowship.

Yours

Lyman E. Johnson[21]

In spite of the letter, a trial was held the following day in Far West with Marsh, Patten, and Young presiding over the high council. George Hinkle testified that Johnson had been "active in urging on lawsuits" against President Smith. Thomas Grover testified

---

20. Cannon and Cook, *Far West Record*, 172-73. D. Michael Quinn, *The Mormon Hierarchy: Origins of Power* (Salt Lake City: Signature Books, 1994), 556, said that Johnson was "fined for assault and battery on B[righam] Y[oung]'s brother in 1838." A Mormon named George Walter posted bail for Lyman Johnson. "I was taken to task & warned that I would suffer for it," he said, "and on leaving town that evening, in company with Johnson, there was a number of guns fired at us. As I heard the balls whistle near us, in a day or two I returned to town and saw [Sidney] Rigdon who took me to task for going Johnson's bail." Mormon Inquest Testimony before Judge Austin A. King, Nov. 1838, 36, Western Historical Manuscript Collection, University of Missouri, Columbia.

21. Cannon and Cook, *Far West Record*, 173.

that Johnson had cheated him out of a parcel of land, and Arthur Morrison complained that the defendant had served as a civil prosecutor in a case against a church member, George Hinkle.

Elder Patten testified that while living with him, Johnson used to take tea and coffee, neglected his prayers, corresponded with dissenters in Kirtland, and complained about "a thousand dollar note against Joseph Smith." Nor did Johnson believe that the high council had jurisdiction over him, according to Patten. Others accused Johnson of drinking in a tavern, not keeping the Sabbath, and riding steamboats without paying.

Brigham Young testified that Johnson had beaten up his brother, Phineas Young, after which Phineas stumbled into John Greene's house "with his head cut[,] the blood running out of his ears, also his stomach was injured, & Phineas said Lyman E. Johnson had fought him." Dimick Huntington said Johnson had bragged about the scuffle, promising "the same sauce" to anyone else who behaved as Phineas had. Hinkle testified that Johnson got a man named Weldon "well shaved," meaning drunk, before Weldon agreed to sell his "large farm with great improvements together with five hundred head of hogs, a good stock of horses and cattle, also a flock of sheep [and] the plows belonging to the farm" for a discount price of $2,250.

"After some few appropriate remarks, by the Councellors, it was decided by the President [Marsh] that Lyman E. Johnson be no longer considered a member of the Church of Christ of Latter Day Saints, nor a member of the quorum of the twelve Apostles of the Lamb and also be given over to the buffetings of Satan untill he learns to blaspheme no more against the authorities of God."[22]

Next the high council considered charges against David Whitmer for not observing the Word of Wisdom, unChristian-like conduct, and referring to himself as president of the church after

---

22. Ibid., 173–76.

his removal from office. Like Cowdery, Whitmer was a Book of Mormon witness and early organizer of Mormonism. His departure would mean that all three of the men who had testified they had seen the Book of Mormon angel would be out of the church. Martin Harris had been purged at the same time Luke Johnson and John Boynton were removed in Kirtland.

Following the example of those who had gone before him, or perhaps reflecting a coordinated effort, Whitmer penned a letter of protest and withdrawal, reiterating his belief that he was being summoned unlawfully. "To spare you any further trouble I hereby withdraw from your fellowship and communion," he fumed, "choosing to seek a place among the meek and humble, where the revelations of Heaven will be observed and the rights of men regarded." In the court session, the members of the high council made a few remarks, then Marsh ruled that Whitmer "be no longer considered a member of the Church of Christ of Latter day Saints."[23]

Neither Lyman Johnson nor David Whitmer would ever return to fellowship with their former colleagues, but Cowdery would take a different path and rejoin in 1848, four years after Joseph Smith's death and two years before Cowdery's death. David Whitmer is interesting for never having changed his mind about Joseph Smith being a fallen prophet, asserting this observation in tandem with his enduring testimony about the Book of Mormon being of divine origin. To many believers today, his alienation from Joseph is evidence that the former really did see the angel holding the golden plates in his hands because if an estranged friend of Joseph Smith would not repudiate the Book of Mormon, it was worth taking a second look at it, or so the argument goes.

Curiously absent from the whorl of judgments against the apostles and witnesses in the spring of 1838 was William McLellin,

---

23. Ibid., 176–78. Ebenezer Robinson, former clerk of the Far West High Council, criticized the trial and treatment of David Whitmer in "Items of Personal History of the Editor," *The Return*, Sept. 1889, 132–33.

who often took unpredictable paths and has been difficult to trace. Whatever his pursuits at that time, he later claimed to have peacefully withdrawn from the church in August 1836. If so, it is strange he would be listed in a March 1837 *Messenger and Advocate* article among those whose ministerial licenses had been renewed.[24] Even stranger, he was sustained as an apostle in November 1837 in Kirtland. Historian Larry Porter concluded that he must have been involved with the church until his trial in 1838, but William Russell disagrees.[25] Whatever the case, whether he was sitting quietly on the sidelines or actively participating in promoting the faith, he managed to avoid drawing attention to himself until April 1838 at a conference in Far West when David Patten declared that he could not recommend him as a standing apostle.[26]

On May 11, according to George Robinson, McLellin attended a trial to determine his membership and confessed that he, McLellin,

> had no confidence in the heads of the Church, beleiving they had transgressed, and had got out of the way, consequently <he> left of[f] praying and keeping the commandments of God, and went his own way, and indulged himself in his lustfull desires. But when he he<a>rd that the first presidency, had made a general settlement and acknowledged their sins, he began to pray again, and to keep the commandments of God.[27]

When pressed at trial by Joseph Smith about whether McLellin had personally seen anything amiss in the actions of the church

---

24. *Messenger and Advocate*, Mar. 1837, 472.

25. Larry C. Porter, "The Odyssey of William Earl McLellin: Man of Diversity, 1806-83," in Jan Shipps and John W. Welch, eds., *The Journals of William E. McLellin, 1831-1836* (Provo and Urbana: *BYU Studies* and University of Illinois Press, 1994), 322-23; William D. Russell, "Portrait of a 'True Believer' in Original Mormonism," in Stan Larson and Samuel J. Passey, eds., *The William E. McLellin Papers, 1854–1880* (Salt Lake City: Signature Books, 2007), 127.

26. Cannon and Cook, *Far West Record*, 160.

27. Dean C. Jessee, Mark Ashurst-McGee, and Richard L. Jensen, eds., *The Joseph Smith Papers: Journals* (Salt Lake City: Church Historian's Press, 2008), 1:268.

president, McLellin said no, that rumor of his criticism was "hear-say." The account in the Scriptory Book ends without telling the outcome of the trial. However, it seems likely that McLellin with-drew from fellowship with the church and the Twelve, meaning that within six months the church lost four apostles and three wit-nesses, among many other pillars from its early history.

The clash between the dissenters and loyalists continued after the excommunications. The critics saw themselves as unaffiliated Mormons, rather than anti-Mormons, and continued to live in the Mormon settlements in a state of unstable rapprochement with friends in the church. The presence of so many influential crit-ics, who watched every move the leadership made and communi-cated their displeasure to non-Mormons, was a thorn in the side of church leaders, who thought they had rid themselves of these pests. John Corrill[28] wrote about the tense interactions between the hier-archy and the apostates:

> Notwithstanding the dissenters had left the church, yet the old strife kept up, and Smith and Rigdon, with others, com-plained much of the ill treatment they had received from the dis-senters and others; they said they had been persecuted from time to time with vexatious law suits; that mobs had arisen up against them, time after time; that they had been harassed to death, as it were, for seven or eight years, and they were determined to bear it no longer, for they had rather die than suffer such things.[29]

What Smith and Rigdon did was to try to insulate themselves

---

28. John Corrill was born in 1794 in Massachusetts. He was baptized in January 1831, served a mission, and became a bishop in Missouri. In 1838 he was elected to represent Caldwell County in the state legislature. After Corrill left Mormonism, he published a history of the church in 1839. Kenneth H. Winn, "'Such Republicanism as This': John Corrill's Rejection of Prophetic Rule," in *Differing Visions: Dissenters in Mormon History*, eds. Roger D. Launius and Linda Thatcher (Urbana: University of Illinois Press, 1994), 45-75.

29. John Corrill, *A Brief History of the Church of Christ of Latter Day Saints* (St. Louis: By the author, 1839), 29.

from the dissidents and to try to undermine the attempts by apostates to limit the church's influence in the Mormon counties. John Cleminson, a Mormon clerk in the Caldwell County court, said he was given instructions by Joseph Smith on which cases to allow to move forward and which ones to quash. In his testimony before Judge Austin King in November, Cleminson said he felt intimidated by Smith, to the point that he complied with his demands.[30] The excommunicated William Phelps was a Caldwell County judge. He similarly testified that Joseph interfered with the issuance of writs.[31] John Whitmer said the same thing, that Joseph "did not intend in [the] future to have any process served on him, and the officer who attempted it should die." Rigdon also made threats, according to the testimony, demanding impunity from prosecution.[32]

The attempt to shield themselves from legal proceedings was one of several steps Smith and Rigdon took to build a wall between themselves and former colleagues. It is interesting that the apostates avoided simply pulling up stakes and leaving. To leave their former companions in the Gospel would have been difficult, even if they had the means to relocate. If they departed, they would leave behind a way of life that was wrapped up in their extended families and friends, which would have been emotionally trying.

By mid-June, Smith and Rigdon were acting out of real fear, having been hounded from Kirtland by dissenting Mormons and arriving in a place where refugees had streamed in from neighboring counties, only to find themselves further harassed. They

---

30. Senate Document 189 (Washington, D.C.: U.S. Government Printing Office, 1841), 15-16. Reed Peck, a former Danite, wrote that the church leaders "would not permit the clerk of the court to issue [writs against] them in Caldwell County." See Reed Peck Manuscript, 1839, in Henry E. Huntington Library, San Marino, California; printed as *Reed Peck Manuscript* (Salt Lake City: Utah Lighthouse Ministry, n.d.), 9.

31. Senate Document 189, 1841, 44.

32. Ibid., 33.

thought if they could banish Lyman Johnson and other presumed troublemakers from Far West, the dissidents would not be able to infect other members. They believed the community needed to be purified. It "would never become [the] pure" land of Zion and a safe haven as long as there were unbelievers, dissenters, and sinners among them, they said. John Corrill explained that "secret meetings were held, and plans [were] contrived" to determine how to push former adherents out of the county.[33] Reed Peck, who wrote about the clash between the institutional church and the apostates, said the "enmity of the two parties from Kirtland" had smoldered to the point that some in Missouri considered killing the church's critics, while Marsh and Corrill registered their objection, being "strenuously opposed" to this option. Against a background of anger and hysteria, Sidney Rigdon delivered his now-famous Salt Sermon on Sunday, June 17, to a large gathering of Mormons.

> S. Rigdon took his text from the fifth chapter of Mat[t]hew: "Ye are the salt of the Earth but if the salt have lost his savour [savor] wherewith shall it be salted, it is henceforth good for nothing but to be cast out and be trodden under foot of men.[34] From this scripture he undertook to prove that when men embrace the gospel and afterwards lose their faith it is the duty of the Saints to trample them under their feet. He informed the people that they had a set of men among them that had dissented from the church and were doing all in their power to destroy the presidency[,] laying plans to take their lives &c., [and] accused them of counterfeiting lying cheating and numerous other crimes and called on the people to rise en masse and rid the country of such a nuisance. He said it is the duty of this people to trample them into the earth and if the country cannot be freed from them any other way I will assist to trample them down or to erect a gallows on the square of Far West and hang them up as they did the gamblers at Vicksburgh [in

---

33. Corrill, *Brief History*, 30, explained that the plans were held in abeyance until "President Rigdon delivered from the pulpit what I call the salt sermon."
34. Cf. LDS D&C 101:39-40; RLDS D&C 98:5.

1835] and it would be an act at which the angels would smile with approbation. Joseph Smith in a short speech sanctioned what had been said by Rigdon, though said he[,] I don't want the brethren to act unlawfully but will tell them one thing. Judas was a traitor and in stead of hanging himself was hung by Peter.

Peck thought the threats were "a farce acted to frighten these men from the country that they could not be spies upon their conduct" or to interfere with the church's hegemony in real estate and government.[35] Even so, Corrill warned John Whitmer that it was possible that his life was in danger. When Whitmer met with Smith, he elicited an acknowledgment that the "excitement is very high" and suggestion that Whitmer put his "property into the hands of the bishop and high council, to be disposed of according to the laws of the church."[36] Whitmer did not think the confiscation of his land was a very helpful compromise.

Whitmer's refusal to surrender provoked a long threatening letter, its authorship credited to Sidney Rigdon and signed by eighty-three individuals, that was presented to the dissenters the day after the salt sermon. The first signer was Danite leader Sampson Avard; other signers included Hyrum Smith, his Uncle John Smith, and "eighty other Danites," according to historian Michael Quinn. The Danites were the extralegal Mormon military society in Missouri organized to protect the church from internal and external opposition. The letter was sent to Oliver Cowdery,

35. Peck, *Reed Peck Manuscript*, 6-7. The July 4 entry of Joseph Smith's "Scriptory Book," kept by George Robinson, justified the sermon: "I would mention or notice something about O[liver] Cowdery, David Whitmer, and Lyman E. John Whitmer who b[e]ing guilty of bace [base] iniquities and that to[o] manifest in all the eyes of all men" and "being often entreated would continue in their course seeking the Lives of the First Presidency and to overthrow the Kingdom of God which they once testified" off [of]. Prest Rigdon preached one sabbath upon the salt that had lost its savour, that it is henceforth good for nothing but to be cast out, and troden under foot of men." Jessee, et al. *Joseph Smith Papers: Journals*, 1: 276, 278.

36. Senate Document 189, 33.

Lyman Johnson, William Phelps, David Whitmer, and John Whitmer.[37] A sampling of the rhetoric includes:

> Whereas the citizens of Caldwell county have borne with the abuse received from you at different times, and on different occasions, until it is no longer to be endured; neither will they endure it any longer, having exhausted all the patience they have, and conceive that to bear any longer [would be] a vice instead of a virtue ... [F]or you there shall be no escape; for there is but one decree for you, which is depart, depart, or a more fatal calamity shall befal[l] you.

Cowdery, Johnson, and David Whitmer were accused of uniting with "a band of counterfeiters, thieves, liars, and blacklegs of the deepest dye, to deceive, cheat, and defraud the saints out of their property by every art and stratagem which wickedness could invent." Cowdery and Johnson were in fact studying to become attorneys, which according to the writer was further reason to distrust them; they had "set up a nasty, dirty, pettifogger's office, pretending to be judges of the law, when it was a notorious fact that [they] are profoundly ignorant of it." Instead of enduring such people among them, "we will put you from the county of Caldwell, so help us God," the writer promised.[38]

According to John Whitmer's account, Joseph and Hyrum, Sidney, and George Robinson arranged to have the dissidents' property confiscated and "threatened to kill" them if they contested this application of eminent domain. The four leading apostates, Cowdery, Johnson, and the Whitmer brothers, went to Clay County "to obtain legal" advice. While they were away, the loyalists forced their families out of their houses. The men returned to find their wives and children on the road, clothing and bedding in their arms. According to the families, "the band of gadeantons," meaning

---

37. Quinn, *Mormon Hierarchy: Origins*, 94. It is not clear that every signer was a Danite.

38. The complete document was printed in Senate Document 189, 6-9.

Gadiantons or Danites, "kept up a guard, and watched our houses" and "threatened our lives if they ever saw us in Far West."[39] John Whitmer took the hint and left, as did others. William Phelps took a different tack and begged for forgiveness. He was the postmaster of Far West, which may have helped convince the authorities to allow his rebaptism by July 8.[40]

Writing in the Scriptory Book on July 4, George Robinson described his perception of the dissenters' flight from Far West: "These men took warning, and soon they were seen bounding over the prairie like the scape Goat to carry of[f] their own sins. [W]e have not seen them since, their influence is gone, and they are in a miserable condition, so also it [is] with all who turn from the truth to Lying cheating defrauding & swindeling."[41] William McLellin had more to say about this in an 1847 reminiscence:

> Near sunset, David, Oliver, John and Lyman bid farewell to their youthful wives, and their little children, their homes and firesides. ... But the darkness of night soon coming on, and being comparative strangers to the way, they directly lost their path. ... But onward see those men wander, until the light of a new day broke in upon that part of the earth, and meeting a stranger, he points them to the road that will lead them to an old and tried friend's who lived about twenty-five miles from Far West. With joy, mixed with sorrow, he received them. Mrs. McLellin soon furnished them with a repast.[42]

The refugees stayed with William and Emeline McLellin for

---

39. Bruce N. Westergren, ed., *From Historian to Dissident: The Book of John Whitmer* (Salt Lake City: Signature Books, 1995), 184. McLellin gave a more impressionistic account of the dissenters' expulsion in the *Ensign of Liberty*, Mar. 1847, 9.

40. Alexander L. Baugh, "A Community Abandoned: W. W. Phelps' 1839 Letter to Sally Waterman Phelps from Far West, Missouri," *Nauvoo Journal* 10 (Fall 1998): 23; Jessee, et al., *Joseph Smith Papers: Journals*, 1:285-86. In March 1839, Phelps was excommunicated again but returned in the summer of 1840.

41. Jessee, et al., *Joseph Smith Papers: Journals*, 1:278.

42. Shipps and Welch, *Journals of William E. McLellin*, 324.

several days until they were reunited with their families from Far West, then found temporary lodging in Richmond. Rigdon followed up with an inflammatory Fourth of July oration, putting non-Mormons on notice that they too would be chased down if they interfered with the affairs of their Mormon neighbors. In his typically hyperbolic style, Rigdon stirred the Mormon crowd. "We will carry the seat of war to their own houses," he shouted, and "a war of extermination" would result if Mormons were harmed. His message was not only applauded by Joseph Smith but printed by the *Elders' Journal* as a pamphlet and advertised for sale.[43]

While the threat of internal dissent faded, Joseph Smith received a revelation in July 1838 reorganizing the Quorum of the Twelve. Thomas Marsh wrote to Wilford Woodruff informing him that he had been chosen to fill one of the vacancies:

> Sir; a fiew [few] days since Prest. Joseph Smith jr. and some others were assembled to attend to some Church business when it was thought proper to select those who was designed of the LORD to fill the places of those of the twelve who had fallen away namely Wm. E Mclellin, Lyman E. Johnson, Luke Johnson, and John F. Bointon [Boynton]. The persons selected were John E. Page, John Taylor, Willford Woodruff and Wil[l]ard Richards. ... Know then brother Woodruff by this that you are appointed to fill the place of one of the twelve apostles.[44]

Like their forerunners, each of the new apostles was a veteran missionary, only Woodruff having been a member of Zion's Camp in

---

43. Richard S. Van Wagoner, *Sidney Rigdon: A Portrait of Religious Excess* (Salt Lake City: Signature Books, 1994), 220–21. Ebenezer Robinson, "Items of Personal History of the Editor," *The Return*, Nov. 1889, 170, wrote: "Let it be distinctly understood that President Rigdon was not alone responsible for the sentiment expressed in his oration, as that was a carefully prepared document, previously written, and well understood by the First Presidency."

44. Thomas B. Marsh to Wilford Woodruff, July 14, 1838, copied in Scott G. Kenney, ed., *Wilford Woodruff's Journal, 1833–1898*, 9 vols. (Midvale, UT: Signature Books, 1983–85), 1:276–77.

1834. Their primary skill was the ability to preach and convert. Of the former apostles, we lose track of John Boynton during this time. His parents were living in Davenport, Iowa Territory, where he eventually visited them, and we know that he studied to become a dentist.

Based on a revelation that was canonized as LDS Doctrine and Covenants 118:4, Marsh's call to lead the quorum "over the great waters" to England must have seemed to him like an answer to a dream. He looked forward to the planned rendezvous at the temple site in Far West nine months in the future in April 1839.[45] Despite the wait, Marsh would have been thrilled to know there was light at the end of the tunnel and that the turmoil and sadness that had accompanied the banishment of half his former colleagues was coming to an end. He had been disappointed not to be included among the few who opened the mission to England in 1837 and had wanted to lead the apostles overseas. This was a reward for his devotion and patience, he would have thought. In any case, within three months—six months short of the planned Far West meeting with the other apostles—he too would be out of the church.

During this period, the Orson Hyde and Heber Kimball families, accompanied by Erastus Snow and perhaps thirty other saints, arrived at Richmond, Missouri, where they encountered Lyman Johnson and his family. In light of Lyman's enmity with the institutional church and the fact that he had recently suffered the loss of property and possessions, Lyman was remarkably friendly. Heber Kimball recorded: "He ordered a dinner at the hotel for all of his old friends, and treated us with every kindness—Brother Hyde and family remained there several days. Wagons were procured there to take us to Far West, where we arrived on the 25th of July."[46]

---

45. The revelation is not in the RLDS D&C.

46. Jeni Broberg Holzapfel and Richard Neitzel Holzapfel, eds. *A Woman's View: Helen Mar Whitney's Reminiscences of Early Church History* (Provo: Brigham Young University Religious Studies Center, 1997), 100.

It was a chaotic time. Mormons were on the brink of all-out war, and other significant events were materializing, making it even more improbable that Marsh, as a popular myth has it, left the church over some milk strippings.[47] Marsh's wife, Elizabeth, shared part of the family's milk harvest every other day with her neighbor, Lucinda Harris, and Lucinda reciprocated on alternate days so each could make a full block of cheese on her appointed day. It went well enough until Lucinda caught Elizabeth holding back the richer last drops of milk from her cow, called the strippings. George A. Smith took a dim view of this after he filled Marsh's vacancy in the quorum and drew an unlikely moral from the story, concluding that Marsh's "apostacy" was "caused by so small a thing as a pint of strippings."[48]

Ten years later the same commentator gave more details, saying the matter was brought before Bishop Partridge for trial and that when Elizabeth was found guilty, an appeal was made to the First Presidency, which failed. Unhappy, Marsh huffed that he would "sustain the character of his wife, even if he had to go to hell for it."[49] There was one eyewitness to the church court who left his impressions. Henry W. Bigler said he attended the trial and heard "the Bishop and others plead with [Elizabeth] to make things right," even offering to "give her time to do so[,] but no[,] for she called on God and angels to witness her innocence[.] At this," Bigler wrote, "the Prophet jumped up and Said, 'Sister Marsh ... you lie like the devil.'"[50]

Wandle Mace later summarized the problem with the husbands,

47. This story has persisted to the present. See Gordon B. Hinckley, "Small Acts Lead to Great Consequences," *Conference Report*, Apr. 1984, 109-12.

48. Qtd. from a report by William Clayton of an address by George A. Smith, Dec. 21, 1845, in George D. Smith, ed., *An Intimate Chronicle: The Journals of William Clayton* (Salt Lake City: Signature Books, 1991), 221.

49. George A. Smith, Apr. 6, 1856, *Journal of Discourses*, 26 vols. (London and Liverpool: LDS Booksellers Depot, 1855–86), 3:283-84. It is not clear if Smith knew firsthand about this incident or heard it from a common report. No high council minutes mention a church trial involving Elizabeth Marsh.

50. Henry W. Bigler Journal [autobiography], Feb 1846-1899, 21-22,

that each "believed his own wife to be truthful and in the right, and the other man's wife was in the wrong."[51] No doubt, Thomas probably supported Elizabeth through the appeals process, but his discontent with the church was not motivated by the amount of cream his wife delivered to her neighbor. It was rather the atrocities Mormons were led to commit in acts of revenge against their non-Mormon neighbors that turned this staunchest of defenders of Mormonism into a lost apostle. The strippings story reduces him, a man of proven judgment and leadership, into a petty and vindictive caricature. In fact, that may be the very reason why the story became popular in the general imagination, since it alleviated the dissonance people experienced when trying to make sense of the mass apostasy of the 1830s.

The conflict known as the "Mormon War" took place over three months and saw the deaths of about twenty-two people, most resulting from the barbaric non-Mormon retaliation at Haun's Mill. Casualties in the battle of Crooked River included anti-Mormon Moses Rowland, killed; six of his companions wounded; and non-Mormon guide Patrick O'Banion, killed. On the Mormon side, Gideon Carter and David W. Patten were both killed. Broadly, the Missourians disliked and distrusted their Mormon neighbors, while the Mormons disliked the older backwoods settlers. Prior to this confrontation, there had been conflict ever since the Yankee emigrants arrived in Missouri, a Southern state, and made mildly abolitionist statements. More seriously, Mormons made brash claims about having been promised the land by God as a pre-millennial inheritance. In support of this surprising theology, the religious pilgrims arrived and almost immediately closed ranks, voting in bloc and doing business with each other.

The opening salvo took place on August 6 in the Election Day

---

microfilm, LDS Church History Library, Salt Lake City. This recollection was evidently written in the 1890s.

51. Wandle Mace Autobiography, ca. 1890, 177, LDS Church History Library.

Battle at Gallatin where the badly outnumbered Mormons were led by John Butler, a Danite, in a fight that ended in a bloody draw. No one was killed, but some had their "sculs cracked." Summarizing it in the Scriptory Book, George Robinson bragged that "about 150 Missourians faut [fought] against from 6 to 12 of our brethren" and that "our brethren faut like tigers" and gained a victory, in his view.[52]

The following day rumors that two Mormons had been killed in Gallatin and that a non-Mormon militia was on the march elicited a Mormon response. A guerilla force headed by three Danite leaders, Elias Higbee, Sampson Avard, and George Robinson, accompanied Joseph and Hyrum Smith, Sidney Rigdon, and others to Adam-ondi-Ahman. The group arrived at the home of a justice of the peace, Adam Black, and forced him to sign an affirmation that "he is not attached to any mob" and will not "attach himself to any such people, and so long as they will not molest me, I will not molest them." On August 10, Black, along with William P. Peniston and others, traveled to Richmond to complain to Judge Austin King of the Fifth Judicial Circuit Court. Peniston testified that Mormons forced Adam Black to sign the document "under threats of immediate death" and said their goal was to "drive all the old citizens" from the areas surrounding Mormon settlements.[53]

A preliminary hearing was held on September 7 to determine

52. Jessee, et al., *Joseph Smith Papers: Journals*, 1:299-300; William G. Hartley, *My Best for the Kingdom: History and Autobiography of John Lowe Butler, a Mormon Frontiersman* (Salt Lake City: Aspen Books, 1993), 51-61; Stephen C. LeSueur, *The 1838 Mormon War in Missouri* (Columbia: University of Missouri Press, 1987), 60-64; see also LeSueur, "Mixing Politics with Religion: A Closer Look at Electioneering and Voting in Caldwell and Daviess Counties in 1838," *The John Whitmer Historical Association Journal* 40 (Spring/Summer 2013): 184-208.

53. Alexander L. Baugh, "A Call to Arms: The 1838 Mormon Defense of Northern Missouri" (PhD. diss., Brigham Young University, 1996), 48-50, describes this encounter. See also Joseph Smith Jr., et al., *History of the Church of Jesus Christ of Latter-day Saints*, 2nd ed. rev., ed. B. H. Roberts, 7 vols. (Salt Lake City: Deseret Book, 1959), 3:60-61. Adam Black's August 28 affidavit condemning the Mormons for their August 8 encounter with him is contained in ibid., 3:64-65.

the nature of the threats said to have been made by Joseph Smith and future apostle Lyman Wight. The circumstances were ambivalent enough that the judge allowed Smith and Wight to post bail of $500 on the promise that they would return to court on November 29 on a misdemeanor charge. Behind the scenes the old settlers pushed the governor to call out the state militia. One of the chief proponents of this was an itinerant Methodist minister from Ray County named Samuel Bogart, who was a rougher individual than one might expect from his profession.[54] He solicited the governor's approval to patrol between Caldwell and Ray Counties, saying he would raise his own militia to do so. When granted permission, he began driving Mormons from Ray County and making incursions into Caldwell.[55]

Through the fall, Marsh urged fellow believers to exercise caution, while he secretly started to feel alienated from them. At a conference in Far West on October 6, he counseled some departing missionaries "not to go forth boasting of their faith, or of the judgments of the Lord; but to go in the Spirit of meekness and preach repentance unto the children of men."[56] It is unlikely that all was well in his mind as he observed the growing aggressiveness of the Mormon defense.

While he struggled with an inner uncertainty about what to do, some 400 non-Mormon vigilantes carried out a siege of the small Mormon town of DeWitt in Carroll County. On October 10, after holding out for two months, the starving, outnumbered, and highly stressed residents bowed to the inevitable and surrendered, then began an exodus to Caldwell and Daviess Counties.[57] The evacuation opened the way for state and county militias to shift

---

54. Baugh, "Call to Arms," 99–100, appraises Bogart.
55. LeSueur, *1838 Mormon War*, 132–34.
56. Cannon and Cook, *Far West Record*, 209–10.
57. Baugh, "Call to Arms," 65–76. LeSueur, *1838 Mormon War*, 109, summarized some of the effects upon the Mormons, who were "still suffering from lack of adequate provisions and shelter." They left DeWitt on the afternoon of October 11. "During the first night at least one Mormon, weakened by the two week siege,

the emphasis of their maneuvers. Leland Gentry explained that "no sooner had the Saints abandoned DeWitt, in fact, then their enemies marched for Daviess County." Simultaneously, other groups, encouraged by the governor's apparent indifference and by the state militia's inability to check unlawful movements, began operating against the Saints, who in response "organized themselves" into their own "military companies."[58]

It was in this context that Marsh may have reached a breaking point. As the violence escalated, Joseph Smith and Sidney Rigdon spoke on October 15 to "nearly all the male inhabitants of Caldwell County" at the town square in Far West to raise a militia to aid the Saints in Daviess County. Joseph reminded the assembly of the Missourians' unjustified aggression and his intent to protect the Mormon settlers from mob action.[59]

Rigdon went further and denounced pacifists, whom he called the "O don't[s]," parodying their arguments with "O don't! O don't! you are breaking the law you are bringing ruin on the Society." They were timid men who were good at "finding fault" as long as they were at home, out of harm's way, but created divisions in society and did nothing to protect themselves or others. If they refused to willingly participate in the Daviess County relief effort, Rigdon said, they should have their "blood spilled" or "be pitched on their horses with bayonets and placed in the front of battle."[60] To Marsh, Rigdon was pointing a finger at him. It was not the first time Rigdon's remarks seemed to be tailored for special criticism of the apostle, but now to have his allegiance to pacifism mocked as cowardice must have been especially disturbing because he finally,

---

died of exposure, and a woman named Jenson died while giving birth. Several young children would later succumb to illnesses contracted during the ordeal."

58. Gentry, "History of the Latter-Day Saints in Northern Missouri," 365.

59. *Reed Peck Manuscript*, 18-19. Concerning Mormon culpability in the ensuing violence in Daviess County, compare Baugh, "Call to Arms," 83-98, and LeSueur, *1838 Mormon War*, 112-30.

60. Sidney Rigdon, qtd. in *Reed Peck Manuscript*, 19.

however reluctantly, agreed to accompany the armed force to Daviess County. There, on October 18, the Mormon forces attacked the small gentile settlements of Gallatin and Millport as payback for DeWitt. They invaded homes, cast women and children out into the snow, plundered both the houses and the commercial buildings, and burned a number of structures to the ground.

Making the excuse that "there was something urgent at home," Marsh returned to Far West and consulted with Orson Hyde, who had been too ill to travel.[61] As the two men evaluated the situation, they doubtless contemplated the inevitable response and possible annihilation of the Mormon settlements. Hyde and Marsh decided to cast their lots elsewhere. John Taylor wanted to reason with them, but Heber Kimball assured him that "if you knew him [Marsh] as well as I do, you would know that if he had made up his mind to go, you could not turn him."[62] That very evening, October 19, Hyde and Marsh gathered their families together, packed supplies into a wagon, and made arrangements for the care of whatever they could not remove, and left Far West.

The more certain end of Marsh's career as president of the Twelve came on October 24 when he agreed to testify to the mayhem he had observed. He did so in Richmond before Justice of the Peace Henry Jacobs, a Mormon who would later marry Zina

---

61. Roger D. Launius, *Alexander William Doniphan: Portrait of a Missouri Moderate* (Columbia: University of Missouri Press, 1997), 54, summarized the Mormon attacks: "On October 18, Mormon troops plundered and burned Gallatin and Millport, looting and burning about two dozen buildings, and then torching an unspecified number of non-Mormon farmhouses." For in-depth descriptions, see LeSueur, *1838 Mormon War*, 117-30; Baugh, "A Call to Arms," 83-98.

62. John Taylor, *The Gospel Kingdom: Writings and Discourses of John Taylor*, ed. G. Homer Durham (Salt Lake City: Bookcraft, 1987), 187-88. Orson Hyde explained that several days after Patten's death, Hyde was sitting with Marsh when some invisible being "smote him on the shoulder, and said, with a countenance full of the deepest anxiety and solicitude, 'Thomas! Thomas! Why have you so soon forgotten?'" Hyde to "Brother Pierce," Mar. 30, 1844, *The Prophet*, June 8, 1844, 3.

Huntington. According to her statement, she later became a plural wife of Joseph Smith and then Brigham Young.[63] According to Marsh, Joseph Smith preached that "Mormons who refused to take up arms ... should be shot or otherwise put to death. ... I have heard the prophet say that he should yet tread down his enemies, and walk over their dead bodies." He described how he accompanied the Mormon militia, how the forces under David Patten "hauled away all the goods from the store in Gallatin, and deposited them at the Bishop's store houses at 'Diahmon.'" He said Mormons carried off "beds, clocks, household furniture, hogs, and cattle" from Millport. Much of this, he explained, was carried out under the direction of the Danites.[64] Orson Hyde added a short concurring statement. "The most of the statements in the foregoing disclosure, of Thomas B. Marsh," he testified, "I know to be true; the remainder I believe to be true."[65]

If they thought their affidavits might have a conciliatory effect, they were wrong. They inflamed the non-Mormons, whose suspicions were confirmed that Mormons were on a medieval-style crusade.[66] Marsh wrote to Far West to his sister and brother-in-law, Anna and Lewis Abbott that "I left the Mormons & Joseph Smith Jr. for conscience sake, and that alone, for I have come to the full

---

63. Todd Compton, *In Sacred Loneliness: The Plural Wives of Joseph Smith* (Salt Lake City: Signature Books, 1997), 71-72.

64. Thomas Marsh's document was printed in *Document Containing the Correspondence, Orders, &c. in Relations to the Disturbances with the Mormons; and ... the trial of Joseph Smith, Jr., and others, for High Treason and Other Crimes against the State* (Fayette, MO.: Missouri General Assembly, 1841), 57-59.

65. B. H. Roberts condensed Thomas Marsh's affidavit in *History of the Church*, 3:167, and reported that Marsh left the saints because he found "a mote in Joseph's eye." When asked by Joseph if he was going to leave the saints, he answered "Joseph when you see me leave the church you will see a good fellow leave it." "History of Thos. Baldwin Marsh," 18.

66. LeSueur, *1838 Mormon War*, 135-37, evaluates the negative effect of Marsh's affidavit on the Missourians. Many contemporaries believed the affidavit was the stimulus for the forced exodus from the state. For example, see George A. Smith, Apr. 6, 1856, *Journal of Discourses*, 3:284.

conclusion that he is a very wicked man; notwithstanding all my efforts to persuade myself to the Contra[ry]. I also am well convinced that he will not escape the just judgements of an offended God[.]"[67] Orson Hyde added to this letter, "I have left the Church called Latter Day Saints for conscience sake, fully believing that God is not with them, and is not the mover of their schemes and projects."[68]

On the day Marsh filed his affidavit, Bogart's militia kidnapped three Mormon men and camped across Crooked River in a defensive position. Apostle David Patten, or Captain Fearnought as he was called, probed the camp early the next morning with a detachment of forty to fifty men, wearing a white blanket as an overcoat and appearing impervious to danger. After exchanges of musketry between the Mormons and the Missourians, he led a charge into the camp and received a fatal wound.[69]

The Mormon militia took him to the home of Stephen Winchester, who lived some four miles from Far West. Joseph Smith, Sidney Rigdon, Heber Kimball, and Phoebe Ann Patten soon arrived to comfort Patten, the dying martyr. Kimball asked to be remembered on the other side of mortality when Patten arrived in heaven and gave a report of his earthly deeds. Patten prayed: "Father, I ask thee, in the name of Jesus Christ, that thou wouldst release my spirit and receive it unto thyself." To those watching, he said, "Brethren, you have held me by your faith, but ... let me go, I beseech you," at which he died.[70]

With the two ranking members of the quorum gone, Brigham Young became the senior member of the Twelve that day. He would see to it, four months later at a quorum meeting in Quincy,

67. Thomas B. Marsh and Orson Hyde to Lewis Abbott, Oct. 25, 1838, copied by James Mulholland about May 1839 into Joseph Smith's Letterbook, 2:18-19, LDS Church History Library.

68. Ibid., 2:19.

69. LeSueur, *1838 Mormon War*, 139-42.

70. *President Heber C. Kimball's Journal: Seventh Book of the Faith-Promoting Series* (Salt Lake City: Juvenile Instructor Office, 1882), 63-64.

Illinois, on March 17, 1839, that Marsh was excommunicated *in absentia*.[71] Meanwhile, Patten's raid and the destruction of Gallatin and Millport convinced Missourians that Mormons must be controlled by militia efforts. On October 27, 1838, Governor Boggs borrowed Rigdon's verbiage and told Mormons they would be "exterminated" unless they left the state. Before his insidious communiqué even reached the field, vigilantes attacked the Mormon settlement of Hawn's Mill and killed seventeen men and boys, an act that would thereafter fester in the Mormon psyche as proof of persecution. In the public relations battle since then, the Missourians have been branded as aggressors. In Mormon circles, Thomas Marsh came to be seen as a villain for refusing to take up arms, for simultaneously defending his wife's theft of cream. Such are the unforeseen results of history and popular mythology, where victims can become perpetrators and vice versa, where crusaders attain a heavenly reward and the meek perish.

The war ended on November 1 with the surrender at Far West, accompanied by the arrest of Joseph Smith and others who were sentenced to be shot. As every Mormon is told in Sunday School, General Alexander Doniphan intervened to spare the prisoners and move them to a jail in Liberty, forty miles south in Clay County. It took a month to get them there because they went by way of Richmond, thirty miles east of Liberty. The jail received its prisoners on December 1: Joseph and Hyrum Smith, Sidney Rigdon, Lyman Wight, Amasa Lyman, and George Robinson, while other Mormon men involved in the Battle of Crooked River or known for their Danite activities fled the area. The remaining Saints were increasingly invited to leave their settlements by throngs of rabble who looted their bedding, clothing, and jewelry.

Kimball said he recognized, among "the men who piloted these mobs into our city," such "former brethren" as William McLellin

---

71. "Extracts of the Minutes of Conferences," *Times and Seasons*, Nov. 1839, 15.

and Lyman Johnson of the Twelve, as well as David and John Whitmer of the Missouri presidency, and hymnist ("The Spirit of God Like a Fire Is Burning") William Phelps.[72] What Kimball failed to mention was that among the looters were some individuals whose own property had been previously confiscated.

Reed Peck wrote that "by permission from Genl Clark the agents for the Whitmers, Cowdery & Johnson searched and recovered most of the property taken from them by Geo W Robinson and others the June before."[73] Several stories emerged out of these dramatic scenes, for instance, of people claiming to have seen McLellin ransacking Joseph Smith's home and stable[74] and taunting Heber Kimball, asking what he thought of "the fallen prophet, now?"[75] People said McLellin appeared at the jail and wanted to beat Joseph Smith while he was in shackles. The sheriff made this known to Joseph, who consented "if his irons were taken off," but McLellin, according to the myth, shied away from this offer.[76]

Elder Timothy Foote said he saw that McLellin "was armed," that he confronted McLellin, who said "the Bible and all religion are matters of speculation and priest craft from beginning to end and 'Joe' [Joseph Smith] is the biggest speculator of them all." Foote reminded McLellin that he had previously testified that Joseph was a prophet. Furthermore, that McLellin had once said the "Book of

---

72. Orson F. Whitney, *The Life of Heber C. Kimball*, 2nd ed. (Salt Lake City: Bookcraft, 1945), 217-18; cf. H. Michael Marquardt, "Judge Austin A. King's Preliminary Hearing: Joseph Smith and the Mormons on Trial," *John Whitmer Historical Association Journal* 24 (2004): 50-51.

73. *Reed Peck Manuscript*, 29.

74. Thomas D. Cottle and Patricia C. Cottle, *Liberty Jail and the Legacy of Joseph*, 2nd ed. (Portland: Insight, 1999), 60-62, 110-11. See also *History of the Church*, 3:215, 286-87.

75. Jeni Broberg Holzapfel and Richard Neitzel Holzapfel, eds., *A Woman's View: Helen Mar Whitney's Reminiscences of Early Church History* (Provo: BYU Religious Studies Center, 1997), 6; cf. Parley P. Pratt, *History of the Late Persecution Inflicted by the State of Missouri upon the Mormons* (Detroit: By the author, 1839), 41.

76. "History of William E. McLellin," *Deseret News*, May 12, 1858, 49.

Mormon was true," so how could he now say the contrary; "and I asked him if he would tell me which time he lied! A crowd having gathered, McLellin slunk away, and I never saw him again."[77] This recollection reminds one of the biblical scene of Peter betraying Christ, which could have been the inspiration for the anecdote. Another strange tale came from Ebenezer Page, a Danite and brother of Apostle John E. Page. Ebenezer's son broke his arm. Dr. Frederick Williams, formerly of the church presidency, repaired the fracture and charged Page two dollars, but since Page could not pay that amount the fee was waived, according to Page. In fact, the IOU was passed on to McLellin, who sought to collect five dollars. McLellin threatened to disclose Page's identity to General Lucas, Page said, and have the Danite shot the following day. Page was apprehended anyway and marched to the Richmond jail with the other unfortunates, where he "got froze, and my toe nails came off," all because, he told McLellin, he "refused to pay you five dollars which I never owed either you or any other man."[78]

These stories of self-justification blur the memory of who did what and when, and show one side as virtuous and the other barbarous. Those who wanted to clear their names must have found the former high-ranking apostles and members of the Missouri presidency to be easy targets of blame for their misfortune. We hear tales of woe from Mormon refugees who relocated to Illinois, but they did not acknowledge that they helped sack Gallitin and Millport and left non-Mormon families homeless in inclement weather. Also conspicuously absent from the Mormon recapitulation of their Missouri experience was their treatment of former members of the hierarchy whose real estate was seized and personal property appropriated.

Joseph Smith joined the chorus of those who blamed the former

---

77. *Deseret Evening News*, June 4, 1868, 2, qtd. in Porter, "Odyssey of William Earl McLellin," 325.

78. *Zion's Reveille*, Apr. 15, 1847, 55-56; cf. Porter, "Odyssey of William Earl McLellin," 324-28.

apostles and Book of Mormon witnesses for the church's misfortune. Writing on December 16 from Liberty Jail, Joseph vented his anger at their betrayal:

> We have waded through an ocean of tribulation and mean abuse, practiced upon us by the illbred and the ignorant, such as [George] Hinkle, [John] Corrill, [William] Phelps, [Sampson] Avard, Reed Peck, [John] Cleminson and various others who are so very ignorant that they cannot appear respectable in any decent and civilized society, and whose eyes are full of adultery and cannot cease from sin. Such characters as [William] M'Lellin, John Whitmer, D[avid] Whitmer, O[liver] Cowdery, & Martin Harris who are too mean to mention[,] and we had liked to have forgotten [Thomas] Marsh and [Orson] Hyde whose hearts are full of corruption, whose cloak of hypocrisy was not sufficient to shield them.[79]

If the tribulations had been a divine test, few had passed it. By December there were seven vacancies in the Quorum of the Twelve alone, and those who remained in the quorum were busy finding suitable replacements for the vacancies. On December 13, Brigham Young and Heber Kimball reorganized the Far West High Council so it could vote six days later to have John Page and John Taylor ordained apostles, which was done by Young and Kimball on December 19.[80] The fallen apostles were equally busy picking up the pieces of their lives, gathering their families together, relocating elsewhere, finding new ways of supporting themselves, adjusting their religious views, and finding new circles of friends and levels of civic engagement.

Thomas Marsh asked David Whitmer if he retained anything of his former beliefs, to which Whitmer "replied as sure as there is

---

79. Joseph Smith to "the Church ... and all the Saints who are scattered abroad," in Dean C. Jessee, ed., *The Papers of Joseph Smith: Journal, 1832-1842* (Salt Lake City: Deseret Book, 1992), 2:298-99.

80. *President Heber C. Kimball's Journal*, 75.

a God in heaven, he saw the angel[,] according to his testimony" published in the Book of Mormon. "I asked him, if so, why he did not stand by Joseph? He answered, in the days when Joseph received the Book of Mormon, and brought it forth, he was a good man and filled with the Holy Ghost." Whitmer considered Joseph to have since fallen into sin and lost the prophetic mantle. "I interrogated Oliver Cowdery in the same manner, who answered similarly," Marsh wrote.[81]

Orson Hyde continued to suffer from bilious fever but eventually settled in Richmond and opened a school. Unlike Marsh, he was tormented about having left the faith. Allen J. Stout, a Danite, encountered him after Stout was released from the Richmond jail in December. Stout gave Hyde a ride in his wagon. Hyde was in agony, Stout said, having experienced a visionary warning that if he did not return to church, "the curse of Cain would be upon him."[82] The emotional pain was not yet sufficient to cause him to seek reconciliation, however. On January 16, 1839, Joseph Smith, Sidney Rigdon, and Hyrum Smith wrote from Liberty Jail that Elders Young and Kimball should ordain George A. Smith and Lyman Sherman as apostles to take the places of Orson Hyde and Thomas Marsh in the quorum. Kimball recorded, "Lyman Sherman was somewhat unwell," and died "several days" later. Kimball specified that "we did not notify him of his appointment."[83]

Brigham Young saw to it that Elders Avard, Corrill, Hinkle, Marsh, Peck, Phelps, and Williams, among others, were removed from the church rolls at a conference on March 17 in Quincy.[84]

---

81. "History of Thos. Baldwin Marsh," 18.

82. Allen Stout Reminiscences and Journal, 1845–89, 15, LDS Church History Library.

83. *President Heber C. Kimball's Journal*, 79. For biographical information about Sherman, see Lyndon W. Cook, *The Revelations of the Prophet Joseph Smith* (Salt Lake City: Deseret Book, 1985), 217; Cook, "Lyman Sherman: Man of God, Would-be Apostle," *Brigham Young University Studies* 19 (Fall 1978): 121–24.

84. "Extracts of the Minutes of Conferences," *Times and Seasons*, Nov. 1839, 15.

Hyde would have been on the list, but he had reached out to Kimball, his previous companion in England, for advice. Kimball told him to gather up his family and move to Illinois, which Hyde did.[85] First he wrote remorsefully to Brigham Young that

> if the church will accept me as a minister, or a soldier, or a door keeper, they can have me, I need not write you that I have litterally died and have been raised from the dead since I was last at Far West. But will tell you more about it when I see you face to face. Keep this part to yourself, if you please. Brigham, will you forgive me? Will the church forgive me? If so, God will forgive me.[86]

Two months later, Heber Kimball and Hyrum Smith spoke in defense of Hyde at a general conference. We "pleaded for him according to the spirit that was in us," Kimball wrote, and requested Hyde to "give an account" of his conduct at the next conference.[87] The apostles met on June 25 in Montrose, Iowa, and heard Hyde's confession that he had acted despicably but now "had a deep sense of his high-handed wickedness," having "humbled himself in the dust." The following day he met with the church presidency to assuage Rigdon's fear that he might "desert the Church" again at the first challenge. After Hyde repeated his confession on June 27, Rigdon was satisfied. Hyde was "restored to the Church and the quorum of the Twelve in full fellowship."[88]

Lyman Johnson took a different path than his brother-in-law and received no such overtures. He and his brother Luke kept their distance from the quorum; probably everyone in the quorum was so exhausted by the Johnsons' vacillations that they no longer considered it worth their while to reach out to them. For

---

85. *President Heber C. Kimball's Journal*, 81.
86. Orson Hyde to Brigham Young, Mar. 30, 1839, Brigham Young Collection, LDS Church History Library.
87. *President Heber C. Kimball's Journal*, 90-91. Kimball spoke on May 4, 1839.
88. Kenney, *Wilford Woodruff's Journal*, 1:340-41.

Thomas Marsh and William McLellin, the wounds were still much too deep to tamper with. William Smith's situation was different. Because of his sense of entitlement, he had alienated others in the quorum, but it was not that he had committed any spectacular new sins or errors in judgment or lost his temper. He had miraculously missed the pitfalls most loyal members of the quorum had fallen into, which were now considered liabilities, such as involvement with the Kirtland Safety Society or riding with the Danites in Missouri. Nor had he affiliated with the dissenters. He had simply been aloof, and remained so, seeking his own advice for now and feeling shut out of the inner circle by Young. No doubt, he thought that when his brother Joseph was back in charge of things, everything would return to normal. This would not happen because the Mormon world had so fundamentally changed. The church was adapting to new realities and creating its own. The most radical period of church history, in terms of theological ideas, social structures, and hierarchical development, was about to begin in Illinois. It would affect William as much as the other apostles.

8. THE NEW TWELVE, MINUS ONE

The departure from Missouri signified a much needed new beginning for the church, considering the severity of its internal, as well as external, problems. The loss of so many prominent leaders in Kirtland and Far West left a troublesome void that Joseph Smith could not fill during his incarceration at Liberty jail. By the time he escaped custody in April 1839 and arrived in Commerce (later Nauvoo), Illinois, the high council had approved ordination of John E. Page and John Taylor to the Quorum of the Twelve, which occurred in Far West on December 19, 1838, "under the hands of Brigham Young and Heber C. Kimball."[1] Wilford Woodruff and George A. Smith were added to the quorum on April 26, 1839, during the apostles' secret rendezvous at Far West prior to their famous year-long mission to England.

A spot was held among the vacancies for Willard Richards, who had lingered in England since July 1837 and was called *in absentia*. He would be ordained on April 14, 1840, when the other apostles arrived in Britain.[2] Richards's ordination marked the only time an apostle would be ordained to office outside the United States. Even after he was added to the quorum, there would be another vacancy

---

1. Donald Q. Cannon and Lyndon W. Cook, *Far West Record: Minutes of the Church of Jesus Christ of Latter-day Saints, 1830-1844* (Salt Lake City: Deseret Book, 1983), 224.

2. James B. Allen, Ronald K. Esplin, and David J. Whittaker, *Men with a Mission, 1837-1841: The Quorum of the Twelve Apostles in the British Isles* (Salt Lake City: Deseret Book, 1992), 83, 134, 246-55.

to fill until April 8, 1841, when Lyman Wight was ordained. This ordination occurred shortly before the apostles returned from their overseas mission and arrived back in Nauvoo.

The eight apostles who served together in the British Isles developed a camaraderie that served them well into the future.[3] Richards was joined overseas by Heber Kimball, the Pratt brothers, George A. Smith, John Taylor, Wilford Woodruff, and Brigham Young, but not yet Orson Hyde, who had been readmitted to the Twelve on June 27, 1839, and would be assigned elsewhere, crossing paths with his brethren in England but briefly. Only William Smith and John Page would remain behind in Illinois and complain of their poverty, difficult family circumstances, and various other inconveniences that prevented them from traveling.

The seven apostles arrived in Liverpool on the tenth anniversary of the church's founding, April 6, 1840, and would stay almost exactly one year, beginning their return trip on April 20, 1841. It was a successful endeavor by any measure. When they departed the British Isles, they left behind a bustling church membership of 5,864, about 2,000 more than the total membership in Illinois at the time. The apostles had overseen the intellectual life of the British church during this period by founding the *Millennial Star* newspaper and publishing new editions of the Book of Mormon and the church hymnbook.[4]

When most of the others returned home, Parley Pratt remained behind to continue his editorship of the *Millennial Star* and oversight of the mission. For his part, Willard Richards had courted a young woman whom he married in September 1838: Jennetta

---

3. For more on this, see Ronald K. Esplin, *The Emergence of Brigham Young and the Twelve to Mormon Leadership, 1830-1841* (Provo: Joseph Fielding Smith Institute and *BYU Studies*, 2006), 163-88.

4. Allen, Esplin, and Whittaker, *Men with a Mission*, 246-55, 300-02; Dean May, "A Demographic Portrait of the Mormons, 1830-1980," in *The New Mormon History: Revisionist Essays on the Past*, ed. D. Michael Quinn (Salt Lake City: Signature Books, 1992), 122-23.

Richards, whose name became Jennetta Richards Richards. The courtship may explain why Willard stayed so long overseas. She was not among his converts, but was baptized by Heber Kimball during his first mission to Preston and was the first person confirmed a member of the church in all of England. They settled down into something of a normal life, Willard spending his time preaching and Jennetta keeping house as their first child was born in Preston in July 1839, but tragically Heber John died five months later of small pox. They soon conceived another child, born in Manchester in October 1840, who was given the same name as his late brother.[5]

While the other apostles sailed to England, Orson Hyde had remained in Nauvoo and had spoken in general conference the same day his colleagues were landing in Liverpool. Joseph Smith also spoke and proposed that Hyde follow the others overseas, with a detour to Palestine to dedicate it for the return of the diaspora Jews. The congregation agreed, so he left nine days later despite the fact that his family was impoverished and sick. He was accompanied by John Page as far as Ohio. There, Page abandoned his assignment as Hyde's companion to the Holy Land and suddenly returned home.[6]

Hyde traveled on to New York and remained several months laboring with the branches of the church before setting sail and arriving in Liverpool in March 1841. On April Fools Day, he caught up with his brethren in Manchester for a spirited and emotional surprise reunion. The next day they held a council meeting, and Hyde was able to spend a few weeks with the quorum members before they began their trek back across the ocean to Illinois, Hyde continuing east to Jerusalem. He arrived there in late October. On

---

5. Allen, Esplin, and Whittaker, *Men with a Mission*, 60-66, 210, 302; Esplin, *Emergence of Brigham Young*, 3, 83, 294.

6. Myrtle Stevens Hyde, *Orson Hyde: The Olive Branch of Israel* (Salt Lake City: Agreka Books, 2000), 114-20; William Shepard, "Shadows on the Sun Dial: John E. Page and the Strangites," *Dialogue: A Journal of Mormon Thought* 41 (Spring 2008): 38-39.

his way back, his circuitous trek through Europe delayed his arrival on native soil until the end of 1842.[7]

As the apostles returned to Nauvoo, the city appeared more or less the same on the outside, despite its rapid rate of expansion, but on the inside something had changed, and the observant apostles could probably sense that their lives were about to change dramatically. Joseph Smith had married the first of his documented plural wives,[8] Louisa Beaman, in 1841. This was three days before Lyman Wight's ordination to the Twelve. He told the apostles about the new doctrine of marriage and gradually invited them to join this ancient order. The first to do so was Heber Kimball, who married British convert Sarah Peak Noon in 1842. Her erstwhile husband, William, had left her soon after coming to America, but without divorcing her. No matter, Joseph said. Civil marriages were subordinate to eternal marriage.[9] On June 14, Brigham Young married Lucy Ann Decker, wife of William Seeley, who apparently continued to live with his wife even though she now had two husbands. Joseph had set a precedent for this; by the time Brigham married Lucy, the prophet is said to have already married eight women who had living husbands. Brigham would acquire another plural wife, Augusta Adams Cobb, while on a mission assignment to Boston. Augusta was married to Henry Cobb and left several children with him in order to move with Brigham to Nauvoo, taking a daughter and infant son with her.[10]

Documentation shows that polygamy was embraced by all the members of the re-established Quorum of the Twelve while in Nauvoo. Young married thirty-nine wives there, Kimball thirty-six,

---

7. Hyde, *Orson Hyde*, 120–22, 131, 148–50.

8. See Todd M. Compton, *In Sacred Loneliness: The Plural Wives of Joseph Smith* (Salt Lake City: Signature Books, 1997).

9. Stanley B. Kimball, *Heber C. Kimball: Mormon Patriarch and Pioneer* (Urbana: University of Illinois Press, 1981), 95.

10. John Turner, *Brigham Young: Pioneer Prophet* (Cambridge: Belknap Press of Harvard University, 2012), 101.

and John Taylor acquired the third largest polygamous family with twelve wives in Nauvoo. Willard Richards ended up with eight plural wives before leaving Illinois. George A. Smith had seven, Parley P. Pratt six, and his brother Orson four. Although Wilford Woodruff would eventually have ten wives, he only had four in Nauvoo, his first wife and three plural ones. Orson Hyde kept to only two plural wives but would later add an additional six women to his family. John Page and William Smith, the two apostles who remained in Nauvoo while the others traveled to Europe, accepted plural marriage. Page took three wives and William about eight wives. Junior apostle Lyman Wight took three.[11]

Additional rituals were also soon added to an expanding Mormon theology. The ordinances that began in Kirtland as washing of feet evolved in Nauvoo into elaborate ceremonies, performed for the first time for Heber Kimball, Willard Richards, Brigham Young, and five other men on the second floor of Joseph's Red Brick Store on May 4, 1842. Before Joseph's death, which occurred two years later, all of the apostles except John E. Page would be initiated into the new rituals, and Page would receive his "endowment" a half year later in January 1845. In all, forty-two men and forty-eight women were endowed between 1842 and 1845 before the formal temple was completed with rooms specially designed for such ceremonies. The elite group that blazed the path for the rest of the church called itself the Quorum of the Anointed. They began with initiatory rites and the endowment ceremony, while later Joseph added ordinances such as marriage sealings for eternity and second anointings.[12]

The new Quorum of the Twelve remained intact throughout the remainder of Joseph's life, after which William Smith, John

---

11. George D. Smith, *Nauvoo Polygamy: " … but we called it celestial marriage"* (Salt Lake City: Signature Books, 2008), Appendix B.

12. Devery S. Anderson and Gary James Bergera, eds., *Joseph Smith's Quorum of the Anointed, 1842-1845: A Documentary History* (Salt Lake City: Signature Books, 2005), xxxix-xliii.

Page, and Lyman Wight were excommunicated from the church in 1845, 1846, and 1848 respectively. The apostles faced the disapprobation of many members who rejected polygamy and other surprising new tenets. For instance, a counselor in the First Presidency, William Law, later rejected these secret ordinances and concluded that Joseph Smith had sinned, that the church needed to be reformed. In May 1844, William Law and his brother Wilson joined with several other prominent residents of Nauvoo in founding a newspaper called the *Nauvoo Expositor*. The first issue, which appeared on June 7 with a print run of 1,000 copies, denounced polygamy and the idea of a plurality of gods, which was said to have been preached by Joseph Smith. The following day, the Nauvoo city council discussed what to do. Two days later it passed a libel law in order to justify intervening in the paper's publication. Mayor Joseph Smith directed the city marshal and Nauvoo Legion to destroy the press, which they did. The firestorm that resulted led to the arrest of Joseph and Hyrum Smith by county officials on a charge of treason and ultimately to their deaths in the jail cell when, on June 27, a mob stormed the facility in nearby Carthage and shot both men dead.[13]

Most of the apostles were away at the time. When they returned home, they focused on trying to help the high council pick up the pieces and begin planning for the future, the most notable question being who Joseph's successor should be. The only surviving member of the First Presidency was Sidney Rigdon, and he was most likely manic depressive.[14] His argument made sense, which was that as a member of the First Presidency, he should at least be recognized as the "guardian" of the church until a permanent replacement could be found. As president of the Twelve, however, Brigham Young saw

---

13. John S. Dinger, ed., *The Nauvoo City and High Council Minutes* (Salt Lake City: Signature Books, 2011), 238-66, 574.

14. See Richard S. Van Wagoner, *Sidney Rigdon: A Portrait of Religious Excess* (Salt Lake City: Signature Books, 1994).

things differently. The decision came to a head at the famous open-air meeting held at 10:00 a.m. on August 8 when Rigdon and Young laid out their respective claims to the presidency. An afternoon meeting was scheduled "to choose a guardian, or trustee for said church."[15]

William Clayton explained the outcome of this meeting. "The Church universally voted to sustain the Twelve in their calling as next in presidency and to sustain Elder Rigdon and A. Lyman as councilors to the Twelve as they had been to the First Presidency. The church also voted to leave the regulation of all the church matters in the hands of the Twelve."[16] A week later, Brigham, "As President of the Twelve," announced that the singular office of church president that Joseph Smith held would not be continued and that the Twelve stood at the head of the church:

> You are now without a prophet present with you in the flesh to guide you; but you are not without apostles, who hold the keys of power to seal on earth that which shall be sealed in heaven, and to preside over all the affairs of the church in all the world; ...
>
> Let no man presume for a moment that his place will be filled by another, for *remember, he stands in his own place*, and always will and the Twelve Apostles of this dispensation stand in their own place and always will, both in time and in eternity, to minister, preside and regulate the affairs of the whole church.[17]

A month later on September 8, the high council held an open-air meeting, this time to consider Rigdon's membership status. Due to illness, Rigdon stayed away, while testimony was given for and against him. When a vote was called, it was acceded to by both the high council and the large number of members gathered

---

15. "Special Meeting," *Times and Seasons*, Sept. 2, 1844, 637.

16. William Clayton Journal, Aug. 8, 1844, cited in George D. Smith, ed., *An Intimate Chronicle: The Journals of William Clayton* (Salt Lake City: Signature Books, 1991), 142.

17. "An Epistle of the Twelve," *Times and Seasons*, Aug. 15, 1844, 618, emphasis retained.

in the congregation that Sidney Rigdon be excommunicated from the church.[18]

Instead of ending the turmoil, the assassination of Joseph and Hyrum and excommunication of Sidney proved to be the beginning of even greater problems, both within and outside the city. The state legislature repealed the Nauvoo charter and withdrew recognition of the city's militia, largely because of alleged Mormon stealing from non-Mormons and Mormon control of county politics.[19] The municipal establishment in Nauvoo refused to recognize arrest warrants from outside the city. Rumors spread that Mormons were going to get revenge by attacking neighboring towns and that anti-Mormons were amassing arms across the river.[20]

As diplomatic efforts deteriorated, Young realized the Mormons had no choice but to abandon Illinois and avoid a repeat of the war in Missouri, leading refugees to cross the iced-over river in February 1846, not yet knowing exactly where they were headed. As they traversed Iowa, they founded both temporary and permanent settlements that would form the nucleus for followers of Young's future rivals. The temple in Nauvoo opened in December 1845 even though construction was not yet complete. With four walls and a roof, it was deemed sufficiently ready to host initiates to the rites that the Quorum of the Anointed had received in the Red Brick Store. More than 5,000 members received their endowments within two months before the temple closed its doors.[21]

During the rise and fall of Nauvoo, the five apostles who had

18. Dinger, *Nauvoo City and High Council Minutes*, 505-25.

19. For an extensive study of factors which led to the forced Mormon exodus from Illinois, see William Shepard, "'Marshaled and Disciplined for War': A Documentary Chronology of Conflict in Hancock County, Illinois, 1839-1845," *John Whitmer Historical Association Journal* 33, no. 2 (Fall/Winter 2013): 79-131.

20. Robert Bruce Flanders, *Nauvoo: Kingdom on the Mississippi* (Urbana: University of Illinois Press, 1965), 324-35.

21. Devery S. Anderson and Gary James Bergera, eds., *The Nauvoo Endowment Companies, 1845-1846: A Documentary History* (Salt Lake City: Signature Books, 2005).

left the church began to put their lives together in social circles that stood outside the church community. Some would keep their distance and others would return to familiar sights and former associations to live nearby or join with the Midwestern remnants. Luke Johnson apparently moved his family to Virginia to be near in-laws and later returned to Kirtland. In 1846, he arrived in Nauvoo and petitioned for rebaptism. This was granted, and Orson Hyde performed the ordinance on March 8. Luke afterward followed the church on its westward migration to Utah. John Boynton moved east to Syracuse, New York. Thomas Marsh liked Missouri and saw no reason not to stay there.

William McLellin settled for a brief time in Hampton, Illinois, over 100 miles northeast of Nauvoo, opposite Davenport, Iowa. He later moved to a variety of locations with his family including back to Kirtland. He was involved with, and joined a number of, Mormon factions and hailed each as holding the true gospel. In Ohio and then in Independence, Missouri, McLellin remained preoccupied with theology, all the while retaining his core beliefs from the time he was an apostle, but fell out of touch with church members elsewhere and mostly kept informed of their movements through newspaper accounts and an occasional letter. As researchers Stan Larson and Sam Passey found in collecting McLellin's letters and essays, "the LDS Church was like a train moving toward an undetermined destination," from which the apostle "had disembarked," and "the train continued on ... McLellin found the progression disconcerting."[22]

William Smith's Circuitous Route to Apostasy

William Smith's falling out occurred differently from the others because he had not found himself theologically opposed to anyone. What he had was what might be called a massive sense of entitlement, which was guaranteed to put him at odds with everyone

---

22. Stan Larson and Samuel J. Passey, eds., *The William E. McLellin Papers, 1854-1880* (Salt Lake City: Signature Books, 2007), xxiii.

he came in contact with. His assumption that he would have a leading role put him at loggerheads with Brigham Young, and it could not have helped that William took advantage of his stature in the church to court plural wives and procure disbursements for private needs. Yet from another perspective, his path was similar to that of the other wayward apostles, if one substitutes Brigham for Joseph and then watches William butt heads with Brigham in much the same way as before. Brigham knew William was grossly unsuited for the job. But looking beyond his erratic behavior and arrogance, he could see that William's claim was not unreasonable, and this probably further unnerved Brigham. In any case, William was not a passive bystander in the drama that played out in the post-martyrdom period of Nauvoo, and it was not any more unreasonable to assume he might lead the church than to think an uneducated frontier carpenter like Brigham Young would.

Three weeks after disposing of Rigdon's claim to the presidency, Brigham wrote to William on September 28, 1844, to hurry to Nauvoo so he could be ordained Church Patriarch.[23] William was still concerned about his personal safety following his brothers' murders and delayed travel until the following spring. It was a strategic mistake because during this time, the other apostles began to see the task at hand and consolidate their grip of the city and church institutions. The membership welcomed the steady leadership of Young and others of the Quorum of Twelve. William Smith wrote an open fourteen-paragraph letter to William W. Phelps from Bordentown, New Jersey, on November 10, 1844, which was published. In it, he referred to his "poor old mother" and his inconsolable distress over his brothers' murders but did not discuss the succession.[24]

On December 1, 1844, the *Times and Seasons* announced that William would be "returning here as soon as circumstances will

---

23. Brigham Young to William Smith, *The Prophet*, Nov. 1844, 2.
24. "Correspondence," *Times and Seasons*, Jan. 1, 1844, 755-57.

permit." The notice was probably written by editor John Taylor or his assistant William W. Phelps. In any case, it continued that it would be William's "privilege when he arrives" to be "ordained to the office of patriarch to the church, and to occupy the place that his brother Hyrum did, when living, and he will stand in the same relation to the Twelve, as his brother Hyrum did to the First Presidency, after he was ordained patriarch."[25]

It was a carefully spelled-out notice that may have seemed laudatory to readers but would have alerted William to the fact that the Twelve had forestalled any claim he might make on the presidency. In writing about the succession crisis, historian D. Michael Quinn found that William had begun giving patriarchal blessings in the East "shortly after mid-July when he learned of the Presiding Patriarch's death."[26] He no doubt saw the need and felt that, as an apostle, he had the authority to do so; but more likely he considered the presidency his right by inheritance and was himself signaling to the Twelve that his authority was plenary due to the fact that he was the heir apparent. When he read in the same issue of the *Times and Seasons* that the Twelve were releasing him as president of the eastern states mission, to be replaced by apostle Parley P. Pratt, he was appalled. He angrily shot off a letter to Heber C. Kimball on December 21, complaining that this was highly inappropriate, nor had he even been acknowledged for his accomplishments in the mission, for instance in saving it from Rigdon's influence. William said explicitly that he held the same authority as Pratt. "I hold my office & power in spite of Earth or hell," he wrote.[27]

If William's administration in the East had been characterized by peace and harmony, it may have been somewhat different,

---

25. "Communication from Elder William Smith," *Times and Seasons*, Dec. 1, 1844, 727.

26. D. Michael Quinn, *The Mormon Hierarchy: Origins of Power* (Salt Lake City: Signature Books, 1994), 214.

27. William Smith to Heber C. Kimball, Dec. 21, 1844, Brigham Young Collection, LDS Church History Library, Salt Lake City.

but in fact, it had been anything but placid. He must have known what a blemish he had been on the church's image. He had publicly battled a church elder, Benjamin Winchester, who was one of the founders of the Philadelphia branch. When Winchester became aware of the practice of polygamy in Nauvoo, he warned the branches of this "evil" that was creeping into the church. For this, he was excommunicated in September 1844 and did not go quietly. In responding, William used characteristic hyperbole in the November 23 issue of the church's periodical, *The Prophet*, published in New York:

> Who appointed Ben Winchester the Prophet, great director and regulator of this church, to direct and dictate to the saints, their faith and doctrine? ... I do not wish any one to infer from my former communication, that B. Winchester would or has stole[n] a horse, or slept with bad women. But I would sooner be guilty of all these crimes and charges than to have my garments stained with innocent blood; ... he has more or less engaged in the Law-infraction at Nauvoo.[28]

Historian David Whittaker looked into this situation and concluded that William's accusation was "tantamount to" saying Winchester had helped with "plotting Joseph's death," which was impossible because Winchester was in the South at the time on a church mission. Winchester was upset enough to sue William in civil court.[29] Hoping to extricate himself from this imbroglio,

---

28. "Mr. Editor," *The Prophet*, Nov. 23, 1844, 2. William must have thought that Winchester was in cahoots with William Law, the Irish-Canadian convert who moved to Nauvoo in 1839 and opened a dry goods store and sawmill. He was called to the First Presidency in 1841 but became distant from Joseph Smith in 1844 when Law learned about polygamy. Law helped found the *Nauvoo Expositor* but had nothing to do with Joseph's death. Lyndon W. Cook, "Law, William," in *Encyclopedia of Latter-day Saint History*, eds. Arnold K. Garr, Donald Q. Cannon, and Richard O. Cowan (Salt Lake City: Deseret Book, 2000), 644-45.

29. David J. Whittaker, "East of Nauvoo: Benjamin Winchester and the Early Mormon Church," *Journal of Mormon History* 21 (Fall 1995): 70-71. William's

William posted bail and printed a retraction: "As much speculation has been had in regard to an article published in the Prophet, some time back, in reference to Mr. Benjamin Winchester &c, I wish to correct the public mind on this subject. ... [I]t was far from my intention of imputing it to him" the charge of being an "accessory to the death of my Brothers." That "was not" the "meaning of the [words] 'Law infraction.'" In other ways his language had been "harsh" and untrue, he wrote.[30]

This avoided the main reason Brigham Young felt compelled to recall William, which was because William was practicing polygamy and using money collected for the Nauvoo Temple for his private use. A dismayed Wilford Woodruff, visiting the east coast churches on his way to England, wrote to Young in October 1844 that the membership had been scandalized by "a variety of subjects, but Kissing Women [and the] Spiritual wife" doctrine were "the most prominent." William Smith, Samuel Brannan,[31] and George J. Adams[32] had become "leagued together" in these things, Woodruff explained. "Elder [Joseph] Ball, has taught[,] as well as William Smith[,] [to] the Lowell girls that [it] is not wrong to have intercourse with the men what they please."[33]

---

legal difficulties were widely noted in news stories, such as in the *Peoria Democratic Press*, Apr. 23, 1845, 2, which informed readers that William was "charged with publishing a libel against B. Winchester" and "held to bail by the mayor in the sum of $3,000, to answer the charge in the court of quarter session."

30. "To the Editor," *The Prophet*, Apr. 5, 1845, 3.

31. Brannan was a leading elder in the New York branch. He would soon attain some notoriety for taking 230 church members to California by ship. Lorin K. Hansen, "Voyage of the *Brooklyn*," *Dialogue: A Journal of Mormon Thought* 21 (Fall 1988): 51-52; Will Bagley, ed., *Scoundrel's Tale: The Samuel Brannan Papers* (Spokane: Arthur H. Clark, 1999).

32. Adams had been a member of the Council of Fifty in Nauvoo. Peter Amann, "Prophet in Zion: The Saga of George J. Adams," *New England Quarterly* 37 (Dec. 1964): 477-500; Reed M. Holmes, "G. J. Adams and the Forerunners," in *Restoration Studies II*, eds. Maurice L. Draper and A. Bruce Lundgren (Independence: Herald Publishing House, 1983): 42-60.

33. Wilford Woodruff to Brigham Young, Oct. 9, 1844, Brigham Young

Woodruff was in Boston on October 7 when the branch tried John Hardy, its presiding elder since February 1843. Hardy had said that Smith, Brannan, and Adams had acquired additional wives, which was in fact true but did not matter because on October 12 the branch ruled that its president had slandered these men. The branch stopped short of excommunicating Hardy for it.[34] Woodruff wrote in dismay to Young that the whole situation was "a stinking mess." "You may look out for a storm in Boston," he predicted.[35] Four days later Woodruff recorded in his journal: "The Saints brought forth their tithing for the Temple all of which Elder William Smith took to the amount of $150 for the Temple and $25 or $30 for his own use."[36]

Next came a separate church hearing, this time for Hardy having allegedly slandered William Smith. The October 22 trial was chaired by none other than George J. Adams, who allowed testimony about William's behavior around women. As an example, a woman said he had been "obscene" and had asked her to "come to bed with him." In response to her alarm, he had allegedly countered that "nothing was too good to give a friend" and that he had personally overcome an aversion to relationships outside of civil marriage by "round[ing] up his shoulders" and doing what God had asked him to do. Despite the explicit nature of the testimony, 95 of 120 members of the branch found Hardy "guilty of slandering Wm. Smith" and voted this time to have him "cut off."[37]

Collection, LDS Church History Library.

34. John Hardy, *History of the Trials of Elder John Hardy ... for Slander, in Saying That G. J. Adams, S. Brannan and William Smith Were Licentious Characters* (Boston: Conway and Co., 1844), 5-9. He said he was found guilty of slandering Brannan by the slimmest of margins, 30-28, as well as for insulting Adams, 33-24, and that only 19 of 53 members wanted Hardy excommunicated.

35. Wilford Woodruff to Brigham Young, Oct. 14, 1844, Brigham Young Collection.

36. Scott G. Kenney, ed., *Wilford Woodruff's Journal: 1833-1898,* 9 vols. (Midvale, UT: Signature Books, 1983), 2:475.

37. Hardy, *History of the Trials of Elder John Hardy*, 9-14.

This was all orchestrated by Smith himself in a purge of any official who opposed him, for instance calling a council together in New York City at the end of October to hear complaints against local church leaders Thomas Braidwood, George Leach, and A. E. Wright. The church court found the three guilty of "abuse to Elder Smith" and excommunicated them.[38] The wreckage inflicted by Smith and Adams motivated Woodruff to write again to Young on December 3, predicting that the two would not act in harmony with the apostles if they came to Nauvoo. They had "set themselves up as great men," he wrote, in order "to gratify their own propensities," with a corrosive effect on the branches under their care.

Woodruff charged that he had "reason to believe they have spent hundreds of dollars of Temple money for their own use. A principle that they call the spiritual wife doctrine is so instilled in the minds of the Elders, where they have been, that if any one says anything against practicing or preaching it, they think he is an old granny and weak in the faith." In what seemed a tone of resignation, or at least pragmatism, he offered that the Twelve would "have to bear it" because there was no remedy. In fact, William Smith told his brother-in-law Jedediah Grant that he did not feel accountable to the Twelve because "he was led by visions and revelations for himself." Woodruff pleaded that if Young wanted to save the eastern churches, he should "delegate some one of the Twelve from Nauvoo that will act with you to come and take charge ... someone besides William or Adams," and then the designated administrator would need to "keep an eye" on the two.[39]

An article in Sidney Rigdon's *Latter Day Saint's Messenger and Advocate* on January 15, 1845, took notice of the hostility between

---

38. "New York Conference," *The Prophet*, Nov. 1844, 2.
39. Wilford Woodruff to Brigham Young, Dec. 3, 1844, in Journal History of the Church of Jesus Christ of Latter-day Saints, microfilm, LDS Church History Library.

William Smith and Wilford Woodruff. It was a "storm in the camp of the spiritual wife devotees," he explained:

> We cannot see, for our parts, if there should be honor among thieves, why there should not also be honor among spiritual wife men. Now if the apostle William did believe and practice what he believes, and apostle Wilford believed, and practiced the same things, we cannot see why the apostle Wilford was not bound to defend the character of the apostle William, in Philadelphia, instead of giving a little more than hints in relation to his (William's) want of propriety. We think with the apostle William, that in all this matter he has been abused. We think the apostle Wilford was bound to pluck the beam out of his own eye, before he undertook to get the post out of the apostle William's.[40]

On January 18, Parley Pratt, who had reached New York City to take over the reins of the mission from William, demonstrated Woodruff's advice to look the other way. In spite of being aware of William's eccentricities, Pratt published a public endorsement of him in *The Prophet*, writing: "I highly approve of the course pursued by Elder Wm. Smith, and the presiding officers in general in this region. ... They seem ... to have taken a decided stand against rebellious, wicked, and corrupt men; ... they have preserved the church in union, by the aid of the Spirit of God."[41]

If Pratt had decided that discretion was the better part of valor,

---

40. "It would seem ...," *Latter Day Saint's Messenger and Advocate*, Jan. 15, 1845, 91.

41. "Mister Editor," *The Prophet*, Jan. 15, 1845, 3; Scot Facer Proctor and Maurine Jensen Proctor, eds., *Autobiography of Parley P. Pratt*, rev. ed. (Salt Lake City: Deseret Book, 2000), 421-22, with this explanation by Pratt: "As we gradually became acquainted with circumstances pertaining to the Church in these parts, we found that Elders William Smith, G. J. Adams, S. Brannan and others, had been corrupting the Saints by introducing among them all manner of false doctrine and immoral practices. ... We, therefore, in accordance with the instructions of the Holy Spirit in President Young before we left home, directed William Smith and G. J. Adams to return to Nauvoo, where, in the process of time, they were cut off from the Church."

the rest of the Twelve in Nauvoo ignored the suggestion that they tread lightly. On April 10 they decided to withdraw fellowship from Adams and Brannan. *The Prophet* trumpeted the news, reporting that the two were "disfellowshipped and cut off" because "their conduct ha[d] ... disgrace[d] them in the eyes of justice and virtue, and we cannot and will not sanction men who are guilty of such things."[42] Behind the gruffness was a hint of undisclosed discretion because no specific reason was given for why Brannan was dismissed. This was because William Smith would have been implicated, having just married Brannan to a plural wife, Sarah E. Wallace, without any action being taken against William.[43]

One person who saw through the slander suits was William's old adversary Thomas Sharp, editor of the *Warsaw Signal,* who editorialized that "the Mormons have disfellowshipped Elders Brannan and G. J. Adams. These scamps have carried the spiritual wife system to such lengths, and were so open and barefaced in their acts of seduction that the church was obliged to cut them off to save itself from ruin. Their crime was not the practice of the system, but the letting out of the secret. Brannan and Adams are also accused of pocketing too much of the church funds." Sharp speculated that "Bill Smith is about on a par with Brannan and Adams, and is guilty of all that can be laid on them. Why don't the Twelve cut him off?" he wanted to know.[44] In fact, it would be only a matter of time.

William returned to Nauvoo with his dying wife, Caroline, on May 4, 1845, and was soon ordained Church Patriarch by Brigham Young and seven members of the Twelve. The next month, Young felt the need to clarify in a sermon that Hyrum Smith, "although he was older than Joseph, had no right to the presidency." It was one

---

42. Bagley, *Scoundrel's Tale*, 59; Quinn, *Mormon Hierarchy: Origins*, 214.

43. Minutes of a Council of Twelve, May 24, 1845, LDS Church History Library, in *Selected Collections from the Archives of the Church of Jesus Christ of Latter-day Saints*, 2 vols. DVD. (Provo: Brigham Young University Press, 2002), 1:18.

44. "Adams and Brannan," *Warsaw Signal*, Apr. 30, 1845, 2.

more rhetorical roadblock to head off William's possible ambitions.[45] A boarder at Emma Smith's house, school teacher James M. Monroe, wrote in his diary about William's arrival with his wife who "was very sick indeed with dropsy" and that William too "had the chills and fever. They came to our house to live for the present."[46] Brigham welcomed them with favorable comments from the stand: "Remember bro. Wm Smith—he has a sick family—Fat[he]r Smith was alive with Sons, and all are gone but bror Wm Smith, be kind to him."[47]

The following day, May 5, William met with six of the apostles at Brigham's house and told Orson Hyde, Heber Kimball, Amasa Lyman, George A. Smith, John Taylor, and Brigham Young that he "was satisfied with the present organization of the church—& state of things in Nauvoo."[48] George A. Smith recorded that "upon the recommendation of William Smith" Sam Brannan would be "restored to the Church" if Brannan gave satisfactory testimony before the quorum. William "bore testimony that Brannan was innocent of the charge brought against him," according to George A.[49] During this honeymoon period, the apostles were willing to make concessions, but significantly Helen Mar Kimball, a teenager, remembered that "the next day after his arrival at Nauvoo, instead of coming to the meeting, which was held by the roadside east of the temple, he rode flauntingly by in a fine carriage dressed in deep mourning with none but himself and driver. He could have taken

---

45. Dean C. Jessee, ed., "The John Taylor Nauvoo Journal: January 1845–September 1845," *BYU Studies* 23 (Summer 1983): 61.

46. James M. Monroe diary, May 4, 1845, 117, Coe Collection, Beinecke Rare Book and Manuscript Library, Yale University, New Haven; also in James M. Monroe journal, LDS Church History Library.

47. "Meeting at Stand," May 4, 1845, Leonard J. Arrington Papers, Series 9, box 12, Special Collections, Merrill-Cazier Library, Utah State University, Logan. William's older brother Samuel had died the previous year, a month after Joseph and Hyrum were assassinated. His younger brother, Don Carlos, had died of malaria in 1841.

48. Willard Richards journal, May 5, 1845, LDS Church History Library.

49. George A. Smith, "My Journal," *Instructor*, Sept. 1948, 418.

any other road as well, but it looked as though he did it just for the purpose of creating a sensation."[50]

James Monroe detected in William's conversation that he was "determined to live up to his privilege and stand in his place, let what would come." William gave a public address calling for civility. The presiding apostle, Brigham Young, spoke "rather coolly" in response, James thought.[51] The *Nauvoo Neighbor* published an epistle from William claiming he had saved the east coast mission from the likes of John Hardy. He prevaricated on the charge of polygamy. Having more than one wife, William wrote, "would destroy the morals of any people." Monogamy was the only acceptable means of living. "I know of no such doctrine in the church of Christ," he continued, "nor have I any allegiance with such a system, neither have I ever practiced or taught any such doctrine."[52]

William's wife died early in the evening of Thursday, May 22, apparently without her husband having attended to her. James Monroe sat with the body.[53] The next day, as preparations for Caroline's funeral were being made, Joseph Smith's former secretary William Clayton wrote that William was "coming out in opposition to the Twelve and in favor of [George J.] Adams." William was claiming to have "sealed some women to men" and was "not accountable to Brigham nor the Twelve nor any one else." Clayton

---

50. Richard Neitzel Holzapfel and Jeni Broberg Holzapfel, *A Woman's View: Helen Mar Whitney's Reminiscences of Early Church History* (Provo: BYU Religious Studies Center, 1997), 260.

51. Monroe diary, May 11, 1845, 121.

52. "Dear Brethren," *Nauvoo Neighbor*, May 14, 1845, 2-3. William reveals in this letter how he perceived his enemies: "John Hardy had become a Rigdonite, and must build himself a reputation, consequently must do it by lying, as this is a spirit peculiar to Rigdonism,—and when this fallen son of Lucifer repents of his lies, slander, and former acts of Sodomy, or abominations, and asks forgiveness, as he has of his spiritual wifery, in profession, I am ready to forgive him; otherwise he must expect to meet his fate with the damned in hell, where all Rigdonites, liars, whoremongers, sorcerers and dogs will meet theirs."

53. Monroe diary, May 22, 1845; "Obituary," *Nauvoo Neighbor*, May 28, 1845, 3; "Funeral of Mrs. Caroline Smith," *Times and Seasons*, June 1, 1845, 918-20.

worried that "there is more danger from William than from any other source, and I fear his course will bring us much trouble."[54] Brannan arrived and met with the apostles in the afternoon of May 23. At some point that day, Heber Kimball heard from Newell Whitney's wife "that Wm. Smith came thare on yesterday" and "expressed enmity against Br. Young and my self, that we had taken rights from him."[55] The day ended with the apostles gathering for an evening meeting in which they discussed the "improper course of Wm. Smith."[56]

The drama in Nauvoo continued on May 24 after Caroline was buried at ten a.m., absent her husband. William said he was afraid of gentile enemies.[57] He was safe enough to walk outside as far as John Taylor's house, though. He had been invited there by Young so the Twelve could ordain him "a Patriarch to the whole church."[58] This was evidently considered an appropriate and necessary means of dampening William's flaring hostility. The specific level of authority promised the aspirant was not recorded, but William seemed satisfied with it and good feelings prevailed. George A. Smith recorded that "the brethren present expressed their feelings" toward William, "to

---

54. Smith, *Intimate Chronicle*, 166. George J. Adams had established an opposition church in Augusta, Iowa. A broadside, "Minutes of a Conference, Held by the Church of Jesus Christ of Latter Day Saints," on March 10, 1845, which resolved "that we (the High Council at Augusta) receive Joseph Smith [III], son of Joseph Smith deceased, as President of the Priesthood of the Church of Jesus Christ of Latter Day Saints, with all the power and authority held by his father. That we receive William Smith, brother of Joseph and Hyrum as the Patriarch, Guardian, and Councillor of the Church, holding the same office and authority as his brother Hyrum."

55. Stanley B. Kimball, ed., *On the Potter's Wheel: The Diaries of Heber C. Kimball* (Salt Lake City: Signature Books, 1987), 114–15.

56. Joseph Smith, *History of the Church of Jesus Christ of Latter-day Saints*, ed. Brigham H. Roberts, 7 vols. (Salt Lake City: Deseret News, 1902-12), 7:417.

57. Linda King Newell and Valeen Tippetts Avery, *Mormon Enigma: Emma Hale Smith*. 2nd ed. (Urbana: University of Illinois Press, 1994), 215; Irene M. Bates and E. Gary Smith, *Lost Legacy: The Mormon Office of Presiding Patriarch* (Urbana: University of Illinois Press, 1994), 86.

58. *History of the Church*, 7:418.

which he responded by lifting both hands to heaven and expressing the same."[59] Willard Richards kept the minutes. "Sister Young came in," he wrote, "& brought a bottle of wine from Sister Clark. The president gave a toast.—and all responded.—Wm Smith asked the views of the council about his patriarchal office.— Prest [President] Young said it was his right.—Wm Smith received his patriarchal blessing by Prest Young."[60]

This was the apostolic meeting at which Sam Brannan's status was reviewed, the evidence seeming to be incontrovertible. A church leader in New England, George B. Wallace, had accused Brannan of having an illicit relationship with Wallace's sister Sarah. A marriage between Sam and Sarah was performed by William Smith in the fall of 1844, two months "after Brannan's legal marriage to Ann Eliza Corwin."[61] George Wallace had testified with specificity that

his sister came to his house in New Bedford, [Massachusetts, and] told him Bro Brannan had waited on her some. one Sunday [when] she staid at home, Bro. Brannan staid at home [too]. On the edge of the [bed?] Brannan accomplished his desire, & went into the kitchen. [My sister?] came in & after reported She was dissatisfied. Wm [Smith] sealed them up. It worried her to think she must be Brannans. Bro [Parley] Pratt told her the sealing was not according to the Law of God. [She] went into consumption & died.[62]

William freely acknowledged having performed the sealing, that he had "married them by all the authority he possessd for time & Eternity, and had a right &c to do as an apostle of J[esus] Christ," he protested. Anxious to soothe the volatile Smith, Young commented that "since Sis Wallace had gone home [died], we could throw the

---

59. George A. Smith, "My Journal," 420.
60. Minutes of a Council of Twelve, May 24, 1845, *Selected Collections*, 1:18.
61. Bagley, *Scoundrel's Tale*, 67.
62. Minutes of a Council of Twelve, qtd. in ibid., 67–68; bracketed additions retained.

mantle over the whole & shut[t]er the subject." William detected a criticism and pressed the issue, asking if the apostles thought he had done anything wrong. Brigham said "he was satisfied with what Wm Smith did in the case of Brannan in marrying him to Sis[ter] Wallace," thereby soothing Smith's pique.[63]

According to Willard Richards, "Wm Smith was ordained Patriarch to the whole church of Jesus christ of Latter Day Saints and to preside over the patriarchs.—All of the Twelve present laying their hands on him except W. Richards—who wrote the blessing. ... There was a warm interchange of good feeling between Wm Smith and the Quorum."[64] It was summer, or else William would have been sustained by the church membership within a few months at a church conference. Even so, he was recognized as being the third patriarch of the church and immediately began to pronounce blessings on individual members in Nauvoo, as his father and brother Hyrum had done before him.[65] His prickly personality continued to be a problem as he freely offered criticisms of other people, nor could he let the controversy that followed him from his eastern mission rest.

Brigham Young gathered leaders together on May 29 in William's absence and prayed "that the Lord would over-rule the movements of Wm. Smith who is endeavoring to ride the Twelve down."[66] William became "wonderfully angry," according to James Monroe, when the *Nauvoo Neighbor* rejected his rant against Parley Pratt. William had broken into an outburst, saying "the Neighbor is a mean little stinking paper, just fit for Jack [shi]t" and added that Brigham was "merely President by courtesy," that the

---

63. Ibid., 68. "Notice," *Nauvoo Neighbor*, May 28, 1845, 3, mentioned William's endorsement of Brannan and the fact that "some one had counselled Br. Brannan wrong."

64. Richards journal, May 24, 1845.

65. H. Michael Marquardt, comp., *Early Patriarchal Blessings of the Church of Jesus Christ of Latter-day Saints* (Salt Lake City: Smith-Pettit Foundation, 2007), 231-430.

66. Smith, *Intimate Chronicle*, 167; *History of the Church*, 7:420.

"whole Twelve are presidents over the Church." Monroe thought this would "seem to portend a rupture between [William] and the Twelve, but I hardly know how it will come out. Most probably to his disadvantage, as the authority of the Twelve is too firmly rooted to be broken up very easily."[67]

A letter William wrote in early June appeared in the May 15 issue of the *Times and Seasons* (the paper was running three weeks late), announcing that he had taken a room with the stake president, William Marks, and was bestowing patriarchal blessings there. He boasted of how much he had endured in the east in overseeing "the eastern churches, in setting them in order," and "teaching them the true principles of virtue and morality."[68] As "the last of the family" and a member of the Quorum of the Twelve, the members of which shared leadership equally, he wrote, he had a right to office: "Support and uphold the proper authorities of the church—when I say authorities, I mean the whole, and not a part; the *Twelve*, and not one, two, six, eight, ten, or eleven, but the whole *Twelve*;—follow me as I follow Christ, God being our judge."[69]

Assistant editor William W. Phelps clarified that "the office of Patriarch over the whole church" implied that its occupant "is to be a father to the church."[70] Taking this to heart, William began telling recipients of blessings that he held "the highest authority in the Church of God now on earth."[71] If Phelps had meant that the patriarchal office was more advisory than administrative, it was lost on William. The other apostles sought several ways, in performing

---

67. Monroe diary, 131-32.

68. William Smith acquired four plural wives during the period he was overseeing the mission: Mary Ann Covington Sheffield, Sarah Ann Libby and sister Hannah Mariah Libby, and Susan M. Cooney. Smith, *Nauvoo Polygamy*, 623.

69. "Patriarchal," *Times and Seasons*, May 15, 1845, 904-5; emphasis in original.

70. "The office of Patriarch" ibid., 905-6.

71. Quinn, *Mormon Hierarchy: Origins*, 216; see also Christine Elyse Blythe, "William Smith's Patriarchal Blessings and Contested Authority in the Post-Martyrdom Church," *Journal of Mormon History* 39 (Summer 2013): 76-77.

the delicate dance they were involved in with William, in which to look the other way to mollify his demands, even indulging his interest in a fifteen-year-old girl, Mary Jane Rollins. Brigham performed this marriage on June 22, 1845.[72]

Caroline had been dead exactly a month, and when the patriarch's old nemesis Thomas Sharp heard about the marriage, he wrote satirically that "Patriarch Bill Smith, brother of the Prophet, whose wife died about four weeks since, was again married on last Sunday week—having been a widower about 18 days. His bride is about 16 and he is 35. Bill will do very well for a father in the church but his wife won't do for [a] mother. Wonder if Bill was not engaged before his former wife died."[73] The printed notice in Nauvoo was inconspicuous for the amount of attention it attracted: "*Married* in this city, on Sunday the 22nd ult. by Elder Brigham Young, Elder William Smith to Miss Mary Jane Rollins."[74] Of course, what the paper reported was only half the story because William, by this time, was also acquiring additional wives, three to whom he had given patriarchal blessings. When he was eventually excommunicated in October 1845, a number of his wives left him, perhaps indicating an existing level of dissatisfaction with their husband. A few of them married another apostle, George A. Smith.[75]

After Phelps's editorial about William Smith, the next issue of

---

72. Quinn, *Mormon Hierarchy: Origins*, 220; Kimball, *On the Potter's Wheel*, 123. Mary Jane left William by the end of August. Helen Mar Kimball Whitney observed that the girl's "character" was "not of the best." Holzapfel and Holzapfel, *Woman's View*, 260. Hiram Stratton commented on "her house keeping with another woman of bad repute at a house of common resort for men of low character." Deposition taken by James J. Strang in Voree, Wisconsin, Mar. 9, 1847, box 93, case 37, Knox County Court House, Galesburg, Illinois.

73. "Patriarch Bill Smith," *Warsaw Signal*, July 2, 1845, 2.

74. "Married," *Nauvoo Neighbor*, July 2, 1845, 3.

75. The additional wives were fourteen-year-old Henriette Rice, Priscilla Mogridge, Mary Jones, and Elizabeth Weston. After his excommunication, William would nevertheless acquire five more wives: Rhoda Alkire, Abenade Archer, Roxie Ann Grant, Eliza Elsie Sanborn, and Rosella Goyette. Smith, *Nauvoo Polygamy*, 623-24, 652; cf. Quinn, *Mormon Hierarchy: Origins*, 594.

the *Times and Seasons* contained a "correction" by John Taylor that emphasized Young's superior authority:

> Since the publication of the last *Times and Seasons*, we have frequently been interrogated about the meaning of some remarks made by Eld. Wm. Smith in an article headed patriarchal, and also concerning some expressions in the editorial connected therewith; and as the nature of the office of Patriarch does not seem to be fully understood, we thought a little explanation on this point might not be amiss.
>
> So far as the editorial is concerned it was written rather hastily by our junior editor, W. W. Phelps, and did not come under our notice until after it was published. There are some expressions contained in it, which might have been worded better and have rendered it less subject to criticism; but he assures us that no such intention was intended to be conveyed as that which is conceived by some. And concerning Brother Wm. Smith, we are better acquainted with him, and with his views, than to believe that he intended to convey any such idea as the one which some persons would put upon, or gather from his sayings. ...
>
> We have been asked, "Does not patriarch *over* the *whole* church," place Brother William Smith at the head of the whole church as president?
>
> Ans. No. Brother William is not patriarch over the whole church; but patriarch TO the church, and as such he was ordained. The expression "over the whole church," is a mistake made by W. W. Phelps. [William Smith] is patriarch TO the church of Jesus Christ of Latter-day Saints. ... And who has the charge of the whole priesthood here? Ans. The presidency of the church; and not the patriarch.

Taylor concluded by reiterating that "Br. William will still retain the same power, priesthood and authority that he did before, and yet will hold[,] in connexion with that[,] the patriarchal office and the keys of that priesthood, and as one of the Twelve [he] must maintain his dignity as one of the presidents of the church, of whom President Brigham Young is the president and head and presides over all patriarchs, presidents and councils of the church."[76] This explanation was not well received by William.

Another inexplicable development on William's part, made to further irritate Brigham, was his support of a local violent criminal gang to which his friends, the Hodges brothers, belonged. The saga will be dealt with in depth in the next chapter, but William's entanglement put him at odds with the Nauvoo police and Brigham Young. The first run-in with the police was when William and Stephen Hodges were pursued for committing burglary and murder, at which William Smith for some reason intervened and counseled them to flee Nauvoo.[77] When they were arrested, William told the Nauvoo police to set them free.[78] He then beat up policeman Elbridge Tufts for testifying against the brothers at their trial, while he secured bail for yet another brother, Amos, who had been arrested in Nauvoo for theft. "It appears [William] is determined to cause us trouble," William Clayton wrote about Smith's strange behavior.[79]

William's physical assault on a Nauvoo policeman and attempt to get Amos Hodges released caused William to subsequently fear for his life. "I am not safe," he complained to Young, and "something must be done," his alarm rising even as he predicted that he could be "murdered in cold blood … and my friends not … the wiser for it." "Who will protect me?" he demanded to know. The "deacons" passed by his house "nightly" with threats, he said, deacons in those days being adults.[80]

---

76. "Patriarchal," *Times and Seasons*, June 1, 1845, 920-21, emphasis in original.

77. William Smith to Brigham Young, June 25, 1845, qtd. in Jessee, "John Taylor Nauvoo Journal," 60. George Q. Cannon was keeping Taylor's journal.

78. Brigham Young, qtd. in ibid., 62.

79. Smith, *Intimate Chronicle*, 169.

80. William Smith to Brigham Young, June 25, 1845, qtd. in Jessee, "John Taylor Nauvoo Journal," 59-60.

He sent this letter to Brigham in the morning; that afternoon, the Twelve met, though without William, and prayed "that God would overrule every evil principle; that [William's] violent spirit might be curbed by the spirit of God, and that we might be enabled to save him."[81] They decided to summon William that evening to the Masonic Hall to meet with the police. William disguised himself and bade his daughters Mary Jane and Caroline goodbye, leaving them with his mother Lucy and predicting that he "might be assassinated before he reached the hall."[82] In fact, he found "some fifty or sixty policemen all armed with Bowie knives, pistols, and hickory clubs" at the hall.[83]

When asked to speak, he said he had gotten into a scuffle with Officer Tufts because the police had "reject[ed] his council" to release Amos Hodges from custody. If William's authority was not appreciated in Nauvoo, he said, "he would go away in to the wilderness or to some more convenient place" and leave everyone in peace. But "he was one of the last remnants of the Smith family to whom the priesthood had come," and "if he went away, he would take [the priesthood] along with him, his sisters, his mother, and the last remains of the family. ... Where he and they went, there the priesthood, authority, and the Church would be."[84]

Brigham Young gave a brusque dismissal of this idea, telling the crowd that if it had been up to William to bring them the priesthood, "we should have been without it till the day of Judgment."[85] Brigham boasted that he "knew as much about the power

---

81. Ibid., 61.

82. Mary B. Smith Norman to Ina Coolbrith, Mar. 27, 1908, Community of Christ Archives, Independence, Missouri. Mary was the daughter of Samuel H. Smith. Josephine Donna Smith, daughter of Don Carlos Smith, changed her name to Ina Coolbrith.

83. William Smith, *Proclamation and Faithful Warning*, reprinted in *Warsaw Signal*, Oct. 29, 1845, 1, 4.

84. Jessee, "John Taylor Nauvoo Journal," 61.

85. Ibid., 61–62.

and authority of the priesthood as William Smith or any other man in the Church." If William left, the priesthood would stay, he assured everyone. Nor was it up to William to decide the guilt or innocence of the Hodgeses. Everyone had lived "in peace here before William Smith came," Brigham said, short on memory but in service of a metaphor, "and since he came there has been the devil to pay." Besides claiming the right to lead the church, Young said, William "told General [Sheriff Minor R.] Deming that I was the instigator of that murder" of Ervine Hodges. "I will not stand such things," he shouted, "nor will I be nosed about by Wm. Smith; … neither shall any of these Police be put out of their office on his account for they are good men, and have done their duty."

Seeing his bluster met by an equal dose from Brigham, and backed up by a show of force from the police, William plead that he had been misunderstood. He had never meant to suggest that he would take away the priesthood, he said, and denied saying "he had a right to the presidency." He had not meant to demean the police, and he supported Brigham as the leading apostle. If Brigham would reciprocate with support for him as the patriarch, everything would be fine, to which Brigham said he would.[86] However, something about the way Brigham said it made William think he meant otherwise. "The conclusion I drew from all this was, that it was an intentional hint to me that I had better leave," he later wrote of the incident.[87]

Following the hanging of William and Stephen Hodges in

---

86. Ibid. See also Smith, *Proclamation and Faithful Warning*, in which he states that Brigham talked for "nearly an hour" and said with boisterous boldness: "I will let William Smith know that he has no right to counsel this Church, for I am the man! I will let William Smith know also, that he shall not counsel the police; furthermore, that where the Smith family goes the church will not go, nor the priesthood either! And I will let William Smith know that I am the president and head of this church and strange to say all the police and the bishops, and the 'Twelve' who were present, said thereunto, 'amen.'"

87. Smith, *Proclamation and Faithful Warning*.

Burlington, Iowa Territory, on July 15, their benefactor, William, apparently had a sister secure plots for them in the Nauvoo cemetery. William said the evidence against them had been insufficient. Brigham responded that "he knew" the Hodgeses were "murderers and not innocent men" and insisted that the bodies be exhumed and moved out of the city cemetery.[88]

Brigham Young complained to Wilford Woodruff that William "seems to think he ought to be President of the Church, and since he was ordained a Patriarch to the whole church he has endeavored to get up an influence among the saints to persuade them that the office of Patriarch necessarily makes him president." More charitably, Young added that even though William was "determined to cause us trouble," their prayers should "continually ascend to our heavenly father to overrule William and save him if possible."[89]

Lucy Mack Smith, William's mother, came to his aid in a convoluted way on the one-year anniversary of Joseph's and Hyrum's murders. At the conclusion of a memorial attended by the apostles and others on June 27, she handed John Taylor's wife Leonora a description of a three-part vision she had received. When John returned home that evening, Leonora showed him the narrative:

> Brothers and Children, I was much troubled and felt as if I had the sins of the whole world to bear … I then heard a voice calling on me saying awake … thy only son that thou hast living, they for his life have laid a snare. … Thy son William he shall have power over the Churches, he is father in Israel over the patriarchs and the whole of the Church, he is the last of the lineage that is raised up in these last days. He is patriarch to regulate the affairs of the Church. He is President over all the Church, they cannot take his apostleship away from him. The Presidency of the Church belongs to William, he being the last of the heads of the Church,

---

88. Jessee, "John Taylor Nauvoo Journal," 78.

89. Brigham Young to Wilford Woodruff, June 27, 1845, qtd. in Bates and Smith, *Lost Legacy*, 88.

according to the lineage, he having inherited it from the family from before the foundation of the world.[90]

The following day, William Clayton summarized what was undoubtedly the interpretation the apostles unitedly gave the vision: "A new revelation has come to light from Mother Smith, corrected and altered by William Smith so as to suit his wishes by representing him as the legal successor of Joseph in the presidency."[91]

Seven of the apostles met with Lucy and other Smiths on June 30 to resolve the issues surrounding her vision. According to John Taylor's journal, they "conversed freely with her" and she responded by claiming ignorance of any implications regarding church administration, saying there must be errors in their copy of the vision and that, in any case, William did not want the presidency. She was a revelator "only for herself and family," she said, not for the whole church. Furthermore, "she wanted peace."[92] William wrote to Brigham the same day: "My proposition is my share of the kingdom, and if you will publish in the Neighbor and Times and Seasons the true state of the case in regard to my office as Patriarch over the whole Church, this will give me a right to visit all branches of the Church ... to attend to all of the ordinances of God, no man being my head[,] [and] I will reconcile all difficulties and Elder Young can stand as the President of the Church."[93]

Unwilling to let William function without the direct supervision of the Twelve, Young responded unequivocally:

---

90. Jessee, "John Taylor Nauvoo Journal," 63–64. In her narrative, Lucy added this charge against Brigham and Heber: "I saw William in a room full of armed men and he having no weapons. They would have crushed him down, if it had not been for the power of God; and many of the family would have been cut off, [but] the Lord having softened their hearts [they retreated]. Two amongst them had blacker hearts than the rest, and I know who they were, and I will tell them if they will come to me. Brigham Young and Heber C. Kimball know it is so, and dare not deny it."

91. Smith, *Intimate Chronicle*, 169.

92. Jessee, "John Taylor Nauvoo Journal," 65–66.

93. William Smith to Brigham Young, June 30, 1845, qtd. in ibid., 66–67.

There are some ordinances in the Church that cannot be administered by any person out of this place at present, but must be done
here. As to your having the right to administer all ordinances in
the world and no one standing at your head, we could not sanction, because the President of the Church and each one of our
Quorums are amenable to the Quorum of which you are a member. But as to your right to officiate in the office of Patriarch, we
say you have the right to officiate in all the world wherever your
lot may be cast, and no one to dictate or control you excepting the
Twelve, which body of men must preside over the whole Church
in all the world.[94]

Although it seemed to be an olive branch in consideration of
what was at stake, the rupture between these two strong-willed
men was even apparent to Thomas Sharp, who gathered from
scraps of information that "the division between Bill Smith and the
Twelve appears to be growing wider every day. A gentleman who
was in Nauvoo, at the time of the late murder [of Ervine Hodges
on June 23] states, that the Twelvites charged the crime on the
Smithites and *vice versa*."[95]

In an effort to decrease the tension, the apostles hosted a ban-
quet for the extended Smith family on July 9, at which William
offered a conciliatory toast: "In the name and in behalf of all my
relatives here assembled, the whole Smith family, I present my
thanks to the President and Bishops for the kind manifestation of
their good feelings toward the remnants of that family."[96] The *Nauvoo Neighbor* editorialized that the social event proved there was
no conflict between the Smith family and the church leadership.[97]
When the article was reprinted in the *New York Messenger*, Brannan

---

94. Brigham Young to William Smith, qtd. in ibid., 60; also in Smith, *Intimate Chronicle*, 172.

95. "Split at Nauvoo," *Warsaw Signal*, July 2, 1845, 2.

96. "Dinner to the Smith Family," *New York Messenger*, Aug. 9, 1845, 44.

97. "Dinner to the Smith Family," *Nauvoo Neighbor*, July 16, 1845, 2.

added a fulsome commentary on "the spirit of union [that] prevails in the hearts of the saints, that can never be broken, and the devil is foiled in his attempt … to bark up a division in the House and Kingdom of God."[98]

William Smith was nevertheless not going to march to the same drummer. He was already constructing outdoor seating in Nauvoo in preparation for a series of services he was planning on holding, featuring himself as the main speaker. His theater would rival the semi-official preaching stand in the grove near the temple, which was preferred by Brigham. But before William could hold his first Sunday morning service, vandals smeared the seats with outhouse waste.[99] He had been warned against holding public meetings without authorization, so he suspected the source of the prank. Since "every seat in that grove had been fouled with outhouse refuse," he could not do otherwise but cancel the services.[100]

William wrote to Brigham on August 9 to complain about the restrictions he was laboring under, which he felt interfered with his ability to function as patriarch: "When the Brethren call on me to be sealed to their wives, their dead friends &c also to get patriarchal blessings for their dead—what shall I say to them?"[101] Brigham responded that it was against church policy to perform patriarchal blessings for the dead "until baptism &c has been attended to for them by proxy" and that the president of the Twelve was the only one who held authority to perform those ordinances:

Joseph [Smith] said that the sealing power is always vested in one man … the president of the Church. Hyrum held the patriarchal

---

98. "Still Later from Nauvoo," *New York Messenger*, Aug. 9, 1845, 44.

99. Isaac Paden to James M. Adams, Apr. 1, 1846, James J. Strang Papers, document 451, Coe Collection, Beinecke Library.

100. Mary B. Smith Norman to Ina Coolbrith, Apr. 24, 1908, Community of Christ Archives.

101. William Smith to Brigham Young. Aug. 9, 1845, qtd. in Bates and Smith, *Lost Legacy*, 91.

office legitimately, so do you. Hyrum was counseller, so are you, but the sealing power was not in Hyrum legitimately, neither did he act on the sealing principle only as he was dictated by Joseph. This was proven, for Hyrum did undertake to seal without counsel, & Joseph told him if he did not stop it he would go to hell and all those he sealed with him.[102]

There could be no resolution to the standoff because William, although he was careful about how he expressed it, believed his authority superseded that of Brigham.

Things may have gone differently if William had not committed a monumental blunder on August 17 in a sermon he delivered at the official stand. Even the title, "The First Chapter of the Gospel by St. William," was off-putting. That aside, he took advantage of the setting to announce that Young, Kimball, and other apostles "were practicing [polygamy] in secret" and that he was "not afraid to do it openly."[103] This speech was a shock to the members of the congregation, most of whom had believed the church's carefully crafted denials. There was disgust on the part of the baffled church members, as well as on the part of the leadership who were trying to hide their practices. It was perhaps the last straw for many non-Mormon neighbors who already suspected that Mormons were fanatics and heretics.

In an unconvincing attempt at immediate damage control, John Taylor stood and said that if William's message were true, it was nothing compared to the fact that "Jacob had four wives and David had several hundred." "Who will say that this doctrine will apply to us?" he asked, adding that if the ancient patriarchs had

---

102. Brigham Young to "Brother Wm. Smith, Patriarch," Aug. 10, 1845, Brigham Young Collection, LDS Church History Library. The letter continues with Brigham's refusal to reimburse William $74.24 because "the Trustees have not one dollar on hand" and William had "already received more assistance from the church funds than all the rest of the Twelve put together."

103. Smith, *Intimate Chronicle*, 178; Bates and Smith, *Lost Legacy*, 91.

many wives, why couldn't a modern Saint have a few? Afterward he poured out his frustration in his journal,

> I felt pained and distressed when William [Smith] was speaking[,] so did a great many of the congregation, and many of the people left, being disgusted at the remarks he made; it was not so much on account of some of the principles advanced by him as the manner in which they were stated, and the unfitness of the congregation to receive such teaching, in the crude manner in which it was thrown forth; it was calculated to lead astray many of the young men, elders and women, and to lead to corruption, adultery and every other wicked thing both in men and women letting loose the reins of government; if not exactly licensing such things.[104]

William Clayton predicted that William Smith's "course today will evidently hurt him in the estimation of the saints more than any thing he has done before."[105] Later that same day, George A. Smith offered a prayer that "the <evils of the> course Wm Smith had pursued might fall on his own head."[106] Thomas Sharp drew information from a mole in the city to gleefully report that "Bill, from the stand, avowed that the Spiritual Wife System was taught in Nauvoo secretly—that he taught and practiced it, and he was not in favor of making any secret of the matter. He said that it was a common thing amongst the leaders and he for one was not ashamed of it. His bold declaration created quite a sensation amongst the Saints and Bill is in hot water in consequence of it."[107]

The Twelve had their own informers. Six days after William's sermon, they sent a spy to his house to ask what his intentions were.

---

104. Jessee, "John Taylor Nauvoo Journal," 83.
105. Smith, *Intimate Chronicle*, 178.
106. Richards journal, Aug. 17, 1845.
107. "From Nauvoo," *Warsaw Signal*, Sept. 3, 1845, 2. In his *Proclamation*, William utilized strange logic to explain why he "preached the so called 'spiritual wife' sermon to allay rumors that I intended ... to bring about a division in the Church." His discourse, he argued, had been "entirely unobjectionable" and was based on "pure principles of morality and religion." He said he wanted to expose hypocrisy.

"By God I'll let this people know who their ruler is," William told the visitor, who claimed to be "privy to the mob" and wanted to warn William that he was unsafe in the city. At that, William left in such a hurry that he neglected to pack. By coincidence, William Hickman appeared and offered to help William "escape," although he was no doubt there to ensure his departure. By September 25, William Smith was twenty miles north of Nauvoo in Augusta, Iowa, hiding out with George J. Adams.[108]

Early in October, William published a pamphlet articulating his claim to be the rightful president of the church. According to his *Proclamation and Faithful Warning*, he believed Brigham Young's only authority was within the Quorum of the Twelve, not over the church generally:

> Brigham Young holds the presidency over the eleven men by age merely; and not by any legitimate authority, neither has he any supreme keys; and the saints will bear in mind that a presidency over twelve men, admitted out of courtesy to age, does not make a man president, prophet, seer, revelator, and perpetual head of the church over a whole dynasty of people to the exclusion to the lawful heir by blood and lineage.

William suspected "a deep laid plan" by the Twelve "to get the power of every thing under their control."[109]

William made his way to St. Louis and before a week or two were out, he had fractured the tranquility of the branch by preaching against Brigham Young and promoting himself.[110] Jedediah

---

108. The spy was an acquaintance of Uncle John Smith, who was unwaveringly loyal to the Twelve. Richards journal, Sept. 16, 1845; William Smith to Brigham Young, Sept. 25, 1845, qtd. in Marvin S. Hill, *Quest for Refuge: The Mormon Flight from American Pluralism* (Salt Lake City: Signature Books, 1989), 164; George A. Smith, "My Journal," *Instructor*, Nov. 1948, 515-16; Kimball, *On the Potter's Wheel*, 123; Norman to Coolbrith, Apr. 24, 1908; Hope A. Hilton, *"Wild Bill" Hickman and the Mormon Frontier* (Salt Lake City: Signature Books, 1988), 12.

109. Smith, *Proclamation and Faithful Warning*.

110. For William's impact on the St. Louis branch, see Stanley B. Kimball,

Grant arrived in late September and said that one of the first things
he heard was that William had "become involved in an illicit affair
with a young woman who was living in the home where he and
his daughter were boarding."[111] Parley Pratt, for one, was less than
surprised by this news because he had observed the same kind of
behavior from William on the east coast. Speaking at the October 6,
1845, conference in Nauvoo, Pratt offered that William's "doctrine
and conduct ... have produced death and destruction wherever he
went." William's one-note doctrine was his "aspir[ation] to uproot
and undermine the legal Presidency of the Church, that he may
occupy the place himself."[112]

The Twelve had clearly had enough of William's influence.
They voted on October 12 to remove him from the quorum, and
on October 19 at a general membership meeting in the temple,
William was excommunicated two weeks after his name had been
successfully presented for approval at general conference. The secretary to the quorum, Willard Richards, published a notice the
next month in the newspaper. The notice read:

> Elder Will[i]am Smith having been cut off from the Quorum of
> the Twelve for apostacy, on the Sunday following [general confer-
> ence], several [l]etters & a pamphlet having been read, showing he
> had turned away from the truth; on motion, it was unanimous[l]y
> resolved by the church of Jesus Christ of Latter-day Saints, that
> the said William Smith be cut off from said church, and left in the
> hands of God.[113]

"The Saints and St. Louis, 1831-1857: An Oasis of Tolerance and Security," *BYU
Studies* 13 (Summer 1973): 503-4; "Bill Smith the Only Surviving Brother of Joe
Smith," *Telegraph and Review*, Oct. 25, 1845, 2.

111. Gene A. Sessions, *Mormon Thunder: A Documentary History of Jedediah
Morgan Grant* (Urbana: University of Illinois Press, 1982), 54.

112. "Conference Minutes," *Times and Seasons*, Nov. 1, 1845, 1,008-09.

113. "Notice," ibid., 1,019; *History of the Church*, 7:483. Orson Hyde, "Cause
for Which William Smith Was Excluded from the Church," *Frontier Guardian*,
Feb. 6, 1850, 2, summarized the charges as a "wish to appropriate the public
funds of the Church for his own private use—for publishing false and slanderous

Samuel Brannan wrote to Brigham Young on October 9, before any action had been taken against William, that the apostle had "written several letters to the different branches in the east, that he should spend the winter in this country. Now I do not believe he will do so, by your willing council—and I would say to you, that if he comes into this country contrary, he will have to go to work on the dock rolling molas[s]es or else starve."[114] Brannan had clearly "abandoned William Smith and cast his lot with Brigham Young and the apostles," as historian Will Bagley commented.[115]

William Smith probably went into a state of depression at receiving word of his excommunication. Not only did some of his wives leave him, he apparently abandoned the others. At least, Mary Ann Sheffield said so in a court case in 1892 when she testified that "Smith treated me very well, until he left the church and me, too. ... I never heard from him while he was gone,—got no letters from him."[116] Amazingly, William sent Thomas Sharp copies of his *Proclamation,* showing that his animosity toward the Twelve had reached such a level, it was greater than his antipathy for his onetime archenemy. Orson Hyde pled with him to stop his militancy and return home: "I beseech you in the name of God to come speedily back to Nauvoo. ... Your mother's heart is grieved and broken. You are her son, she feels for you, and all the church feel for you. We feel that you have aimed a deadly blow at us, still we fear no evil therefrom; but all would be glad to forgive you, if you will only come within the reach of our forgiveness, in your person and your spirit."[117]

statements concerning the church: and for a general looseness and recklessness of character which ill comported with the dignity of his high calling."

114. Samuel Brannan to Brigham Young, Oct. 9, 1845, qtd. in Bagley, *Scoundrel's Tale*, 93.

115. Ibid., 97-98.

116. Mary Ann [Sheffield] West, Deposition, *Complaint's Abstract of Pleading and Evidence in the Circuit Court of the United States* (Lamoni, IA: Herald Publishing House and Bindery, 1893), 381.

117. Orson Hyde to William Smith, Oct. 28, 1845, qtd. in *Warsaw Signal*, Nov. 26, 1845, 1.

The gleeful Thomas Sharp willingly devoted the complete front page of the October 29, 1845, issue of the *Warsaw Signal* to William's pamphlet, completing the reproduction of it on page 4. A scathing attack against the Nauvoo hierarchy, written in haste, it stated that William had saved the eastern churches from Sidney Rigdon, and that George Adams and Samuel Brannan had been unjustly disciplined. The Nauvoo hierarchs had rejected his "royal blood," he explained, adding that "little Joseph" (III) was the ultimate successor to the church presidency. Young and Pratt "were the first to preach, and to practice the 'spiritual wife' doctrine in the city of Boston and other places," he claimed, evasively adding that his "dissent from any such doctrine of course gave annoyance."

The pamphlet charged that Young, Kimball, and Richards were dipping into the tithing money to support their wives and children in Nauvoo. Incredibly, this was the charge they had hurled at him. He said his brother Joseph had warned him against Brigham, saying the carpenter turned apostle "was a man, whose passions, if unrestrained, were calculated to make him the most licentious man in the world."[118] Sharp editorialized that the pamphlet "established beyond a doubt, the utter depravity of the Mormon leaders and the dangerous nature of the secret combinations existing in Nauvoo."[119]

William wrote a hostile response to Orson Hyde's private letter and sent both to Sharp, who again obliged by publishing them on his front page. William called Orson "a fallen angel whose heart is sufficiently black even to darken the gloomiest prison of *hell* (not one of your present colleagues excepted.)" He charged the Twelve with inflicting emotional pain on his mother, weakening his esteem among eastern church members, and committing gross immoralities, among which was the authorization of his murder in Nauvoo.[120]

---

118. Smith, *Proclamation and Faithful Warning*.
119. "Proclamation of Bill Smith," *Warsaw Signal*, Oct. 29, 1845, 2.
120. William Smith to Orson Hyde, Nov. 12, 1845, *Warsaw Signal*, Nov. 26, 1845, 1; emphasis retained.

Three days later a conference was held in New York City. The eastern Saints were in the middle of preparations to "move to the west," but among a number of resolutions, Brannan added a repudiation of William's pamphlet and an endorsement of William's excommunication, with a warning that William should avoid the eastern Saints, that "if he wishes to keep himself from trouble, shame, and disgrace," then he should "stay where he is, or go where he is not known."[121]

---

121. "New York Conference," *Times and Seasons*, Nov. 15, 1845, 1,037.

9. FROM HEIGHTS
TO GREATER HEIGHTS

In July 1838, about thirty church members encountered Lyman Johnson and his family on the streets of Richmond, Missouri. Even though Johnson had been threatened and driven from the Mormon community in Far West, "he ordered a dinner at the hotel for all of his old friends, and treated us with every kindness," according to Heber Kimball. "Brother Hyde and family remained there several days," hosted by Johnson, while "wagons were procured there to take us to Far West, where we arrived on the 25th of July."[1]

Other stories of encounters with the former apostles indicate that they did not consider themselves enemies and were saddened by the events that had contrived to separate them from their friends. True, they continued to maintain and publicize that the church hierarchy had wronged them, but their affection for each other seemed a constant, human emotion. Four of the six would ultimately explore a return to some form of Mormonism, but John Boynton and Lyman Johnson discovered they were as content out of the church as they had been in it. Reflecting the skills that had made them leaders in the first place, they had the ability to forgive and remain busy, engaged in business and community affairs, and become successful. They were not the type to withdraw and lick their wounds in ascetic

---

1. Jeni Broberg Holzapfel and Richard Neitzel Holzapfel, eds., *A Woman's View: Helen Mar Whitney's Reminiscences of Early Church History* (Provo: BYU Religious Studies Center, 1997), 100.

self-abnegation. They were outgoing, rugged, forward-looking individuals who seemed to always land on their feet.

Lyman Johnson

One of the first things Johnson did in his post-Mormon life was to file charges in the Ray County Circuit Court on August 30, 1838, against one of the Danites, Daniel Kern, who had broken into Johnson's house and stolen his property. Johnson enumerated what had been taken: clothing, tools, utensils, a rifle, a carriage harness, furniture, luggage, food, "stove pipe, ... one clock, one Book Case, ... three port barrels," razors, buttons, eye glasses. In other words, Kern had cleaned out Johnson's house, to the extent that Lyman claimed the missing chattel was worth about $1,000.[2] But when Kern asked for the writs to be quashed "in this cause," the judge did so and dismissed the suit.[3]

Even though the former apostles had spiritually separated themselves from the church, they had enough family still among the faithful to keep them close by for the time being. As the Saints crowded the roads through northern Missouri to Illinois in the middle of winter, 1838–39, the dissenters followed the paths their extended families took, ending up north of Nauvoo as far as Davenport, Iowa Territory. Boynton's sister Olive Boynton Hale and her husband, Jonathan, remained in the church, both eventually dying in September 1846 in Council Bluffs. John's parents, Eliphalet and Susan, remained within the church's orbit of influence in Scott County, Iowa.[4] A history of Scott County noted that "Johnson and

2. "Legal Instruments Re: Mormons in Utah," Mss. 707, L. Tom Perry Special Collections, Brigham Young University, Provo; D. Michael Quinn, *The Mormon Hierarchy: Origins of Power* (Salt Lake City: Signature Books, 1994), 480. Kern's name was variously spelled in documents as Karn, Karns, Cairn, Cairns, Carnes, Carn, Carns, Carr, and Garn.

3. *Daniel Kern vs. Lyman E. Johnson*, Ray County Circuit Court Record, Apr.-June 1839 Term, A:362, microfilm no. 959,749, LDS Family History Library, Salt Lake City.

4. Olive Boynton Hale to Martha Hale, ca. Mar. 1841, LDS Church History

Boyington were among the settlers of 1839" who built "a distill-
ery, the first, it is believed, ever introduced into Scott County. Like
many others who have undertaken the manufacture of spirituous
liquors, they failed in the enterprise, and removed to other parts."[5]

All was not lost, however. In addition to distilling alcohol,
Johnson began his legal practice.[6] He eventually settled in Keokuk,
Iowa, at the foot of the Des Moines Rapids twelve miles downriver from Nauvoo. It must have been partly due to being nearer
his extended family that he moved. At that time, Keokuk was a
small village of about 150 settlers. It had potential for growth,
being situated below the rapids which had always required river-
boats to lighten their loads to get past.[7] In the documents relating
to Keokuk's early history, Lyman is mentioned as having built a log
house overlooking the river. It was said to be "a most comfortable
little place, with a lean-to at the back and a small yard at the side,"
not to mention a "clear cold spring" that provided culinary water.[8]

Lyman's father died in July 1843 of prostate blockage of the uri-
nary passage.[9] The *Painesville Telegraph* reported his death:

> He was a man noted for his characteristic precision in all his deal-
> ings with others, always cheerful, and at the same time reserved
> and very exemplary; always ready to alleviate the necessities of

---

Library, qtd. in Janiece Lyn Johnson, "'Give It All Up and Follow Your Lord':
Mormon Female Religiosity, 1831-1843" (master's thesis, Brigham Young University, 2001), 147.

5. *History of Scott County, Iowa* (Chicago: Inter-State Publishing, 1882),
1189. Our thanks to Elaine Speakman, Johnson family genealogist, of Mt. Pleasant, Utah, for calling our attention to this reference.

6. Ibid., 350.

7. See Ben Hur Wilson, "Over the Rapids," *The Palimpsest*, Nov. 1923, 361-78.

8. Virginia Wilcox Ivins, *Yesterdays: Reminiscenses of Long Ago* (N.p.: By the
author, 1914), 43. The site of the Johnson house is now under the new Mississippi
River Bridge.

9. William E. McLellin, "Reasons Why I Am Not a Mormon," ca. 1880, in
Stan Larson and Samuel J. Passey, eds., *The William E. McLellin Papers: 1854-1880*
(Salt Lake City: Signature Books, 2007), 420.

the destitute, his generosity never withheld from doing good to his fellows when required, and from an acquaintance with him, all were his friends. He was very devoted and affectionate in his family, and seemed most happy when seated with them around his domestic fireside. In him, the widow and family have truly lost an affectionate and devoted husband and father.[10]

There is no evidence Lyman attended the funeral, no doubt because the distance was prohibitive.

Lyman not only defied the stereotype of a bitter apostate, he and John Boynton seem to have briefly entertained plans to return to the church in late 1840. Joseph Smith and some others bought a steamboat in September, the *Des Moines,* and renamed it the *Nauvoo,*[11] with stops up and down the river north and south of the city. It allowed for easy access to Nauvoo for people who lived on either side of the river and within the general region. In December there was "good news" when Boynton and Johnson were found among the passengers, as Vilate Kimball relayed it to her husband, Heber, in England:

> I mentioned in my last to you, that our people had bought a boat; they have named her Nauvoo, the last trip she made up the river President Smith went with her, and when he returned who should accompany him but John F Boynton and his wife, and Lymon Johnson. They [stayed at] home to Joseph Smiths all the time they were here. I never saw Joseph appear more happy; said he, I am a going to have all my old friends around me again. [T]hey both bought [city] lots and calculate to build and move here the ensuing Season. As

---

10. Death notice, *Painesville Telegraph*, Aug. 9, 1843, 3.

11. Vilate Kimball to Heber C. Kimball, Oct. 11-13, 1840, LDS Church History Library; Joseph I. Bentley, "In the Wake of the Steamboat Nauvoo: Prelude to Joseph Smith's Financial Disasters," *Journal of Mormon History* 35 (Winter 2009): 23-30 (one passenger described Joseph Smith as having "long light hair, light skin, light blue eyes, large mouth, long teeth several gone"); Daniel P. Kidder diary, Nov. 14-15, 1840, typescript, Kidder Papers, Special Collections and University Archives, Archibald Stevens Alexander Library, Rutgers University, New Brunswick, New Jersey.

to their faith, I have not heard much about it, but I conclude they have got some, or they [would] have no object in comeing here. I never saw any body that appeared glad[d]er to see me than John['s] wife, they all called us brother, and sister, and appeared as friendly as I ever saw them. Lymon called her the day that the English sisters were here, he had quite a chat with them. That is a day long to be remembered by me, it was quite a Paradice.[12]

Brigham Young heard that Boynton and Johnson had been rebaptized and forwarded this misinformation to his wife, Mary Ann, writing that "sister [Leonora] Taylor says in hir letter that John Boyington is Baptised a gan, my hart leeps for joy to see those men coming back."[13] Two weeks later Brigham wrote, "I am thankful to here of the returne of J Boying & L Jonson returne[d] to the church."[14] The rumor, although incorrect, indicates how friendly the two former apostles were with the remaining leaders.

Johnson met with five of the apostles at Brigham Young's house on July 19, 1841. Joseph Smith and Sidney Rigdon also briefly made an appearance at the council meeting and good feelings were expressed on all sides. Johnson was even invited to address the assembled men. Years later, Young remembered the event and said about it:

> Lyman E. Johnson said, at one of our Quorum meetings, after he had apostatized and tried to put Joseph out of the way … "Brethren—I will call you brethren—I will tell you the truth. If I could believe 'Mormonism'—it is no matter whether it is true or not—but if I could believe 'Mormonism' as I did when I traveled with you and preached, if I possessed the world[,] I would give it. I would give anything, I would suffer my right

---

12. Vilate Kimball to Heber C. Kimball, Dec. 8, 1840, LDS Church History Library.

13. Brigham Young to "my beloved companyan," Feb. 11-14, 1841, qtd. in Ronald O. Barney, "Letters of a Missionary Apostle to His Wife: Brigham Young to Mary Ann Angell Young, 1839-1841," *BYU Studies* 38, no. 2 (1999): 184.

14. Brigham Young to "beloved wife," Mar. 1, 1841, qtd. in ibid., 186. The letter "L" stands for Lyman; the published version misidentifies this as Luke.

hand to be cut off, if I could believe it again. Then I was full of joy and gladness. My dreams were pleasant. When I awoke in the morning my spirit was cheerful. I was happy by day and by night, full of peace and joy and thanksgiving. But now it is darkness, pain, sorrow, misery in the extreme. I have never since seen a happy moment."[15]

Although the story, when told thirty years after the Saints fled Nauvoo, probably reflects a need to project unhappiness onto unbelievers, it still captures the friendship and harmony that had reappeared in the wake of the interpersonal friction in Kirtland and Missouri. It is possible that Johnson, in a sentimental moment, confessed to unhappiness and darkness of mind, but it was probably exaggerated somewhat by Brigham in the retelling.

In June 1842, Johnson visited the *Times and Seasons* office. Wilford Woodruff saw him there and wrote to Parley Pratt that Lyman had just come "into the office" and was "well in health."[16] The next month Brigham told Parley that the former apostle was in Nauvoo at Marinda Hyde's being nursed to health and that "John Boyington is in this cou[n]try as a dentest."[17]

In 1842, Johnson built a more permanent house in Keokuk on the corner of Main and Second Streets and put aside any thoughts of moving to Nauvoo. The construction involved transporting loads of bricks across the Mississippi on a flatboat.[18] Before long, the stately house had become such a landmark that it was later

---

15. Brigham Young, June 17, 1877, *Journal of Discourses*, 26 vols. (Liverpool: LDS Booksellers Depot, 1855–86), 19:41.

16. Wilford Woodruff to Parley P. Pratt, June 12, 1842, LDS Church History Library.

17. Brigham Young to Parley P. Pratt, July 17, 1842, LDS Church History Library.

18. The boat was connected to a rope, and a horse on either side of the river, "working on a treadmill," pulled it across. "Keokuk History," *The Constitution-Democrat*, Sept. 29, 1906, 62, microfilm no. 960,049, item 1, Family History Library; see also Virginia Wilcox Ivins, *Pen Pictures of Early Western Days* (Keokuk: By the author, 1908), 33–34. The home was torn down about 1987.

remodeled as a bank, the size indicating Johnson's financial security. He was practicing law and dealing in real estate, as Elaine Speakman documented in finding that Johnson drew up over sixty deeds and mortgages in Keokuk.[19] Jonathan Dunham mentioned that Lyman and Sarah Johnson were regular customers on his ferry from Nauvoo in August through November 1843.[20]

There is no record of Lyman uniting with any religious denomination. It is possible that when he joined the Nauvoo Masonic lodge, it filled his religious and social needs. Historian Kenneth W. Godfrey explained:

> In the early summer of 1841, after considerable urging by Judge James Adams, a number of Mormon Masons petitioned Bodley Lodge at Quincy for permission to establish a lodge at Nauvoo. This petition was apparently signed by all the known Masons in the church. It was refused on the ground that these persons were unknown to the Quincy lodge as Masons, but on October 15, 1841, a recess dispensation was granted by Jonas, the newly elected grand master, to George Miller, John D. Parker, and L[ucius] N. Scovil. The Masons in Nauvoo began to hold meetings almost immediately. These meetings were conducted early in the morning one day a week.[21]

By joining the lodge, Lyman intentionally associated with some of his former quorum members. Non-Mormons included Johnson, "aged 30, Attorney at Law," along with Jacob B. Backenstos, "aged

19. Elaine Speakman, comp., "Lyman E. Johnson," 1994, with revisions through 2007, 7, photocopy in our possession.

20. Jonathan Dunham Account Book, 1825-1844, LDS Church History Library. This record was brought to our attention by Joseph Johnstun.

21. Kenneth W. Godfrey, "Joseph Smith and the Masons," *Journal of the Illinois State Historical Society* 64 (Spring 1971): 83; see also Michael W. Homer, "'Similarity of Priesthood in Masonry': The Relationship between Freemasonry and Mormonism," *Dialogue: A Journal of Mormon Thought* 27 (Fall 1994): 27-33; "Nauvoo Masonic Records, Minutes and List of Members October 15, 1841 to September 15, 1845," LDS Church History Library.

30, Merchant of Carthage." Among the applicants were apostles Amasa Lyman (who had been converted by Johnson and Orson Pratt in Vermont), Willard Richards, William Smith, Brigham Young, and Lyman Wight; stake president William Marks; and Joseph Smith's brother Samuel.[22]

At an April 7 meeting of Masons, several LDS luminaries sat alongside Johnson, including the entire church presidency: Joseph Smith, John C. Bennett, William Law, and Sidney Rigdon; church patriarch Hyrum Smith; medical doctor Robert Foster; and apostles John Page, John Taylor, and Wilford Woodruff. On April 20, Lyman Johnson and William Marks were "duly initiated" as "entered apprentice" Masons.[23] Later Johnson became a charter member of Eagle Lodge No. 12 in Keokuk and served as senior warden, the second highest position in the lodge, and then worshipful master in 1849.[24] A Masonic symbol prominently adorns his tombstone.

His career as an attorney offers a glimpse into his post-church years. In a legal history of early Iowa, Edward Stiles described a trip by four attorneys from Keokuk to the Mormon settlement in Kanesville. Lyman Johnson, John F. Kinney, J. C. Hall, and William Thompson were asked to take "a little ride of 250 miles through an almost unbroken wilderness" to document the vote in the 1847 election between Daniel F. Miller and William Thompson for the Southern District of Iowa.[25] Stiles said nothing about the Mormons

---

22. Mervin B. Hogan, *The Founding Minutes of the Nauvoo Lodge* (Des Moines: Research Lodge No. 2, 1971), 10-22; correspondence with Nauvoo Masonic historian Nick Literski.

23. Hogan, *Founding Minutes*, 34.

24. *History of Lee County, Iowa* (Chicago: Western Historical Co., 1879), 656; Speakman, "Lyman E. Johnson."

25. "The Miller-Thompson Contested Election," in *History of Des Moines County*, 432-37. According to Edward H. Stiles, *Recollections and Sketches of Notable Lawyers and Public Men of Early Iowa* (Des Moines: Homestead Publishing, 1916), 256, the Mormons in Kanesville had voted almost solely for Miller. However, the poll books from Kanesville disappeared and Thompson was elected. The results of the canvass are not known.

who were involved in the controversy but concentrated on the lawyers' preoccupation with their liquor supplies. At the start, Johnson
was driving the two-horse wagon when Kinney "pulled out a bottle
of brandy which I had taken the precaution to provide myself with,"
Kinney said, "and as I held it up in my hand, I cried out 'I have got
the advantage of you fellows.' 'Not by a great sight,' says Hall, and as
he spoke he raised from the bottom of the wagon a one-gallon jug.
Thus equipped we started."[26]

Stiles related the outcome of a poker game Johnson and Hall
indulged in along the way:

> While they were at the river, they fell in, at the tavern, with a
> French trader by the name of Percha, who induced Hall and John-
> son into a game of cards, at the end of which through his trickery,
> they found their exchequer in a very famished condition. They
> came to where Judge Kinney and Miller were and related their
> misfortune, stating that the Frenchman had through his cheating
> and manipulation of the cards reduced them to the condition they
> were in. Up spake Kinney, 'See here, boys, I can beat that fellow
> and if you'll say nothing about it, I will.' Of course, they prom-
> ised. Kinney and the Frenchman played, and strange to say, he
> won back all the money Johnson and Hall had lost and some forty
> dollars besides.[27]

These stories hint at Johnson's success in Keokuk, to the extent
that he was selected as one of four lawyers to document the election
results. Even though the description of him paints a less than flatter-
ing picture of his attraction to alcohol and gambling, these are por-
trayed with humor and as more or less harmless. There was sterner
criticism from the authors of *The History of Lee County* against Lyman
and two others for defending three thieves, alleged to be from Nauvoo. According to the authors, the attorneys "produced a host of

---

26. Ibid., 256–58.
27. Ibid., 333.

perjured witnesses," disguised as "farmers and laboring-men," who were "strangers to the Court" but provided an alibi.[28] In another case Lyman was involved with, a similarly hostile critique surfaced, although its portrayal of Isaac Galland, who sold property to Mormons to build Nauvoo, is unsupportable.[29] The county history correctly said that Galland had converted to Mormonism but incorrectly identified him as "one of the twelve apostles," which was wrong, and then curiously accused Johnson of having "raised a mob to attack him at his house" and having backed down when personally challenged by Galland because "Johnson had no personal courage."[30] Whatever the facts surrounding this strange tale are, it suggests that Lyman was not universally loved, which is not necessarily negative. If he was principled enough, he may have thereby made enemies.

As strange as these two accounts are, Johnson would play a role in another drama of genuine greed and crime surpassing any others for drama and intrigue. In the late 1830s and early 1840s, criminal elements plied their trade along the Mississippi River from Wisconsin to Missouri, and by the time Nauvoo took shape the leader of the infamous William W. Brown gang of Bellevue, Iowa, had been killed and a few surviving gang members had made Nauvoo their new base of operations.[31] It was a logical relocation. As Mormon writer Truman Madsen observed, "At this time Nauvoo was the largest city in Illinois; hence, counterfeiters, blacklegs, bootleggers, slave traders, gamblers, and every other disreputable type of person found their way there, trying to exploit the possibilities for

---

28. *History of Lee County*, 482.

29. Lyndon W. Cook, "Isaac Galland—Mormon Benefactor," *BYU Studies* 19 (Spring 1979): 261-84.

30. Col. J. M. Reid, *Sketches and Anecdotes of the Old Settlers, and New Comers, the Mormon Bandits and Danite Band* (Keokuk: R. B. Ogden, 1876), item 3, 149.

31. Susan K. Lucke, *The Bellevue War: Mandate of Justice or Murder by Mob?* (Ames, IA: McMillen Publishing, 2002), gives as information about criminals in the Mississippi River towns, especially the discussion of Aaron and John Long and Judge Fox, accomplices of the Hodges brothers.

dishonest profits, trying to gull recent and sometimes naïve converts who had come from far and near."[32] It was also true that there were a few Mormons who were willing to engage in the same sorts of activities in spite of the concerted efforts of Joseph and Hyrum Smith to cull them from the Mormon society in Illinois.[33]

Philip D. Jordan, an authority on violence in frontier America, wrote in the introduction to the 1963 edition of Edward Bonney's *The Banditti of the Prairies*: "During the 1840s, counterfeiters, horse thieves, stage robbers, and murderers plagued western Illinois and eastern Iowa. Singly and in well-organized bands, desperadoes disrupted the peace not only in the immediate vicinity of Nauvoo but also in the trans-Mississippi towns of Fort Madison, Montrose, Burlington, and Davenport in Iowa Territory."[34] It was a violent time on the frontier. The *Western World*, a newspaper in Warsaw, Illinois, reported in 1840 about a negro named Nat, who in Dubuque, Iowa, was literally lashed to death after being falsely accused of stealing a small amount of clothing.[35] Non-Mormons in Nauvoo repeated the process when the Key Stone Store of Rollison and Finch was robbed in the spring of 1844. A negro known only as Chism was blamed for the robbery and was savagely lashed. Mormons, to their credit, unsuccessfully attempted to prosecute the offenders.[36]

At the time Chism was brutalized, there were some 11,000

---

32. Truman G. Madsen, *Joseph Smith the Prophet* (Salt Lake City: Bookcraft, 1989), 112.

33. The issue of Mormon stealing is outlined in William Shepard, "'Marshaled and Disciplined for War': A Documentary Chronology of Conflict in Hancock County, Illinois, 1839-1845," *John Whitmer Historical Association Journal* 33, no. 2 (Fall/Winter 2013): 79-131.

34. Edward Bonney, *The Banditti of the Prairies or the Murderer's Doom! A Tale of the Mississippi Valley* (1850; Norman: University of Oklahoma Press, 1963), ix.

35. "Horrid! Horrid!!" *The Western World*, Oct. 7, 1840, 2.

36. See "Robbery and Lynching," *Nauvoo Neighbor*, Apr. 3, 1844, 2. On March 30, 1844, Joseph Smith heard that Chism was lacerated "from his shoulders to his hips with 20 or more lashes." Scott H. Faulring, ed., *An American Prophet's Record: The Diaries and Journals of Joseph Smith* (Salt Lake City: Signature Books, 1989), 461.

Mormons in Nauvoo,[37] and within this extensive population there were a few hardened, habitual criminals who cooperated with another small number of non-Mormons in one particular gang whose specialty was "midnight robberies" in the neighboring counties in Illinois and Iowa. Because they were opportunists, the thugs would sometimes also accost Mormons. The gang was bound by secrecy and the commitment to do all within their power to obtain the release of any member who was incarcerated. The Mormon thieves included four brothers—Amos, Ervine, William, and Stephen Hodges—whose parents had converted to Mormonism in Erie County, Pennsylvania, and were baptized in Kirtland, Ohio, in late 1832.[38] The family moved to Missouri with the body of the Saints and were forced, with others, to leave Clay County in 1836. They were driven from Caldwell County during the 1838 Mormon War.[39] Curtis Sr., Curtis Jr., and an unnamed son were participants in the Battle of Crooked River, where the father survived a gunshot to the side.[40] In 1842 two of his sons, William and Stephen, and brothers-in-law Darius Campbell and Truman Waite were accused of stealing a horse in Des Moines County. Stephen was convicted.[41] Curtis Jr. was

---

37. Susan Easton Black, "How Large Was the population of Nauvoo?" *BYU Studies* 35, no. 2 (1995): 93.

38. The best information about the Hodgeses becoming Mormons is found in Marietta Hodges Faulconer Walker, *With the Church in an Early Day* (1911; Independence: Price Publishing, 2000), who became a popular RLDS author, writing about "the Clark family," her mother's maiden name. The surname, Hodges, is sometimes given as Hodge in contemporary reports, and Ervine has been alternately referred to as Arvine, Irvine, and Irvin. He signed his name to legal documents as Ervine or E. C. Hodges.

39. Their losses in Missouri are listed in Clark V. Johnson, ed., *Mormon Redress Petitions: Documents of the 1833-1838 Missouri Conflict* (Provo: BYU Religious Studies Center, 1992), 464-65, 590-91, 706.

40. Walker, *With the Church*, 229-31.

41. Incomplete trial documents, Des Moines County Court House, District Court, box A, 176, Burlington, Iowa. Stephen was found guilty, but his sentence is unknown.

cut off from the church in 1843 for bigamy, and Curtis Sr. was accused of stealing from the Saints in Tennessee.[42]

After Joseph Smith's death, Curtis, his wife Lucy, son Curtis Jr., daughter Marietta, and other family members left Nauvoo in the spring of 1845 for Pennsylvania, where they fellowshipped with Sidney Rigdon. William and Stephen remained in Nauvoo and lived with Amos and wife Lydia in the poorer section of town near the Mississippi River. Although Amos was president of the Thirteenth Quorum of Seventy,[43] he could not enter Iowa "because he had been indicted for robbery."[44] Ervine and wife Luzette lived in Mechanicsville some thirty miles from Nauvoo. Apostle John Taylor referred to him as having "a poor character for unrightness," by which was probably meant that he had an inclination to sin.[45]

Rumors reached the Hodges gang that a stash of $1,000 was available for the taking in West Point, Iowa, where they had heard a Mennonite family had stored the money in their house. Twenty-five-year-old William Hodges, twenty-three-year-old Stephen Hodges, and two fellow Mormons, thirty-six-year-old Artemus Johnson[46] and twenty-one-year-old Thomas Brown,[47] planned the robbery.[48]

---

42. *History of the Church*, 5:350; "To the Editor," *Times and Seasons*, Mar. 1, 1844, 461.

43. The Seventies Record, 13th Quorum, Book B:43, LDS Church History Library. This record also lists William Hodges as an elder.

44. Judge Charles Mason, qtd. in Charles Mason Remy, ed., *Life and Letters of Charles Mason: Chief Justice of Iowa, 1804-1882* (Washington, D.C.: Charles Mason Remy, 1939), 91.

45. Dean C. Jessee, ed., "The John Taylor Nauvoo Journal: January 1845–September 1845," *BYU Studies* 23 (Summer 1983): 21, 36, 59.

46. Artemus Johnson was ordained an elder in November 1839 and was identified as a "notorious thief" in "Beware of Thieves," *Times and Seasons*, Dec. 15, 1840, 256.

47. In the article "Shocking Murder," *Illinois State Register*, May 23, 1845, 3, a person using the pseudonym "Alpha" said "Brown, though scarce twenty-one is notorious in Hancock and the adjoining counties. He has been in jail, in Brown County, for stealing. His father [Alanson Brown] was expelled from the Mormon Church, six years ago, and forcibly driven from the community."

48. Stephen Hodges apparently did not hold priesthood in the church. At

Deciding they needed to do some surveillance, they went to the Millers' house and asked for directions, even asking if they could change a large bill. They also contacted neighbors to ask about a lost ox and to see what people knew of the family's financial situation. They asked one young man named John Walker if he would join their gang and threatened to kill him if he told anyone of their conversation.[49]

The erstwhile thieves made their move near midnight on May 10, 1845, creeping quietly outside the house, forcing their way in, and encountering the stout Mr. Miller and son-in-law Henry Leisi. In the ensuing melee, Miller was killed and Leisi mortally wounded. One of the brothers left behind a hat that proved he had been there. While Johnson and Brown were fleeing the area, William and Stephen Hodges brazenly returned to Nauvoo and told Brigham Young what they had done and asked for protection. When Young told them to turn themselves over to the law, they made an even bigger blunder by threatening to harm him. Two days later a mixed party of Nauvoo police and Iowa officials arrested the Hodgeses at Amos's house and the brothers were turned over to officials in Iowa, who took them to Fort Madison and then Burlington.[50]

---

twenty-three, two years younger than William, he was nevertheless the dominant brother.

49. Testimony of John Walker in "Trial for Murder," *Burlington Hawk-Eye*, June 12, 1845, 2-3.

50. Edward Bonney, who lived opposite Nauvoo in Iowa near Montrose, recorded many first-hand events relating to the murder of the Mennonites, the arrest of William and Stephen Hodges, and their trial and execution in his 1850 book, *The Banditti of the Prairies or, the Murderer's Doom!! A tale of the Mississippi Valley.* See Bonney, *Banditti*, 27-35; Juanita Brooks, ed., *On the Mormon Frontier: The Diary of Hosea Stout*, 2 vols. (Salt Lake City: University of Utah Press, 1962), 1:38-39; Jessee, "John Taylor Nauvoo Journal," 48-49. Bonney was born to Jethro M. and Laurana Webster Bonney in 1807 in New York. He married Maria L. Van Frank in 1832. The family lived in Nauvoo from 1840 to 1845, before moving to the outskirts of Ft. Madison where Bonney became a bounty hunter and possibly a counterfeiter. Philip D. Jordan, introduction to *Banditti*, vii-xxi. Quinn, *Mormon Hierarchy: Origins*, 127, found that Bonney was a Mason in Nauvoo, a member of the Council of Fifty, and Joseph's aide-de-camp in the Nauvoo Legion. He was dropped from the Council of Fifty on February 4, 1845.

Looking for a reputable lawyer, they turned to Lyman Johnson. He may not have known, even if he sensed, that this would become one of the state's most famous criminal trial proceedings. Hawkins Taylor joined Johnson in Nauvoo during two weeks in June taking depositions of criminal associates and friends of the two brothers. Taylor had been a member of the Iowa legislature. The lawyers asked the District Court in Burlington, Des Moines County, Iowa, to delay the trial so additional witnesses could testify that William and Stephen Hodges were in Nauvoo on the night of the murders. The request was denied at about the same time three of the would-be-witnesses, Judge Fox (Judge was his given name) and John and Aaron Long, murdered the celebrated Colonel George Davenport at Rock Island, Illinois, on July 4.[51] Hawkins Taylor cynically observed that "there probably never w[as] a worse lot of thieves testifying in any one court than in this [one]."[52] Johnson may have decided he was in over his head and deferred the case to two attorneys in Burlington, thereafter acting in a supporting role in convincing friends of the Hodgeses to transfer $1,000 in property to support the attorneys. Non-Mormon gang members William F. Louter and R. Blecher (alias Robert H. Birch)[53] joined with Mormons Ervine and Amos Hodges, William

---

Quinn, "The Council of Fifty and Its Members, 1844 to 1945," *BYU Studies* 20 (Winter 1980):193. Bonney's book is also valuable as it tells of the arrest, trials, and execution of three of the murderers of George Davenport.

51. Hawkins Taylor autobiography, 56, typescript, Archives and Special Collections, Western Illinois University Library, Macomb. Period histories and newspaper accounts unanimously reported that the attempt to get the Longs and Fox to give alibis for the brothers was proof that they were in the Hodgeses' criminal gang. For example, see "The Murder of Miller and Leiza by the Hodges," *Gate City*, Keokuk, Iowa, May 24, 1876, 2.

52. Taylor autobiography, 56.

53. Bonney identified William W. Louter as having been on a stealing expedition with Mormon criminal Return Jackson Redden and of having joined with others to plan the robbery of Colonel George Davenport. Bonney, *Banditti*, 214. Also Robert H. Birch was identified as a former member of the William W. Brown gang. Birch, among those arrested for Davenport's murder, used the aliases Blecher and

(Bill) Hickman, Return Jackson Redden, and W. Jenkins Salisbury in transferring property to pay the lawyers.[54]

The trial began on June 19 with jury selection. Amazingly, it concluded three days later with death sentences, having taken a total of only six weeks from the commission of the crime to the execution of the convicts. The guilty parties were hanged in Burlington on July 15. Amos Hodges's wife, Lydia, did not testify, but told attorney Jonathan C. Hall in confidence that she had been told to testify that William and Stephen were in Nauvoo the night of the murder, and "were gone all night, came home in the morning, said they had been unsuccessful, and perhaps got themselves into trouble."[55]

The execution of the prisoners did not dissuade the criminal underworld in Nauvoo even though the trial riveted the city and entire region. Even while the trial was in session, Amos Hodges, Robert Birch, and Judge Fox planned to rob the store of Rufus Beach, a Mormon merchant in Nauvoo. For some reason, Amos told Brigham Young what they were planning, and Brigham tipped off Beach in time to station armed guards in his store to deflect the robbery.[56] Birch and Fox escaped, but Amos was apprehended. John Taylor recorded on June 21 that he was afraid of "a man of the

---

Bleeker. Bonds and Mortgages, 1844-48, 2:66-67, Hancock County Courthouse, Carthage, Illinois, microfilm no. 954,776, LDS Family History Library.

54. William Hickman was a leading member of a criminal gang operating in and around Nauvoo. Hope A. Hilton, *"Wild Bill" Hickman and the Mormon Frontier* (Salt Lake City: Signature Books, 1988), 10-11. Bonney, *Banditti of the Prairies*, frequently refers to Hickman in conjunction with the Hodgeses. Return Jackson Redden was born in 1817 in Hiram, Ohio, and would have known the Johnson family from his youth. Jenkins Salisbury was a brother-in-law of Joseph Smith. Other than joining in this endeavor, there is no evidence he was a criminal associate of the gang. For general information, see Lavina Fielding Anderson, ed., *Lucy's Book: A Critical Edition of Lucy Mack Smith's Family Memoir* (Salt Lake City: Signature Books, 2001), 861-62.

55. Remy, *Life and Letters of Charles Mason*, 91-93.

56. Bonney, *Banditti*, 55-56. "A Brother of the Murderers Murdered," *Iowa Territorial Gazette and Advertiser*, Burlington, June 28, 1845, 2, tells of betrayed thieves seeking vengeance and killing Ervine, whom the paper confuses with Amos.

name of Amos Hodges ... I am afraid he is connected with a gang of villains that are lurking about, stealing on our credit."[57]

Ervine Hodges publicly proclaimed in Burlington on June 22 that unless Brigham helped get his brothers out of jail, he would reveal all he knew about Mormon involvement in theft. The following day Ervine appeared at Young's door in an agitated state. Zina Diantha Huntington Jacobs, who was married to both Henry Jacobs and Joseph Smith simultaneously, and later to Brigham Young, recorded that Hodges arrived "direct from Burlington" and was "a man of unbounded temper," who threatened Brigham Young's life.[58] When Ervine took a short cut through a corn field near Brigham's house the next evening at about ten o'clock, it was the worst decision of his life because when he re-emerged, he had been beaten and savagely cut with a bowie knife and was nearly dead.

What is known about this is that policemen Allen Stout and John Scott heard "a few blows struck as if someone was beeting an ox with a club, which was followed by shrieks." Ervine limped out of the field and climbed over Brigham's fence, then collapsed near the apostle's door.[59] Officer Scott asked what happened, and Ervine said, "They were men whom he took to be friends, from the river." Scott asked their names, but Ervine's strength failed and he went dumb. A crowd gathered around. A non-Mormon asked the same question: who had done this? Ervine's response was that "he could not tell."[60]

---

57. Jessee, "John Taylor Nauvoo Journal," 53. After being arrested following the murder of Colonel Davenport in Rock Island, Birch, in an effort to get his sentence reduced, testified that "Fox and myself attempted to rob Beach in Nauvoo, and would have succeeded, had not Brigham Young told Beach the plan. We came near being caught, but escaped, and crossed the [Mississippi] river to Old Redden's." Bonney, *Banditti*, 215.

58. Maureen Ursenbach Beecher, ed., "'All Things Move in Order in the City': The Nauvoo Diary of Zina Diantha Huntington Jacobs," *BYU Studies* 19 (Spring 1979): 314.

59. Allen Stout reminiscences and journal, 1845-89, 24, LDS Church History Library.

60. Jessee, "John Taylor Nauvoo Journal," 58.

D. Michael Quinn examined Ervine's murder and concluded that Hosea Stout, captain of the Nauvoo police, and brother Allen Stout were involved.[61] It was the same conclusion drawn by people in and around Nauvoo at the time. William Hall, for instance, a former Mormon who published a sensational narrative about the church in 1852, claimed that Hosea Stout had boasted he had participated in the murder and "intimated that it was done by the order of Brigham Young."[62]

Whether or not the story was true, Hosea Stout was not above committing such an act. More realistic evidence indicates that fellow gang member Return Jackson Redden may have murdered Ervine to keep him from revealing gang secrets. The *Territorial Gazette and Advertiser* of Burlington reported on June 28 that "the supposition of many is that he was murdered by a gang of scoundrels to which he and his brothers are supposed to have belonged, to prevent disclosures which it was feared the execution of Stephen and William might provoke."[63] The following day the local sexton, William Huntington, wrote that Ervine was murdered "by some ruffians—as Hodge[s] was supposed to be of the same gang."[64] A month later, Attorney D. F. Miller of Lee County, Iowa, wrote Judge Charles Mason, who presided at the trial of William and Stephen Hodges, that Ervine "was killed unquestionably by one of the Band because he threatened exposure."[65]

Another Hodges brother, Amos, was bailed from custody in Nauvoo on June 24 by William Smith. This intensified William's

---

61. Quinn, *Mormon Hierarchy: Origins*, 217n169-71, 427-28.

62. William Hall, *The Abominations of Mormonism Exposed; Containing Many Facts and Doctrines ... from 1840-1847* (Cincinnati: L. Hart & Co., 1852), 30-34.

63. "A Brother of the Murders Murdered," *Territorial Gazette and Advertiser*, June 28, 1845, 2.

64. William Huntington autobiography, typescript, Brigham Young University, *LDS Family History Suite,* CD-ROM (Provo: Infobases, 1996).

65. "Hon. Charles Mason," July 23, 1845, typescript, Iowa State Historical Society, Des Moines.

power struggle with the other apostles.[66] Interestingly, Amos then disappeared. William suspected that members of the Nauvoo police had taken his friend to Iowa and murdered him.[67] The *Warsaw Signal* announced on July 23 that Amos had not been seen since Ervine's murder,[68] and as he was never seen again, he was probably murdered by Robert Birch or Judge Fox for betraying them. Reverend R. A. Gurley, who was attending a Territorial Convention of Universalists in Burlington, said "a fourth brother who was taken up for the same offence [stealing] but who afterwards was bailed out of prison, mysteriously disappeared; and the general belief is the Mormons murdered him also to prevent a full revelation of their dark deeds."[69]

In this desperate environment, associates of the Hodgeses met at an isolated cabin belonging to Grant Redden some five miles from Montrose, Iowa, to plan the robbery of Colonel Davenport, who was a wealthy fur trader and founder of the town that bears his name. Known participants included Grant Redden,[70] his son William, Robert Birch, John and Aaron Long, and John Baxter. Another thief named Granville Young joined them in Rock Island where Davenport lived. It was Granville Young who accidentally killed Davenport during the commission of the robbery when his gun discharged. It was another botched crime resulting in another

---

66. George D. Smith, ed., *An Intimate Chronicle: The Journals of William Clayton* (Salt Lake City: Signature Books, 1995), 169.

67. "Letter from Wm. Smith, Brother of the Late Prophet," *Sangamo Journal*, Nov. 5, 1845, 2.

68. "Irvine Hodges," *Warsaw Signal*, July 23, 1845, 2.

69. For Gurley's account, see "The Mormons," *Trumpet and Universalist Magazine*, Boston, Sept. 13, 1845, 1.

70. George Grant Redden was born in 1790 in Bernardstown, New Jersey, and married Adelia Higley in 1816 in Ohio. They had eight children, including Return and William Harrison. Father Grant and son William, both baptized Mormons, were allied with the Hodgeses. An account of the criminal meeting at Redden's is contained in "The Davenport Murderers," *Burlington Hawk-Eye*, Nov. 13, 1845, 2.

corpse, once more credited to the Hodges gang. Word of this development reached William and Stephen in jail where they were awaiting execution. One of the brothers reportedly attempted suicide the day after Ervine's murder but survived.[71]

Judge Charles Mason agreed to commute William's sentence to a fixed number of years if he would give up the gang's membership list. At first the prisoner agreed, then he changed his mind, saying his confession would jeopardize the lives of his family, especially of Amos's widow, Lydia, and his own parents in Pittsburgh.[72] So the next day, the executions took place, accompanied by eight thousand spectators who brought picnic lunches and gathered to see the brothers die. Public officials made speeches and there was music from brass bands. The *Burlington Hawk-Eye* enthused that it had "never ... seen more decorum or better behavior exhibited at a public execution."[73] The prisoners were brought out in manacles, dressed in shrouds, and led to their coffins, where they were seated while four ministers spoke and uttered prayers.[74] The prisoners' chains were then removed and the ropes adjusted on their necks. After hoods were pulled over their faces, the trap doors were opened and William died instantly of a broken neck. For Stephen, because the platform sagged on his side, he twisted and twitched for a while as he was slowly strangled to death.[75]

---

71. "Irvine Hodge[s]," *Lee County Democrat*, June 28, 1845, 2.

72. Remy, *Life and Letters*, 91–94. William is described on several occasions as being "tender," by which was meant childlike in intelligence. For instance, he was not able to sign his name. A second account of the brothers refusing to save their lives in exchange for evidence against the criminal associates was given by Reverend R. A. Gurley attending a Universalist Conference in Burlington. He said he visited William at the jail and maintained he "gave as a reason for not exposing the whole band of robbers and murderers, that it would implicate so many, and among the number the rest of his family." "The Mormons," *Trumpet and Universalist Magazine*, Sept. 13, 1845, 1.

73. "The Hanging," *Burlington Hawk-Eye*, July 23, 1845, 2.

74. "Remarkable Story of the Hanging of the Hodges[es]," *Burlington Hawk-Eye*, Jan. 25, 1914, 1.

75. "The Execution," *Burlington Hawk-Eye*, July 17, 1845, 2. "An Old Time Letter Discovered Telling of the Hodges Tragedy," *Burlington Hawk-Eye*, Jan. 25, 1914, 1.

William Hodges undoubtedly believed he had done the honorable thing by refusing to divulge the names of accomplices, but the popular opinion, as expressed in the newspapers, was that he was wrong to go to the gallows without setting the record straight, that this confirmed what an utterly evil man he was.[76] We can imagine Lyman Johnson's task as he continued to work with the defense lawyers while Edward Bonney's pursuit of Davenport's murderers led him to check the list of witnesses who had agreed to testify in the Miller trial. Bonney came to the deduction that John and Aaron Long and Judge Fox had probably implicated themselves by their willingness to testify. Bonney also learned that Robert Birch had joined the others at Grant Redden's cabin.

Bonney visited the cabin and began trailing the group's movements from there, going so far as to pose as an outlaw on the run, enabling him to infiltrate the group. His cunning won out, and he arrested Birch, Fox, and John Long. Other lawmen arrested John Baxter, Aaron Long, and Granville Young. Grant and William Redden were indicted "as accessory to the murder of Davenport before the fact" and were arrested.[77] Birch testified during his trial that the plan for the robbery "was held in Joseph Smith's old council chamber in Nauvoo," a claim that defies logic. However, more realistically, he said Return Jackson Redden murdered Ervine Hodges "out of his fear" that Ervine would confess.[78] Birch and Fox avoided punishment by escaping from jail, probably by bribing their guards. After a "hung jury" in a trial of Grant and John Redden, the two were retried on lesser charges. Grant was released and John was imprisoned for one year.[79] In separate trials, Baxter

---

76. "The Two Hodges," *Quincy Whig*, July 23, 1845, 2
77. Bonney, *Banditti*, 212.
78. Ibid., 214; "The Murder at Rock Island," *New York Sun*, Oct. 27, 1845, 2. *The Illinois State Reporter*, Oct. 31, 1845, 2, carried a similar statement reprinted from the *Missouri Reporter*.
79. Bonney, *Banditti*, 238.

was sentenced to life in prison. John and Aaron Long and Granville Young were convicted and hanged on October 19, 1845.

Shortly after the trial of the Longs and Young, Lyman Johnson notified Bonney by letter that he too had been indicted by a Grand Jury in Ft. Madison, Iowa, for counterfeiting and being in league with the Hodges. It turned out that William Hickman and other gang members were behind the allegations. Bonney characterized Hickman "as one of the most notorious rascals unhung" and alleged he was wanted for "several larcenies he had committed in the county of Lee."[80]

Based on Birch's testimony, Return Jackson Redden was indicted "as accessary before the fact" in the murder of Colonel Davenport. The disclosures of Mormon involvement in such heinous crimes further inflamed public opinion against Nauvoo and its inhabitants. The *Warsaw Signal* printed a short statement from the *Lee County Democrat* of Fort Madison, Iowa, which noted that "a gentleman residing at Nauvoo called on us this week, and in the course of conversation about the Hodges, said he was persuaded that the man who killed Irvine Hodges is well known to many of the elect in that place." Thomas Sharp, the editor of the *Signal*, concluded: "Proofs multiply so rapidly, of the many acts of villains which are perpetrated, or originated in Nauvoo, that our decided opinion is, that the presence of the Mormons is incompatible with the safety and well being of those in their vicinity."[81]

Meanwhile, aggressive acts by non-Mormons in the countryside were being met with deadly force by Hancock County sheriff Jacob Backenstos, aided by all-Mormon posses, which did little to tamp down public opinion. In the middle of this turmoil, Iowa law officials were unable to proceed through normal channels and have Redden delivered to them. They turned to Lyman Johnson for help.

Johnson had not only represented the Hodgeses as an attorney,

---

80. Ibid., 229-30. Bonney was subsequently cleared of the charges.
81. "The Mormons," *Warsaw Signal*, Sept. 17, 1845, 2.

he had apparently known the family in Ohio and was distantly related through an aunt.[82] Edward Bonney said that "L. E. Johnson was deputied under authority of a warrant issued by Miles W. Conway, Esq., justice of the peace."[83] Lyman agreed to a ploy to lure Redden to the stone house on Nauvoo's wharf in order to "consider arrangements for bailing his father and brother out of jail."[84] On October 25, 1845, the steamboat *Sarah Ann* churned up to port, with Sheriff James L. Bradley of Rock Island on board, equipped with a warrant for "Jackson Redden, charging him with the murder of Col. Davenport in July last."[85] Johnson was talking with Redden when Bradley attempted to arrest Redden, who resisted. The sheriff received assistance from some of the crew and passengers, but a number of Mormons rushed to Redden's side, and in the resulting melee Johnson and Sheriff Bradley were both badly injured.

Adding to the confusion, one passenger on the steamboat, Robert D. Foster, fired a pistol into the air. He was know as one of the publishers of the alternative *Nauvoo Expositor,* and was responded to by Mormons hustling Redden off. The *Sarah Ann,* perceiving danger, backed into the river and began moving downriver. The *History of the Church* recorded this without mentioning that Redden had been served with a warrant for murder:

> The steamer *Sarah Ann* passed up the river. Doctor Foster and Lyman E. Johnson were on board. ... Dr. R. D. Foster got a number of men from the boat and undertook to haul Redden on board and take him off with them. Redden knocked the first man down that undertook to lay hands on him; a few of the brethren who were not far off ran to Redden's assistance and with sticks and

---

82. Redden was the nephew of Nancy Jacob Redden.

83. Bonney, *Banditti,* 217.

84. "Affray at Nauvoo—Rescue of a Prisoner," *Bloomington Herald,* Nov. 1, 1845, 2; Bonney, *Banditti,* 217.

85. "The Nauvoo Fracas," *Territorial Gazette and Advertiser,* Nov. 1, 1845, 2.

stones soon drove the whole crew on board; the captain started immediately, without unloading; the clerk left the bills of lading with a man who handed them to Albert P. Rockwood, but appeared not to know what he did. After the boat started Doctor Foster shot his pistol at the brethren but hurt no one. One of the brethren was cut on the back of the neck with a stone.[86]

The *Warsaw Signal* gave a different view:

When the boat, on which they were, landed, Mr. Johnson, went up into the City and decoyed Red[den] to the landing and endeavored to get him on board the boat; but he would not go. The Sheriff then arrested him on shore; he however resisted him and he would not go on the boat. He was then seized by the Officer and his aids, and while they were in the act of forcing him on the boat, they were attacked, by a mob, who assailed them with brick bats and other missiles, which soon disabled them so that they were compelled to let their prisoner go. Mr. Bradley was severely wounded on the head and also on the knee. Mr. Johnson was struck with great violence with a brick-bat on the side of the face.[87]

Three days later, three officers in the Illinois state militia arrived in Nauvoo and asked to meet with the Twelve. In the resulting conference, Major William B. Warren and Captains James D. Morgan and M. Turner conversed with Elders Heber Kimball, Amasa Lyman, George Smith, John Taylor, and Brigham Young. According to the *Warsaw Signal*, the officers wanted Redden to surrender, but the apostles "replied that Redding had gone to Michigan."[88] Young defended Redden by insisting that when the sheriff approached the twenty-eight-year-old Mormon, "there was nothing said about a

---

86. *History of the Church*, 7:486–87.

87. "Outrages in Nauvoo," *Warsaw Signal*, Oct. 29, 1845, 2.

88. "Last Visit of Major Warren to Nauvoo," *Warsaw Signal*, Nov. 5, 1845, 2. Our thanks to Bryon Andreasen for information on James D. Morgan and M. Turner.

Writ [arrest warrant]—a man came up, grabbed him by the arms & said I have got the man—hundreds will swear it." Major Warren mentioned that Lyman Johnson was recovering and would not suffer permanent damage.[89]

People in Fort Madison prepared a proclamation objecting to what they considered Mormon obfuscation in trying to protect Redden, signed by seven of the riverboat's crew and nineteen passengers who testified that the sheriff was prevented from making the arrest by some forty Mormons. The sheriff and several others had received serious cuts and abrasions from rocks thrown by Mormons.[90] Even William Smith wrote in the *Sangamo Journal* that Ervine Hodges was "running at large in Nauvoo" under protection of Brigham Young.[91]

William Clayton wrote that "Lyman Johnson, one of the old Twelve, headed a party of the mob from Keokuk" that plundered the city, although Clayton was on the western side of Iowa by September 25, 1846, and could not have known this himself.[92] Although hearsay, was it true that Johnson took part in the Battle of Nauvoo? Did he succumb to emotion, after having been beaten by the Mormons the previous year? Perhaps he responded to a civic call for volunteers when his community rallied a militia. This was the course his friend Hawkins Taylor took, who said he regretted acting "most foolishly and wickedly" in going "over from Keokuk and join[ing] the anti-Mormon army."[93]

A year later, Johnson sold his brick home to John A. Graham, but not because he was abandoning the town. He wanted to build

89. Minutes of the Quorum of the Twelve Apostles, Oct. 28, 1845, typescript, Leonard J. Arrington Papers, Series 9: Mormon History Topics, Special Collections and Archives, Merrill-Cazier Library, Utah State University Libraries.

90. "Public Meeting," *Burlington Hawk-Eye*, Oct. 30, 1845, 2.

91. "A Faithful Warning to the Latter Day Saints," *Sangamo Journal*, Nov. 6, 1845, 2.

92. Smith, *Intimate Chronicle*, 291.

93. Taylor, Autobiography, 57.

an even larger mansion at 204 N. Second Street, which like its predecessor would become a landmark for many years.[94] We get a glimpse into Johnson's high social status from the size and prominence of his houses, as well as from an 1876 history in which the author explained that "in early times," it was customary "to select for every character of any special note in the place, some soubriquet or nickname—such as the whim of its donor might deem appropriate." Johnson was called "heels," in reference to his deliberate dance steps. Society leader Kate Hughes wrote a poem entitled "Invitation to the Grand Fancy Ball" to explain that Johnson "in the dance you will see, and all surely must feel / That light are his movements and heavy his heel, / His dress well becomes him, and all persons say, / In the figure he cuts he makes a display." The poem compared him to an "old honest Quaker ... in thought and in deed, in word and in action." In other words, he was trustworthy but not much fun at a party. Even so, the overall tone was positive and wryly worshipful, in it comically expressing fondness for a revered friend.[95]

The 1850 census showed still that a teenage daughter, Sarah, and young son, John, age six, were living with Lyman and Sarah Johnson.[96] The value of their house was $8,800, which today would be about $240,000. As good as life seemed, they were struck with tragedy on February 3, 1851, when Lyman's wife died.[97] The family seemed to go into free fall after this, the daughter, Sarah Marinda,

---

94. Ivins, *Yesterdays*, 44.

95. Reid, *Sketches and Anecdotes*, 72-74. The nickname "heels" also could refer to someone who had run away from danger, "took to his heels," or was known to empty a liquor bottle down to the last drop. See Timothy R. Mahoney, *Provincial Lives: Middle-class Experience in the Antebellum Middle West* (New York: Cambridge University Press, 1999), 96.

96. John E. Johnson was born in Keokuk on April 19, 1844, and died of pneumonia on February 6, 1917, at the Iowa Soldiers Home in Marshaltown. Elaine Speakman, comp., Family Group Sheet Record, Apr. 2005.

97. Sarah Johnson obituary, *Valley Whig & Keokuk Register*, Feb. 6, 1851, 2; the Caleb F. Davis Papers, Keokuk Public Library, 1:59, indicate that she "died of consumption."

marrying her father's law partner, Joel Matthews, before the year was out (October 14) even though she was only fifteen years old. She joined her new husband in attending the Episcopal Church. A year later Lyman sold his stately house to his daughter Sarah and son-in-law Joel.[98]

When Lyman remarried in 1853, little was recorded about his wife, Mary, except that the couple seemed restless, moving to St. Louis, then Chicago, and then Vermont in pursuit of business opportunities. In St. Louis they acquired half interest in the *Patrick Henry* steamboat and lived on a tract of land they called Prairie Place.[99] They had a daughter, Kate, born in 1854 in Missouri. By October 25 of the following year, they were in Chicago, and with each move they sold more land in Iowa to finance additional acquisitions elsewhere.[100]

Eventually things fell apart in Chicago, and the next we learn of them they were the owners, by August 1857, of a small hotel in Clarendon, Vermont, named Union Hall. Lyman was given a loan with easy installments of three equal payments,[101] but even at that he was unable to meet the terms and had to sell the hotel.[102]

---

98. Lee County Deeds, Lyman E. Johnson to Joel Matthews, Nov. 30, 1852, microfilm no. 959,244, 13:242, LDS Family History Library. Joel Matthews and wife Sarah sold the property to J. E. Burke on June 7, 1853 (ibid., 13:672). There is a 1985 photograph in the Office of Historic Preservation (Photo Roll 5256), Iowa State Historical Department, Des Moines, captioned "This house is a standard version of the Gable-front & Wing National style, with decorative pedimented window heads." The house was demolished after 1985.

99. Lyman E. Johnson to Joel Matthews, Feb. 10, 1853, St. Louis (Independent City), Deeds Book 6:261, microfilm no. 531,610, LDS Family History Library. We are indebted to Elaine Speakman for her research in the land transactions relating to Lyman Johnson.

100. Lee County Deeds, 14:611, Lyman and Mary A. Johnson to Hugh T. Reid, Jan. 13, 1854, microfilm no. 959,245, LDS Family History Library.

101. Rutland County Deeds, Reuben R. Throll and Enoch Smith to Lyman E. Johnson, Aug. 6, 1857, Book 15:331, microfilm no. 982,549, LDS Family History Library. The purchase price was $1,800.

102. Rutland County Deeds, Lyman E. Johnson and Mary A. Johnson to Andrew J. Lang, July 22, 1858, Book 15:338, microfilm no. 982,549, LDS Family History Library. The selling price was $1,634.28.

Mary gave birth to another daughter, Nettie, while in Vermont. Lyman ran for justice of the peace, or at least he appeared on the ballot but he had probably been recruited against his wishes and was not a serious candidate, since he only received three of 1,432 votes cast.[103]

They moved again in late 1858, this time to Prairie du Chien, Wisconsin, on the east side of the Mississippi River. Probably operating with limited funds by now, they managed to rent the one-and-a-half-story Prairie Hotel, built in 1835, and renovate it, without ownership changing hands. Of four hotels in town, it was the only one that didn't advertise in the local newspaper. The *Courier* reported the grand re-opening on November 10, 1858:

> This well known Hotel has recently been taken, fitted up, and refurbished by Mr. L. E. Johnson who has successfully prosecuted this line of business for many years. ... Previous to the recent change of proprietors, this fine hotel was favorably known to the traveling public as a public house of good accommodating capacity[,] and with a gentleman of kind and obliging manners we have no doubt but it will command an exclusive patronage. The house is to be formally "opened" this evening by an Oyster Supper Party, to which our citizens have been cordially invited by the Proprietor.[104]

Lyman may have liked the peace and quiet he would have found in Prairie du Chien, away from the bustle of the city or the increasing tensions between the northern and southern states in the run-up to the Civil War, just a few years off. But the nation's woes were not that far away, after all. The man who in three years would become president of the Confederate States of America, Jefferson Davis, had been stationed at nearby Fort Crawford in the 1830s. The year previous to the Johnsons' arrival, the town had been added

---

103. Speakman, "Lyman E. Johnson," 7-9.
104. "The Prairie Hotel," Prairie du Chien *Courier*, Nov. 10, 1858, 3.

to the railroad line to Milwaukee, which suddenly opened that part of the country to the rest of the world. This was only twenty-five years after the first steam-powered trains made their appearance on American tracks. Despite all of this, Prairie du Chien was not Chicago or New York, and Wisconsin was not Bleeding Kansas. It was restful, albeit with a promise of future visitors. The future looked promising for the one-time apostle.

Yet, the dream was not meant to be. On December 20, 1859, Lyman and a riding companion, perhaps a Christmas guest at the hotel, started across the frozen Mississippi River on a horse-drawn sled and hit a patch of thin ice, which cracked and broke beneath them. As they plunged into the depths of the river, their heavy coats and furs weighed them down. Lyman was unable to make it back to the surface, and his body was not recovered until March.[105] His wife, Mary, undeterred, took over the business and continued to run the hotel.[106]

To the end of Lyman's life, we can see evidence of an irrepressible spirit. He was independent-minded, unable to live under artificial constraints such as were beginning to be constructed by Joseph Smith. He had been drawn to the faith because of doubts about mainstream Christianity, and once the shield of faith in Mormonism had been pierced, he cast around for an alternative society that would allow him to put his undeniable talents to work, although now in pursuit of wealth and standing. He had decided he would enjoy the benefits of his own industry from then on, and it is unlikely that he

---

105. "Drowned," *Courier*, Dec. 22, 1859, 3; Mar. 8, 1860, 3. Apostle Matthias F. Cowley, speaking at the October 1901 general conference, reported "hearing President Lorenzo Snow say on more than one occasion how determined Lyman E. Johnson was to see an angel from the Lord. He plead[ed] with and teased the Lord to send an angel to him, until he saw an angel; but President Snow said that the trouble with him was that he saw an angel one day and saw the devil the next day, and finally the devil got away with him." Matthias F. Cowley, *Conference Report*, Oct. 1901, 18.

106. Speakman, "Lyman E. Johnson," 7.

would have followed the example of Luke Johnson and rejoined the church. Far from being dormant, his testimony had probably died.

What is touching about his story is the bond he felt with the other apostles, especially Amasa Lyman, Heber Kimball, Orson Pratt, and Brigham Young. Even in the face of institutional abuse, his ties to these men transcended their difficulties for a while. He and the other apostles had labored alongside each other in the trenches, and they continued to respect each other. We see the best and worst of the Restoration Movement personified in Lyman, with an abundance of faith, endurance, and selflessness on one hand and independence, commitment to truth over collegiality, and trust in one's own thinking on the other hand.

John Boynton

Like Lyman Johnson, John Boynton followed the Saints from Missouri to Illinois and Iowa Territory, probably being caught up in the migration alongside family and friends but finally breaking free to become a celebrated scientist and society mogul. Like Lyman, he was friendly with his former colleagues in the church. One story illuminates Boynton's willingness to help his former friends and tormentors. In early September 1842, he called on Joseph Smith in Nauvoo, and scribe William Clayton recorded that Joseph was "at home in company with John Boynton" until Sheriff James M. Pitman and two companions, all of whom were armed, came into the house looking for Smith. Clayton wrote: "John Boynton happened to be the first person discovered by the Sheriffs and they began to ask him where Mr Smith was. He answered that he saw him early in the morning; but did not say that he had seen him since. While this conversation was passing, president Joseph passed out at the back door and through the corn in his garden to brother Newel K. Whitney's."[107] The officials were unable to locate him.

---

107. Book of the Law of the Lord, Sept. 3, 1842, Andrew H. Hedges, Alex

Boynton's occupation was dentistry, and he traveled around to various small towns in Illinois, placing advance ads to notify people that he would be available on pre-determined days. An ad in the *Warsaw Signal* in 1841 promised "all the necessary operations for the preservation of the health and beauty of the Teeth." Tellingly, his ad reassured his potential patients that he was always governed by the "scientific principles of Dentistry" and that "Examinations of the Teeth and professional advice" would be given gratuitously.[108] Brigham Young mentioned in 1842 that Boynton was working as a dentist.[109] Writing about himself, Boynton remembered some forty years later that

> while visiting in Salem, Massachusetts in the thirties, I called on Dr. Peabody, who I think had just returned from England. He was the first dentist I had ever seen, and he kindly allowed me to examine his instruments, and witness his operations, saying he "thought I would make a skillful dentist." In a few days I returned to my native town, and assisted in the manufacture of a set of instruments. With these I operated for many years, and after I had obtained extensive sets of instruments would frequently return to the old ones, as they would apply in many cases better than the new ones that others had made. Between 1835 and 1850 I operated in nearly all the western and southern states.[110]

There is a glaring omission from Boynton's history in his

D. Smith, and Richard Lloyd Anderson, eds., *The Joseph Smith Papers: Journals* (Salt Lake City: Church Historian's Press, 2011), 2:124–25.

108. "Dr. J. F. Boynton, Surgeon Dentist," *Warsaw Signal*, Aug. 18, 1841, 3. Our thanks to Joseph Johnstun for providing this reference.

109. Brigham Young to Parley P. Pratt, July 17, 1842, LDS Church History Library.

110. Qtd. from an 1884 letter in John Farnham Boynton and Caroline Harriman Boynton, comps., *The Boynton Family: A Genealogy of the Descendants of William and John Boynton, Who Emigrated from Yorkshire, England, in 1638, and Settled at Rowley, Essex County, Massachusetts* (Groveland, MA: J. F. & C. H. Boynton, 1897), xx. It should be remembered that there were only twenty-eight states in 1850, and by "western" he would have meant Arkansas, Iowa, and Missouri.

avoidance of any mention of Mormonism. Although he initially maintained cordial relations with church leaders, he became more silent about this aspect of his past life as time wore on, leading to the unavoidable conclusion that he must have become embarrassed by his sojourn with the Mormons. At the very least, he apparently never again volunteered information about that time of his life. Maybe he became more skittish as church members in the West disclosed that they wanted to remain independent from the United States and openly live in polygamy.

After keeping close by, in Illinois and Iowa, John and Susan Boynton decided to move to Missouri, so John could attend the St. Louis Medical College, where he graduated in 1843, to become a traveling practitioner.[111] By the time their daughter, Tululah Josephine, was born in December 1845, the Boyntons were living in Syracuse, New York. Later they moved to Saco, Maine, but returned to Syracuse again in 1851 and remained there for the next thirty years.

As John took an increasing interest in science, he began inventing solutions to technological questions involving geology and chemistry. The hobby began occupying increasingly more of his time and brought him into contact with other inventors. Samuel Morse hired him to deliver public lectures regarding the telegraph. Boynton found that he enjoyed lecturing so much that he added it to his offerings in the towns where he provided medical and dental services. In 1849 he departed for California with dispatches for Commodore Thomas Jones, and along the way he stopped in Utah to see old friends. While there he showed off one of his inventions. Since Utah Mormons had yet to announce their belief in plural wives, Boynton probably felt comfortable enough socializing with them. Wilford Woodruff wrote that "Br Boynton had with him A model of A machine which he Had invented for cutting out soles for

---

111. Ibid., xxi.

making shoes which is A vary ingenious peace of work." Boynton was going to apply for a patent, Woodruff noted.[112] In spite of a lingering feeling of friendship, John showed no inclination to stay in Utah Territory. After he had returned from the west coast, Abigail Holmes talked with him about Mormonism, and he said it was "all a humbug from first to last."[113] He was apparently more interested in science now and more attentive to his family and day-to-day concerns than questions of religion. Susan gave birth to two sons in the early 1850s, Randolph Hamilton in February 1851 and John Willard in September 1853, but John Willard died the next year in July. It must have been difficult to see such a young child expire. It would not have been a cure for John's growing skepticism, in any case.

Through the 1850s, Boynton transformed himself into something of a renaissance man who would be mentioned in retrospect in the *National Cyclopedia of American Biography* for his lectures on "Geology and the Natural History of Creation," as well as for presentations on "various other scientific as well as medical subjects." A stimulus for his interest in geology was his discovery in the 1840s of a large copper vein on the shores of Lake Superior. He indulged in some speculation when he traveled to California in 1849. He was equally interested in the accounts he heard from the legendary explorer Kit Carson, with whom he became friends. As he began solving problems in mining and manufacturing, according to the encyclopedia, he hit on some useful inventions such as a chemically based fire extinguisher, a process for production of steel, and an improved type of cement. He patented his discoveries during the war that were intended to aid the north, including the "oil well torpedoes."[114]

---

112. Scott G. Kenney, ed., *Wilford Woodruff's Journal, 1833-1898,* 9 vols. (Midvale, UT: Signature Books, 1983-84), 3:425.

113. Abigail D. Holmes to James J. Strang, Oct. 6, 1850, James Jesse Strang Collection, Ms. 447, box 2, fd. 42, Beinecke Rare Book and Manuscript Library, Yale University, New Haven.

114. "Boynton, John F.," *The National Cyclopedia of American Biography* (New

It seems his favorite lecture topic was the relationship of geology to the biblical account of the Creation. The *New York Times* announced in 1853 that he would be lecturing on geology and creation at Metropolitan Hall and that he had "acquired a high reputation as a popular lecturer on scientific subjects, and has been successful in attracting and satisfying very large audiences wherever he has lectured."[115] His intellect and diversity of interests were highlighted in an article about the University of Rochester library, where Boynton was a benefactor. In one instance he donated "the proceeds of a lecture on Egypt" so they could purchase books on Egyptian topics.[116]

In June 1859, John and Susan had their fifth child, Susan Helen, and then the mother died less than two months later of complications from heart disease. It was just before her forty-third birthday. Around the same time, John's father passed away, possibly as early as 1858. Despite the grief and added responsibility of raising children as a widower, John continued traveling and lecturing, researching, and setting up a chemical firm in Utica. This may have been his way of sublimating his grief into more focus on work.[117] He spent six years juggling child-rearing, traveling, lecturing, and earning a living. Then he met Mary West Jenkins, whom he married in November 1865 at a high-society wedding in New York City. It was held at the Fifth Avenue Hotel and performed by the famous Reverend Henry Ward Beecher, after which the couple departed for their honeymoon in a hot air balloon. *Harper's Weekly* mentioned that Boynton's bride was less than half his age, he being fifty-four and she twenty-two. She nevertheless impressed the reporters with her education, having studied at Monticello Female Seminary in Illinois. She also

York: James T. White & Company, 1897), 6:91-92.

115. "Lectures on Geology," *New York Times*, Feb. 28, 1853.

116. Catherine D. Hayes, "The History of the University of Rochester Libraries," *University of Rochester Library Bulletin*, spring 1970, available at www.lib.rochester.edu.

117. *Syracuse Journal*, June 16, 1864, Onondaga Historical Society, Syracuse, New York.

"displayed great ability in drawing and music. She has a fresh and clear complexion, hazel eyes, and in figure is tall and commanding," the magazine explained. When the balloon lifted off from Central Park, there were 6,000 people on hand to observe the spectacle.[118]

The six-year interregnum between the death of his first wife and subsequent remarriage to Mary must have been long and difficult. One assumes that John hired domestic servants to help watch over and care for the children while he was away. It would be interesting to know if the youngsters traveled with him during school breaks. The strain of responsibility must have been lightened somewhat when he married a second time and his new wife assumed some of the duties involved in raising children, some of whom were approaching adulthood. The oldest was fourteen at the time of the marriage. For Mary, it might have been a strain to step into a ready-made family of four, judging from the fact that the marriage lasted four years and then John and Mary separated. She moved away and took a position teaching school but did not obtain a divorce until 1880.[119] After they separated, she filed suit against John in December 1879, accusing him of committing adultery with Rebecca Smith. Both John and Rebecca denied the charges. It was ruled that the charges were not established, and the complaint was dismissed.[120]

In 1872, John visited Utah Territory a second time, bringing his nephew Alma Helaman Hale with him.[121] They arrived on the evening of April 6 and called on President Brigham Young, who was under house arrest at the time. They met with apostles Orson Pratt, Erastus Snow, and other officials, all of whom "called him

---

118. "The Balloon Bridal," *Harper's Weekly*, Nov. 25, 1865, 746.

119. Supreme Judicial Court, May Term 1880, 36:222-23, Maine State Archives, Augusta.

120. "A Lady's Fair Name: Involved, in Proceedings for a Divorce," *Syracuse Daily Courier*, Jan. 21, 1881, 4.

121. Alma H. Hale journal, Apr. 6, 1872, LDS Church History Library. His parents were Jonathan and Olive Boynton Hale.

Brother John," the nephew noted with satisfaction.[122] It would be interesting to know if John still viewed them the same way or whether he was making an obligatory courtesy call without feeling any lasting attachment. They used to have common passions, but John no longer obsessed about theological issues.

Boynton's patents testify to the fact that he was a man of varied interests and talents and that he was able to successfully navigate the transition into a different realm of activities. His submissions for patents in Onondaga County, New York, from 1856 to 1870 showed that he had an imaginative but practical bent. His patents weren't daydreams but offered real-world solutions to actual problems, often small improvements on existing designs. He had already tested them. Some of the more interesting patents were for producing carbonic acid for soda fountains, a carburetor design for mixing gas and oxygen for city lights, salt evaporators, explosive devices for oil wells, improved methods of oil refining, recipes for industrial lubricants, production of oil-based roofing materials, a new type of telegraph insulation, ideas for steel production, improvements in steam generators, fire suppression devices, and lightning rods.[123] His status as a scientist was demonstrated in 1880 when he met with railroad magnates, inventors, and bankers at College Point on Long Island to witness the trial use of a synthetic fuel for steam locomotives.[124]

John took an interest in his family genealogy beginning about 1852, then more seriously in 1879 when his daughter Tululah began acting as his recorder.[125] When she died in 1880, this brought

---

122. Alma Hale wrote that when Boynton "visited Utah in 1872, he called on President Brigham Young twice, in my company," qtd. in Andrew Jenson, "The Twelve Apostles," *Historical Record*, Apr. 1886, 53. The article confuses his first name, giving it as Ariot.

123. "Onondaga County Patentees: July 1, 1790-June 30, 1875," www.rootsweb.ancestry.com.

124. "Water as a Fuel: An Experiment," *New York Times*, May 7, 1880, 8.

125. John Farnham Boynton, comp., *American Boynton Directory, 1638:*

an end to his "researches until the close of 1882" and his meeting of Caroline Foster Harriman, his brother-in-law's niece, whom he ended up marrying midwinter on January 20, 1883. She took an interest in his genealogical hobby and accompanied him to libraries to collect probate records, deeds, and pension rolls. In 1883 he began devoting significant resources to genealogical research and referred to himself as a "Genealogist and Historian of the Boynton Family, Secretary of American Boynton Association."[126]

In April 1884 John spoke to the Syracuse *Sunday Herald* about his genealogical travels and lifelong interests in minerals and the history of the earth's crust. He and renowned geologist Sir William Logan once traveled together on a research excursion to the south shore of Lake Superior, he explained, and then made their way through Wisconsin to Elgin, Illinois, where they were impressed by the watch factory, the condensed milk plant, and the "magnificent system of illumination" in downtown Elgin where seven towers supported bright lanterns that kept the streets lit.[127]

His interest in science made him skeptical about exaggerated claims to knowledge but not immune to the scams that were part of American cultural history in the nineteenth century. A celebrated American hoax involved the Cardiff Giant that was unearthed south of Syracuse in 1869. The artifact had been manufactured out of gypsum by New York cigar maker George Hull, whose interest was apparently in making money and challenging religious dogma about the peopling of the Americas. He buried the human-like form on

---

Containing the Address of All Known Boyntons … in the United States and British Dominions (Syracuse, NY: Smith and Bruce, 1884); Boynton and Boynton, *The Boynton Family.*

126. Boynton, *American Boynton Directory,* 5, 92. John's sister Clarissa married Henry Harriman, Caroline Harriman's uncle. She was born in 1843 and died in 1913.

127. "Dr. J. F. Boynton: Telling of His Six Weeks' Trip in the Western Country Hunting for Members of His Family," Syracuse *Sunday Herald,* Apr. 27, 1884, 8.

land near Binghamton, New York, and then stood back to watch the experts argue over whether it was a petrified man or an ancient statue. Almost immediately crowds began flocking in to view the discovery and eagerly paid an entrance fee. Hull eventually sold the item for $37,000 to a group of investors who moved it to Syracuse. Asked if it was a petrified man, Boynton said no and "showed conclusively that the alleged prehistoric man was a fake."[128] However, it was an authentic ancient statue, he said, that was "carved some 250 years before," probably "by a French Jesuit priest" who wanted "to awe the local Indians. 'The chin is magnificent and generous,'" clearly "the Napoleonic type," he said.[129]

An 1869 pamphlet on the topic quoted Boynton at greater length, identifying him as "a celebrated Geologist." He repeated his theory that the "American Goliath" was crafted a hundred years or earlier to "impress inferior minds or races" of the superiority of caucasians after their invasion, "and for this purpose only was sculptured of colossal dimensions." He recommended that it be preserved by the Onondaga Historical Society as "one of the greatest curiosities of the early history of Onondaga County."[130]

Boynton was also connected, at least in print, to a famous forty-day fast undertaken by New York physician Henry Tanner, who wanted to prove that Jesus could have fasted that long, as the Bible says. The experiment has been largely forgotten, but at the time it was a national *cause célèbre*. Mark Twain was among the commentators who followed it closely. It took place in Clarendon, New York, about twenty-five miles west of Rochester, in rooms set aside for that purpose in the city hall. Tanner soon lost his commitment to going without water but went the distance without

128. Dr. John Farnham Boynton: Death of an Old and Remarkable Resident of Syracuse," *Syracuse Standard*, Oct. 21, 1890, 6.

129. Stephen W. Sears, "The Giant in the Earth," *American Heritage*, Aug. 1975, 98.

130. John F. Boynton to Henry Morton, Oct. 18, 1869, qtd. in *The American Goliah: A Wonderful Geological Discovery* (Syracuse: Redington and Howe), 1869, 4-6.

food, losing a total of about forty pounds, or a pound a day. Several reports claimed that Boynton stood by Tanner's side and provided the news media with "daily bulletins," or even that Boynton joined in the fast for a short time. Boynton was probably an observer like many others who offered support but were not directly involved. He was not mentioned in a book-length treatment of the experiment, in any case.[131]

No doubt, Boynton wove details of the experiment into his lectures. He had become a naturalist, and like other scientists of his day, he may have retained a core belief in the New Testament as a guide for living, thinking that Tanner had vindicated the biblical narrative about Jesus. In any case, he delivered a total of more than 4,000 lectures during his lifetime, introducing people to empiricism and reason. With the perspective of time, looking at his involvement in New York society, his participation in civic events, his family activities, and his scientific research, we can see that in many ways he lived a charmed life, even with the heartbreak of family losses and various setbacks. Ten years after observing and possibly commenting on the forty-day fast, he died in his home across from Highland Park in Syracuse. It was October 20, 1890, one month after he turned seventy-nine and a month after the Utah church announced its intent to discontinue plural marriage. Boynton was buried in Woodlawn Cemetery.

A colleague paid high tribute to his memory:

John F. Boynton breathed the atmosphere of investigation. Nothing escaped his attention. Born a great man, his restless spirit led him into every field of science, art and letters. He relied upon evidence, on demonstration, upon experience. He endeavored to examine only that which was capable of being examined. He had a brain full of the dawn, the head of a philosopher, and his inventive

---

131. "American Obituaries," *Appletons' Annual Cyclopaedia* (New York: D. Appleton and Company, 1891), 636; Robert A. Gunn, M. D., *Forty Days without Food! A Biography of Henry S. Tanner M. D* (New York: Albert Metz & Co., 1880).

genius led him into every field of scientific study. His attention was
forever turned toward things that were to benefit his fellow men.[132]

Printed obituaries similarly mentioned Boynton's divergent
interests, but all of them kept a deafening silence on his five-year
association as a missionary and service as one of the original apostles
of the Restoration. By the time of his death, few would probably
have remembered that he had ever traveled physically or spiritually
with the Latter Day Saints. Etched on the marker for his and Caroline's headstones are quotes from English poet Philip James Bailey
(1816-1902): "He most lives who thinks most, feels the noblest, acts
the best" and "A better heart God never saved in heaven."

The Syracuse *Evening Herald* announced Boynton's passing on
the front page of its October 20 edition, adding that the "city of
Syracuse lost, not only one of its oldest residents, but one of the
most remarkable men who ever lived in it."[133] The next day the
Syracuse Standard described the deceased as a man whose "figure
was commanding, his character of marked individuality, his mind
powerful, unique and inventive." It added that he was, for a short
time, president of *Father Columbia* newspaper in New York City,
and that he more recently attended weekly lectures at the Onondaga County Farmers' Club.[134]

Due to his medical training, he was able to diagnose his own
ailment as a ruptured blood vessel in his chest. He predicted that
he would die, sat down, and wrote a letter to Caroline, who was
visiting her cousin in Massachusetts, then collapsed. The Syracuse
obituaries reported from the family's biographical information that
he married Susan Lowell in Saco, Maine—not in Kirtland, Ohio,

---

132. "John Farnham Boynton: Tribute to His Memory by F. M. Terry," in
Boynton and Boynton, *The Boynton Family*, xxxii.
133. "John Farnham Boynton: Death of This Brilliant and Versatile Man,"
Evening Herald, Oct. 20, 1890, 1.
134. "Dr. John Farnham Boynton: Death," 6.

on January 20, 1836, in a ceremony conducted by Joseph Smith.[135] The *Syracuse Standard* said he studied at Columbia school in New York City and then went to medical school in St. Louis, skipping his religious interval.

The *Daily Standard* wrote that he was able to sell a patent for as much as $15,000. Far from being "depressed at the thought of death," the *Evening Herald* added, he was excited about the prospect of showing "his characteristic zeal in the cause of science," expressing "willingness to have his body examined before the students of the Medical college to determine the cause of death."[136] Although some of what was reported was probably overstated, his inventions having been of passing utility more than permanent impact, for instance, it is clear that he was the best educated and most intellectually gifted of any of the men who constituted the first Quorum of Twelve Apostles.

In the 1830s, Boynton began to see a logical deduction about religious truth. One of the attractions for men with his bent of mind when they encountered the doctrines of the Restoration was that, unlike ancient creeds founded in superstitious assumptions, the new movement was based entirely on a rational approach to faith. "The glory of God is intelligence," one of the early revelations declared (D&C 93:36). Joseph Smith preached that the Bible should be interpreted in a way that makes sense, although with the help of modern prophetic insight, and Boynton responded well to that message. At first, he was completely dedicated to Joseph Smith. The blond-haired farm boy who spoke with angels met Boynton's perceived expectation of what a prophet should be—that is, until Joseph asked him to be obedient to guidelines in conflict with his rational understanding. At that, John found the need to look elsewhere for enlightenment and found it in science.

---

135. Dean C. Jessee, Mark Ashurst-McGee, and Richard L. Jensen, eds., *The Joseph Smith Papers: Journals* (Salt Lake City: Church Historian's Press, 2008), 1:165.

136. "John Farnham Boynton: Brilliant," 1.

10. FROM PRAIRIE TO DESERT

Reflecting the waning days of the church in Ohio, Joseph Smith could not have escaped being incarcerated without the help he received from recently excommunicated apostle Luke Johnson. As the "new year dawned upon the Church in Kirtland in all the bitterness of the spirit of apostate mobocracy," Joseph wrote in explaining the circumstances, "Elder Rigdon and myself were obliged to flee from its deadly influence."[1] Then the constable, an avowed dissenter and fallen member of the Quorum of the Twelve Apostles, came to the rescue.

Explaining it from his own perspective, Johnson wrote:

I learned that Sheriff [Abel] Kimball was about to arrest Joseph Smith, on a charge of illegal banking, and knowing that it would cost him an expensive lawsuit, and perhaps end in imprisonment, I went to the French farm, where [Joseph] then resided, and arrested him on an execution for his person, in the absence of property to pay a judgment of $50, which I had in my possession at the time, which prevented Kimball from arresting him. Joseph settled the execution, and thanked me for my interference.[2]

---

1. Joseph Smith Jr., et al., *History of the Church of Jesus Christ of Latter-day Saints*, 2nd ed. rev., ed. B. H. Roberts, 7 vols. (1902-32; Salt Lake City: Deseret Book, 1959), 3:1. Manuscript History of the Church, B-1:780, written by Willard Richards in Feb. 1844, LDS Church History Library, Salt Lake City.

2. "History of Luke Johnson (By Himself)," *Deseret News*, May 26, 1858, 57; Marvin S. Hill, C. Keith Rooker, and Larry T. Wimmer, "The Kirtland Economy Revisited," *BYU Studies* 17, no. 4 (Spring 1977): 414-30.

Luke Johnson

Luke's story, following his ouster from the quorum, initially mirrored that of his brothers, but it took an abrupt turn in 1846 when he did the unexpected and joined the westward-wending Saints in Nebraska. After his rehabilitation, he left some personal thoughts in a brief history, intent on convincing readers of his penitence. As such, this narrative omits details of his life for the eight-year gap when he was not a church-goer. He included only stories that showed his willingness during that time to still help out Saints in danger. Even so, the significance of his good will cannot be overstated. Like others of the apostles, his feelings may have been ambivalent but they were not hostile. His next good turn for the Smith family, after helping Joseph and Sidney escape, occured the very next day, January 13, 1838,[3] when he helped Joseph Sr. leave a room where he was held captive, with assistance from John Boynton and Hyrum Smith.

Father Smith had performed a marriage without civil authorization, according to his wife, Lucy. "Luke Johnson, an apostate," was sent to arrest him, but afterward Johnson "bustled about, pretending to be very much engaged in preparing [documents] for the money, and making other arrangements, such as were required of him by the party to which he belonged." In fact, he stalled for time while "get[ting] the window out" where her husband was held. "By the help of Hyrum [Smith] and John Boynton," she wrote, her husband "escaped from the window."[4]

Luke added details:

The court not being ready to attend to the case, I put [Joseph Sr.]

---

3. Johnson reminisced that he "told John F. Boynton, to go and assist Father Smith out of the window. Hyrum got out first, then he and Boynton assisted the old man out." "History of Luke Johnson," 57; cf. Eliza R. Snow Smith, *Biography and Family Record of Lorenzo Snow* (Salt Lake City: Deseret News, 1884), 24.

4. Lavina Fielding Anderson, ed., *Lucy's Book: A Critical Edition of Lucy Mack Smith's Family Memoir* (Salt Lake City: Signature Books, 2001), 616-18.

in a small room adjoining the entrance from the office. I also allowed his son Hyrum to accompany him. I took a nail out from over the window sash, left the room and locked the door, and commenced telling stories in the court room, to raise a laugh, for I was afraid they would hear Father Smith getting out of the window; when the court called for the prisoner, I stepped into the room in the dark and slipped the nail into its place in the window, and went back and told the court that the prisoner had made his escape. [John] White and others rushed into the room, and examined the fastenings and found them all secure, which created much surprise how the prisoner had got out.[5]

At the same time he was helping the Smith family, Luke Johnson was aiding the dissenters in their criticism of Joseph Jr. on theological and administrative grounds. It might be thought that Johnson ran from one position to another and back again, but it is more likely that he retained loyalty to the principles he had been taught in the church and felt had been violated by the prophet. From his point of view, the church had wandered afield and needed guidance, but not a revolution. He seems to have been convinced that Joseph was a fallen leader who had mismanaged church funds and altered revelations in Kirtland. This is not to say that Johnson was possessed of blood lust, because far from it, he detested violence, persecution, and in this case a frivolous lawsuit. Remembering that the Johnson family had close ties to the Smiths in Ohio, Luke must have seen himself as coming to the rescue of old friends, including Joseph's wife and children who were especially vulnerable in the middle of winter, rather than that he was rendering any service to the church.

The Kirtland separatists seized the temple and printing office. In court, the printing office was transferred to Grandison Newel as part of a "judgement ... against the Presidents" in Kirtland, wrote

---

5. "History of Luke Johnson," 57.

Hepsy Richards to her brother Levi. The press building was "nailed up and kept guarded every night," she explained, and only "John Johnson has the key. Luke Johnson [is the] Constable."[6] Despite the precautions taken, the defenders of these symbols of church ownership who were loyal to Joseph Smith set the printing building on fire in the early morning of January 16. The loyalists were intent on preventing the dissenters from publishing their own views or giving the appearance that they, not those who had left for Missouri, represented the status quo. The dissidents resorted to circular letters. One written on February 5 by Warren Parrish and endorsed by Luke contained a statement of facts according to his best recollection. Another letter penned on March 18 by John Boynton was witnessed by Luke.

Then Luke disappeared into the fog of history for eight years. Instead of joining the other dissenters who were traveling west or remaining in Kirtland, he went the other direction, traveling east to what is now West Virginia where his wife Susan's relatives lived. "From this time up to the death of Joseph Smith," he later explained in an autobiographical sketch, "I spent my time in teaching school in Cabal [Cabell] Co., Virginia, for about a year, devoting my leisure time in reading works on medicine." Even when he was drawn back to Ohio, it was not to join the diaspora in the Kirtland area. What attracted him, besides the presence of family in the state, was a medical school in Cincinnati, about 250 miles southwest of Kirtland where he was able to study the "botanical" approach to medicine under a professor whose surname, Curtis, is the only thing known about him. Johnson received a certificate to vouch for his time spent studying medicine and then returned to Kirtland, where he mostly "engaged in various [other] occupations to enable me to

---

6. Hepzibah Richards to "Dear Brother" [Levi Richards], Jan. 10, 1836 [correct year 1838], Papers of the Philip Blair Family, Manuscripts Division, J. Willard Marriott Library, University of Utah, Salt Lake City.

obtain a living," he wrote, significantly adding that he "did not officiate in any religious duties."[7]

In early 1846, Luke determined to travel to Nauvoo to rejoin
the church, as he was still deeply attached to the movement. On
Sunday, March 8, 1846, he was rebaptized by his brother-in-law,
apostle Orson Hyde. Willard Richards, traveling with the refugees
who had fled Nauvoo and were camped at Indian Creek, recorded
that "Alexander Merill arived from Nauvoo & stated that Luke
Johnson made a publick confession to the church at Nauvoo yesterday & wanted to be united with them again."[8] On March 10, Hyde
wrote to Brigham Young and confirmed that Johnson had been
rebaptized and would start the next day for Kirtland to retrieve his
family so he could take them back to Illinois. Hyde included an
incident involving Johnson and John E. Page, who had replaced
Johnson in the Twelve. The latter "called on Page a few days ago,"
Hyde wrote, "and Page did not know him." "You are my successor
in office," Johnson explained, saying he had "come to call you to
an account for your stewardship." What Johnson did not know was
that Page had been expelled from the quorum the previous month.
Page "colored up and hung his head. Thus was an innocent joke
converted into the most cutting truth by unknown circumstances."[9] Whether the news was all that "cutting" or not, there was

---

7. "History of Luke Johnson," 57. Cabell County was originally in Virginia
but became part of West Virginia when that state was created in 1863.

8. Willard Richards journal, Mar. 9, 1846, LDS Church History Library.
Richards's journal was a source for the Manuscript History of Brigham Young,
but the quoted portion was omitted; cf. "History of Brigham Young," Mar. 9,
1846, LDS Church History Library.

9. Orson Hyde to "Dear Brethren," Mar. 10, 1846, Brigham Young Collec-
tion, LDS Church History Library, with quotation marks added and a crossed-
out word retained for clarity. Page was removed from the Quorum of Twelve on
February 9. Johnson left on March 13 to retrieve his family, according to Eliza
Snow. Maureen Ursenbach Beecher, ed., *The Personal Writings of Eliza Roxcy Snow*
(Logan: Utah State University Press, 2000), 120. Orson Hyde, who had been
placed over Nauvoo, debated Page on March 3 over the rightful successor to
Joseph Smith. Page had sided with James J. Strang. Benjamin E. Park and Robin

more to come when Page, after being removed from the quorum, was excommunicated from the church.

Johnson's decision to fellowship with the majority of the apostles appears to have been genuine and deeply grounded, aided by having a brother-in-law, Hyde, who understood what it was like to leave the church and be readmitted. Luke gave full allegiance to Brigham Young. The timing was inconvenient because the members were strung out across Iowa. Brigham was fending off other claimants to lead the remnants of Joseph's church. The instability was in stark contrast to the order Johnson had achieved in his own personal family life. He had been practicing medicine and pursuing other business interests while he and Susan continued to have children, ranging in age from two to twelve at this point. Just as he was beginning to enjoy a life that was free from the interruptions of mission assignments and factional squabbles, he threw aside the comfort of Ohio and set out with his large family for the bluffs overlooking the Missouri River where Omaha is now located. It was September 1846. He would soon discover just how difficult the challenge was that lay before him.

Before they even reached Council Bluffs, and as incomprehensible as it must have been to Luke, his wife contracted some disease and died. Susan was buried in St. Joseph, Missouri. With six children, Luke could do little more than continue on alone, reaching Nebraska Territory on the evening of December 12.[10] A man with children was expected to remarry as soon as possible, and accordingly Luke wasted little time connecting with twenty-three-year-old America Morgan Clark and marrying her on March 3, 1847. They

---

Scott Jensen, "Debating Succession, March 1846: John E. Page, Orson Hyde, and the Trajectories of Joseph Smith's Legacy," *Journal of Mormon History* 39 (Winter 2013): 181–205; William Shepard, "Shadows on the Sun Dial: John E. Page and the Strangites," *Dialogue: A Journal of Mormon Thought* 41 (Spring 2008): 40–41.

10. Will Bagley, ed., *The Pioneer Camp of the Saints: The 1846 and 1847 Mormon Trial Journals of Thomas Bullock* (Spokane: Arthur H. Clark, 1997), 106. Susan had given birth to seven children and lost one.

would have another eight children themselves, nearly doubling the size of the family.[11] A month after his wedding, Luke was called to be part of the vanguard pioneer company that was leaving to explore the Rocky Mountains. He was trusted enough to be named a captain of ten in the wagon train that rolled out of Omaha on April 7, personally led by Brigham Young.

It turned out that Luke's training in dentistry proved useful as he was able to extract infected teeth from men who were, incredibly, a thousand miles from civilization. We know he became adept at killing buffalo too, as well as rattlesnakes. In the evenings, the camp engaged in music and drama, and Johnson participated in the camp frolics, including, as William Clayton recorded on May 22, a mock trial of James Davenport "for blockading the highway and turning ladies out of their course." Johnson served as prosecuting attorney and an Elder Whipple represented the defense. "We have many such trials in the camp which are amusing enough and tend among other things to pass away the time cheerfully during leisure moments," Clayton wrote in his journal.[12]

Luke was among nine men who stopped short of traveling all the way to the Great Basin so they could establish a ferry across the North Platte River near what is now Casper, Wyoming.[13] It was

---

11. Born in Council Bluffs, Pottawattamie County, Iowa: Susan Marinda, August 9, 1848; Orson Albert, February 14, 1850; Mark Anthony, November 10, 1851; and Charlotte Elizabeth, January 13, 1853. Family Group Record prepared by John and Carol Cluff, copy in our possession.

12. *William Clayton's Journal: A Daily Record of the Journey of the Original Company of "Mormon" Pioneers from Nauvoo, Illinois, to the Valley of the Great Salt Lake* (Salt Lake City: Deseret News and Clayton Family Association, 1921), 176; George D. Smith, ed., *An Intimate Chronicle: The Journals of William Clayton* (Salt Lake City: Signature Books, 1991), 320. The accused, James Davenport, was a forty-five-year-old convert from Vermont and no apparent relationship to George Davenport. However, the fact that Return Jackson Redden was asked to serve as the mock judge, with the added hilarity of him frequently interrogating "Mr. Davenport," gives the show a slightly sinister cast.

13. Scott G. Kenney, ed., *Wilford Woodruff's Journal, 1833–1898*, typescript, 9 vols. (Midvale, UT: Signature Books, 1983–85), 3:207–8; Bagley, *Pioneer Camp*

no small endeavor, and it meant that he would not be able to build a cabin or plant crops in the Salt Lake Valley in anticipation of his family joining him there. Months later he was still at the ferry when the pioneers returned in September on their way back to Nebraska. Johnson joined them going east. Wilford Woodruff said that one night Johnson "came near being killed by a herd of Buffalo" when "a large herd came upon" him "suddenly & he was caught in the midst of thems & could not get out." The herd was so large, it took about fifteen minutes to pass. "The ownly way He kept them from treading on him was by hollowing [hollering] & striking & punching them with his cane ... as they came along" on either side. By diverting them in this way, "they would open Just wide enough for him to stand as they passed along."[14] He arrived home at Winter Quarters, Nebraska, on October 31, 1847, pleased to be reunited with his large family.

The Council of the Twelve approved Luke's re-ordination to the office of elder on December 6 in Kanesville, Iowa, then discussed re-installing him into the Quorum of Twelve Apostles in another meeting toward the end of the month.[15] But when replacements were chosen on February 12, 1848, for the vacancies created by the appointment of three apostles to the First Presidency and to fill a vacancy left by Lyman Wight's defection in Texas, they were Charles C. Rich, Lorenzo Snow, Erastus Snow, and Franklin D. Richards. Luke would not hold another prominent position in the church or be connected to the LDS hierarchy in the future despite being called one of the "four principal Elders" by Arthur Conan

---

of the Saints, 194n65. While ferrying he also performed more dentistry and was paid "$3.00 for cleaning teeth & Doctoring" which was put into the general fund. William H. Empey journal, July 8, 1847, cited in Richard L. Saunders, ed., *Dale Morgan on the Mormons: Collected Works, Part 1, 1939-1951* (Norman, OK: Arthur H. Clark, 2012), 302

14. Kenney, *Wilford Woodruff's Journal,* 3:284.

15. Quorum of Twelve Minutes, Dec. 6, 25, 1847, typescript, Leonard J. Arrington Papers, Special Collections, Merrill-Cazier Library, Utah State University, Logan.

Doyle in his Sherlock Holmes story, *A Study in Scarlet*. The book was published in 1887 and had to do with the Utah period, portraying the foremost elders as white slave traders who abducted women into seedy polygamous relationships, so Johnson would have felt more resentment than flattery over the misidentification.[16]

When he turned forty-five in 1853, Johnson was still living in Council Bluffs, Iowa. He may have been asked to help other emigrating Saints prepare for the trek west. His reaction to being passed over for the Quorum of Twelve Apostles is not known. Finally in early June, he and America and their combined ten children, ranging from five months to nineteen years old, left for the Salt Lake Valley, arriving in September. Initially they settled in West Jordan, where Luke, because of his medical training, became known as "Dr. Johnson."

The next spring on May 22, 1854, Luke and neighbor Nephi Loveless became enmeshed in legal trouble after adopting a stray spotted pony that John M. Montgomery claimed was his. The pony was probably a pinto or Appaloosa, one of the preferred breeds among Native Americans, and assumed to have been abandoned.[17] Not wanting to give it up, Johnson and Loveless proceeded to county court with Orson Hyde as their attorney, who squared off against future apostle Albert Carrington representing the plaintiff. County probate judge Elias Smith ruled that the pony should be delivered to Montgomery. Failure to do so would result in John having to pay $75 and court costs of $18.50.[18]

---

16. Although Conan Doyle does not mention Luke specifically, he refers to a "Johnston," whom one Doyle expert has identified as Luke. Leslie S. Klinger, ed., *The New Annotated Sherlock Holmes: The Novels* (New York: W. W. Norton, 2005), 139n212.

17. *John M. Montgomery vs. Luke Johnson and Nephi Loveless*, Salt Lake County Probate Court, Civil and Criminal Case Files, Microfilm Series 373, reel 2, box 2, fd. 30, Utah State Archives, Salt Lake City.

18. Salt Lake County Probate Court, Civil and Criminal Case Docket Books, Microfilm Series 3944, Reel 3, Docket A-1, 1852-1860, p. 179, Salt Lake City.

It is hard to interpret what happened next, but apparently Hyde counseled his clients to keep the horse and pay the fine, which Carrington thought was "a miserably mean proceeding." He was speechless over "the utter meanness of Johnson." Hyde even solicited help from Pratt's family, asking them to cover half the court costs even though they "had no more to do with it than the man in the moon," Carrington complained.[19] There are no other sources, outside of Carrington's notes, to explain what may have really happened, but "meanness" suggests how high the emotions ran and what a personal turn the case took.

In the fall of 1855, the Johnsons built a home fifty miles southwest of Salt Lake City in Rush Valley, located at the southern end of what is now Tooele County on the other side of the Oquirrh Ridge from the Salt Lake Valley. A few other families settled in the same area and began calling it Johnson's Settlement. They built a fort for protection, which became known as Johnson's Fort.[20] The valley was used mostly for pasturing cattle. Wilford Woodruff arranged to have people lend their cattle to a common herd and charged them for the privilege of having their livestock winter in that area. He received grazing rights from the legislature, along with partners Samuel Bennion, James W. Cummings, William A. Hickman, Jesse C. Little, Claudius V. Spencer, and Brigham Young.[21] While Luke helped with the herd, America added two sons and two daughters to their family.[22] Although Luke is often referred to as a bishop,

19. Albert Carrington, "Albert Carrington's Memorandum Book, Law Business, Mineralogy, Geology & Recipes," 1854, photograph, Albert Carrington Papers, Manuscripts Division, J. Willard Marriott Library, University of Utah, Salt Lake City.

20. Kenney, *Wilford Woodruff's Journal*, 4:430–31; 5:252.

21. Thomas G. Alexander, *Things in Heaven and Earth: The Life and Times of Wilford Woodruff, a Mormon Prophet* (Salt Lake City: Signature Books, 1991), 162.

22. The children were John Joseph, born January 11, 1855; Lavina Ann, November 8, 1856; Phebe W., May 5, 1858; and Luke, April 10, 1861. Family Group Record prepared by John and Carol Cluff, copy in our possession.

Woodruff organized the settlement and appointed Luke as "president" of the local branch.[23]

Luke did some farming as well as ranching, assisted in the latter endeavor by the notorious rifleman William, or Bill, Hickman. Over time the Johnson and Hickman families became close enough that "Wild Bill" asked for the hand of Luke's seventeen-year-old daughter, Sarah Eliza, and married her on March 28, 1856, as the outlaw's seventh wife. Soon enough, however, Bill's violent past caught up with him; he was "disfellowshipped" (in this case, excommunicated from the church) and most of his wives left him.[24] Sarah Eliza married a man named Frank Moreno. Her new husband did his best to shelter her and her children from her violent husband, but he ended up being killed by a shotgun blast. Rumor was that he was killed by Hickman, but the gunslinger swore he did not do it.[25]

Johnson became a manager of the Rush Valley herd in mid-1858. The cattle company assigned Claudius Spencer to oversee operations in the northern part of the valley and Johnson to oversee the southern half.[26] The next year, Luke was appointed probate judge for the short-lived county of Shambip, an Indian name meaning marshland reeds.[27] Confirming the wild nature of the West at that time, Luke's son James was involved in a gunfight on May 26, 1859. He and Deloss Gibson began to fight in a bar and then stepped outside where James tried to extricate himself from the scuffle and walk away, but Deloss pulled a revolver and shot

---

23. Kenney, *Wilford Woodruff's Journal*, 4:431.

24. [John H. Beadle, ed.,] *Brigham's Destroying Angel: Being the Life, Confession, and Startling Disclosures of the Notorious Bill Hickman* (New York: Geo. A. Crofutt, 1872), 171-72, 183, 194-95.

25. Ibid., 187-89, 218.

26. Kenney, *Wilford Woodruff's Journal*, 5:219.

27. Ibid., 5:273. Shambip County was created in 1856 with a population of less than two hundred and was absorbed back into Tooele County in 1862. John W. Van Cott, *Utah Place Names: A Comprehensive Guide to the Origins of Geographic Names* (Salt Lake City: University of Utah Press, 1990), 84, 336.

him. James struggled for a few hours and died the next day. At the inquest, Myron Brewer, a witness to the shooting, reported that James was "shot on Thursday evening about 10 O'clock in front of the Empire Saloon" in Salt Lake City.[28]

His father was heartbroken and could barely function. Elder Woodruff recorded that "Brother Luke Johnson arived at about dark having rode some 75 miles" and was physically and emotionally spent—"thoroughly used up," as Woodruff said. James was buried in Orson Hyde's lot. The next day, Wilford Jr. drove Luke home to Rush Valley.[29] Deloss Gibson was indicted, escaped from jail, and was captured after a $300 reward was posted for his return. At the trial, he avoided the death penalty by being sentenced to ten years of hard labor.[30]

It is unknown if Luke attended the trial or if he avoided the emotional drain from seeing the killer tried. In any case, his son's death was devastating to him. For the next two years, he struggled with one illness after another until he acquired his final affliction in July 1861. While his health deteriorated, he stayed at Orson Hyde's home in Salt Lake City and died on December 9 at the age of fifty-four.[31] The Church Historian's Office Journal recorded that he died at 12:30 a.m., after having "lived to the truth to the best of his ability" since his return to the church and that he "died in the faith."[32] His wife, America, lived another thirty-nine years and was buried in Ogden.

---

28. Inquest on the Body of James Johnson, May 27, 1859, Coroner's Records, Salt Lake County, 1858-81, microfilm number 485,535, LDS Family History Library. Our thanks to Elaine Speakman for calling this to our attention.

29. Kenney, *Wilford Woodruff's Journal*, 5:338-40.

30. *Deseret News*, June 1, July 27, Aug. 17, 1859; *The Mountaineer*, Oct. 6, 1860.

31. Kenney, *Wilford Woodruff's Journal*, 5:587. The modern grave marker in the Salt Lake City Cemetery has his death as December 6, which is wrong. Four children of Luke and America Johnson are buried in the St. John Cemetery in Rush Valley.

32. Church Historian's Office Journal, 26:11, Dec. 9, 1861, LDS Church History Library.

This son of a well-to-do farming couple would have remained in Ohio if fate had not brought Joseph Smith and Sidney Rigdon into his life when he was twenty-four. He ardently believed the Mormon gospel. Leaving his comfortable home and loving family, he traded everything he had for a peripatetic life of scorn and ridicule as he introduced the new faith into regions where it had never been heard of before. Like his brother Lyman, he was dedicated, courageous, and fully committed through 1836. He preached, counseled, healed, and ministered to the rapidly evolving church.

Unlike his brother Lyman, whose belief apparently died in him, Luke's testament burned on even through his apostasy. In later years, he exhibited the same devotion he had manifested in his earlier ones. In between these two periods of loyalty to the church, his commitment began waning in early 1837. To his credit, he took the higher path and refused to burn any bridges with former colleagues, demonstrating such strength of character that it gives us an idea of what elevated him to a position of trust in the first place. He helped Joseph Smith and Sidney Rigdon and then Joseph Sr. escape antagonists who wanted to harm them, then he endorsed the complaints enumerated by Warren Parish and John Boynton as a matter of principle to him.

By not having severed ties, he was still susceptible to their effects. After being rebaptized in 1846, he demonstrated a renewed sense of purpose, dedicating the rest of his life to the church, absorbing the discouragement of not being renamed to the apostleship, and proving to be an asset in less conspicuous ways. He carried out local church assignments and worked hard as a farmer and rancher to support his family. He worked for respected partners like Wilford Woodruff and got along with the notorious Bill Hickman. He died with all his church blessings intact, having been loyal for two-thirds of the time since his conversion in 1831, taking a vacation from church in between.

Thomas B. Marsh

As president of the quorum, Thomas Marsh was older than all but one of the other men who filled the quorum's ranks, and that being the case, he was also married and had children, which further set him apart from the others. There were other ways in which he was different, since he spent most of the 1830s in Missouri, away from the internal discord that characterized Kirtland in the second half of the decade. Like the others, however, he had walked hundreds of miles without purse or scrip and had endured the same persecution. He took seriously his role as the quorum leader and the one primarily responsible for spreading the gospel around the world.

It is ironic that in spite of his service to the church, the negative response to his apostasy was greater than for Oliver Cowdery, Lyman Johnson, William McLellin, David and John Whitmer, or other once prominent Mormons at Far West. The October 24, 1838, affidavits of Thomas Marsh and Orson Hyde in Richmond, Missouri, had a devastating effect on Joseph Smith and the church. According to historian Stephen LeSueur, "The affidavits, which Marsh wrote and they both signed, detailed the Mormon military operations in Daviess County, confirmed the existence and activities of the Danite band, and told of the threats against dissenters and others who refused to take up arms in the conflict." Marsh's accusations included an electrifying statement :

> The plan of said Smith, the prophet, is to take this State, and he professes to his people to intend taking the United States, and ultimately the whole world. This is the belief of the church, and my own opinion of the prophet's plans and intentions. ... I have heard the prophet say that he should yet tread down his enemies and walk over their dead bodies; that if he was not let alone he would be a second Mahomet to this generation, and that he would make it one gore of blood from the Rocky Mountains to the Atlantic Ocean.

LeSueur said the affidavits contributed to "near panic" among area "gentiles" as they believed a Mormon attack was imminent.[33] Historian Leland H. Gentry said Marṣh and Hyde's testimony "cannot be overstated" as "it fastened in the public mind concepts already placed here by lies and exaggerations."[34] The directness of Marsh's published accusations convinced many Mormons to believe they were what persuaded Governor Boggs to issue his "exterminating order" and usher in the forced exodus from Missouri. Wilford Woodruff labled the affidavits "high handed wickedness" that "jepordized the church by bearing false witness against the presidency & the church before authorities of the state of Missouri which was the leading cause of the Governor calling out thirty thousand of the Militia against the Church."[35]

It is little wonder Joseph Smith would write from Liberty Jail on December 16, 1838, "Marsh & Hyde whose hearts are full of corruption, whose cloak of hypocrisy was not sufficient to shield them or to hold them up in the hour of trouble, who after having escaped the pollutions of the world through the knowledge of God and become again entangled and overcome[,] the latter end is worse than the first."[36] Seventeen years later, church historian George A. Smith expressed his feelings about Marsh's action. "He went before

---

33. Stephen C. LeSueur, *The 1838 Mormon War in Missouri* (Columbia: University of Missouri Press, 1987), 135-37.

34. Leland H. Gentry and Todd Compton, *Fire and Sword: A History of the Latter-day Saints in Northern Missouri, 1836-39* (Salt Lake City: Greg Kofford Books, 2011), 290.

35. Kenney, *Wilford Woodruff's Journal*, 1:340. Regarding Woodruff's assessment, historian Marvin Hill explained: "Actually, there is no evidence that the testimony of the two apostles before Justice Henry Jacobs on the 24th had any influence on Boggs. Boggs's letter to General Clark on the 26th demonstrated that it was the Danite raids on Gallatin and Millport that caused him to call out the militia. It is also evident that the extermination order on the following day came in the wake of reports that the elders had attacked Bogart. Military retaliation by the Mormons, not apostolic testimony, had once and for all turned Missouri state officials against the Saints." Marvin S. Hill, *Quest for Refuge: The Mormon Flight from American Pluralism* (Salt Lake City: Signature Books, 1989), 96.

36. Joseph Smith to the church in Caldwell County, Dec. 16, 1838, qtd. in Dean C. Jessee, comp and ed., *Personal Writings of Joseph Smith* (Salt Lake City, Deseret Book, 2002), 421.

a magistrate and swore that the 'Mormons' were hostile towards the State of Missouri. That affidavit brought from the government of Missouri an exterminating order, which drove some 15,000 Saints from their homes and habitations, and some thousands perished through suffering the exposure consequent on this state of affairs."[37]

Unlike Orson Hyde who rejoined the Mormons within a year, Marsh remained aloof from the Mormons and stayed in Missouri for eighteen years. Lyndon Cook found that he settled in Howard County, about 100 miles east of Jackson County, in the middle of the state. Later Marsh moved to Grundy County in the northern part of Missouri, where he apparently earned a living teaching Bible classes.[38] He and Elizabeth appear in the Bonne Femme, Howard County, census of 1840 with three sons and one daughter living with them.[39] It would have been an interesting and trying time to be in Missouri, which was awash with slavery and crops that relied on slave labor. Howard County was in the heart of what was called Little Dixie, where cotton, hemp, and tobacco were farmed on plantations along the Missouri River. One wonders to what extent the Marshes took part in that culture. Thomas penned a brief autobiography for the *Deseret News* in 1858 without mentioning a single word about his years wandering in the wilderness of doubt.

The assumption one might draw is that he experienced a change of heart, except that it was initially more literal than metaphorical when, in the summer of 1856, he had a stroke and was forced to consider his life's trajectory in light of the fact that his wife left him and he had become aware of his limited life expectancy. On May 5,

---

37. George A. Smith, Apr. 6, 1856, *Journal of Discourses,* 26 vols. (London: Latter-day Saints Book Depot, 1854–86), 3:284.

38. Lyndon W. Cook, "'I Have Sinned against Heaven, and Am Unworthy of Your Confidence, But I Cannot Live without a Reconciliation': Thomas B. Marsh's Return to the Church," *BYU Studies* 20, no. 4 (Spring 1980): 396. Cook's sense that Marsh struggled to get by, living "on the edge of survival," might be inferred but cannot be verified.

39. U.S. Census, 1840, Missouri, Howard County, 33.

1857, he wrote to Heber C. Kimball to say that, having lost his wife, he had no reason to stay in Missouri and wanted to make his way "to Salt Lake, God being my helper, & there throw myself at the feet of the apostles and implore their forgiveness." He pleaded with Kimball to allow him to return:

> I cannot live long so without a reconciliation with the 12 and the Church whom I have injured O Bretheren once Bretheren!! How can I leave this world without your forgiveness[?] Can I have it[?] Can I have it? Something seems to say within yes. ... I know what I have done[,] a mission was laid upon me & I have never filled it and now I fear it is too late but it is [filled] by another [and] I see, the Lord could get along very well without me.[40]

He stayed for a short time in Council Bluffs with Wandle Mace, whom he told he had experienced "a Stroke of Par[a]lysis" the previous summer "and for six weeks he was unable to help himself, or turn over in bed." He was "completely paralyzed, [so] they had to move him in a sheet, and while in this condition he said he made a determination if the Lord spared his life, and he received sufficiently to help himself[,] he would return to the Church. And as soon as he was able to travel He left his home in Missouri."[41]

His former colleagues, doubtlessly remembering the damage caused by his affidavits at Richmond, did not welcome his return in the manner they did Luke Johnson and Orson Hyde. Public humiliation would be dished out as he re-entered the church. What Kimball told a congregation on July 12, 1857, at the bowery in Salt Lake City, where the tabernacle would later be built, was that Marsh's wife was "dead and damned," incorrectly assuming from Marsh's

---

40. Thomas B. Marsh to Heber C. Kimball, May 5, 1857, LDS Church History Library, qtd. in Cook, "'I Have Sinned against Heaven,'" 396–97, terminal punctuation added.

41. Wandle Mace Autobiography, ca. 1890, 178, LDS Church History Library; initial capitals and terminal punctuation added.

correspondence that she had died. "She led him some eighteen years," Kimball said, "and as soon as she died he came to Winter Quarters."[42] Despite Kimball's assumption that she was gone, Elizabeth was very much still alive. It is unknown whether Kimball was corrected on that score, but he was not the last of the apostles to imply this and mock both Thomas and Elizabeth in cruel ways.

Speaking at the same venue a month later on August 9, John Taylor claimed Marsh had spent the last few years "afraid of his life—afraid the 'Mormons' would kill him; and he durst not let them know where he was." He called Marsh "a poor, decrepit, broken down, old man. He has had a paralytic stroke—one of his arms hangs down. He is coming out here as an object of charity, destitute, without wife, child, or anything else."[43] The description exaggerated Marsh's condition since the former apostle had begun his pilgrimage to Utah by walking about 200 miles from Grundy County, Missouri, to Florence, Nebraska.

When Marsh arrived in Florence in July 1857, he asked to be rebaptized. Amos Milton Musser described the scene at Papillion Creek, which empties into the Missouri River, when about twenty-seven immigrants on their way to Utah lined up to be immersed in the creek. "Among the candidates for this ordinance," Musser wrote, "appeared the venerable Thomas B. Marsh, once President of the Twelve Apostles. He received this holy rite in all humility, and is now on his way to Zion, rejoicing in the salvation of the Lord."[44]

The pilgrim arrived in Salt Lake City on the afternoon of Friday, September 4, with the William Holmes Walker freight train, just ahead of U.S. troops on their way to the territory under orders from U.S. President James Buchanan, who had decided to remove Brigham Young from office as governor and replace him. Buchanan

---

42. Heber C. Kimball, July 12, 1857, *Journal of Discourses*, 5:29.

43. John Taylor, Aug. 9, 1857, Ibid., 5:115.

44. "Correspondence from the Plains," Amos M. Musser to President [William] Appleby, July 16, 1857, *Millennial Star*, Sept. 26, 1857, 620.

found the Utah settlers to be in rebellion against the country and in need of supervision. Hosea Stout summarized Brigham Young's sermon two days later, in which Young said the thread "was cut between us and the U.S." and that "the Almighty recognised us as a free and independent people." Having severed its ties with the eastern states, "no officer apointed by gover[n]ment ... should come and rule over us from this time forth," he thundered.[45] Nine days later Young declared martial law.

As Stout watched Marsh and Young on the speaker's stand, he found himself in agreement with the observation that Marsh presented "a sad spectacle of the effects of apostacy." The former president of the Quorum of the Twelve had gone gray, had a head tremor, used a cane, and was emaciated, all of which gave "the appearance of a very old man" when he was "but little more than one year older than Brigham & Heber both of whom look to be in the prime and bloom of life." More than that, wrote Stout, "his intellect presents a still more deplorable spacticle of apostate degeneracy which seems to be in the last stage of dotage."[46]

Marsh was invited to address the congregation, and he chose a self-deprecating stance, saying he had received what he deserved in life as a result of his sins. He said that God

> loved me too much to let me go without whipping [me]. I have seen the hand of the Lord in the chastisement which I have received. I have seen and know that it has proved he loved me; for if he had not cared anything about me, he would not have taken me by the arm and given me such a shaking. ... Many have said to me, "How is it that a man like you, who understood so much of the revelations of God as recorded in the Book of Doctrine and Covenants, should fall away?["] I told them not to feel too

---

45. Juanita Brooks, ed., *On the Mormon Frontier: The Diary of Hosea Stout 1844-1861*, 2 vols. (Salt Lake City: University of Utah Press and Utah State Historical Society, 1964), 2:636.

46. Ibid.

secure, but to take heed lest they should also fall; ... You will not then think nor feel for a moment as you did before you lost the Spirit of Christ; for when men apostatize, they are left to grovel in the dark. ... I have frequently wanted to know how my apostasy began, and I have come to the conclusion that I must have lost the Spirit of the Lord out of my heart.

He remarked that he "now [had] a better understanding of the Presidency of the Church than I formerly had. I used to ask myself, What is the difference between the President of our Church and a Pope? True, he is not called a Pope, but names do not alter realities, and therefore he is a Pope." The audience was probably somewhat stunned by this remark but took it as a compliment, assuming Marsh had been away too long to remember the stigma Mormons attached to the supreme Catholic leader.[47] Stout noted that the congregation nevertheless "voted to recieve [Marsh] into the Church."[48] The penitent apostate had felt a compulsion to show humility in order to receive forgiveness, which he received, and for the grateful congregation, it was a sermon the Saints needed to hear at a time of such uncertainty with an army of 2,500 troops at their doorstep.

Rather than graciously accept Marsh's apology, however, Brigham Young, maybe to convince people he was not overly burdened in running both church and state, could not resist heaping further humiliation upon his former quorum leader and drawing a comparison between Marsh's infirm physical health and his own fitness:

Brother Thomas considers himself very aged and infirm, and you can see that he is, brothers and sisters. What is the cause of it? He left the Gospel of salvation. What do you think the difference is between his age and mine? One year and seven months to a day; ... "Mormonism" keeps men and women young and handsome; and when they are full of the Spirit of God, there are none of them

---

47. Thomas B. Marsh, Sept. 6, 1857, *Journal of Discourses*, 5:207-9.
48. Brooks, *Mormon Frontier*, 2:636.

but what will have a glow upon their countenances; and that is what makes you and me young; for the Spirit of God is with us and within us.[49]

After saying that Marsh had told him he was troubled about polygamy, Young jeered: "Look at him. Do you think it need [bother him]? … I doubt whether he could get one wife. Why it should have troubled an infirm old man like him is not for me to say." On the following day, Marsh dedicated everything to God: "I Thomas B. Marsh, do hereby, this day, Sept. 7th AD 1857 consecrate and dedicate myself soul, body and spirit <with all I possess on earth> to the Lord."[50] The next month, despite Young's mockery, Marsh married Hannah Adams on October 4. It was indeed possible for a man of Marsh's age to find a new wife.[51] He was ordained an elder on March 11, 1859, and later that year became a high priest.[52] He was present on the stand at the conference held October 6, listed with the high priests: "John Young [president of the high priests quorum], Edwin D. Wooley, Samuel W. Richards, John M. Bernhisel, William W. Phelps, Samuel L. Sprague and Thomas B. Marsh."[53]

One of Marsh's sons, Thomas Emerson Marsh, immigrated to the West in 1852 and acquired about 160 acres in Santa Clara

---

49. Brigham Young, Sept. 6, 1857, *Journal of Discourses*, 5:211. In fact, Young looked fairly robust in 1857, his long hair having receded only slightly and not yet having grayed. He was clean shaven. It is possible that he was self-conscious about having put on weight. Richard Neitzel Holzapfel and R. Q. Shupe, *Brigham Young: Images of a Mormon Prophet* (Salt Lake City: Eagle Gate and BYU Religious Studies Center, 2000), 136.

50. Dedication, 1857 Sept. 7, LDS Church History Library.

51. "Records of Early Church Families," *Utah Genealogical and Historical Magazine*, Jan. 1936, 29–30. The article stated that Elizabeth Marsh "probably died just prior to 1857," but this is incorrect.

52. Spanish Fork Branch, Record of the Genealogies of the Elder's Quorum, Spanish Fork City, LDS Church History Library. This record indicates that Marsh had gone into the high priest quorum, but contains no ordination date.

53. "Semi-Annual Conference," *Deseret News*, Oct. 12, 1859.

County, California.[54] He was followed by his mother, Elizabeth, who was still in Missouri at the time of the 1860 census but was in California, near her son, by the next ten-year census.[55] She died on May 20, 1878, in Saratoga, California.[56] When her son, Thomas E., died in 1904, he was buried near his mother.[57] Apparently she never received a formal divorce from Thomas B., nor can it be documented that she corresponded with him.

Marsh became a school teacher, according to the 1860 census of Spanish Fork.[58] In November 1858, a year after reaching the valley, he wrote Brigham Young, saying he was "teaching Geography & history, by lecture."[59] In other letters to Young, he asked for help obtaining such essentials as clothing, as he was too poor to purchase any for himself. For his part, Young kept repeating his negative characterizations of his defeated foe, uttering insults from the pulpit. "I can call Thos. B. Marsh, who is now in the congregation," Young said, "to witness: he was once the President of the Quorum of the Twelve Apostles. Soon after the selection of that Quorum, brother Marsh felt to complain. I said to him, brother Thomas, if we are faithful we will see the day in the midst of this people, that we will have all the power that we shall know how to wield before God. I call him to witness if I have not already seen that day."[60]

These repeated jabs are hard to understand today when the

---

54. Thomas E. Marsh, Notice of Claim, Santa Clara County, Research Library, San Jose History Museum, San Jose, California.

55. U. S. Census, 1860, Missouri, Jasper County, Center Creek Township, 131; U.S. Census, 1870, California, Santa Clara County, Redwood Township, 95.

56. The short obituary read, "MARSH—in Saratoga, May 20th, 1878, Mrs. Elizabeth Marsh, aged 79 years," *San Jose Daily Herald*, May 23, 1878, 2.

57. Bradley Clark Jenkins, "Madronia Cemetery Tombstone Inscriptions," Eagle Scout Service Project, 1982, LDS Family History Library, Salt Lake City.

58. U.S. Census, 1860, Utah Territory, Utah County, Spanish Fork, 210.

59. Thomas B. Marsh to Brigham Young, Nov. 10, 1858, Brigham Young Collection, LDS Church History Library.

60. Brigham Young, Oct. 7, 1860, *Journal of Discourses*, 8:197.

chapel commands more reverence, but in the nineteenth century the derision was part of the whole pulpit theater, of which Young was a master. He considered Marsh to have been a Judas who betrayed the church in Missouri and caused the church to be expelled from that state. Marsh was different from any of the other former apostles, having sunk far lower than any other in the estimation of the surviving quorum members. His regret was no doubt genuine, but he must have also remembered clearly the revulsion he had felt at seeing Danites assault non-Mormons and ransack their homes, so one has to question whether he came to feel desperate enough that he was willing to endure any indignity to survive. It was, at best, a complicated situation, exploited by the apostles who had remained in the church and felt superior to Marsh.

In his final years, Marsh suffered from a mental disorder and hallucinations. Wilford Woodruff recorded in June 1861 that Marsh was "quite Crazy" and had been "Chained up. He was now better"; he had named "different Devils which He says are tormenting him."[61] The former quorum president died on January 25, 1866. His brief obituary read: "Died.—Last Thursday, at Ogden, Thomas B. Marsh. The deceased was once the President of the Twelve Apostles—more we have not to say."[62] Even his obituary seemed to contain an expression of contempt.

About ten months before his death, Marsh attended a mission conference in Salt Lake City for the Reorganized LDS Church, referred to by Thomas Job, an elder in the Reorganized Church, a few months after Marsh's death. Job said he had thought of "something more to say" than the Salt Lake *Telegraph* had to offer, where the editor had given little information:

[I have] something more than the editor of that paper, to say about T. B. Marsh, that Thomas had been in the Josephite Conference

---

61. Kenney, *Wilford Woodruff's Journal*, 5:584.
62. "Died," *Semi-Weekly Telegraph,* Salt Lake City, Feb. 1, 1866, 3. Thomas B. H. Stenhouse was editor and proprietor.

in Salt Lake City, and bore a strong testimony to the truth, and necessity of the re-organization, and when a revelation through young Joseph [Smith III] was read to him he said that it was the voice of God, and again testified that he knew it, and desired us to write to the young prophet to send for him back from here, that he had faith that he would bear the journey, and join the young prophet, if he could go that (last) spring that such was the reason that the editor of the *Telegraph* had so little to say about him.[63]

The detail about Marsh's view of the RLDS was assumed to be the secret that had tied the editor's tongue.

One might have expected a tug-of-war over Marsh's remains after his death, but in fact no one seemed to notice his modest internment. He was buried in the Ogden City Cemetery under a simple wooden marker with the initials T.B.M. on it.[64] Eventually in 1893, David Stuart, president of the Bench District, Weber Stake, arranged to replace the marker with a marble column with the following inscription: "Thomas B. Marsh, First President of the Twelve Apostles of the Church of Jesus Christ of Latter Day Saints. Born in Acton, Masssachusetts, November 1, 1799. Died January, 1866. Erected by his friends, July 17, 1893;"[65] with a foot marker inscribed "Thomas B. Marsh." The sandstone and marble maker was replaced by a granite one with similar wording, omitting "Erected by his friends, July 17, 1893." This modern marker, which still stands, was placed about 1920.

In this remarkable man, we find an individual who devoted almost eight years of his life, at great personal sacrifice, to spreading the Restoration. Unlike apostles John Boynton, Luke Johnson, Lyman Johnson, and William McLellin, he survived the "great apostasy" of 1837 and was undeterred in his ardent devotion to

---

63. "Utah Conference," *True Latter Day Saints' Herald*, May 1, 1866, 139. Job's sermon was delivered at a conference in Goshen, Utah Valley, March 4-5, 1866.

64. Andrew Jenson, "The Twelve Apostles," *Historical Record*, Feb. 1886, 19.

65. "The Grave of Thomas B. Marsh," *Saints' Herald*, July 24, 1895, 470.

Joseph Smith. Under the prophet's orders, he led the attack against the Missouri church presidency. His stomach turned when he saw the Mormon deprivations against "gentiles" in Missouri and he removed himself from the church for nearly two decades. But unlike John Boynton, Lyman Johnson, and William McLellin, he later made peace with the church and acknowledged his wrong in opposing it. In what was a sacrifice perhaps as great as any earlier test, he humbled himself to the point of being rebaptized, then made his way to Utah, spending his last few years living in subordination to the elders he had once commanded.

11. AN ENDLESS SEARCH

Even before Joseph Smith's death in 1844, the Mormon schisms began forming. The religiously dispossessed began coalescing around a few leaders in Ohio and Missouri and banding together into small groups in Illinois and Iowa that attracted some of the prominent leaders from the past. Some of the diaspora moved from one small faction to another in undulating waves, everyone searching for a true version of the Restoration. Some appeared to be looking for that elusive "spirit of truth" they felt when they first encountered Mormonism. William McLellin was one of those who moved from one group to another, each time becoming more frustrated and generally more unforgiving and caustic in his own views and jaded in his critique of others.

William E. McLellin

The McLellins moved up the Mississippi River to Hampton, Illinois, across from Davenport, Iowa, where William's experience in medicine allowed him to earn a living. He was not too close to Nauvoo and yet far enough away that he would not be identified with, or contaminated by, the innovative doctrines reshaping Mormonism in Nauvoo. Like others who had made episodic heroic sacrifices, McLellin felt the need to congregate with other like-minded individuals. That need was briefly satisfied when he fellowshipped in the church founded in June 1840 by George M. Hinkle, called the Church of Jesus Christ, the Bride, the Lamb's Wife.

Hinkle was a thirty-eight-year-old former high councilor in Far West, Missouri, and leader of the Latter Day Saint settlement in DeWitt who was excommunicated in 1839 for surrendering Far West to the Missouri state militia. He did so to prevent a massacre of Latter Day Saints. With the hindsight of history, it was fortuitous that Hinkle, a colonel in the Missouri militia, was also a Latter Day Saint and was able to plead the church's case with the other militia officers. The militia was the equivalent of today's national guard. Rather than feeling regret for his action, Hinkle came to think of himself as being more competent than Joseph Smith in running a church, and in November 1842 the Hinkleites held a general conference in Moscow, Iowa, about forty miles west of Davenport. The next year, in September, McLellin attended one of their conferences and agreed to edit their newspaper, the *Ensign*, which appeared in 1844.[1]

When a Latter Day Saint from Nauvoo visited McLellin in 1845, hoping to collect on a debt, he said McLellin "gave me a severe lecture on Mormonism, he having apostatized during the troubles in Far West, Missouri, being at that time one of the Twelve Apostles."[2] McLellin was clearly not reconsidering joining the main faction of Latter Day Saints at that time. As someone who firmly believed the core doctrines, however, he wrote to Sidney Rigdon on December 23, 1844, suggesting that Rigdon and William Law, both recently of the First Presidency, unite together, saying enough people were waiting in the wings who would follow them that their action

---

1. Larry C. Porter, "The Odyssey of William Earl McLellin: Man of Diversity, 1806-83," in Jan Shipps and John W. Welch, eds., *The Journals of William E. McLellin, 1831-1836* (Provo and Urbana: BYU Studies and University of Illinois Press, 1994), 330.

2. Lorenzo Brown journal, Jan. 27, 1845, typescript, LDS Church History Library. In McLellin's defense, Brown was trying to collect on a note given to his father in 1835. Brown said the former apostle told him "many things that were true and a great many that were absolutely false and I had the independence of mind to tell him so and advised him to repent," although not enumerating which topics they disagreed on.

would meet with success. He knew this because he had received a revelation, he told Rigdon, that "all the honest in heart among the Latter Day Saints and throughout the world will UNITE also, and form that company who will follow the saviour robed in white linen 'clean and white.' ... I am with you, henceforth in the great work," he wrote.[3] Thus would begin McLellin's next phase, after his revelation of January 7, 1845, directing him to proceed "speedily unto the east" with Law to "unite with my servants who are willing to forsake all for Christ's truth" and to fellowship with "mine elders who have kept themselves from the abominations which I hate, who have kept their priesthood unspotted."[4]

Law had already joined with James Blakeslee in forming a church, but decided to defer to Rigdon, as did Hinkle. When McLellin accompanied Law to Pittsburgh at the end of January 1845, the two joined with Rigdon in a new association of Latter Day Saints that met in conference in April.[5] At the conference, McLellin was accepted as an apostle.[6] Immediately, McLellin was sent on a mission to Tennessee, where he baptized his father, whom he had not seen since 1829. On his return, he joined Blakeslee and

---

3. William E. McLellin to Sidney Rigdon, Dec. 23, 1844, *Latter Day Saint's Messenger and Advocate*, Jan. 15, 1845, 91-92. After William Law (1809-92) was excommunicated in 1844, he and James Blakeslee participated in the organization of a rival church, while Law helped print the only issue of the *Nauvoo Expositor*. William Shepard, "James Blakeslee: The Old Soldier of Mormonism," *John Whitmer Historical Journal* 17 (1997): 113-32.

4. Debating McLellin on October 19, 1847, James Strang cited two revelations McLellin had received in Hampton, Illinois, on January 7 and 18, 1845. The quotations are from the January 7 revelation. "Mormon Discussion," *Gospel Herald*, Nov. 4, 1847, 142. The Strangites printed at Voree three periodicals: *Voree Herald*, monthly from January through October 1846; *Zion's Reveille*, monthly for November and December 1846, then it was printed weekly from January 14 through September 16, 1847; followed by the *Gospel Herald*, weekly from September 23, 1847, through June 6, 1850.

5. James Blakeslee journal, Jan. 30, 1845, Community of Christ Archives, Independence, Missouri.

6. "Minutes of a Conference of the Church of Christ, held in the City of Pittsburgh," *Messenger and Advocate of the Church of Christ*, Apr. 15, 1845, 172.

Hinkle in preaching locally. His most satisfying accomplishment was converting Harvey Whitlock, who along with David Whitmer had converted McLellin in 1831.[7]

The McLellins moved to Pittsburg in June so William could fulfill his ministerial duties there, as well as in nearby New Jersey and New York. In October, at another conference in Philadelphia, he declared that "his intention was to devote himself entirely to the cause," saying he had full "faith and confidence" in the direction Rigdon was taking the church.[8] McLellin may have gone out of his way to overstate his support for Rigdon in spite of the fact that he soon determined Rigdon's claims as Joseph Smith's successor were flawed. At a meeting of the Grand Council on December 13, McLellin bristled at Rigdon's rebuke of his friend and fellow apostle Benjamin Winchester. Winchester and Richard Savary, a member of the Grand Council, were charged with transgression, and McLellin strongly objected to the prodeedings. Historian Richard Van Wagoner said McLellin was dropped from Rigdon's Council of Apostles "apparently for physically threatening Rigdon." The latter was told he could ask for forgiveness at the April conference.[9] Rather than face his accusers, though, McLellin informed the council on December 30 that he would not "stand his trial, and vacated his seat."[10] His position in the Grand Council was filled by William Bickerton, who years later would lead a separate faction that would absorb Rigdon's organization, and his position as apostle would be filled by Ridgon's seventeen-year-old son Algernon in 1848.[11]

Rigdon penned a stinging rebuke of McLellin in the *Messenger*

7. Porter, "Odyssey of William Earl McLellin," 335.

8. "Minutes of a Conference of the Church of Christ held at Philadelphia,"*Messenger and Advocate of the Church of Christ*, Nov. 1845, 398.

9. Richard S. Van Wagoner, *Sidney Rigdon: A Portrait of Religious Excess* (Salt Lake City: Signature Books, 1994), 387n54; "From the minutes of a meeting of the grand council," *Messenger and Advocate of the Church of Christ*, Jan. 1846, 425.

10. "Dec. 30th, Council met," ibid., 427.

11. Porter, "Odyssey of William Earl McLellin," 337-38.

and Advocate of the Church of Christ in February 1846, probably in response to a critique McLellin probably made against Rigdon. How could McLellin, who had recently testified that "God had revealed to him" that Ridgon was the proper successor, now retract that testimony, Rigdon wanted to know. None had borne a "stronger testimony that the kingdom of heaven was set up in Pittsburgh than William E. M'Lellin," Rigdon reminded readers, "and on this point he has so committed himself, that he has no escape." Rigdon had McLellin's written testimony of why he had "united with the church of Christ."[12] Unfazed by this, McLellin wrote that Rigdon's choice of the Cumberland Valley as a gathering place demonstrated how uninspired the onetime Baptist preacher was.[13] McLellin now found Rigdon's prophetic claims based on "hypocrisy, dishonesty and fanaticism," he wrote his longtime friend David Whitmer.[14]

The McLellins had no particular reason to remain in Pittsburg after being severed from the Rigdon fold, nor did they have reason to return to Hampton, having pulled up stakes there and bid their neighbors good-bye, so they returned to the Kirtland area, forty miles to the south in Shalersville, where William once again practiced medicine. Every time he and Emeline moved, they had to consider their children. They now had three sons and two daughters ranging in age from ten months to twelve years of age. William liked being near enough to Kirtland so he could follow developments there, for instance, a four-day conference in August 1846 that attracted a diverse group of individuals retaining Mormon identities. The congregation considered options for the future and heard sermons from men like James J. Strang and prized convert William Smith. Their message resonated and a stake was formed in Kirtland. One conference resolution stated that Strang was the "duly appointed successor

---

12. Sidney Rigdon, "The Distinctive Character of the Religion of Christ," *Messenger and Advocate of the Church of Christ*, Feb. 1846, 437.

13. See William E. McLellin to Leonard Soby, Feb. 1, 1846, ibid., Mar. 1846, 464.

14. William E. McLellin to David Whitmer, Dec. 2, 1846, *Ensign of Liberty*, Apr. 1847, 17.

of Joseph Smith." Strang appointed Jacob Bump, one of Kirtland's original members, as bishop of Kirtland and Leonard Rich, Amos Babcock, and Sylvester Stoddard as the stake presidency. Martin Harris was appointed to the high council.[15] McLellin received a letter of introduction to Strang from John C. Bennett, a former assistant in the First Presidency under Joseph Smith. Apparently, McLellin was sufficiently impressed to accept Strang's invitation to continue his ministry as an apostle. Strang ordained him to be a "special witness of the Lord Jesus Christ to the nations of the earth."[16]

The *Voree Herald* of September 1846 trumpeted the spread of Strangism and acquisition of "the Temple at Kirtland," which was now "in possession of our Brethren of the true order."[17] The acceptance of Strang's version of Mormonism in Philadelphia, New York, Boston, and Pittsburgh was then topically explained,[18] the newspaper proclaiming:

---

15. "Kirtland," *Voree Herald*, Sept. 1846, 1-2. James J. Strang, a recent convert to Mormonism from Burlington, Wisconsin, claimed he had not only been ordained by an angel at the time of Joseph Smith's death, he produced a letter he claimed was written by the late prophet which appointed him his successor. To many Latter Day Saints who were bewildered by the ascension of the Twelve Apostles to church leadership, Strang represented "primitive Mormonism" and had ascended to church leadership in accordance with church law. Strang maintained he was "called of God" and ordained by angels to the prophetic office, and translated "sealed" plates by use of the urim and thummim. The best information on Strang's calling, ordination, and early ministry is in monthly issues of Strang's newspaper, the *Voree Herald*, from January to October 1846. Essential reading includes Robin Scott Jensen, "Gleaning the Harvest: Strangite Missionary Work, 1846-1850" (Master's thesis, Brigham Young University, 2005), 1-72 and Vickie Cleverley Speek, *"God Has Made Us a Kingdom": James Strang and the Midwest Mormons* (Salt Lake City: Signature Books, 2006), 1-71.

16. Andrew F. Smith, *The Saintly Scoundrel: The Life and Times of Dr. John Cook Bennett* (Urbana: University of Illinois Press, 1997), 157; Conference Minutes, Oct. 6-19, 1846, qtd. in John J. Hajicek, ed., *Chronicles of Voree, 1844-1849* (Burlington, WI: JJRR Publishing, 1991), 113; "Conference Minutes," *Voree Herald*, Oct. 1846, 1; "Message to the Conference," *Zion's Reveille*, Apr. 1, 1847, 52.

17. "The Temples," *Voree Herald*, Sept. 1846, 2.

18. Under the headings, "Philadelphia," "New York," "Boston," and "Pittsburgh," ibid., 2.

All the organized branches of the Church, [from] which we can hear in Wisconsin, Michigan and Ohio, ack[n]owledge President Strang and the true order of the church.—In Pennsylvania, we can hear of but one Rigdonite, and one Brighamite organization[.] All Northern and central New York is with us. A large majority of the Saints in the New England States, New Jersey, Indiana, Illinois and Iowa are with us and the work is progressing far and wide in the southern States and in England. There are engaged and in the faith with us nearly all the best preachers of the church[,] all the living witnesses of the book of Mormon save one [Oliver Cowdery], and every surviving member of the family of Joseph Smith.[19]

The *Herald* overstated its case, but Strangism was clearly in the ascendancy.

What Strang was unaware of was the depth of McLellin's dissatisfaction and the pattern that emerged in which McLellin would enthusiastically join with a faction, accept a calling in it, and then find himself plagued by doubts and swear off the whole endeavor. He repeatedly came to see the various leaders, and Mormonism itself, as misrepresenting what he believed. But then he would wonder if he had been too hasty in his judgment and if he had been right to doubt. He would restate his loyalty to Mormonism's key foundational tenets and begin searching for a new faction to join. One of the paradoxes of his life was that even though he was looking for the rightful heir, he believed it was vanity that made anyone presume to be Christ's representative on earth.

It is not surprising that within weeks of his ordination as a Strangite apostle, McLellin was on the prowl again to find a replacement for the Wisconsin prophet. By the end of November, he had concluded that David Whitmer might be the heir, having been ordained president of the church in Missouri in July 1834. McLellin was "willing to confess that these matters had passed

---

19. "Progress of the Work," ibid., 3–4.

from our minds," he wrote to Whitmer, until "our recollections were roused up by the visitation of holy messengers standing in our presence, and causing us to understand great and marvelous things," meaning that he (referring to himself in the plural) had been visited by an angel.[20] McLellin dated his letter December 2 but mailed it after a gathering in Kirtland in mid-December where the congregation reversed itself and decided to reject Strang's leadership. Historian Milo M. Quaife cynically, but correctly, observed that the reorganization of August 1846, "within the space of four months, was so completely lost," that Strang pronounced a curse upon it.[21] McLellin's attack on Strang was the chief reason Strang was rejected in Kirtland.

Strang's periodical, *Zion's Reveille,* denounced his critic's indecision, drawing people's attention to McLellin's fourth apostasy. "O, William, arch-apostate! Who can hereafter have the least confidence in such a perfidious monster of iniquity?" It was like an "adulterous propensit[y]," the article added, for a man who was never satisfied with the woman he was with.[22] Not one to take such insults sitting down, McLellin started his own newspaper, the *Ensign of Liberty,* to attack the imposters non-stop and perhaps lull David Whitmer into stepping in as head of the church. McLellin attracted a small following but not the acquiescence of Whitmer until he visited the Book of Mormon witness in September 1847 at his home in Richmond.[23]

Whitmer suggested that he and McLellin and a brother, Jacob Whitmer, travel to Far West, where their brother John Whitmer

---

20. "The Successor of Joseph, the Seer," *Ensign of Liberty,* Mar. 1848, 78.

21. Milo M. Quaife, *The Kingdom of Saint James: A Narrative of the Mormons* (New Haven: Yale University Press, 1930), 53.

22. "William E. McLellin's Fourth Apostasy," *Zion's Reveille,* Jan. 14, 1847, 3. *Zion's Reveille* was edited for Strang by John Greenhow from October 1846 to April 15, 1847.

23. "Our Tour West in 1847," *Ensign of Liberty,* Aug. 1849, 99-104. McLellin edited the *Ensign of Liberty* for seven issues, from Mar. 1847 to Aug. 1849.

lived. Once there, McLellin was able to convince David of his calling. All three Whitmers were baptized by McLellin and re-ordained to the priesthood. David chose John Whitmer and Oliver Cowdery as counselors in the new presidency and McLellin as an assistant president.[24] Strang was again badly wounded when the witnesses, who had tenuously given their allegiance to him, now upheld the work of McLellin.

While William wooed the Whitmers, he and Strang exchanged a series of scathing letters, Strang informing McLellin that the high council had excommunicated him on October 7, 1847, for "apostasy and falsehood" and had conveyed him "to the buffetings of Satan."[25] Strang was currently with his community of loyalists in Voree, Wisconsin, eighty miles north of Chicago, where he had been sent in 1844 to establish an outpost. McLellin parried with a bold move by traveling there himself and commiserating with people who had rejected Strang's leadership. They were derisively called "pseudos" by Strang loyalists. While there, McLellin and Strang held a debate at the schoolhouse beginning October 19, 1847. When asked about his own fleeting commitment to Strang, McLellin hedged, and discredited himself by denying any former interest, including a specific denial that he had communicated with John Bennett about his intent to join the Strangites or that he had allowed Strang to ordain him: "I never had any confidence in him. I never wrote that I had. ... I was not ordained one of his apostles. He never had his hands on my head."[26]

During the debate, Strang produced McLellin's correspondence with Bennett and the minutes of the meeting in which McLellin was ordained.[27] In the *Gospel Herald*, John E. Page, who was

24. David Whitmer to Oliver Cowdery, Sept. 8, 1847, qtd. in ibid., May 1848, 93.

25. Hajicek, *Chronicles of Voree*, 150.

26. "Mormon Discussion," *Gospel Herald*, Nov. 25, 1847, 155.

27. Ibid., Dec. 2, 1847, 164-66.

with Strang at the time, mocked McLellin's prevarication, as well as his attempt to "wake up" David Whitmer "to a remembrance" that he was "a prophet." Page took note of the fact that McLellin had pursued one claimant to the prophet's mantle after another and that, "after all this chase to find Smith's successor, lo and behold! [McLellin] rises up as out of a snooze and says, 'O, I *forgot* that Smith ordained Whitmer;' and further says, 'that God has manifested it unto him by *revelation*.' O! how forgetful such prophets are."[28] Despite the pushback, McLellin gained the temporary allegiance of about forty pseudos in the Voree area and added them to his congregation of about the same number in Kirtland and a few in Missouri, including the Whitmers and Hiram Page, and for a short time it seemed that McLellin's dream of picking up where Joseph Smith had left off might become a reality.

One problem was that David Whitmer was keeping strangely aloof. Then in June 1849, Hiram Page broke the silence in a communication from the Whitmers, saying they had decided McLellin's organization was not "in accordance with the order of the Gospel Church." It was McLellin's turn to have a taste of his own medicine. The offenses the Whitmers and Page had detected were threefold: that McLellin was ordaining people to the office of high priest when "the office of High Priest does not belong to the church of Christ under the gospel dispensation, and that all offices filled exclusively by High Priests are null and void"; that "the office of a Seer is not, nor has been the means by which the Lord intended his church should be governed"; and "that the gathering dispensation has not come."[29] This rebuff, coming from Missouri, doomed McLellin's Church of Christ, leaving the one-time apostle "completely overthrown by the letter from his friends in Missouri," as

---

28. "Forgetful Prophets," ibid., Dec. 9, 1847, 176; emphasis Page's.

29. Hiram Page to Alfred Bonny, Isaac N. Aldrich, and M. C. Ishem, June 24, 1849, qtd. in the *Olive Branch, or Herald of Peace and Truth to all Saints*, Springfield, IL, Aug. 1849, 27-29.

James Brewster's rival group in Kirtland exulted. In their newspaper titled the *Olive Branch*, they reported with glee that McLellin's Church of Christ had "passed out of existence."[30]

Strang's *Gospel Herald* of July 5, 1849, contained a request from Austin Cowles, a member of the Church of Christ in Kirtland, to publish the minutes of the trial held on June 3, 1849, in which Martin Harris and others withdrew "all fellowship from the aforesaid Wm. E. McLellin both as an Elder or member of the church of Christ." Charges included that McLellin had employed "abusive language," engaged in "quarreling and fighting," and refused to do "as instructed" by the church presidency.[31]

Whether McLellin defended himself or just decided to move on is unknown. One can imagine him rationalizing that he once again had been unjustly treated by the Mormons. He and his family remained in the Kirtland area as the 1850 census listed William as a "botanic physician." By March 1853, they were living in Chester Township, Ohio.[32] A year later McLellin received an overture from Orson Pratt, who wanted to renew their friendship, to which McLellin responded equivocally that he would be open to it but would not want to go all the way to Utah "to learn the will of God concerning myself." He enumerated some of his objections to the church in the Rocky Mountains, instructing Pratt to "take this letter to the Valley, and show it to the Leading men in the church; especially those of the original council of the 'Twelve.' There is not one of them as men for whom I entertain the least personal ill feeling."[33] The outcome

---

30. Editor, ibid., Aug. 1849, 30; "Confounding False Leaders," ibid., June 1850, 190.

31. "President J. J. Strang: Truly Honored and Respected," *Gospel Herald*, July 5, 1849, 74.

32. U.S. Census, 1850, Ohio, Lake County, Kirtland, 225; Porter, "Odyssey of William Earl McLellin," 346. The census information lists McLellin's birth date ten years off and his birthplace on the Isle of Man instead of Tennessee.

33. William E. McLellin to Orson Pratt, Apr. 29, 1854, in Stan Larson and Samuel J. Passey, eds., *The William E. McLellin Papers, 1854-1880* (Salt Lake City: Signature Books, 2007), 433, 438.

of the correspondence was that it stimulated McLellin in compiling personal thoughts about his faith and theology generally in a series of notebooks he kept until about 1880.

He appears to have lain dormant in his public profile for a decade before he corresponded with Granville Hedrick in 1864. Hedrick, a farmer and schoolteacher, coalesced a few Latter Day Saints scattered in Woodford County, Illinois, near Blooming-ton and at Vermillion, Indiana, into an organization that declared they were the true remnant of the Restoration. Their major attraction was that they were devoid of what they called the fol-lies of Brighamites, William Smithites, or Strangites. Hedrick defended Joseph Smith's purity and perfection, but then he dis-covered Joseph's polygamy and concluded the church had been led astray beginning in 1834 with the failure to redeem Zion. He rejected the Reorganized Church, which was formally orga-nized in 1860, over the doctrine of lineal descent.[34] He had him-self ordained a prophet, seer, revelator, and translator by John E. Page, an ex-Brighamite and ex-Strangite, without seeing any con-tradiction in that history. Despite the conflicted path Hedrick had taken, it probably reminded McLellin of his own disorganized search for truth and felt familiar to him. He joined the Hedrickites in June 1869.

In explaining this action to acquaintances in July, McLel-lin wrote that Hedrick relied on the "original principles as taught at first in 1830." He liked Hedrick's teaching that Joseph Smith had gone astray in 1834, the same year McLellin had pinpointed. McLellin had not approached this latest decision without first fully investigating the group. He had traveled to Independence to hear Hedrick preach and see him in action, which is what made him

---

34. William Shepard, "The Concept of a 'Rejected Gospel,'" in *Mormon History: Part 2,*" *Journal of Mormon History* 35 (Summer 2008): 158-65; and R. Jean Addams, *Upon the Temple Lot: The Church of Christ's Quest to Build the House of the Lord* (Independence: John Whitmer Books, 2010), 7-21.

"willing to believe Hedrick was a Prophet ... Hence I united with them."[35] McLellin was asked to preach on June 6, the first time in about twenty years he had delivered a sermon. It went well, and he seemed utterly content in his new religious environment for the space of about a half a year before, as usual, he was unable to escape the disillusionment that began to set in.[36] This time he chose not to align himself with any other group and remained aloof until his death in Independence in March 1883, although he continued to write extensively in letters and notebooks about what he thought Mormonism was and should have been.

He came to have an ever more jaded sense of the church's past, but retained a soft spot for people he encountered who belonged to one of the various offshoots of Mormonism. Mark Forscutt, a member of the Reorganization, found McLellin "very bitter against Joseph, against the Reorganization, against the Hedricketes, against everybody and against everybody's views but himself and his views," and yet he "very kindly obtained two horses and saddles" so they could ride out to see two members of the RLDS Church.[37]

Interestingly, McLellin began writing about what he had witnessed and had not commented on at the time in his journal, leading some to believe that he filled in the gaps as he wished. "I myself attended the Amherst Conference," he wrote, "and know positively that [Joseph Smith] was only ordained President of the church. Priesthood was not mentioned in his ordination at that time and place."[38] McLellin's assertion that "Priesthood was not mentioned

---

35. William E. McLellin to "Our Very Dear Friends," July 12, 1869, in Larson and Passey, *William E. McLellin Papers*, 450-51.

36. Ibid., 452; Inez Smith Davis, *The Story of the Church* (Independence: Herald Publishing House, 1964), 123.

37. Mark Hill Forscutt journal, Aug. 20-21, 1871, L. Tom Perry Special Collections, Harold B. Lee Library, Brigham Young University, Provo.

38. William E. McLellin to Mark H. Forscutt, Oct. 1, 1871, in Larson and Passey, *William E. McLellin Papers*, 477-78. McLellin originally wrote this letter to Isaac Sheen in October 1870.

in his ordination" is almost certainly in error since priesthood was definitely implied. He came to see that Joseph had invented the concept of a higher priesthood at a later date. It may be an example of selective memory, by which McLellin made the facts fit a theory he later developed, over a period of thirty-seven years. But in this case, he didn't record in his journal any conference business, only his commission to "go to the South" with Luke Johnson to preach, so the rest is open to interpretation.[39]

In early 1872, McLellin indicated to friends that he had been working on a manuscript concerning Mormonism: "I have my book almost finished, but no means to print it."[40] He intended it to be something of an exposé, or at least a comparison between his feelings about what the true restoration of primitive Christianity would look like and what he had encountered in the Latter Day Saint movement. The 264-page manuscript was purchased in 2008 by Brent Ashworth, a collector of historic documents. McLellin had corresponded with an admirer, John L. Traughber, about his manuscript and some troublesome issues in church history. For instance, he told Traughber he had seen a revelation in Martin Harris's possession that had directed Oliver Cowdery and others to travel to Kingston, Ontario, where they would be able to sell the foreign copyright to the Book of Mormon and raise funds for the first printing of the Book of Mormon. "They went, but did not succeed; and the revelation proved so false," McLellin wrote, "that Joseph" declined to publish it.[41] Was McLellin telling the truth? David Whitmer knew

39. William E. McLellin journal, Jan. 25, 1832, in Shipps and Welch, *Journals of William E. McLellin*, 70.

40. William E. McLellin to "My Old Friends," Feb. 22, 1872, in Larson and Passey, *William E. McLellin Papers*, xvi, 482.

41. Dawn House, "The McLellin Papers, Clues from the Past," *Salt Lake Tribune*, Jan. 24, 2009, C3; William E. McLellin to John L. Traughber, Feb. 19, 1877, handwritten copy, in "Some Statements by Dr. W. E. McLellan," Traughber Papers, Manuscripts Division, Marriott Library, University of Utah, Salt Lake City; McLellin to Traughber, May 7, 1877, Larson and Passey, *William E. McLellin Papers*, 503-04.

of the revelation too. Recently, a copy of the revelation was found in a handwritten collection of early revelations and was published in 2009 by the Church Historian's Press, an official imprint of the LDS Church in Utah.[42]

Over the years, as McLellin received visitors from the main branches of the Restoration, time allowing some of the animosity and conflict to ebb away, he became a curiosity more than an enemy. In September 1878, LDS apostles Joseph F. Smith and Orson Pratt called on him at his home in Independence. Elder Smith described him as being a "very tall, strong man, quite grey, but well preserved. He says when younger he measured 6 feet 3 inches in his stockings." On McLellin's gospel understanding, Smith recorded:

> He avowed his disbelief in the Book of Doctrine and Covenants, in polygamy, in the Lesser Priesthood, and in all offices in the Higher or Lesser Priesthood; but he believes in the Apostleship, but no man could confer it. He disavowed his belief or faith in his own ordination to the Apostleship and in that of all of the first Twelve. ... He said Emma Smith told him that Joseph was both a polygamist and an adulterer, and what was most strange to him was that she should join in with her son Joseph [III] in his theory of religion which holds up the Prophet as the founder of their faith.[43]

His memory spurred by this conversation, McLellin related to Traughber in December that "Mrs. [Emma] Smith told me that she knew her husband practiced both adultery and Spiritual Wifery!" and "had the Polygamic revelation."[44]

---

42. Robin Scott Jensen, Robert J. Woodford, and Steven C. Harper, eds., *The Joseph Smith Papers: Revelations and Translations: Manuscript Revelations Books, Facsimile Edition* (Salt Lake City: Church Historian's Press, 2009), 30–33.

43. Joseph F. Smith, qtd. in his son's compilation, Joseph Fielding Smith, *Life of Joseph F. Smith* (Salt Lake City: Deseret News Press, 1938), 239. McLellin and Joseph F. Smith corresponded with each other from November 1878 to January 1883.

44. William E. McLellin to John L. Traughber, Dec. 14, 1878, in Larson

A few years later, in January 1882, RLDS apostle William H. Kelley told of visiting McLellin in Independence:

> The doctor was able to point out the identical spot where Joseph stood when he first visited [the temple site], and which is the place of the corner stone. He visited it soon after himself, when it was all covered with young poplars thickly standing. Joseph cut his way in through this thick growth of trees, brush and saplings, and marked the spot by blazing a tree near by, cutting away the under brush for a few feet around and setting up a small stone that had been picked up in the ravine below. This was all the corner stone that was ever laid upon it, and it only to mark the place of the corner.[45]

Joseph Smith III wrote of meeting McLellin at a conference in Independence in April 1882. At the opening session, McLellin interrupted to exclaim, "That's wrong; that's wrong!" President Smith chastised him for the outburst, but at the conference's end,

> as McLellin was passing, I greeted him and extended my hand. He withdrew his and spoke quite decidedly, "No, sir; I will not shake hands with you. You have rebuked me publicly!" To which I replied, "Do as it pleases you, sir! I did rebuke you; you deserved it for interfering when you had no right to do so." He answered, "No, I did not interfere."
>
> Looking straight in the face I repeated my statement: "Sir, you did interfere. When that motion was made, you said aloud, that it was wrong and I heard you say it. It is bad enough for you to interfere without your making it worse by lying about it." Almost involuntarily he answered, "I did not know you heard me," whereupon he offered his hand, which I took, and the episode passed.
>
> The opinion I then formed of his disposition was confirmed

---

and Passey, *The William E. McLellin Papers*, 515.

45. William H. Kelley letter, Jan. 16, 1882, *Saints' Herald*, Mar. 1, 1882, 67. In 1879, Mark Forscutt visited the temple area and McLellin indicated he "knows it is within ten feet of it, [w]here the dedication of it was made for a Temple." Mark Hill Forscutt journal, Feb. 17, 1879, L. Tom Perry Special Collections, Harold B. Lee Library, Brigham Young University, Provo.

by later acquaintance. He proved to be meddlesome and irritating, with a tendency to find fault with others and to strongly resent any suggestion of his own shortcomings.[46]

At another time McLellin was heard to ask, "Why does not the Prophet's son preach on the subject of the Book of Mormon? He has preached here several times, but not once has he presented the book. Is he afraid to attempt to discuss the subject?" The next evening, President Smith did speak on the topic. Walking down the aisle afterward, he shook McLellin's hand and said, "Doctor, you see that the son of the Prophet is not afraid to preach about the Book of Mormon!" With "tears rising to his eyes," McLellin responded, "I perceive that you are not only ready to talk upon the subject, but that you can talk about it exceedingly well."[47]

McLellin died in Independence on March 14, 1883, at age seventy-seven. Joseph Smith III commented that he was "in many respects a remarkable man of some attainments, and a fertile brain, active temperament, loose attachments, and strong and persistent enmities; which most likely gives the key to his estrangement from the men of the Church in the rise of it. He was a strong believer in the Book of Mormon, and probably in the mission of Joseph Smith up to a certain date, which he fixed somewhere in 1834; but discarded much or all the work after that date."[48] By his death, McLellin had rejected many of the doctrines he had once held sacred but still believed fiercely in the Bible and Book of Mormon. Emeline McLellin joined the RLDS Church in 1888, five years after her husband's death.

William's legacy continued after he passed away as his widow

---

46. Mary Audentia Smith Anderson, ed., *The Memoirs of President Joseph Smith III (1832-1914)* (1959; rpt., Independence: Price Publishing, 2001), 199. This autobiography was first published in the *Saints' Herald* from Nov. 6, 1934, through July 31, 1937.

47. Ibid., 199.

48. "Extracts from Letters," *Saints' Herald*, Mar. 31, 1883, 194.

shared his writings and the contents of his library with interested admirers. Joseph Smith III purchased a complete set of the *Evening and Morning Star* from Emeline for fifty dollars.[49] She gave a copy of the Book of Commandments to John Traughber, along with her husband's diaries and some of his notebooks. Traughber sold manuscript copies of Joseph Smith's revelations and some other notebooks to Samuel Bennion, president of Utah's Central States Mission, in February 1908. Bennion forwarded this material to the LDS First Presidency. The remaining notebooks and correspondence remained in the Traughber family until 1995, in the possession of John's son Otis.[50]

Of the six apostles treated herein, McLellin is the most difficult to interpret and appreciate for his contributions. Utah historian Dale Morgan famously called him "Mormonism's stormy petrel." What he meant by that was that McLellin was a sign of trouble, just like the seabird that acts as a forecast of bad weather for sailors because it hides onboard ship when a storm is approaching. In a later article, RLDS Church Historian Richard P. Howard agreed with Morgan's characterization, and it has remained the caricature of the former apostle.[51] But as Utah historian D. Michael Quinn cautioned, McLellin "cannot be dismissed as someone who did not know what he was talking about" because he was "present at many of the crucial events in early LDS history." McLellin "conveniently edited himself out of scenes he later came to despise," Quinn conceded, but "this is not to say there is not some truth in what he

---

49. Anderson, *Memoirs of President Joseph Smith III*, 199.

50. Richard E. Turley, Jr., *Victims: The LDS Church and the Mark Hofmann Case* (Urbana: University of Illinois Press, 1992), 213, 248-50; Larson and Passey, *William E. McLellin Papers*, xv. Another notebook was published as *William E. McLellin's Lost Manuscript*, ed. Mitchell K. Schaefer (Salt Lake City: Eborn Books, 2012), augmenting what is already in print through Shipps and Welch and Larson and Passey.

51. Richard P. Howard, "William E. McLellin: 'Mormonism's Stormy Petrel,'" in *Differing Visions: Dissenters in Mormon History*, eds. Roger D. Launius and Linda Thatcher (Urbana: University of Illinois Press, 1994), 76-97.

chose to report, at least from his later perspective." It is nonetheless unfortunate "that the passage of time and a healthy ego tended to accentuate [McLellin's] own virtue and cast others as definite villains," Quinn wrote. But in the end, Quinn concluded this simply meant that, "as with any source we consider, McLellin's selective memory must be checked against other eyewitness reports."[52]

RLDS historian William D. Russell wrote more charitably about McLellin as an individual who was truly converted to the Restoration and sought a "manifestation of the religion he loved and the book he treasured [Book of Mormon], while he simultaneously became disenchanted with the church he had enthusiastically joined and the prophet who had brought forth the Nephite record."[53] In his quest, McLellin showed himself to be a "true believer" in Joseph Smith's ministry to 1834, so we should pay attention to his critique, even as McLellin revisited his original assumptions. According to Russell, McLellin raised five points of criticism about what the church had become. He believed it had taken a wrong turn when Joseph: (1) had himself ordained a prophet, seer, and revelator; (2) presumed to convey God's literal thoughts and words; (3) claimed that he and Oliver Cowdery were apostles; (4) assumed he was the head of the church; (5) and restricted church-wide revelation to one person when the "genius of Mormonism" was that everyone had "equal access to God."[54] These are not such unreasonable comments, Russell thought. They are issues we may disagree with, but they are reasoned disagreements from someone who was there and saw these principles in action.

So even though McLellin's esoteric musings are easy to write off, where he sometimes seems to split hairs, and even though

---

52. D. Michael Quinn, "'My Eyes Were Holden in those Days': A Study of Selective Memory," in Larson and Passey, *William E. McLellin Papers*, 59-60.

53. William D. Russell, "Portrait of a 'True Believer' in Original Mormonism," in ibid., 105.

54. Ibid., 118-19.

McLellin was crabby and impossible to get along with, we should keep in mind, as Quinn wrote, that somewhere between 40 to 50 percent of the membership of 1844 left Mormonism within ten years of Joseph Smith's death over such issues.[55] The matter of succession was not a bureaucratic issue as we sometimes think of it today, but it was one of the most important theological questions contemplated, in which the answer lay with God, not with a quorum or committee. If Quinn's estimate is correct, thousands were unhappy with the options they were offered, yet many retained their belief in the Book of Mormon and gravitated toward the restorationist churches, hoping to find the same spirituality they had once experienced when they first converted to the church. The greatest number of Midwestern Saints regrouped in 1860 under the leadership of Joseph Smith III. Many others went with Sidney Rigdon or James Strang. Some, like William McLellin and John Page, continued to quibble about what may seem to us like minutiae, but it shows how devoutly they continued to hold to their original hopes and beliefs, however unrealistic they may now seem to have been.

William Smith

William Smith's five-month sojourn in Nauvoo ended on September 12, 1845, when he slipped out of the City of Joseph at night with his brother-in-law Jenkins Salisbury.[56] Both men left Nauvoo under a cloud of suspicion because of their interactions with the Hodges criminal gang. For example, Brigham Young said on April 2, 1846,

---

55. D. Michael Quinn, *The Mormon Hierarchy: Origins of Power* (Salt Lake City: Signature Books, 1994), 241–42.

56. Kyle R. Walker, ed., *United by Faith: The Joseph Sr. and Lucy Mack Smith Family* (American Fork, UT: Covenant Communications, 2005), 279. Born June 6, 1809, in Lebanon, New York, Jenkins Salisbury married Katharine Smith in 1831. His stormy Mormon membership is outlined in Lavina Fielding Anderson, ed., *Lucy's Book: A Critical Edition of Lucy Mack Smith's Family Memoir* (Salt Lake City: Signature Books, 2001), 861–62.

"that he had become satisfied that William was in [on] the murder with the Hodges in Iowa."[57] There is no suspicion Salisbury was involved in criminal activities in Nauvoo, but the fact he transferred money to lawyers to defend William and Stephen Hodges suggests he participated as the agent of William Smith.[58] It put him in company with Amos and Ervine Hodges, William Hickman, Return Jackson Redden, William Louter, and Robert Birch.

Thomas Bullock recorded on March 8, 1846, what could be called William's "closing act" in Nauvoo. He said "William Smith landed in Nauvoo with a parcel of drunken rowdies" who "commenced firing guns in air." At a time when area anti-Mormons were threatening Nauvoo, these actions "created a disturbance and alarm." However, when the Mormons became aware William was involved, Bullock said "not a single person took any notice of him." He added that when William offered to shake hands with "Sister Phelps," she sharply responded, "Don't Sister Phelps me!"[59]

It was an embittered William who spread his message of hate against the twelve apostles in St. Louis, Cincinnati, and in the eastern branches of the church. He said it was his God-given mission to act as a spokesman for his nephew Joseph Smith III until the boy assumed church leadership. This is not to say he did not emphasize that his own "royal blood" entitled him to special ecclesiastical privileges and being sustained financially by others.

William was probably drawn to Knox County, Illinois, because Caroline's parents, Joshua and Athelia Grant, lived in the area, and William may have targeted them to help raise grandchildren Mary Jane born in 1835 and Caroline L. born in 1836. Another possibility

---

57. Juanita Brooks, ed., *On the Mormon Frontier: The Diaries of Hosea Stout 1844-1861*, 2 vols. (Salt Lake City: University of Utah Press, 1964), 1:147.

58. See Bonds and Mortgages, 1844-48, June 16, 1845, 2:66-67. Original in Hancock County Courthouse, Carthage, Illinois, microfilm no. 954,776, Family History Library, Salt Lake City, Utah.

59. Greg R. Knight, ed., *Thomas Bullock Nauvoo Journal* (Orem, UT: Grandin Book, 1994), 61.

is he traveled there when his mother and sister visited Arthur and Lucy Milliken, to spend the fall and winter in Knoxville as the hostilities associated with the "battle of Nauvoo" played out.[60] William was familiar with the area, as he had presided over about one hundred of the brethren in Walnut Grove, Knox County, in January 1841.[61] Area president Isaac Paden informed James Strang in May 1846 that there were seven priesthood holders in the Knoxville branch and nine priesthood holders in the Spoon River branch.[62] William would have fit in well with these Mormons, as they had essentially rejected the twelve apostles and acknowledged Strang as their leader.[63]

At first William appears to have found solace and rejuvenation under James Strang, along with a significant number of former leaders from Nauvoo who had found their way to Strang's camp. Strang's claim was based on a letter of appointment Joseph Smith had written to him in June 1844, charging Strang to lead the church in Wisconsin, as one might interpret it, or as he and his followers understood it, to oversee the entire church as Joseph's successor. When the letter arrived, Joseph was dead, so a clarification was impossible. In any case, at the instant of Smith's death, angels appeared to Strang and, as he said, ordained him to assume the church's leadership. He was shown the burial spot of a second ancient record like the Book of Mormon which he unearthed and

---

60. Anderson, *Lucy's Book*, 791.

61. Walker, *United by Faith*, 267.

62. Isaac Paden to James J. Strang, May 17, 1846, Document 30, James J. Strang Collection, Beineke Rare Book and Manuscript Library, Yale University, New Haven, Connecticut.

63. The *Voree Herald* in "Conference in Knox Co., Ills.," Sept. 1846, 3, reported: "We received sometime since the proceedings of a large Conference in Knox Co. at which all the branches in that section of the state were represented, and which we intended to lay before our readers in this number but the article is mislaid. Jehiel Savage of the Twelve and several other distinguished Elders, were in attendance. The Conference were unanimous in sustaining the true authorities of the Church and the principles of the Gospel."

translated, thereby establishing his *bona fides* as the new prophet leader. From then on, he proceeded under the assumption that his group was the official church, so that anyone who had been a member in Nauvoo was automatically a member and did not need to be re-baptized. He offered to keep the existing Quorum of the Twelve, although he requested that the apostles move from Nauvoo to Voree, a settlement that bordered the village of Burlington, Wisconsin. When most of the apostles declined, the Voree high council charged them with apostasy and excommunicated them, with three exceptions: William Smith and John E. Page, both of whom were on the outs with Brigham Young, and Wilford Woodruff, who was in England and had not heard of his appointment, or at least chose not to dignify the invitation with a response.[64] But Smith and Page temporarily became part of Strang's church.

William may have been intrigued by the possibility of ecclesiastical authority in a new arena, away from the people he had clashed with. In the spring and summer of 1846, he conducted extensive correspondence with Strang, who published one of William's letters in the July issue of the *Voree Herald*, in which he stated that he had examined Strang's claims and found them logical and believable. William provided signatures from his family "to certify that the Smith family do believe in the appointment of J. J. Strang," specifically attaching the names of his mother Lucy Smith, brother-in-law Arthur Milliken, sister Lucy Milliken, brother-in-law Jenkins Salisbury, sister Catherine Salisbury, and sister Sophronia McCleary.[65]

---

64. The best biography on Strang is Milo M. Quaife, *The Kingdom of Saint James: A Narrative of the Mormons* (New Haven: Yale University Press, 1930) in spite of its cynical portrayal of Mormons. Speek, *God Has Made Us a Kingdom*, provides a wealth of new information about the movement and Strang's plural wives.

65. Letter, Mar. 1, 1846, *Voree Herald*, July 1846, 3. The newspaper nevertheless made some slight mistakes, identifying William's sister as Nancy Milliken and misspelling Sophronia's married name as McLerie. At a later date, Sophronia denied ever having told her brother that she supported Strang. Gracia N. Jones, "Sophronia Smith Stoddard McCleary," in Walker, *United by Faith*, 185; also "Correspondence," *Friends' Weekly Intelligencer*, Philadelphia, Oct. 17, 1846, 226.

When Woodruff returned from England in April 1846, he found his stepmother, Azubah Hart Woodruff, together with his brother-in-law Dwight Webster, stepsister Eunice Webster, and Mother Lucy Smith "advocating the cause of Strang" and "some unplesant feelings were manifest upon the subject."[66] Woodruff, of course, hastened to join the migration to the Great Salt Lake.

Mother Smith wrote favorably about the Wisconsin movement to an official in England, Reuben Hedlock, while complaining that "the Twelve (Brighamites) have abused my son William, and trampled upon my children; they have also treated me with contempt. The Lords hand is in this to save the church; now *mark it*; these men [under Brigham] are not right, God has not sent them to lead this kingdom; I am satisfied that Joseph appointed J. J. Strang. It is verily so."[67]

Based on his mother's enthusiasm for the direction the church was taking in Voree, William considered helping move her there.[68] Scouting out the situation on June 11, he received a warm reception from Strang, who offered him the possibility of remaining Church Patriarch and one of the Quorum of the Twelve. Strang also suggested that they travel to Kirtland together, where Strang secured the allegiance of the Saints still living in Ohio, including those in temporary possession of the Kirtland Temple.[69]

The October *Voree Herald* announced that a committee had been appointed to take Mother Smith to Voree. Unfortunately, the Strangites were virtually destitute due to losses in Missouri and Illinois

---

66. Scott G. Kenney, ed., *Wilford Woodruff's Journal, 1833–1898*, typescript, 9 vols. (Midvale, UT: Signature Books, 1983–85), 3:49. For other encounters of Woodruff with Dwight and Eunice Webster see ibid., 39-40, 53. William Smith wrote to Reuben Hedlock in England that "the whole Smith family excepting Hyrum's widow uphold Strang, and say this wilderness move [by Brigham Young] is not of God." "Opinions of the Smith Family," *Voree Herald*, June 1846, 1.

67. "My dear Son," ibid.

68. "Brother William Smith is Making Preparation," ibid., 3.

69. "Kirtland," ibid., Sept. 1846, 1.

and unable to raise funds quickly.[70] William traveled back to Voree from Kirtland and boarded with Benjamin and Sarah Ellsworth for an unknown period of time in their primitive home. In a late July letter, published in the December 1846 issue of *Zion's Reveille*, William reconfirmed his support of Strang, about whom he "entertain[ed] no doubt whatever." He was convinced of Strang's "appointment" and "confirmation by angelic administration," for "God has revealed [it] to me," he disclosed. William concluded with, "I therefore, as your spiritual father, bear witness to you all of the truth of these declarations." He signed the letter "Patriarch to the whole church."[71]

Brigham Young heard of Mother Smith's conversion and, in a late January 1847 letter to members at Punca Camp, Nebraska, dismissed it as irrelevant. And if she had been on her way to Voree, she became stuck in between, about eighty miles east of Nauvoo in Knoxville, he said.[72] She was still there three months later, the committee still not having raised sufficient funds for her travel.[73] At this time William was living in Knox County[74] and was in good fellowship in the church until it was disclosed by Sarah Ellsworth on April 23, 1847, that in July 1846, he had slept with Abenade Archer, a female employee of the Ellsworths in Voree, in the room which adjoined the Ellsworths' sleeping

---

70. "Conference Minutes," ibid., Oct. 1846, 2.

71. William Smith "To the Church," *Zion's Reveille*, Dec. 1846, 3.

72. Brigham Young, "The Twelve Apostles to the Saints at Punca," Jan. 27, 1847, qtd. in Elden J. Watson, comp., *Manuscript History of Brigham Young, 1846-1847* (Salt Lake City: By the compiler, 1971), 516.

73. "Annual Conference of the Church of Jesus Christ of Latter Day Saints, at Voree," *Zion's Reveille*, Apr. 1, 1847, 7.

74. "William Smith," in *Zion's Reveille*, Dec. 1846, 3, said: "He [William] is now at Knoxville with his mother, waiting for spring, to come to Voree. And that the pseudoes [sic] may know what his faith is, we will inform them that he has just sent us a correspondence between himself and an influential BRIGHAMITE ... [who] urged [him] to join the emigrating party. His answer given in that letter concludes with these words. 'Candour and truth will prevail, and the honest saints will find it hard to kick against it. Mormonism is of God, and James J. Strang is his prophet.[']"

quarters. The Ellsworths waited months to come forward before Sarah's conscience got the best of her and she filed a formal complaint, explaining that Abenade had stayed two nights in William's room. Sarah said she had "heard some things that disgusted me and I mentioned it to Mr. Ellsworth: After a short time I sent [Abenade] away." To her amazement, the girl returned the following Saturday and William again spent the night "with her[,] not going to his own bed at all, and while in bed ... had carnal knowledge of her."[75]

Strang allowed some time for William to respond to the accusation and clear his name, but to no avail. William was preoccupied, having just married Roxie Ann Grant, the younger sister of his first wife, on May 19, 1847, in Knoxville. On September 21, 1848, Roxie Ann gave birth to their first child, Thalia Grant, in Altona, twenty miles from Knoxville. Two years later in August 1850, they had a boy, Hyrum Wallace, but by that time William had become restless and abandoned his wife and children in March 1850, halfway through Roxie Ann's pregnancy.[76]

While trying to dodge Strang's inquiry into his illicit sexual behavior, William wrote from the Knoxville area to Orson Hyde in June 1847 to ask for rebaptism and restoration to the Quorum of the Twelve. In one letter, William fatuously expressed "hope [that]

---

75. "John C. Gaylord accuser vs William Smith accused: Complaint for Adultery," Apr. 23, 1847, James J. Strang Papers, Doc. 181. Ironically, the Ellsworths would be excommunicated at the October 1847 conference for "teaching and practicing the spiritual wife system," as recorded in the *Chronicles of Voree*.

76. Roxie Ann Grant was born March 16, 1825, in Naples, New York, and died March 30, 1900, in Lathrop, Missouri, where she and her two children had been living for thirty years. Our thanks to Erin Metcalfe for this information. A complaint was issued against William Smith on February 14, 1853: "On or about the said 4th day of March AD 1850, the said William Smith wickedly disregarding the solemnity of his marriage vows, and the sanctity and contract of matrimony, and the marriage State hath wickedly and willfully deserted an[d] absented himself from the bed and boar[d] of your Oratrix without any reasonable cause for the space of more than two years." Knox County Circuit Court, April Term 1853, Galesburg, Illinois, box 93, case 37.

Brother Brigham will forgive me for I have said many hard things concerning him and yet I know him to be a man of God[.] He shall never complain of me hearafrter [hereafter] for I have decreed that my toung shal no more speak evile of the ruler of my people."[77] The Brighamites rejected William's overtures, and when Hyde learned of William's sexual misadventures he ridiculed him for wanting to use his position in the church "as a key to sensuality, avarice and ease."[78]

At the October 1847 conference in Voree, President Strang reviewed the testimony against William from Sarah Ellsworth, William Marks, and Ebenezer Page and ordered William "excommunicated from the Church and delivered over to the buffitings of Satan."[79] Furious, Smith attacked Strang with as much vengeance as he had Young, saying Strang tricked people by anointing their heads with oil and phosphorus so they glowed with a supernatural haze.[80] Strang brushed this off and said he had "been cursed with the friendship of such men as Wm. Smith."[81] William began touring eastern Illinois and giving lectures on the "corruptions of the Mormon leaders," according to the *Gospel Herald*, and charging men a variable admission price, the *Herald* suggested tongue-in-cheek, depending on how many loose women were in attendance.[82]

Casting about for a congregation that would appreciate him, Smith traveled east to Philadelphia. While there, he ran into a Strangite, Peter Hess, who forwarded to the Voree church president some criticisms William had offered: "He says you made the [Voree] plates yourself, out of an old brass kettle," Hess wrote. Hess

---

77. William Smith to Orson Hyde, June 1847, qtd. in Quinn, *Mormon Hierarchy: Origins*, 224.

78. Orson Hyde, qtd. in ibid.

79. "General Conference of the Church at Voree," Oct. 6, 1847, *Chronicles of Voree*, 157; "Conference of the Church," *Gospel Herald*, Oct. 14, 1847, 122.

80. "Mormonism," *Carrollton Gazette*, Oct. 8, 1847, 3, rpt. *Davenport Gazette*, Nov. 4, 1847; see also the Strangite rebuttal in "A Late Mormon Miracle," *Gospel Herald*, Dec. 23, 1847, 186.

81. James J. Strang, "An Appeal," *Gospel Herald*, Aug. 21, 1848, 98.

82. "Crimes," ibid., June 15, 1848, 51.

reported that William claimed Strang preached "that Christ turned the water into wine by having some dough cakes in his pockets." "All miracles were done by natural means," Smith allegedly told Hess. William was the rightful "prophet and the great head of the Mormon church," he had insisted. The *Gospel Herald* commented satirically that anyone who believed William would receive punishment enough and was deserving of everyone's sympathy. It was an honor to be maligned by him, they wrote. "We know of few who could turn away more ungodliness," they mused, "than he did when he turned himself away." They would have their revenge when William abused those who thought well of him.[83]

After receiving a cold shoulder in Philadelphia, William headed west to an enclave of Latter Day Saints residing in several settlements in Lee County, Illinois: Pleasant Grove, Rocky Ford, and other rural towns about 150 miles from Chicago. When Smith tried to pitch in with some physical work and broke his arm, he told the doctor, Ephraim Ingals, that he was "never blessed when [he] engaged in manual labor. I think I have another work to perform," he said, which elicited a smile from the doctor.[84] A sizable body of non-aligned Mormons was organized in the county under the nominal leadership of Aaron Hook,[85] who had been baptized and ordained an elder before Joseph Smith's death. In March 1848, Hook published a broadside, *Zion's Standard: A Voice from the Smith Family,* with a letter from William. True to custom, instead of offering inspirational encouragement, William used the space to report how Brigham had tried to "ruin the Smith family." William,

---

83. "William at It Again," ibid., Jan. 4, 1849, 226.

84. Inez A. Kennedy, *Recollections of the Pioneers of Lee County*, ed. Seraphina Gardner Smith (Amboy, IL: Lee County Columbian Club, 1893), 392. Reference supplied by Erin Metcalfe.

85. For information on Aaron Hook, see Janet Burton Seegmiller, "The Succession Crisis: A Family View," *John Whitmer Historical Journal* 20 (2000): 94-110; also Frank E. Stevens, *History of Lee County, Illinois*, 2 vols. (Chicago: S. J. Clarke, 1914), 1:273.

not Brigham, was the true "Apostle and Prophet of the Most High God," he insisted. He must have been persuasive in person, however, because five members of the northern Illinois congregations testified that "the spirit of God has borne witness with our spirits that he is a servant of God." They were Nathaniel Berry, Aaron Hook, John Landers,[86] Alva Smith (no relation),[87] and Thomas Tourtillott.[88] Mostly the group was interested in forming a defense against Strang's growing popularity, but they were also pleased to have a Smith family member in their midst.

A founder of the RLDS Church, Jason W. Briggs, wrote that William was able to convince Mormons in southern Wisconsin and northern Illinois to take him on despite his considerable baggage by making them believe that he was standing in for Joseph III as his regent and mentor. By this tactic, William was able to unite people, and "there seemed a general acquiescence on the part of the Saints among whom he labored," Briggs wrote, that this was

---

86. Respectfully referred to as "Father" John Landers, he was born on August 20, 1794, in Leeds County, Ontario, Canada. He was baptized by John E. Page on October 7, 1836, and was ordained an elder a month later. He later united with the Strangites and then with William Smith. After joining the RLDS in 1860, Landers actively served in the church until his death at over 97 years in Lamoni, Iowa. As he requested, Joseph Smith III preached at his funeral. "Father Landers Dead," *Saints' Herald*, Jan. 30, 1892, 65; Inez Smih Davis, *The Story of the Church*, 4th ed. rev. (Independence: Herald Publishing House, 1948), 235-37.

87. Alva Smith (1804-?) converted to Mormonism in Dickson, Illinois. In 1861 he joined the Reorganization. Joseph Smith and Heman C. Smith, *History of the Reorganized Church of Jesus Christ of Latter Day Saints* (Independence: Herald House, 1967), 3:297; Edmund C. Briggs, *Early History of the Reorganization* (Independence: Price Publishing, 1998), online at restorationbookstore.org.

88. "To the Scattered Saints," *Zion's Standard: A Voice from the Smith Family* (Palestine, IL: Printed by P. Lynch, 1848). William said that "during that time my preaching was in the county of Lee, State of Illinois. ... There was no one went with me except Aaron Hook. He was an elder in the church ... a separation had taken place (1845) between me and the balance of the Quorum of the Twelve." Testimony of William Smith in Temple Lot Suit, typescript, 92, Inez Smith Davis Papers, P23, f47, Community of Christ Library Archives, Independence, Missouri.

the solution to the succession crisis. William chose Aaron Hook and Lyman Wight as "Counselors *pro tem*" (counselors for the time being) to serve under a president *pro tem*, with Joseph Wood serving as a counselor and spokesman.[89]

As William's influence grew, he was fined $33.28 in late August 1848 by a justice of the peace in Lee County for assaulting a man named Stephen Little. William "beat" and "bruise[d]" him, according to the complaint.[90] This is important only in indicating that the volatile Smith brother had probably not yet shaken his old temper, which could flare up at minor irritations. He was in an unusual situation as titular head of about two hundred Mormons, since most of them at that time were half a continent away in a settlement called Zodiac, overseen by Lyman Wight in Texas, seventy miles north of San Antonio. Wight's adherents, like Young's, practiced polygamy, while the eastern Saints did not. At first, the Texans were discreet about their anomalous domestic arrangements, but the secret eventually leaked out.[91]

In 1849, Smith brought Isaac Sheen into the alliance. Sheen had left the church in Nauvoo over none other than plural marriage.[92]

---

89. Jason W. Briggs, "History of the Reorganization," *The Messenger*, Nov. 1875, 1. Joseph Smith III was appointed head of the church at a conference in Palestine Grove, Illinois, on October 6, 1848, with William filling in for "little Joseph till he takes his place." Lyman Wight was sustained as president of the Twelve, and James Strang and Brigham Young were excommunicated. "An Extract of Conference Minutes," *Melchisedek and Aaronic Herald*, Covington, KY, Sept. 1849, 4.

90. General Record 11, Criminal Book B, Circuit Court, Lee County, Illinois Regional Archives, DeKalb, Illinois. Stanley B. Kimball, "New Light on Old Egyptiana: Mormon Mummies, 1848-71," *Dialogue: A Journal of Mormon Thought* 16 (Winter 1983): 87n31, cited additional relevant files at the DeKalb archives, but Bill Shepard found them missing, presumably stolen, when he visited the facility in March 2009.

91. Melvin C. Johnson, *Polygamy on the Pedernales: Lyman Wight's Mormon Villages in Antebellum Texas, 1845 to 1858* (Logan: Utah State University Press, 2006), 124-32, includes information on the temporary Smith-Wight alliance.

92. Isaac Sheen was born in Leicestershire, England, in December 1810 and immigrated to America when he was nineteen. He was baptized in the

The anti-polygamy crusader led a group in Covington, Kentucky, located near Cincinnati. After joining with Smith, the two began editing a periodical titled the *Melchisedic and Aaronic Herald*, a medium for attacking Strang and Young, among others. Cut from the same cloth as Smith, the editor reveled in the bellicose rhetoric Smith was known for. One can only imagine what Lyman Wight thought of the attacks on polygamy, even though he probably agreed that Young was the "man of sin, the son of perdition" prophesied in the Bible.[93] In his own column, Smith called Strang a "booby," "rotten trash," and a "vicious impostor." The *Gospel Herald* was called a "filthy, dirty, half-penny sheet," lacking "the least plausibility of truth."[94]

Nobody was surprised to encounter this type of polemic from Smith, but people were caught off guard when Sheen suspended the invective long enough to announce that William was "the prophet Elijah," based on a revelation Sheen and Smith had received in Covington in July informing them that Smith was "the Elijah of this dispensation."[95] Whether Smith was *like* Elijah or *literally* Elijah was a detail that would be worked out later, apparently. One can imagine that since William was in the

---

Philadelphia area by Erastus Snow ten years later, ordained an elder the next year, and moved to Illinois in 1842. When he dissented from Brigham Young over polygamy, he relocated to Cincinnati and briefly joined with William Smith, then with the proto-RLDS in 1859. With the RLDS, he became a gifted editor, publisher, and church recorder.

93. 2 Thess. 2:3; "The Man of Sin," *Aaronic Herald*, Feb. 1, 1849, 1. William Smith asserted in the *Melchisedek & Aaronic Herald*, Feb. 1850, 1, that Salt Lake Mormons were dressing like Indians "for the purpose of robbing the emigrants" on their way to Oregon and California. "Many murders and robberies have already been committed by these demons in human shape," he said of the Utah settlers. Readers should know that the spelling of Melchizedek in the masthead often changed.

94. "Strang's Consistency," *Melchisedek & Aaronic Herald*, Oct. 1849, 1.

95. "The Elijah," ibid., Aug. 1849, 1; also "A Revelation, Given to William Smith and Isaac Sheen," ibid.; "Covington, Ky., June 14, 1849: A Proclamation to the Saints," ibid.

audience in Kirtland when Elijah was said to have appeared to his brother Joseph behind the curtain, the meaning was probably that William was more *like* the ancient Hebrew prophet than a literal reincarnation knowing that the Brighamites had begun taking oaths against the United States to "avenge the blood of Joseph Smith on this nation,"[96] Smith and Sheen protested in a petition to the Federal Committee on Territories in late 1849, adding that those in Utah were guilty of "blasphemy." In doing so, William neglected to mention that he was himself a modern incarnate of the prophet Elijah.[97]

Delegates from Zodiac attended a church conference in Covington in early April 1850. The primary representative, forty-nine-year-old Otis Hobart, found the trip trying and died before the conference began. Saddened by this, the leaders nevertheless pressed forward and received a positive vote for the suggestion that all church members relocate to Texas. It was determined that Isaac Sheen would replace Aaron Hook as second counselor.[98] A few eager members left immediately, but most were still making preparations when Wight suddenly broke with Smith, according to a now common storyline. Smith responded by having Wight disfellowshipped.[99] If Smith thought this would render a crippling blow, the script went differently than imagined and turned out to be the beginning of the end for Smith. The next issue of the *Melchisedic and Aaronic Herald* in February 1850 would be the last. The editors devoted the issue to an attack on Mormon schismatic leader James Colin Brewster.[100]

---

96. Quinn, *Mormon Hierarchy: Origins*, 179.

97. "Petition of William Smith, Isaac Sheen, et al., of Covington, Kentucky, against the Admission of Deseret into the Union, December 31, 1849," rpt. in the RLDS *Journal of History* 7 (Oct. 1914): 453-57; also in the *Congressional Globe* 21 (1849): 92.

98. Johnson, *Polygamy on the Pedernales*, 127-28.

99. Ibid., 131-32.

100. "Brewsterism," *Melchisedek & Aaronic Herald*, Feb. 1850, 3, promised to

Years later a son of Isaac Sheen published an anti-polygamy booklet that gave insight into the demise of the *Melchisedic and Aaronic Herald*. With the arrival of the representatives from Zodiac, "it was learned that the 'devil' [polygamy] was in Texas and that William was not above suspicion."[101] Father Sheen determined to lay "a plan to entrap him, and succeeded in getting a polygamous letter from William, who was then in Illinois." By this means, Sheen "exposed 'the Elijah of the last dispensation': withdrew his name from the petition against the 'State of Deseret' and pulled up the 'Stake of Zion' in Covington."[102]

The "polygamous letter" Isaac elicited from William laid out the doctrine of polygamy and probably confided that he had been sealed to multiple women. We don't know what Sheen's initial response to Smith was, but Smith sent a follow-up letter on April 29, 1850, from Shelburn (Rocky Ford), Illinois, begging Sheen to not cast him off, saying he had been "quite sick" when he penned his previous letter and was, in any case, provoked by Sheen's importunity and arrogance in assuming the authority for "correcting what was wrong in doctrine," revealing the probable trap Sheen's son mentioned. William promised to turn his life around, "set my face against all sin," and let "every evil … go by the board." "So give me a chance, and I will do all that is in my power to reconcile your feelings," he wrote, begging Sheen not to show his letters to Roxie Ann. That alone is interesting in that it confirms that Smith had mentioned her to Sheen. Then Smith showed his true inner self by

---

follow up with an article exposing the "nonsense" of the faction "for the purpose of saving a few of its deluded victims," but the paper folded. For information on Brewster, see Dan Vogel, "James Colin Brewster: The Boy Prophet Who Challenged Mormon Authority," in Launius and Thatcher, *Differing Visions*, 120-39. In the February issue, the editors included a crude insult to Brigham Young, saying Joseph Smith had pronounced his lineage to be "of Cain through the loins of Ham," 3.

101. John K. Sheen, *Polygamy: The Veil Lifted* (York, NE: John K. Sheen, 1889), 14.

102. Ibid., 14-15.

assuming the guise of a victim and saying he could "do no more than to offer my life as a sacrifice."

Instead of accommodating Smith's request for confidentiality, Sheen publicly denounced him. True to form, the modern Elijah struck back, dropping the façade of repentance and crying that Sheen had betrayed him. The apostate should leave, Smith suggested. The collapse in their relationship was so unexpected that it attracted widespread attention. It was announced in two Cincinnati newspapers. The *Daily Cincinnati Commercial* reported that Smith had sent them a letter identifying himself as the "true representative of God on earth."[103] Feeling equally desperate, Sheen went public with a response in the *Daily Nonpareil* under the heading, "Wm. Smith—The Imposter," to which he attached for the editor's eyes a letter Smith wrote, which Sheen thought would be enough to convince the editor of Smith's villainy:

Eds. Nonpareil:—The subjoined letter will show that the statements which the imposter, Wm. Smith, is now circulating concerning me are false, and will in some degree explain the cause of my renunciation of him and his Church. The iniquity spoken of in the [attached] letter is a vindication of adultery and fornication by Wm. Smith. He claims that he has authority from God to raise up posterity from other men's wives, and says it will exalt them and their husbands in the eternal world. His repentance is base hypocrisy, which he proves by his late conduct.[104]

Even more blunt was a communication to the *Daily Cincinnati Commercial* two days later, in which Sheen wrote:

Wm. Smith has not cut me off from his church. I have cut myself off, and intend to remain cut off eternally from such a hypocritical

---

103. "A Prophet Robbed and Deserted: Excommunication of Elder Sheen," *Cincinnati Daily Commercial*, May 20, 1850, 1.

104. "Wm. Smith: The Imposter," *Daily Nonpareil*, Cincinnati, May 20, 1850, 2.

libertine. He has professed the greatest hostility to the plurality wife doctrine, but on the 18th ult., he told me that he had a right to raise up posterity from other men's wives. … He said it would be an honor conferred upon them and their husbands, to allow him that privilege, and that they would thereby be exalted to a high degree of glory in eternity.[105]

Brewster's newspaper, the *Olive Branch*, announced from Springfield, Illinois, that "Wm. Smith's organization is now entirely overthrown." The Brewsterites found it especially rich that Smith had "promised an expose of 'Brewsterism,'" when instead of that, Sheen was "exposing the iniquity of Smith through the public papers."[106] In Voree, the *Gospel Herald* announced with equal satisfaction the information they had received "from Isaac Sheen that Wm Smith has been at his old tricks again." They knew of no one "who talks so much of his own virtue and other men's vices as Wm. Smith."[107]

Like James Brewster, Orson Hyde reprinted Smith's letters in his newspaper, the *Frontier Guardian* out of Council Bluffs, Iowa, prefacing them with an impressive salvo of denunciations for the "lying, deception, laziness, intemperance and debauchery" of their author. Not that anyone in the circles Sheen ran in had experienced second thoughts about William Smith in the past, Hyde wrote, at least not while William was "attacking the Brighamites." Only after William had "invaded [Sheen's] domestic circle, and the fangs of the monster [had] pierced the fountain of his most sensitive feelings, he cries against Br. William!" The pretended prophet had always been a "scoundrel," Hyde wrote, "lying against the [Utah] church and slandering it" the whole time.

---

105. "William Smith: Fornication, Adultery," *Cincinnati Daily Commercial*, May 22, 1850, 4. The same paper printed an "Extract from Wm. Smith's Fornication Letter," also on May 22: "My wife [William's wife Roxie Ann Grant] says that she will not go to Texas for fear of the spiritual doctrine. I have told her better, but all to no avail."
106. "Confounding False Leaders," *Olive Branch*, June 1850, 190.
107. "Since the First," *Gospel Herald*, May 30, 1850, 87; emphasis in original.

As surprising as it was, William found a well-off adherent in Lee County, Joseph Wood, who joined with him in 1851 in publishing a twenty-four-page pamphlet entitled *Epistle of the Twelve.* The pamphlet touted Smith's prophetic credentials in a new church, of which Smith was "First President, Prophet, Seer, Revelator, Translator, and Patriarch." Wood was identified as senior apostle and co-prophet with "the keys of the ministry of this latter day dispensation, equal to and jointly with the said William Smith."[108]

Wood called the Utah apostles "sons of perdition," showing himself to be an attentive student of Smith, also calling Young the biblical "man of sin." In this onslaught of ridicule, Strang fared no better, receiving an equal dose of invective. Wood defended the familial approach to succession by saying the rightful successor to Jesus was his stepbrother James, not Peter.[109] The pretenders were everywhere pushing their claims, but "President William Smith," by contrast, was blessed with "vision, ... humility, ... forbearance, and charity." Joseph Smith himself had told William he had "all the necessary ordinations to lead the church," and after ordaining William a "Prophet, Seer, Revelator, and Translator," Joseph had "leaped" up in joy and "smote his feet" to celebrate having finished what was required of him, observing that "it was done," and "in a few days Brother William started on his mission and saw his Brothers no more," Wood wrote.[110] After circulating the epistle, Smith and Wood visited the Beloit area of southern Wisconsin and found the scattered remnants of the church in that area suspicious

<hr />

108. Joseph Wood served a mission in Illinois, was disfellowshipped in November 1840, and later became an attorney. "Elder Joseph Wood," *Times and Seasons,* Mar. 1, 1841, 335; Joseph Smith Jr., et al., *History of the Church of Jesus Christ of Latter-day Saints,* ed. B. H. Roberts, 2nd ed. rev., 7 vols. (Salt Lake City: Deseret Book, 1959), 6:136; Joseph Wood, *Epistle of the Twelve* (Milwaukee: Sentinel and Gazette Steam Press, 1851), 3.

109. Wood, *Epistle,* 6–18.

110. Ibid., 20, 24. Wood included a hymn, "The Elijah," by William Smith, with the line in apparent self-reference, "The Prophet Elijah at last has appeared" (24).

that they were practicing polygamy in secret.[111] Smith and Wood had no sooner returned to Illinois in October than they "threw off the mask in a council called to Priests' Lodge and confessed to the belief and practice of polygamy in the name of the Lord," according to Jason Briggs.[112]

Briggs said he received a vision the following month in which God assured him that William was the intended successor but had violated the trust given him and had forfeited his right. "As Esau despised his birthright, so has William Smith despised my law," the voice of God articulated. Smith and Wood were "degraded in their lives, and shall die without regard," the revelation continued, "for they have wholly forsaken my law, and given themselves to all manner of uncleanness, and prostituted my law and the keys of power entrusted to them, to the lusts of the flesh, and have run greedily in the way of adultery. ... Behold, that which ye received as my celestial law is not of me, but is the doctrine of Balaam."[113]

Smith responded with a letter "denying that which had been

---

111. Roger D. Launius, *Joseph Smith III: Pragmatic Prophet* (Urbana: University of Illinois Press, 1998), 98. Wood received a revelation for Jason Briggs: "Thou hast not trusted to my word, nor given heed to the counsel of my Spirit; nor was it justifiable in thee, to give way to a fearful Spirit while listening to the bickerings of enemies; and also to the lying slanders of secret conspirators against my servants." Joseph Wood to Jason W. Briggs, Palestine Stake of Zion, Sept. 30, 1851, Miscellaneous Letters and Papers, P13, f80, Community of Christ Archives.

112. Briggs, "History of the Reorganization," 1. The Priest's Lodge appears to have been an unfinished structure being built in Palestine Grove. Wood's September 30 letter also mentioned that "President William Smith has a bad cold. $20.00 has been raised on the credit for the Lodge to finish purchasing materials for finishing his house."

113. Ibid. A decade later, Briggs wrote to J. T. Clark from Wheeler, Iowa, on February 18, 1888: "We dropped Strang, and in 1850-51 accepted William Smith as the successor, so so;—but in less than one year he exhibited the cloven foot and boomed polygamy afresh in the name of God and his brother Joseph. This Beloit Branch was the largest perhaps of any that accepted William Smith— and at the conference called by him Oct. 1851 at Palestine, near Amboy Ill., his true character was discovered by many of us; and we went home dissatisfied." In "J. W. Briggs Letters," *The Return*, Davis City, IA, Dec. 1, 1895, 3.

charged," countering with an excommunication of Briggs for his "slanderous" claim.[114] In a letter to David Powell, a colleague of Briggs, Smith confided that the "full right of [his] authority" had dawned on him slowly, beginning as a small idea at first, "and so increased by degrees." Unimpressed, the officers of the Wisconsin branches severed their connection with him and Wood in February 1852, proclaiming with united voice their "duty to warn and forewarn all men, and especially all Saints, of their wiles." The two deposed evangelists were "guilty of teachings and practices against morality and hospitality, violating herein; both the law of God and man—base and hypocritical beyond any with whom we have had the misfortune to be acquainted."[115]

Things could not get worse, it seemed, but in September 1852, Smith was indicted in Lee County for raping Rosanna Hook,[116] a niece of Aaron Hook, on March 1. State attorney William Miller charged that Smith had used "force ... upon one Rosanna Hook," that he "violently and feloniously did make an assault [upon] her and ... then and there forcibly and against her will feloniously did ravish and carnally know" her.[117] As stark as the charges were, the incident has remained shrouded in some mystery because she later retracted her accusation. Whatever the truth of the matter, one can see a possible blending of William's propensity toward violence and disregard for boundaries with young women. If true, it was an appallingly new low that came on the heels of another disclosure in the newspaper that "one of the female members of the church ... had

---

114. Briggs, "History of the Reorganization," 6.

115. Ibid., 5-6.

116. Rosanna and her twin sister Rhoda Hook were born in 1837 in Maine to William Lorenzo Hook and his first wife, Mercy. The 1850 census for Amboy, Lee County, Illinois, documents Rosanna and Rhoda living with Uncle John Hook; William Smith and daughter Mary Jane lived next door with Uncle Aaron Hook. Erin Jennings (Metcalfe) to Bill Shepard, Apr. 2, 2009.

117. *The People v. William Smith*, Indictment for Rape, State of Illinois—Lee County, signed by States Attorney William T. Miller, Lee County Criminal File Records, General number 12, Illinois Regional Archives, DeKalb, Illinois.

been induced to believe that it was necessary for her salvation that she should become [William's] spiritual wife." The witness failed to appear in court, so William took the opportunity to berate her for persecuting him and criticize the court for "persecution." The charges were brought up because he was in the middle of a divorce, he said. The newspaper explained that Roxie Ann was one of the women William had taken "in spiritual wifery."[118]

At this point, things took an even stranger turn when the Illinois *Telegraph* published Rosanna's reversal: "I sincerely and honestly clear William Smith from all the charges made in my affidavit ... before Squire Dutcher." A note from her father, Aaron Hook, and Jotham T. Barrett, stated that she had been pressured by William's enemies to submit dishonest information about him.[119] The newspaper had also obtained a July 1851 letter from Smith in which he disclosed that a certain woman "belong[ed]" to "Brother Wood" and that it was not Smith's "province to interfere with any of [Wood's] wives."[120] On September 21, 1853, Hyra Axtell, presumably a supporter of William Smith, posted a $350 bond for Smith to appear in court at a later date on the charge of "bastardy."[121]

The next year the *Telegraph* reported that Joseph Wood, who had "lately resumed the practice of law," refused to represent William in court unless he paid him his normal retainer. Otherwise, the former co-prophet had warned, he might "appear against" William "and

---

118. "Mormonism in This County," *Telegraph*, Dixon, IL, April 9, 1853, 2. Roxie Ann divorced William on April 25, 1853. See State of Illinois, Knox County Circuit Court, April Term 1853, Galesburg, Illinois, box 93, case 37.

119. "Slander Refuted," *Telegraph*, Apr. 30, 1853, 2.

120. William Smith letter, ibid., 2. The newspaper replaced names by blank lines in publishing the letter. The newspaper also received a letter, presumably from Isaac Sheen, that was so acerbic the editor decided not to publish it. "Mormonism Again," *Telegraph*, May 7, 1853, 2.

121. "September Term 1853. Wednesday 21st," Lee County Circuit Clerk's Office, Chancery Book B, 399, Dixon, Illinois. An untitled document in the same case jacket, dated Sept. 21, 1853, and signed by Sheriff Ozias Wheeler, said: "Arrested the within named William Smith and discharged him on his giving Bond with Security."

could send him to the Penitentiary."[122] Historian Stanley B. Kimball found that Smith left the jurisdiction for Saint Louis and was apprehended there as a fugitive.[123] The *Missouri Republican* described him as genteel, "with good manners," notwithstanding he was "a large and powerfully built man."[124] Sheriff Ozias Wheeler wrote on a subpoena on April 7, 1854, that Rhoda and Rosanna Hook's family and others had raised the $1,000 bond for William's release from jail, at which the trial record went cold, presumably meaning that the charges were dismissed.[125]

By now, William had become a non-factor in the Restoration movement. A visitor from Utah, Thomas Colburn, wrote to the *St. Louis Luminary* in 1855 that he had run into William in Springfield, Illinois, and found the former apostle "evasive" about which church he was loyal to, saying "he and the authorities" in Utah had experienced "some misunderstanding, the same as Peter and Paul" in the Bible, but was "willing to abide" anything Brigham had to say in regard to William's situation.[126] Spurred on by this conversation, Smith wrote five days later to Young that if he had the funds, he would move to Utah.[127] There is no indication that Young responded to this not-so-subtle hint.

Later that year, three men (William Smith, Martin Harris, Chilion Daniels) sent an announcement to several Midwestern factions asking them to "send delegates to a conference" in Kirtland on October 6.[128] The idea was originally pitched to Smith and Harris

---

122. "More Trouble in the Church," *Telegraph*, Mar. 9, 1854, 2.

123. Kimball, "New Light on Old Egyptiana," 87-88.

124. "Important Arrest," *Missouri Republican*, St. Louis, Apr. 28, 1854, 2. Our thanks to Erin Metcalfe, who located this newspaper.

125. Both documents are from the folder, "State of Illinois v. William Smith"; Kimball, "New Light on Old Egyptiana," 87, came to the conclusion that the case was dismissed.

126. Thomas Colburn to editor, *St. Louis Luminary*, May 5, 1855, 94.

127. William Smith to Brigham Young, May 7, 1855, Brigham Young Collection, LDS Church History Library.

128. "Post to James J. Strang," n.d., *Northern Islander*, Saint James, Beaver

through a clairvoyant in Cleveland who had channeled Moses, Elias, Elijah, and John.[129] The conference was held, but those in attendance were unable to come to a consensus. Afterward, William moved to Turkey Creek, Iowa, for a year, then found himself back in Pennsylvania, marrying Eliza Sanborn on November 12, 1857, a woman sixteen years his junior. Her parents had died in Nauvoo in 1839.[130] At some point William became affiliated with the Baptists and apparently preached for them. When asked whether he had been a Mormon, he denied any personal affiliation with the sect.[131] Yet even his attempt to settle into a non–Mormon environment failed. He was "about to be tried by its vestrymen for teaching what they considered was heresy, when he resigned his pastorate and came out openly for 'mormonism,' preaching it as he understood it."[132]

Brigham Young expressed sympathy for William's encounter with the school of hard knocks and predicted that if William lived long enough, he might yet still "become a good humble man." Smith sent the Utah leader additional entreaties about being accepted into the Utah church, showing that William must not

---

Island, Lake Michigan, Nov. 1, 1855, 1. The *Northern Islander* responded that anyone who had not figured out what made William Smith tick, "on proof of a long series of fornications and adulteries," must be themselves "in the gall of bitterness and the bonds of iniquity."

129. Stephen Post journal, Oct. 5, 1855, LDS Church History Library.

130. Eliza Sanborn was born on April 16, 1827, in Cattaraugus, New York. Other researchers (Erin Metcalfe, Connell O'Donovan) have traced her family's movements from Kirtland in 1836 to Missouri and then Illinois in 1838. William and Eliza Smith are in the 1860 census for Erie County, Pennsylvania. William was forty-nine and Eliza thirty-three. Their son, William Enoch, was born in Pennsylvania on July 24, 1858.

131. Walker, *United by Faith*, 281; "Mormonism: A Letter from William Smith, Brother of Joseph the Prophet," *Illinois State Chronicle*, Decatur, June 11, 1857, 1. William's accusation that Utah Mormons killed the territorial secretary, Almon W. Babbitt, has been refuted by Omer W. Whitman and James L. Varner, *Neither Saint Nor Scoundrel: Almon Babbitt, Territorial Secretary of Utah* (Baltimore: Publish America, 2009).

132. Anderson, *Memoirs of President Joseph Smith III*, 184.

have believed his own rhetoric about how dangerous Young was.[133] William's cousin, George A. Smith, said in a sermon in Utah in August 1857, "The Saints could have carried William upon their shoulders; they could have carried him in their arms, and [could] have done anything for him, if he would have laid aside his follies and wickedness, and would have done right."[134]

To William's rescue came Martin Harris in 1858 in Kirtland. Harris called the local believers together and "appointed Wm. Smith their Leader Prophet Seer & Revelator." But even this last-ditch effort lasted only a "few days" before "Harris drove Wm. Smith out of the place & damned him to Hell," according to Enoch Beese, a Utah missionary who was passing through at the time.[135] The next thing, surprisingly, is that William said he allowed himself to be baptized into the Utah church. Albert Carrington of Brigham Young's office staff read aloud a letter indicating that William "desired to come to the [Salt Lake] valley and be restored to his former associations. He stated he [had] been rebaptised." "Another letter was also read from a J. J. Butler stating he had baptized Wm. Smith, and that [William's] course had been to sustain the authorities of this Church."[136] Again, nothing happened. William was not joined by his wife Eliza in his religious feelings, and she may have prevented them from moving to Utah. In this light, it is still interesting to see that they traveled far enough west to end up in Iowa by 1860.[137]

Joseph Smith's son, Joseph III, became aware of his uncle's

133. Quinn, *Mormon Hierarchy: Origins*, 225; Kenney, *Wilford Woodruff's Journal*, 5:58.

134. George A. Smith, Aug. 2, 1857, *Journal of Discourses*, 26 vols. (London: Latter-day Saints Book Depot, 1854–86), 5:102.

135. Kenney, *Wilford Woodruff's Journal*, 5:198–99.

136. Brigham Young Office Journal, May 14, 1860, LDS Church History Library.

137. Two children were born at Elkader: Edson Don Carlos Smith on September 6, 1862, and Loie May on May 8, 1866. Our thanks to Kyle R. Walker for this information.

misbehavior and how the congregations in Lee County "fell to pieces" for "reasons not necessary to be given here," as he thinly camouflaged the incidents in his memoirs. He added:

> In 1856, when the missionaries of the Reorganization, Elders E. C. Briggs and Samuel H. Gurley, came to me at Nauvoo, there was placed in my possession quite an amount of documentary evidence concerning [William] and his several religious movements. Some of this evidence dealt largely with his career ... in Lee County, and his work in connection with one Joseph Wood, Aaron Hook, and others. It was placed in my hands without reservation, or obligation on my part to make any specific use of it.
>
> Uncle William learned that I had these documents and he came to Nauvoo and demanded their surrender. This I refused, with the result that he remained aloof from me until several years after I identified myself with the Reorganization.[138]

Soon after Joseph Smith III stepped into office as president of the Reorganization on April 6, 1860, he received a demand from William "to be received into the church upon his former membership, to be allowed to retain his standing as an apostle." Joseph replied that the church "might be willing to receive him into fellowship on his original baptism" but said that anything else would have to be discussed and approved at a church conference.[139] The matter was still unresolved when William enlisted to fight in the Civil War. To improve his chances of being accepted, he said he was forty-four, concealing the fact that he was actually fifty-two and maybe partly explaining why he only served half his three-year enlistment, February 1864 to July 1865, before returning home to file for an invalid's pension.[140] Under the influence of Eliza, he seemed finally willing to settle down to a quieter existence, but

---

138. Anderson, *Memoirs of President Joseph Smith III*, 184.

139. Ibid.

140. Information supplied by Erin Metcalfe.

neither was he incapacitated. As he adjusted to his life as a veteran, he exhibited a more gentle temperament, according to later reports. Gone were the days of flitting from one sect to another, of moving frequently, of finding himself in serious trouble due to temper and unrestrained sexual appetite.

He continued to petition the Reorganized Church for admittance as Church Patriarch, but President Smith rebuffed him.[141] The two remained at a standoff until April 1878 in Plano, Illinois, where it was decided that William would be recognized as a high priest.[142] In that capacity, he was told, they wanted him to preach throughout Iowa and neighboring states at regular worship services. People wanted to know the details of the church's formative years, and he could fill that need by relating inspirational stories about the founding. In the summer of 1880, two Utah missionaries, Hyrum Jensen and Brigham Roberts, visited William and Eliza Smith at their home in Elkader, Iowa, and found Eliza hostile but William welcoming. Eliza "dominated the household," Roberts reported. The sixty-nine-year-old William, tall and emaciated, directed them to the house of an acquaintance where he thought they might stay, rather than in his own home.[143]

William started to think he should write about his early experiences. Hearing of this, his nephew Joseph III wrote: "I have long been engaged in removing from Father's memory and from the early church, the stigma and blame thrown upon them because of Polygamy; and have at last lived to see the cloud rapidly lifting. And I would not consent to see further blame attached, by a blunder now."[144] William understood what was expected of him. In his

---

141. Paul M. Edwards, "William B. Smith: The Persistent 'Pretender,'" *Dialogue: A Journal of Mormon Thought* 18 (Summer 1985): 132-38.

142. Anderson, *Memoirs of President Joseph Smith III*, 184-85.

143. Gary James Bergera, ed., *The Autobiography of B. H. Roberts* (Salt Lake City: Signature Books, 1990), 103-5. Roberts began writing this autobiography about January 1933 and died in September that year.

144. Joseph Smith III to "Uncle William" Smith, Mar. 11, 1882, Joseph Smith

forty-five-page booklet, *William Smith on Mormonism*, he told about his brother's experiences with an angel and about his own early life without saying anything about polygamy. In listing the faith and doctrines of the church, he went so far as to state that "the doctrines of a plurality and a community of wives are heresies, and are opposed to the law of God."[145] He and Eliza lived out their lives devoid of further scandal, with financial help from the RLDS Church and a Civil War pension. When Eliza died on March 7, 1889, William married a widow named Rosa Surprise on December 21, 1889.

The newlyweds moved to nearby Osterdock in 1890. William continued to preach for the Reorganization. When he was eighty years old, he gave testimony in a court hearing in Kansas City in the Temple Lot Case, pitting the RLDS Church against the Hedrickites who possessed the temple site in Independence.[146] He took advantage of the media megaphone to denounce Utah Mormons over doctrinal issues, saying he "never, prior to the death of my brother, or subsequent to his death, taught or preached the doctrine of polygamy."[147] Interestingly, Mary Ann West, whom William married and deserted in Nauvoo, testified by deposition that she was married to William in Nauvoo by Brigham Young. When asked if she was sealed to William for eternity, she replied "I do not think Smith will ever come where I am to claim me; I do not think they will let him in where I will be."[148]

In 1893 on a speaking assignment in Minnesota, William caught a cold, he took it home with him, and died in Osterdock on November 13, 1893. He was eulogized in the newspaper for his service in

---

III Letterbook 3, Community of Christ Archives; Launius, *Joseph Smith III*, 208-09.

145. William Smith, *William Smith on Mormonism* (Lamoni, IA: Herald Steam Book and Job Office, 1883), 31.

146. *Complaints Abstract of Pleading and Evidence*, Circuit Court of the United States, Western District of Missouri, Western Division at Kansas City (Lamoni, IA: Herald Publishing House and Bindery, 1893), 91-105.

147. Ibid., 98.

148. Ibid., 381.

the Civil War and years of service to his community and church. Judge Samuel Murdock lionized him in this way:

> For nearly a third of a century this good man lived in and about Elkader known and respected by all, and it was here that we would often see him at the reunion of the soldiers, the reunion of old settlers, sitting on both grand and petit juries, then at the beds of sickness, now in the pulpit and then opening assemblies with prayer and dismissing them again with a benediction, or perhaps hastening to the house of mourning to whisper consolation to weeping friends, and never did there fall from his lips a single word or sentence that would cause even a child to shudder.[149]

It is possible to read into the eulogy a backhanded acknowledgement of William's past trouble due to his temper—a possible defensiveness about the turbulent life he led—but one can also detect that he had become a respected and valued member of the community. This was probably due, in no small part, to Joseph III's way of honoring him with a role in the church as a homilist.

The impression most people today have of William Smith is that he was caustic and difficult. It is true enough. However, it is also true that he believed in his brother's divine appointment, believed that his brother saw angels and miraculously translated ancient records. William was an effective missionary. He participated in Zion's Camp. His actions in the Illinois legislature helped preserve the Nauvoo Charter. One can imagine that, in his own way, he tried to live up to the standards espoused by the church but was ultimately unable to control his passions and emotions. Even more disturbing than his temper was his limitless desire to exact retribution against those who crossed him in word or deed. His insistence that Abraham Burtis be excommunicated in 1843 showed an incredible level of intolerance of what he considered to be insubordination.

---

149. "In Memorium: The Rev. William B. Smith," *Elkader Register*, Nov. 23, 1893. Our thanks to Erin Metcalfe for providing the obituary.

Even though Burtis and John Hardy were accurate in their complaints, William denounced them just the same and excommunicated Hardy in October 1844, savagely attacking his character in the *Nauvoo Neighbor* the following year.

His inability to admit when he was wrong made it impossible for people to develop a trusting relationship with him. He prevaricated when it was in his interest to do so. Even the most dispassionate historians struggle with their dislike of him since there is much to be offended by in his behavior.[150] To think of his involvement with the psychopaths in the Hodges family is enough to poison one's feelings, let alone his abuse of women. The long-term effect of his provocative acts was a downgraded view of the office of patriarch in the various churches of the Restoration.

In some ways, one can feel sorry for William as he darted from one group to another. In the wake of his brothers' assassinations, he clearly felt unmoored at sea. Kyle Walker summarized his allegiances with various Mormon factional leaders: "William's connections during this twelve-year period read like a who's who of Mormon dissidents—James J. Strang, Isaac Sheen, Martin Harris, William McLellin, George J. Adams, John C. Bennett, and Lyman Wight. In all of his forays into new movements, his need was the same—personal validation of his perspective—and the continued longing for the recognition a prominent position would provide."[151] The most sympathetic assessment came from RLDS theologian Paul M. Edwards, who wondered why William did not "leave as so many others had done?" It was because, Edwards wrote, he and his relatives were under such "pressure to be a royal family. The family

---

150. Lavina Fielding Anderson, in *Lucy's Book*, 784, states: "Although it is true that William was in a sorry financial plight himself, it is also true that there is no record of his contributing in any way to Lucy's support. Rather, his public expressions of pity and concern for his 'poor old mother' can be read, without any great stretch of the imagination, as designed to raise funds and to bolster his own claims to authority in the church."

151. Walker, "William B. Smith," 280.

must account for, and maintain, the sacred mantle, to wear the royal robes. But the robes of prophetic vision are not the common garment, even of prophets; and men and women have carried those garments with them through six generations because they were not called to wear them and they had no place to lay them."[152]

---

152. Paul M. Edwards, "William B. Smith: 'A Wart on the Ecclesiastical Tree,'" in Launius and Thatcher, *Differing Visions*, 154.

FINAL THOUGHTS ON
APOSTASY AND INTEGRITY

Mormon historian Leonard J. Arrington, in trying to prepare church members for some of the "harsh" and "ruthless" aspects of Brigham Young's administration, warned readers that the president of the Utah church was a man of contradictions. People "like their heroes and villains clearly labeled," he wrote, even though such simplicities are at odds with the realities of history.[1]

We have attempted to faithfully deal with the realities of the past in tracing the lives of the original members of the Quorum of the Twelve. When we previously wrote in 2010 about Lyman Johnson, a vista of possibilities opened to view as we contemplated details about early Mormonism. Our published article showed a great missionary laboring successfully from 1832 to mid-1836.[2] His contribution to this period of church history was immense, and his need to spread the message about the restoration of the gospel dominated his every waking thought. The fact that he claimed angelic confirmation of the truth of the Book of Mormon, and the success of his evangelism, made him a revered man in the church. However, when he rejected Joseph Smith and the religion he helped establish, he was relegated to obscurity in church historical narratives.

To varying degrees, the same was true for the other five

---

1. Leonard J. Arrington, *Brigham Young: American Moses* (New York: Knopf, 1985), xvi-xvii.

2. William Shepard and H. Michael Marquardt, "Lyman E. Johnson: Forgotten Apostle," *Journal of Mormon History* 36, no. 1 (Winter 2010): 93-144.

primary apostles we examined for this book. They were down-graded in importance because apostates were thought to be evil, no matter their previous accomplishments. We have not attempted to either heroize or demonize them, but only to document as nearly as possible the truth we could perceive in their apostolic service and the details of how they left the fold, adding our own obvious commentary along the way for readers to approve or disagree with.

We know that thousands of early Mormons followed similar paths, for which the lives of the dissenting apostles are representative. The others may not have reached high ecclesiastical status, but their conversions and departures were comparable. They range from little-known Saints to members of the First Presidency; collectively their participation was essential to the success of the movement. If it is possible to detect the forces which motivated their sacrifices, it would probably be the conviction deep in their hearts, or the holy spirit whispering in their ears that what they were doing was right. In more secular terms, they longed for a better life, for justice in the world, and for eschatological meaning. In some cases the spiritual truths they responded to in Mormonism sustained them despite the fact that they were troubled by leaders' actions, despite the fact that the simple doctrines of salvation had become more convoluted over time.

Our lost apostles could not sustain the spirit of conversion and commitment and became spiritual wanderers. At least one of them turned his back on religion altogether. Like many other frontier people, the apostles were stubborn, but they could also be contrite and open-minded. Sometimes they were united, other days they bumped into and scraped against each other. They were flawed heroes in the classical sense, each with hidden weaknesses. We found that their acts of altruism sometimes sent a tingle up the spine, for instance, when Luke Johnson helped Joseph Smith Sr. escape from an unjust arrest, even though the church had excommunicated the prison-break facilitator. Luke's brother Lyman treated church leaders as guests of honor after his house and property had been confiscated and he was run out of town.

Just as often as not, the apostles could be officious, jealous of infringements on their privileges, and intractable in policies. All of them had been tested in the mission field before they were called to high office and were promoted because of their extraordinary success. But they soon found the central church to be bogged down in internal conflicts, and they were unable to maintain the level of commitment necessary to continue their terms as apostles. One of the apostles who decided to stay, Parley P. Pratt, went through a period of discontent but found his faith rekindled. David Patten died in full fellowship in Missouri but was not in harmony with Joseph Smith when they engaged in an angry confrontation in Ohio. Orson Pratt and Orson Hyde lost their apostolic standing and had to humble themselves before they could resume their positions in the quorum. Remarkably, there is no record of Brigham Young or Heber Kimball ever publicly dissenting against Joseph Smith, but knowing their reputations for being strong-willed, one can imagine that things did not always go smoothly.

We noticed a few common characteristics. When the apostles spoke to congregations, people responded well to their persuasive charisma. They were possessed of natural leadership and demonstrated an unflinching commitment to simple moral and theological concepts. They constantly testified to a belief in Joseph Smith's calling, even after they became disillusioned in his leadership. There were also differences in the apostles' personalities. Some were incapable of bitterness; others harbored longtime resentments. Two of them turned their backs on Mormonism without exhibiting the slightest hint of regret. Others of the six reunited with whatever branch of the church they were drawn to and then endured the same difficulties again.

Looking at all the evidence together, from our current vantage, we see the first apostles of the church as essentially frontiersmen whose most prized asset was freedom, whether in religion, occupation, or general lifestyle. They were men who believed Jesus was about to return, as soon as the earth's inhabitants created a society that was worthy of receiving him. No wonder they clashed when they tied to avoid the conformity of tradition, or that they bristled when the church began formulating rules and regulations, infringing on their liberty. They had, after all, met one another in the mid-1830s when the national emphasis was Manifest Destiny, small farmer rights, and personal freedom.

As the nation was coalescing around the re-election of U.S. president Andrew Jackson, the apostles were drawn like a moth to the flame by the populism of Joseph Smith. The prophet's stated intent was to break down barriers between tradition and reason, the canon and new revelation, old social mores and new ones. People were tired of eastern intellectualism and thought it could be replaced by common sense and hard work. Joseph Smith brought together those who were searching for something new. "What many people call sin is not sin," he summarized at one point. "I do many things to break down superstition, and I will break it down."[3] Even though he said this in 1841 after five of the apostles had already left, it was his attitude from the beginning. The apostles joined a church that was on the move, both geographically and theologically, and they were more than eager to lend their considerable talents to spreading the word.

It was probably inevitable that conflict would result from establishing two different administrative bodies: a high council to oversee the stakes of Zion and the Quorum of Twelve to look after the mission field. Many people today are unaware of this duplication and assume the church was founded in 1830 with three men at the

---

3. Joseph Smith, et al., *History of the Church of Jesus Christ of Latter-day Saints*, ed. B. H. Roberts, 7 vols. (Salt Lake City: Deseret News, 1902-1912), 4:445; Scott G. Kenney, ed., *Wilford Woodruff's Journal, 1833-1898*, typescript, 9 vols. (Midvale, UT: Signature Books, 1983-85), 2:136.

head and twelve apostles to support them, that the first high council operated only within a stake organization. But until 1832 there were not even two separate priesthoods, let alone a presidency or twelve apostles.[4] The various offices of the church were added as needed, as the church grew and encountered difficulties in its lines of authority and communication. After establishing a quorum of apostles, Joseph sent individual members of the quorum oversees without consulting the quorum president, Thomas Marsh. The apostles operated out of their jurisdiction in the Far West Stake.

The genius of Joseph's administrative style was equally a drawback, in that his pronouncements had to be systematized by others. He was better at long-range thinking than shuffling paperwork, a leader more than an organizer. However, the lack of attention to details sometimes led to ruin, especially in the case of the Kirtland Safety Society. With the bank's collapse, the Smith family suffered as much as anyone else, their money suddenly becoming as worthless as anyone else's. Still, it was Joseph's fault because he should have known better, so the logic went. It was a difficult conclusion to avoid. At least, it forced the apostles to reassess their assumptions about what a prophet was: infallible or an interpreter of more general inspiration. Was he the same as everyone else, only with a more finely tuned ability to interpret the promptings?

As members of the Twelve confronted the shock of realizing that Joseph was as human as they were, they re-evaluated their beliefs and responded variously. John Boynton walked away, never to look back except to stop in on his former friends when he passed through Salt Lake City. It seems that he did not speak again about his time as an apostle, at least not that we could find in the historical record. He lost confidence in all organized religion, which made him unlike the other lost apostles who either affiliated with some

---

4. Gregory A. Prince, *Power from on High: The Development of Mormon Priesthood* (Salt Lake City: Signature Books, 1995), 27.

faction of Mormonism or retained their testimony in the Book of Mormon. Instead, Boynton treated the church as a youthful indiscretion and great mistake.

At the other extreme, Luke Johnson was rebaptized and traveled to Utah, where he was considered for reappointment to the Quorum of the Twelve. When that failed to materialize, he settled in a remote area west of Salt Lake City and lived out his life as a cowboy, his son tragically dying in a saloon fight. It was a long way from the comfortable life he was born into, in a family home in Hiram, Ohio, where his parents were prominent and respected.

When the turmoil in Ohio migrated to Missouri on a larger and more lethal scale, Joseph Smith determined to prevent history from repeating itself and tried to stamp out all dissent. It must have been painful to call for the excommunication of his oldest allies whose loyalties should not have been in question. Lyman Johnson demonstrated more Christ-like behavior while being shunned than the church's Danites, who denounced him. Like Boynton, Johnson soon landed on his feet and was on course to become well situated in Richmond after having been forced out of Far West with only the possessions he could carry. After the death of his wife, he remarried and continued experimenting with business ventures until one day in December 1859 his sled fell through the ice on the Mississippi River and he drowned.

William McLellin harbored uncertainties about some church doctrines from the beginning, but he was a staunch public defender of the faith. He left shortly after Lyman Johnson and spent the rest of his life thinking about it. It has been said that he had a selective memory. His claim was that he did not waver, but that his church did, that it was impossible to remain loyal to teachings that were in flux, a new theological tenet introduced every few weeks and sometimes in direct opposition to what had been previously taught. We were unable to pinpoint exactly when he fell away because he remained committed to core beliefs even though he had separated himself from the organization. As he launched a search for the divinely appointed successor to the original 1830s church, he fell into a cyclical pattern of embracing and then finding fault with each new group he discovered. The notion that he could simply walk away did not seem to occur to him.

Thomas Marsh suffered the most damage in reputation over the years from people who, unlike Arrington, wanted their history to have clear-cut heroes and villains. Marsh was faithful to the church until he witnessed the Mormon sacking of Gallatin and Millport, at which his stomach turned. Ever since then, he has been maligned as a pitiful example of cowardice and pride, as a man who could not control his wife or referee a dispute with a neighbor over the sharing of cream. Eventually his wife abandoned him and he took to the road and settled in Utah. Instead of finding a utopia there, he embarked on a new kind of torment as church leaders ridiculed him for his faithlessness. He died a pauper in Ogden.

After the first desertion in 1837, when Luke Johnson was excommunicated, four more defections occurred within a year. The only reason William Smith stayed was because of his brother's efforts to placate him. After Joseph and Hyrum Smith were assassinated, William found he was less able than before to control his acerbic tongue or need to dominate others. Brigham Young did his best to accommodate the volatile apostle but eventually shunted him to the children's table, so to speak, for which William set about trying to convince the other branches of the Restoration to recognize him as his brother's rightful heir. He ended up being excluded from all the churches and engaging in an exchange of insults that were even shriller than his past examples of character assassination. He managed to find peace only in old age when his nephew, Joseph III, was wise enough to keep him at arm's length.

If things had gone differently in Kirtland or Missouri, one wonders, would at least five of the lost apostles have stayed true to the church? Neither Boynton nor Luke Johnson had been looking for an exit when they were forced out due to the unreasonable demands made of them. One cannot imagine today being submitted to the tests of faith and emotional turmoil they endured. Brigham Young survived by becoming hardened to anything but the task at hand. Where Joseph Smith had encouraged diversity, Young stamped out any hint of disagreement and created an unwelcome environment for those who had thrived on Joseph's creative thinking and encouragement of individual initiative.

In the case of William Smith, we do not have to hypothesize about how he would have fared because he set about testing the reaction to his temperament. It is interesting that those who vied to be Joseph's successor were all demanding men who would not have done well sitting in an office. It is no wonder none of them could get along with William Smith, who felt competitive and, like the others in the improbable circle of apostles, had only served the church because it had touched his soul. His brother had shown him a vision of heaven, and after that, there were few thoughts of returning to his former life. In later criticizing church governance, none of the apostles said they were rejecting the divine hand that had touched them or the miracle of the Book of Mormon, nor were they rejecting the revelations Joseph Smith had received for them. They were only rejecting the later changes to the revelations, John Boynton and Lyman Johnson excepted, who may have convinced themselves it had all been self-delusion from the start, although they did not explicitly say so.

These were mostly young men at the outset, who were unmarried, free to devote their all, and unrealistically idealistic. Life's rhythms inevitably pulled them toward a greater desire for peace and quiet, stability, and consensus as they grew older. Today the various branches of Mormonism have become more accepting of diversity. There is more tolerance of the changes that occur in a person's life, from youthful dissent to midlife crisis. However, the churches still occasionally betray their Ohio heritage by excommunicating someone or encouraging someone to resign because of a misstep. The churches themselves are in a kind of midlife point in their development, which is something McLellin would have noticed and disapproved of even if it meant greater acceptance of himself.

The real miracle in the epic story of the church's founding is that any of these independent-minded men were able to cooperate with each other. It was the spiritual spark inside them that united them. What were temporal concerns when the end of the world was imminent? Jesus would soon descend in glory and nothing else would matter. The world would become a celestial paradise. So they willingly endured the "slings and arrows of outrageous fortune" that were part and parcel with the church because every day brought new spiritual ecstasies, compensating for daily challenges. It didn't matter that Joseph's orders seemed contradictory and belittling. One might even say that the apostles were temporarily blinded to the corruption and deception that had already crept into the church administration; eventually it would prove to be too much for them.

We feel that we have gained by investigating these men's lives and hope others will come to appreciate their significance to Mormon history. Joseph Smith is often given the benefit of the doubt. What if we could extend that same degree of charity toward these lesser figures in Mormon history? It might even make some of the rest of us feel better about our own awkward efforts in life, as we stumble along. Our approach has been to try to see the world the way the founders might have, in the context of the experiences and surroundings that were part of their makeup. Having done that, we feel satisfied that these men are not entirely lost to history anymore.

Photograph of John F. Boynton, ca. 1860. Courtesy LDS Church Archives.

A painting of Luke Johnson, ca. 1845, unknown artist. Courtesy International Society Daughters of Utah Pioneers, Salt Lake City.

Lyman E. Johnson, ca. 1850. Courtesy LDS Church Archives.

Grave marker for Thomas B. Marsh, Ogden City Cemetery. Photograph by H. Michael Marquardt, April 2008.

William B. Smith, ca. 1880. Courtesy Community of Christ Archives.

William E. McLellin, ca. 1870. Courtesy BYU Harold B. Lee Library.

An illustration from *Harper's Weekly* showing the balloon used by John Boynton and his second wife, Mary West Jenkins, to celebrate their marriage. Courtesy J. Willard Marriott Library Special Collections, University of Utah.

MIDWESTERN UNITED STATES ca. 1850

MINNESOTA TERRITORY

WISCONSIN

IOWA

• Prairie du Chien

Elkader •

Voree
•

Beloit,

Bellevue •

Elgin
•

Dixon •
Davenport • Hampton
Rock Island

Rocky Ford
Palestine Grove

Winter Quarters
• Council Bluffs

• Knoxville

Fort Madison
Montrose
Keokuk —

• **Nauvoo**
• Carthage
Warsaw

ILLINOIS

Adam-ondi-Ahman
Gallatin •• Millport
St. Joseph •
• Far West
Richmond •
• Liberty
Independence

Quincy

• Springfield

• DeWitt

Jefferson City •

St. Louis •

MISSOURI

N

Notice that settlements were clustered along the banks of rivers and lakes, which was necessary for transportation, agriculture, communication, and industry, as well as for hygienic and culinary purposes.

The John Johnson home in Hiram, Ohio. This and other photos of the Johnson home courtesy Devery S. Anderson.

The Johnson farm, including (l-r) the residence, attached carriage house, two barns, and silo.

The room where the Smiths stayed in the Johnson home.

An office and workspace inside the Johnson home.

The front door and foyer inside the Kirtland Temple. Photo by Val Brinkerhoff, courtesy Community of Christ Archives.

Joseph Smith's office inside the Kirtland Temple. Photo by Val Brinkerhoff, courtesy Community of Christ Archives.

The Newel K. Whitney Store in Kirtland, ca. 1910. Courtesy LDS Church Archives.

Prairie du Chien, Wisconsin, ca. 1830, including Fort Crawford, built in 1816. Due to frequent flooding of the Mississippi River, a second Fort Crawford was built on higher ground and occupied about 1831. Courtesy Wisconsin Historical Society.

Appendix A

NEWSPAPER ACCOUNTS

Articles from non-LDS newspapers reporting on the evangelism of the six men we track in this book are interesting for their outside perspective. We offer these six articles to readers for that reason.

Mormonism[1]

The Mormonites.—A Preacher of this sect [William E. McLellin] visited us last Saturday. We heard a part of his lecture, which occupied more than two hours. From his account, this sect came into existence a little more than a year since in the following manner:—A young man about 23 years of age somewhere in Ontario county, N. Y., was visited by an *angel*! (here the preacher looked around him apparently to see if the credulity of the people in this enlightened age, could be thus imposed on) who informed him three times in one night that by visiting a certain place in that town he would have revealed to him something of importance. The young man was disturbed, but did not obey the summons until the following day, when the angel again visited him. At the place appointed he found in the earth a box which contained a set of thin plates resembling gold, with Arabic characters inscribed on them. The plates were minutely described as being connected with rings in the shape of the letter D, which facilitated the opening and shutting of the book. The preacher said he found in the same place two stones with which he was enabled by placing them over his eyes and putting his head in a dark corner to decypher the hieroglyphics on the plates!—This we were told was performed to admiration, and now, as the result, we have a book which the speaker informed

---

1. *New-Hampshire Gazette*, Portsmouth, Oct. 25, 1831, p. 4, rpt. *Illinois Patriot*.

us was the Mormon Bible—a book second to no other—without which the holy bible, he seemed to think, would be of little use.

It appears from his statement, that three of the offspring of Joseph, by his youngest son Ephraim, whose names were Laman, Nephi and Lehigh, as near as we could understand, were the persons from whom sprang Mormon.—Laman and Nephi rather declined from walking in the right way, but Lehigh was firm in the faith. Mormon, who was a prophet, led them eastward until they came to the sea, as we suppose, where they built a ship and came to the western world. To prove this, the preacher referred us to Genesis, 49th chapter and 22d verse, and said the branches running over the wall was neither more nor less than the progeny of Joseph, leaving their own and coming to this country! He went into a detail of the reasons which induced him to join himself to this people—that on account of so many sects being in the world, and the discrepances in their opinions, he became sceptical—that hearing of these people in July last, he joined himself to them, believing them to constitute the true Church—and that he came this way to meet a convocation of elders in Jackson county, Missouri, which is to be their New Jerusalem, but was disappointed in not seeing them there. He insisted on the bible being joined with his book, by quoting the 16th and 17th verses of the 37th chapter of Ezekiel, and comparing the bible and Mormon's book to the two sticks there spoken of. We thought this part of his subject too ludicrous to be refuted by any man in his right mind. We cannot now enter into the merits of his discourse, nor should we have given this hastily written sketch, had we not been requested to say something on the subject. Some of these men may be sincere; but does this prove they are in the right? The worshippers of Juggernaut are sincere, or they would not sacrifice their lives by throwing themselves under the wheel of its life destroying car.[2] As far as we

---

2. A juggernaut is a huge chariot-like-wagon, about 45-feet-high, that carries a sculpture of the Hindu deity Lord Jagannath on it, its wheels large enough

are acquainted with the bible we now have, we are satisfied that the Mormonites are a deluded sect of men, whose doctrines are not only dangerous—but, notwithstanding all their professions, they are calling down the curse of God on their own heads.

The Mormonites[3]

On Wednesday, the 8th of this month [March 1832], two strangers [Lyman E. Johnson and Orson Pratt] called at my house and stated that they were sent by God to preach the gospel to every creature, and said if a number should be convened they would deliver a discourse. On the question, what is your profession? they answered, the world call us Mormonites; this excited my curiosity, and at early candle light they commenced an address to the people convened. The substance of which I took down while they were speaking, and afterwards in conversation.

"We are commanded by the Lord to declare his will to effect his intended purpose.—In 1827 a young man called Joseph Smith of the state of New York, of no denomination, but under conviction, inquired of the Lord what he should do to be saved—he went to bed without any reply, but in the night was awakened by an angel, whiter and shining in greater splendor than the sun at noon day, who gave information where the plates were deposited;—Smith awoke, and after due preparation and agreeably to the information given by the angel, he went into the township of Manchester, and there, on the side of a hill, found in a stone box, or a square space inclosed by stone on every side, the plates on which the revelation was inscribed. The box in thickness was about 6 inches, and about 7 by 5 otherwise, the plates themselves were about as thick as window glass, or common tin, pure gold, and well secured by silver

---

to crush anyone who stumbles in front of it, according to early western descriptions of the Chariots of the Gods festival in Puri, India.

3. B. Stokely, *The American Sentinel*, Philadelphia, Feb. 25, 1832, 2, rpt. *The Western Press*, Mercer, Pennsylvania.

rings or loops in the box as an effectual defence against all weather. Smith, being entirely ignorant of any language but the English, and knowing that itself in a very imperfect manner, was unable to read or decipher a single word—he therefore sent the plates to the city of New York to be translated by *Professor Anthony*, who could make nothing of them;—here seemed to be an insurmountable difficulty.

It was supposed that the language of the plates was Arabiac, Chaldean, and Egyptian; but God by his goodness inspired Smith himself to translate the whole.—Smith, however, not being qualified to write, employed an amanuensis, who wrote for him— they thus translated about two thirds of what the plates contained, reserving the residue for a future day as the Lord might hereafter direct. Six hundred years before Christ a certain Prophet called *Lehi* went out to declare and promulgate the prophecies to come; he came across the water into South America, who with others, went to Jerusalem; but there they were divided into two parties; one wise, the other foolish; the latter were therefore *cursed* with yellow skins; which is supposed to mean the Indians of the Rocky Mountains.—In 500 years before Christ the wise ones gave a sign, or was to give one, that there should be a total darkness two days and one night, but the people refused to take warning; and when Jerusalem was destroyed, the righteous only were saved—all the teaching of the Mormonites is comprised in this book (their Bible) price one dollar twenty-five cents. The greater part of the people were converted for a time, but were again divided and destroyed 400 years after Christ. The last battle that was fought among these parties was on the *very ground* where the plates were found; but it had been a running battle, for they commenced at the Isthmus of Darien and ended at Manchester. The plates state that we shall drive back the Indians to the South and West; with a promise, however, to be brought back in the fulness of time; and all the unbeliefs existing can never prevent these prophecies from fulfilment. Iniquity will shortly be swept from the Earth.—Smith, when required by the Lord to translate, read, and publish the plates, excused himself as being unlearned, and could not even read.

The use of the Mormonite Bible is to connect and fulfil the prophecies of Isaiah; it comes also to fulfil the Scriptures and to restore the house of Israel to their lawful rights. The servants of this religion will fish and hunt up Israel and put them into possession of their promised land—(The speaker) himself is specially commanded to go forth and warn the people to flee from the wrath to come—were it not for this injunction he would rather work at the hardest labor. They have gone forth like the disciples of old, without money or scrip, taking no thought what they shall say—and when they are not well received shake off the dust of their feet as a testimony against the people who thus reject the holy spirit. He has left his father, mother, brothers and sisters, the farm and neighborhood of friends, to declare the will of God and the revelation of John who saw the angel flying through Heaven—An angel brought the Mormonite Bible and laid it before him (the speaker;) he therefore *knows* these things to be true. Being sent to call on all to repent —he has come to fulfil the commands of Heaven; he has cleared his skirts of our blood."

I have made some remarks, and given a few particular traits from the Mormon bible—"Christ appeared to 3000 and they all put their hands into his side and believed " (What a host of Thomases.) The books of this Bible are in number 14, under the following names, viz; 1 Nephi, 2 Nephi, Books of Jacob, Enos, Jarem, Omni, Mormon, Masiah, Almo, Helaman, Nephi, jr., Mormon, (again,) Ether, and Morni—translated by Joseph Smith, junior, by pure inspiration—certified to be true by Oliver Cowdry, David Whitmer and Martin Harris, who declare, "That an angel of God came down from heaven and brought the plates and laid them before your eyes and we beheld and saw the plates."—Another certificate is added, signed by eight more, viz: Christian Whitmer, Jacob Whitmer, Peter Whitmer, jr, John Whitmer, Hiram Page,

Joseph Smith, senr. Hiram Smith, and Saml H. Smith, who declare that J. Smith, jr. laid the plates before them, to the truth of which they certify.—One of the young men called himself Lyman Johnston, from Portage county, Ohio. The other was called Arson Pratt; no fixed place of abode. They were going North East, intending to preach the gospel to every kindred, tongue and nation:—They appeared to have very little learning, to be sincere in all they said. They had good manners—had been well raised—were decent and unassuming in every thing I saw, or heard them say.—They said what I could hardly believe: "that John the Revelator was yet alive and about in the world." I thought for certain he had been dead for more than fifty years, and observed that I should be gl[a]d to see the old man; to which they made no reply. Arson Pratt repeating his reluctance to an itinerant life and (but for the mandate of God) he had rather work at any thing else however hard. I observed perhaps on application he could compromise with providence, get another in his place, and he himself [re]locate—he made no reply.

Mormonism[4]

We of this place were visited on Saturday last [March 1832] by a couple of young men [Lyman Johnson and Orson Pratt] styling themselves Mormonites. They explained their doctrine to a large part of the citizens in the court house that evening. They commenced by reading the first chapter of Paul's Epistle to the Galatians: also by giving an account of their founder, Joseph Smith, then an inhabitant of the state of New-York, county of Ontario, and town of Manchester. Having repented of his sins, but not attached himself to any party of Christians, owing to the numerous divisions among them, and being in doubt what his duty was, he had recourse [to] prayer. After retiring to bed one night, he was visited by an Angel and directed to proceed to a hill in the neighborhood where

---

4. *The Fredonia Censor*, New York, Mar. 7, 1832, 4, rpt. *Franklin Venango Democrat*, Pennsylvania.

he would find a stone box containing a quantity of Gold plates. The plates were six or eight inches square, and as many of them as would make them six or eight inches thick, each as thick as a pane of glass. They were filled with characters which the learned of that state were not able to translate. A Mr. Anthony, a professor of one of the colleges, found them to contain something like the Cyrian Chaldena or Hebrew characters. However, Smith with divine aid, was able to translate the plates, and from them we have the *Mormon* bible, or as they stated it, another *Revelation* to part of the house of *Joseph*. The Revelation commenced about 600 years before Christ, with a prophet of the name of Lehi, of the tribe of Joseph, and a contemporary of the prophet Jeremiah, who had also warned the inhabitants of Jerusalem of their idolatry, & becoming unsafe in the city, was ordered by God to leave Jerusalem and journey toward the Red Sea. He with another family who accompanied him, built themselves a ship and landed on the coast of South America, where they increased very fast, and the Lord raised up a great many prophets among them. They built cities, and encouraged the arts and sciences.—Their prophecies foretold the appearance of the Messiah on the other continent, and gave as a sign that they should have two days without a night—also of his death, which was the cause of the terrible earthquakes, which rent all the rocks in our hills into the different shapes they now are. After our Savior's ascension to heaven, that he came down to this continent and appointed twelve disciples, and that Christianity flourished for three or four generations.—After that the inhabitants divided and wars ensued, in which the pagans prevailed.—The first battle was fought nigh to the straits of Darien, and the last at a hill called Comoro, when all the Christians were hewn down but one prophet.* He was directed to hide the plates in the earth, and it was intimated to him that they would be found by a gentile people. The last entry on the plates is 420 years after the commencement of the Christian era. The whole history contains their account of 1020 years. The balance of their discourse was on repentance, and quotations from our prophets to prove their doctrine, and the return of the Jews to Palestine, which was to be done by the gentile nations, accompanied with power from above, far superior to that which brought their fathers out of Egypt. They insisted that our Savior would shortly appear, and that there were some present who would see him on the earth—that they knew it—that they were not deceiving their hearers; that it was all true. They had one of their bibles with them, which was seen by some of our citizens who visited them. *This prophet they say was Mormon.

Mr. Editor—I have compiled the foregoing from memory. If you think it worth publishing, it will probably give some outline of the doctrine of this new sect.

Mormonism in the East[5]

I have this day [Sunday, April 29, 1832] attended a Mormonite meeting in Bath, N. H. It was held in a school-house, which was crowded to overflowing. The speakers were two young men recently from Ohio; one named [Orson] Pratt, apparently about 19 years of age; the other named [Lyman] Johnson, who was probably about twenty-five. The house was filled at an early hour, by an assembly in whose features a love of the marvelous seemed [s]trongly delineated. When the young missionaries arrived (for such I learn they claim to be, sent out by the prophet, Joseph Smith,) the younger arose, and commenced speaking without the usual previous ceremonies of praying or singing. He began by saying it was a great work in which he was engaged, and dwelt somewhat at large on the impropriety and injustice of condemning his doctrines, without giving them a fair hearing. He said he should tell them, first, the manner in which this revelation made by God to man, in these latter days was brought to light. Second, he would give them a brief

---

5. I.W.T., *Boston Investigator*, May 11, 1832, 2.

account of its contents. He then proceeded to relate the story of the angel appearing to Smith, and his subsequent discovery and translation of the plates, and ended with a brief sketch of the adventures of the prophet, Lehi, his escape from Jerusalem and arrival to this continent in a ship which he was taught, specially by Providence, to build, some 700 years before Christ, the subsequent prosperity of himself and his descendants here, their rebellion against God, and the curses consequent upon that rebellion, one of which was a red skin, which they wore to this day.

Johnson then addressed the audience, labouring to show that the present signs of the times, and the incidents attendant upon the discovery of this latter revelation, were plainly and unequivocally predicted in the old and new testaments.

He said that Christ was coming a second time and that before this generation passes away. That it was all important (but he did not say why) that we should believe this testimony. I asked one of their converts, (of whom, by the way, they had already made four, who were dipped in the Connecticut yesterday,) what would be the consequence to the present generation of denying or rejecting their doctrines. He replied, in solemn tone, *famine, pestilence, bloodshed*, and *devastation*—said I, do you give us any proof of this? There is the same proof, said he, as we have for the rest of it. We had no time to continue the conversation. I was not a little amused by the sage speculations of the audience, who were parcelled out into small groups, before and after the meeting, discussing the evidences on which the new doctrine was based. It brought to my mind a very just remark of Mr. Owen's—"How cooly can we examine all theories, how dispassionately discuss all dogmas, save our own." The converts to whom I have alluded, are said not to be under par, for common sense and discretion, in the ordinary concerns of life. This report as it respects some of them, I have the authority of a personal acquaintance, for believing. The speakers were obvious ignorant young men, and the Christians had little to fear. I thought, from their exertions to make the old delusion give place to the new. They gave no precepts by which they would have men govern their conduct, either in relation to God or each other, but only made the modest demand of their audience, that they implicitly believe the Mormon bible.

As a man devoted to the interests of truth and free-enquiry, that [reason is] the best touch stone by which to test it; I do not regret the progress of this modern delusion. Notwithstanding it would seem there were examples enough before the world, show-ing the facility with which men may be led into error and delusion, yet they do not suffice to put them upon their guard and teach them to reason. So long as mankind believe it a sin to reason, so long as they can be made to believe it their duty to approach the mysteries of religion, with a "prostration of intellect" and receive without examination, the *ipse dixit* of the priest, just so long will the undis-cerning many, be the easy victims of the ambitious and crafty few.

Mormonism in New England[6]

I left the White Mountains on the 17th [July 1835], for Mon-treal, via Stanstead, L[ower] C[anada]. Before arriving at this place [in Vermont] (St Johnsbury) we passed through the towns of Beth-lehem and Littleton. The first mention is eleven miles from Den-ninson's Hotel, and is a small uninteresting town. Littletown is a pleasant and flourishing village, located in the east bank of the Connecticut, five miles from Bethlehem. Tourists to the White Mountains usually pass through this place. Leaving Littleton, we crossed the Connecticut at Waterford, a small agricultural town, five miles from Littleton. From there we came to this place, for the purpose of attending a Mormon meeting, now being held here. The Mormon Society here is probably more numerous than in any other village in New England; between thirty and forty persons

---

6. *Maine Farmer and Journal of the Useful Arts*, Winthrop, Maine, Oct. 9, 1835, 288.

are included in the church. An Old barn, standing by the road-side, has been fitted up as a temporary place for assemblage, and on entering it, we found quite a numerous audience collected, the majority of which were females. On the scaffold of the barn were seated the twelve Mormon Apostles, so called by believers, from Ohio. They looked fresh from the back-woods. A brother of Joe Smith, the chief prophet, composed one of the number. We had been seated but a short time before the service commenced. After singing two or three hymns, one of the Apostles arose and com-menced murdering the King's English, in an address on the abuse of gifts. He said that God in his mercy, had vouchsafed "to the church of the latter-day saints," i.e. the Mormons, certain peculiar gifts—and among these were "the gift of tongues," and "the gift of healing." It was considering the abuse of these two gifts, especially, that he wished to address the audience, at the present time; inas-much, as that through the abuse of them, by the saints, great harm had resulted to the church. For instance, "if a saint had the gift of tongues come upon him," he would at once speak out, without regarding the time or place; sometimes half a dozen saints would be moved by the gift at one time, and all would speak out together. This, said the Apostle, is wrong; it creates confusion, and affords the ungodly an opportunity to taunt the church with speaking "unmeaning gibberish." No saint, he continued, however strongly moved by the gift of tongues, should speak out, unless the occasion warranted it, and not even then, if an interpreter were not present. After having lectured the church sufficiently on the abuse of the gift of tongues, the Apostle proceeded to speak concerning the gift of healing, which he said had been abused by the church to as great an extent as the first mentioned gift—even some of the Apostles were deserving of reprehension for their abuse of this gift. They had attempted to exercise it on "adulterous people"—on persons devoid of faith, and therefore had failed—thus bringing disgrace upon themselves and subjecting the whole church to the derision of the unrighteous. The saints, he continued, should be cautious how they exercised this gift; if they were applied to by any one, they should first inquire if he were full of faith, and firmly believed the latter-day saints competent to do all which they professed. If he were a believer, it was proper to attempt, a cure; but if he were an unbeliever, the saints should never attempt to heal him, as a want of faith, on the part of the applicant, unfitted him for the reception of the gift. In conclusion, the Apostle observed, that he hoped the saints would take heed how they abused the two gifts, concerning which he had spoken. In traveling through Ohio and Missouri, he had found the abuse of these two gifts prevalent, to a degree which threatened the prosperity of the church, and it was necessary that the saints should be warned of their danger. The Apostle occupied about half an hour in the delivery of his homily. At times we thought he was about being moved by the gift of tongues, as his discourse, from the looseness of its construction bordered so closely on "*unmeaning gibberish*," that we were much puzzled to comprehend the meaning. The above, however, is the substance of it.

After this Apostle had taken his seat, a second arose who spoke more intelligibly. For the benefit of those of the audience who were unacquainted with the Mormon faith, he entered into an exposition of it, and then attempted to defend the system. Without going into detail, we give below a brief outline of his remarks. He said the latter-day saints believed the bible to be a divine revelation, and that so far as its precepts extended, it was sufficient and worthy of all observance. But the old revelations were not suited to the present condition of mankind. The state of society had altered—manners and customs had changed—mankind had become more enlightened, and had new wants. To meet the wants engendered by a more civilized state of society, said the speaker, fresh revelations were needed, and these in mercy to man had been gracefully supplied. In doing this, continued the speaker, the ALMIGHTY had but granted us the same which he had bestowed on mankind in former ages. Every successive generation, said he, from the creation of the world to the time of Christ, has had its prophet, its revealer, to make revelations suited to the condition, or conditions of mankind at these periods. He would urge this fact as argument against those who said that the old revelations were sufficient, and that it was contrary to the designs of Providence to give new revelations for the instruction of the people. The speaker then proceeded to read from the Book of Mormon various passages, the purport of all which was, that the Almighty had set apart a tract of country in the "westward bounds of Missouri," for the inheritance of the latter-day saints; that it was to be called "the New Jerusalem"—that although it belonged to the saints by right, yet they were to obtain the lands by purchase, in order that they might rest in quiet. Here, said he, the latter-day saints are to be gathered from all quarters, and they are commanded to dispose of their flocks and herds, purchase land, and take up their abode in the New Jerusalem. These revelations, said the speaker, were made in the year 1831, "and I am witness that they were made."

It is evidently the intention of the twelve Mormon Apostles to prevail upon the members of the church in this place to dispose of their property, and proceed with them to the West, and from the profound respect with which their nonsense was listened to, I have no doubt but that they will prevail upon many of the believers to pursue this course. We were both amused and disgusted in listening to observe the fallibility of human reason displayed in the almost crouching reverence with which their discourse was received by the believing portion of the audience. We had not thought it possible to find in one small town in New England the boasted land of intelligence, so large a number of persons who could be led astray by doctrines which at first glance appear so very absurd and ridiculous; but it has been truly remarked that no system of religious faith, however absurd or ridiculous, can be devised, which will not find *some* staunch believers and supporters among men. Among the audience we noticed several aged men. One of them told us that he had come 150 miles, from Maine, for the purpose of attending this meeting.

The Mormons and Their Prophet[7]

Messrs Editors—Permit me in your columns to spread before the public what I consider an authentic account of the new sect called MORMONS, and its acknowledged PROPHET, *Joseph Smith*. As I was ascending the Ohio river, on the 18th of April last [1841], among my fellow passengers was the Rev. William Smith of Nauvoo, a Mormon preacher, and brother to Joseph Smith, the Mormon prophet. Curiosity led me to make many inquiries, all of which he promptly answered, and apparently with great ingenuousness. I then retired and committed to writing the substance of his statements. The next day, I read to him what I had written. He pointed out one or two slight mistakes, added some things not before mentioned, which I noted down, and he then pronounced the whole correct. That entry in my Journal, with some enlargement to render it more intelligible, is as follows:

Joseph Smith, now 35 years of age, is the eldest of five brothers, all born at Norwich, in the State of Vermont. The family originated in the south part of New England, but my informant could not tell precisely where. In the year 1816 or 1817, the whole family removed to the State of New York, and lived sometimes in Palmyra, and sometimes in the adjacent town of Manchester. They were in rather low circumstances, and followed farming. About the year 1823, there was a revival of religion in that region, and Joseph was one of several hopeful converts. The others were joining, some one church, and some another in that vicinity, but Joseph hesitated between the different denominations. While his mind was perplexed with this subject, he prayed for divine direction; and afterwards was awaked one night by an extraordinary vision. The glory

---

7. James Murdock, *The Congregational Observer*, Hartford, July 3, 1841, 1.

of the Lord filled the chamber with a dazzling light, and a glorious angel appeared to him, conversed with him, and told him that he was a chosen vessel unto the Lord to make known true religion. The next day he went into the field; but he was unable to work, his mind being oppressed by the remembrance of the vision. He returned to the house, and soon after sent for his father and brothers from the field; and then, in presence of the family, (my informant one of them,) he related all that had occurred. They were astounded, but not altogether incredulous. After this, he had other similar visions, in one of which the existence of certain metallic plates was revealed to him and their location described—about three miles off, in a pasture ground. The next day he went alone to the spot, and by digging discovered the plates in a sort of rude stone box. They were eight or ten inches long, less in width, about the thickness of panes of glass; and together, made a pile about five or six inches high. They were in a good state of preservation, had the appearance of gold, and bore inscriptions in strange characters on both sides. He brought them home, but was unable to read them. He afterwards made a facsimile of some parts of the inscription, and sent it to professor Anthon of New York city. The professor pronounced the characters to be ancient Hebrew corrupted, and the language to be degenerate Hebrew with a mixture of Egyptian. He could decypher only one entire word. After this Joseph Smith was supernaturally assisted to read and understand the inscription; and he was directed to translate a great part of it. The pages which he was not to translate were found to be sealed together, so that he did not even read them and learn their contents. With an assistant to correct his English, he translated so much of the inscription as now makes the book of Mormon. He kept the plates a long time in his chamber, and after translating from them, he repeatedly showed them to his parents and to other friends. But my informant said, he had never seen them. At length he was directed by a vision to bury the plates again in the same manner; which he accordingly did.

The *book of* MORMON is Mr. Smith's professed translation of the inscription on the plates; and it bears the name of MORMON, because a Jewish Christian of the fourth century bearing the name of *Mormon*, is the alleged author of the inscription. The book is historical. It gives account of a company of Jewish Christians of the tribe of Joseph, who left Judea by divine direction, a little before the destruction of Jerusalem by Titus, under the guidance of Lehi their priest and prophet. This little band after wandering long and far, came at last to America, and planted themselves in the western part of the present State of New York. So long as their Christian characters remained unsullied, they were prosperous. But when their piety degenerated, they became split into parties, were assailed by their heathen neighbors, conquered and either exterminated or enslaved, and thus ceased to be a Christian people. Of these divine judgments upon them they were forewarned by their prophets, but without effect. Before their overthrow, in the fourth century, Mormon their priest and prophet, was directed to write their history, to inscribe it on plates, and to bury those plates in the place where in 1827 a revelation guided Joseph Smith to search for them and to find them. ...

Appendix B

ORDINATIONS TO THE TWELVE

The following text is copied from the Kirtland High Council Minutes, provided by Richard E. Turley Jr., ed., Selected Collections from the Archives of the Church of Jesus Christ of Latter-day Saints, *2 vols.* DVD *(Provo: BYU Press, 2002), 1:19. The first ordination is from February 14, the next four from February 15, and the last from April 26, 1835. The headlines and a synopsis of the ordination blessings were recorded in 1836 onto pages 149-50, 152-54, and 157-58 of the minute book.*

The Blessing of L[yman] Johnson was

in the name of Jesus Christ, that he should bear the tidings of salvation to nations, tongues and people, until the utmost corners of the earth shall hear the tidings, and that he shall be a witness of the things of God, to nations & tongues, and that Holy Angels shall all minister to him occasionally and that no power of the enemy shall prevent him from going forth and doing the work of the Lord. And that he should live until the gathering was accomplished, according to the Holy Prophets. And that he should be like unto Enoch. And your faith shall be like unto his, and he shall be called great among all the living, and Satan shall tremble before thee, and that he shall see the Saviour come and stand on the Earth with power and great glory,

Luke Johnson's blessing

Our Father, in Heaven, look down in mercy upon us and upon this thy servant whom we ordain to the ministry of the twelve. He shall be prepared and preserved and become like those we have blessed before him, The nations shall tremble before him, He shall hear the voice of God: he shall comfort the hearts of the saints always. The angels shall bear him up till he shall finish his minis-try. He shall be delivered and come forth with Israel. He shall bear testimony to the kings of the earth, and hold communion with the Father, with the son and with the general assembly and church of the first born. If cast into prison he shall be able to comfort the hearts of his comrades His tongue shall be loosed and he shall have power to lead many to Zion, and set down with them, and the Ancient of Days shall pronounce this blessing, That you have been faithful. He shall have strength wisdom & power. He shall go among the covenant people and speak all their tongues where he shall go. All these blessings we confirm upon him in the name of Jesus. Amen.

Wm. E. McLel[l]in's blessing.

In the name of the Lord, Wisdom & intelligence shall be poured out upon him, to enable him to perform the great work, that is incumbent upon him. That he may be spared until the saints are gathered, that he may stand before Kings and Rulers to bear testi-mony and be upheld by holy Angels, and the nations of the earth shall acknowledge that God has sent him. He shall have power to overcome his enemies, and his life shall be spared in the midst of pestilence and destruction, and in the midst of his enemies. He shall be a prince and a saviour to God's people. The Tempter shall not overcome him, nor his enemies prevail against him. The Heavens shall be opened unto him as unto men in days of old. He shall be mighty in the hands of God, and shall convince thousands that God has sent him, and his days may be prolonged until the coming of the son of man. He shall be wafted as on eagles wings, from coun-try to country and from people to people and <be able> to <do> wonders in the midst of this generation, Even so Amen.

John F. Boynton's blessing

Thou hast prevailed, and thou shalt prevail and thou shalt

declare the gospel unto many nations. Thou shalt be made mighty before God. And although thou shalt be cast out from the face of men, yet thou shalt <have> power to prevail, thou shalt lead the Elect triumphantly to the places of refuge. Thou shalt be like thy brethren who have been blessed before thee. Thou shalt stand in that day of calamity when the wicked shall be consumed, and present unto the Father, spotless, the fruits of thy labor. Thou shalt overcome all the evils that are in the world. Thou shalt have wisdom to put to silence all the wisdom of the wise, and thou shalt see the face of thy Redeemer in the flesh. These blessings are pronounced and sealed upon thee even so Amen.

William Smith's blessing

That he may be purified in heart, that he may have communion with God. That he may be equal with his brethren in holding the keys of this ministry That he may be kept and be instrumental in leading Israel forth, that he may be delivered from the hands of those who seek to destroy him: that he may be enabled to bear testimony to the nations, that Jesus lives. That he may stand in the midst of pestilence and destruction, he shall be mighty in the hands of God. in bringing about the restoration of Israel. The nations shall rejoice at the greatness of the gifts which God has bestowed upon him, That his tongue shall be loosed, he shall have power to do great things in the name of Jesus. He shall be preserved and remain on the earth, until Christ shall come to take vengeance on the wicked. Confirmed

Thomas B. Marsh's Blessing by O. Cowdery

Dear Brother, You are to be a minister of righteousness and to this ministry and Apostleship you are now to be ordained: and May all temporal and spiritual blessings attend you, your sins are forgiven you, and you are to go forth and preach the everlasting Gospel. You shall travel from kingdom to kingdom and from nation to nation.

Angels shall bear the[e] up, and thou shalt be instrumental in bringing thousands of the redeemed of the Lord to Zion. President David
Whitmer sealed the above blessing upon him, even so Amen.

Select Bibliography

"Adams and Brannan." *Warsaw Signal*, Apr. 30, 1845, 2.

Alexander, Thomas G. *Things in Heaven and Earth: The Life and Times of Wilford Woodruff, a Mormon Prophet.* Salt Lake City: Signature Books, 1991.

Allen, James B., Ronald K. Esplin, and David J. Whittaker. *Men with a Mission, 1837-1841: The Quorum of the Twelve Apostles in the British Isles.* Salt Lake City: Deseret Book, 1992.

Amann, Peter. "Prophet in Zion: The Saga of George J. Adams." *New England Quarterly* 37 (December 1964): 477-500.

Anderson, Devery S., and Gary James Bergera, eds. *Joseph Smith's Quorum of the Anointed, 1842-1845: A Documentary History.* Salt Lake City: Signature Books, 2005.

Anderson, Lavina Fielding, ed. *Lucy's Book: A Critical Edition of Lucy Mack Smith's Family Memoir.* Salt Lake City: Signature Books, 2001.

Anderson, Mary Audentia Smith, ed. *The Memoirs of President Joseph Smith III (1832-1914)*, 1959. Independence: Price Publishing, 2001.

"Annual Conference of the Church of Jesus Christ of Latter Day Saints, at Voree." *Zion's Reveille*, Apr. 1, 1847.

Backman, Milton V., Jr. *The Heavens Resound: A History of the Latter-day Saints in Ohio, 1830-1838.* Salt Lake City: Deseret Book, 1983.

Bagley, Will, ed. *Scoundrel's Tale: The Samuel Brannan Papers.* Spokane: Arthur H. Clark, 1999.

Bates, Irene M., and E. Gary Smith. *Lost Legacy: The Mormon Office of Presiding Patriarch.* Urbana: University of Illinois Press, 1994.

Baugh, Alexander L. "A Call to Arms: The 1838 Mormon Defense of Northern Missouri." PhD. dissertation, Brigham Young University, 1996.

————. "A Community Abandoned: W. W. Phelps' 1839 Letter to Sally Waterman Phelps from Far West, Missouri." *Nauvoo Journal* 10 (Fall 1998): 19-32.

Bean, Cheryl Harmon. "LDS Baptisms in Erie County, PA, 1831-1833." *Nauvoo Journal* 5 (Fall 1993): 57-102.

Beecher, Maureen Ursenbach, ed. *The Personal Writings of Eliza Roxcy Snow.* Logan: Utah State University Press, 2000.

Bergera, Gary James, ed. *The Autobiography of B. H. Roberts*. Salt Lake City: Signature Books, 1990.

Bill of Complaint, February 14, 1853, Knoxville County Circuit Court, Galesburg, Illinois, box 93, case 37.

"Bill Smith." *Frontier Guardian*, June 26, 1850.

"Bill Smith the Only Surviving Brother of Joe Smith." *Telegraph and Review*, Alton, Illinois, Oct. 25, 1845.

Blythe, Christine Elyse. "William Smith's Patriarchal Blessings and Contested Authority in the Post-Martyrdom Church." *Journal of Mormon History* 39, no. 3 (Summer 2013): 60-95.

Bonney, Edward. *The Banditti of the Prairies or, the Murderer's Doom!! A Tale of the Mississippi Valley*, 1850. Norman: University of Oklahoma Press, 1963.

Boynton, John Farnham. *American Boynton Directory, 1638: Containing the Address of All Known Boyntons, Boyingtons and Byingtons in the United States and British Dominions*. Syracuse, NY: Smith and Bruce, 1884.

Boynton, John Farnham, and Caroline Harriman Boynton, comps. *The Boynton Family: A Genealogy of the Descendants of William and John Boynton, Who Emigrated from Yorkshire, England, in 1638, and Settled at Rowley, Essex County, Massachusetts*. Groveland, MA: J. F. & C. H. Boynton, 1897.

Briggs, Jason. "History of the Reorganization of the Church of Jesus Christ of Latter Day Saints." *The Messenger*, Nov., Dec. 1875.

"Brother William Smith is making preparation ..." *Voree Herald*, June 1846.

Brunson, Seymour, to "Dear Brethren in Christ," May 6, 1833. *The Evening and the Morning Star*, June 1833.

Bushman, Richard Lyman. *Joseph Smith: Rough Stone Rolling*. New York: Alfred Knopf, 2005.

Cannon, Donald Q., and Lyndon W. Cook, eds. *Far West Record: Minutes of the Church of Jesus Christ of Latter-day Saints, 1830-1844*. Salt Lake City: Deseret Book, 1983.

Colburn, Thomas, to "Elder Snow, Editor of the *Luminary*," May 2, 1855. *St. Louis Luminary*, May 5, 1855.

Collier, Fred C., and William S. Harwell, eds. *Kirtland Council Minute Book*. Salt Lake City: Collier's Publishing, 1996.

Coltrin, Zebedee. Journal, June 1832-Mar. 1833, LDS Church History Library.

Complainants Abstract of Pleading and Evidence. Circuit Court of the United States, Western District of Missouri, Western Division at Kansas City. Lamoni, IA: Herald Publishing House and Bindery, 1893.

Compton, Todd. *In Sacred Loneliness: The Plural Wives of Joseph Smith.* Salt Lake City: Signature Books, 1997.

"Conference Minutes." *Times and Seasons,* Nov. 1, 1845.

"Conference Minutes." *Voree Herald,* Oct. 1846.

"Continuation of Elder Rigdon's Trial." *Times and Seasons,* Oct. 1, 1844.

Cook, Lyndon W. "'I Have Sinned against Heaven, and Am Unworthy of Your Confidence, But I Cannot Live without a Reconciliation': Thomas B. Marsh Returns to the Church." *BYU Studies* 20 (Summer 1980): 389-400.

———. *David Whitmer Interviews: A Restoration Witness.* Provo: Grandin Book, 1991.

"Correspondence." *Times and Seasons,* Jan. 1, 1844.

"Correspondence." *Friends' Weekly Intelligencer,* Philadelphia, Oct. 17, 1846, 226.

Corrill, John. *A Brief History of the Church of Christ of Latter Day Saints, (Commonly Called Mormons) Including an Account of Their Doctrine and Discipline, with the Reasons of the Author for Leaving the Church.* St. Louis: Author, 1839.

Cottle, Thomas D., and Patricia C. Cottle. *Liberty Jail and the Legacy of Joseph,* 2nd ed. Portland, OR: Insight, 1999.

"Covington, Ky., June 14, 1849: A Proclamation to the Saints." *Melchisedeck and Aaronic Herald,* Aug. 1849.

Cowdery, Oliver, to Warren and Lyman Cowdery, Feb. 4, 1838. Oliver Cowdery Letterbook, 83-84, Henry E. Huntington Library, San Marino, California.

"Crimes." *Gospel Herald,* June 15, 1848, 51.

"Dinner to the Smith Family." *New York Messenger,* Aug. 9, 1845.

Dudley, Todd L. "All But Two: The Disaffection of Ten of the Original Twelve Modern Apostles." Honors thesis, Brigham Young University, 1994.

Duffy, John-Charles. "Reinventing McLellin: A Historiographical Review." In Stan Larson and Samuel J. Passey, eds. *The William E. McLellin Papers, 1854-1880*. Salt Lake City: Signature Books, 2007, 83-104.

"Elder Joseph Wood was ..." *Times and Seasons*, Mar. 1, 1841.

"The Elijah." *Melchisedeck and Aaronic Herald*, Aug. 1849.

"An Epistle of the Twelve." *Times and Seasons*, Aug. 15, 1844.

Esplin, Ronald K. "Thomas B. Marsh as President of the First Quorum of the Twelve, 1835-1838." In *Hearken, O Ye People: Discourses on the Doctrine and Covenants*. Sandy, UT: Randall Book, 1984, 167-90.

Esplin, Ronald K., and Sharon E. Nielsen. "The Record of the Twelve, 1835: The Quorum of the Twelve Apostles' Call and 1835 Mission." *BYU Studies Quarterly* 51, no. 1 (2012): 4-52.

"An Extract of Conference Minutes." *Melchisedek and Aaronic Herald*, Covington, Kentucky, Sept. 1849.

"Extract from Wm. Smith's Fornication Letter." *Cincinnati Daily Commercial*, May 22, 1850.

"Extracts of the Minutes of Conferences." *Times and Seasons*, Nov. 1839.

"For the Neighbor." *Nauvoo Neighbor*, May 15, 1844.

"For Zion's Reveille." *Zion's Reveille*, Apr. 15, 1847.

Forscutt, Mark Hill. Journal. L. Tom Perry Special Collections, Harold B. Lee Library, Brigham Young University.

"From Nauvoo." *Warsaw Signal*, Sept. 3, 1845.

"Funeral of Mrs. Caroline Smith." *Times and Seasons*, June 1, 1845.

Garr, Arnold K., Donald Q. Cannon, and Richard O. Cowan, eds. *Encyclopedia of Latter-day Saint History*. Salt Lake City: Deseret Book, 2000.

Gentry, Leland Homer. "A History of the Latter-Day Saints in Northern Missouri from 1836 to 1839." Ph.D. diss., Brigham Young University, 1965.

Godfrey, Kenneth W., Audrey M. Godfrey, and Jill Mulvay Derr, eds. *Women's Voices: An Untold History of the Latter-day Saints, 1830-1900*. Salt Lake City: Deseret Book, 2000.

Grandstaff, Mark R. "Having More Learning Than Sense: William E. McLellin and the Book of Commandments Revisited." *Dialogue: A Journal of Mormon Thought* 26 (Winter 1993): 23-48.

Gunn, Stanley R. *Oliver Cowdery: Second Elder and Scribe*. Salt Lake City: Bookcraft, 1962.

Hale, Alma H. Journal, April 6, 1872. LDS Church History Library.

Hardy, John. *History of the Trials of Elder John Hardy, before the Church of Latter Day Saints in Boston, for Slander, in Saying That G. J. Adams, S. Brannan and William Smith Were Licentious Characters.* Boston: Conway and Co., 1844.

Hartley, William G. *My Best for the Kingdom: History and Autobiography of John Lowe Butler, a Mormon Frontiersman.* Salt Lake City: Aspen Books, 1993.

Hill, Marvin S. *Quest for Refuge: The Mormon Flight from American Pluralism.* Salt Lake City: Signature Books, 1989.

Hill, Marvin S., C. Keith Rooker, and Larry T. Wimmer. "The Kirtland Economy Revisited." *BYU Studies* 17 (Summer 1977): 391-475.

Hilton, Hope A. *"Wild Bill" Hickman and the Mormon Frontier.* Salt Lake City: Signature Books, 1988.

"History of John F. Boynton." *Deseret News,* June 16, 1858.

"The History of Luke Johnson. (By Himself)." *Deseret News,* May 26, 1858.

"History of Thos. Baldwin Marsh." *Deseret News,* Mar. 24, 1858, 18.

Holmes, Reed M. "G. J. Adams and the Forerunners." In *Restoration Studies II,* Maurice L. Draper and A. Bruce Lundgren, eds. Independence: Herald Publishing House, 1983, 42-60.

Holzapfel, Jeni Broberg, and Richard Neitzel Holzapfel, eds. *A Woman's View: Helen Mar Whitney's Reminiscences of Early Church History.* Provo: BYU Religious Studies Center, 1997.

Hyde, Orson, to William Smith, Oct. 28, 1845. Qtd. in *Warsaw Signal,* Nov. 26, 1845.

"Important Arrest." *Missouri Republican,* St. Louis, Apr. 28, 1854.

Ivins, Virginia Wilcox. *Pen Pictures of Early Western Days.* Keokuk, Iowa: Author, 1908.

———. *Yesterdays: Reminiscenses of Long Ago.* N.p.: Author, 1914.

"J. W. Briggs Letters." *The Return,* Davis City, Iowa, Dec. 1, 1895, 4.

Jenson, Andrew. "The Twelve Apostles." *Historical Record,* Feb. 1886.

———. *Latter-day Saint Biographical Encyclopedia: A Compendium of Biographical Sketches of Prominent Men and Women in the Church of Jesus Christ of Latter-day Saints.* 4 vols. Salt Lake City: Andrew Jenson History Company, 1901–30.

Jessee, Dean C., ed. "The John Taylor Nauvoo Journal: January 1845-September 1845." *BYU Studies* 23 (Summer 1983): 1-96.

————. *The Papers of Joseph Smith: Journal, 1832-1842.* Salt Lake City: Deseret Book, 1992.

————. comp. and ed. *Personal Writings of Joseph Smith.* Rev. ed. Salt Lake City and Provo: Deseret Book and Brigham Young University Press, 2002.

Jessee, Dean C., Mark Ashurst-McGee, and Richard L. Jensen, eds. *The Joseph Smith Papers, Journals, Volume 1: 1832-1839.* Salt Lake City: Church Historian's Press, 2008.

"John C. Gaylord accuser vs William Smith accused: Complaint for Adultery," April 23, 1847. James J. Strang Papers, Document 181, Coe Collection, Beinecke Library, Yale University.

Johnson, Benjamin F. *My Life's Review.* Mesa, AZ: Twenty-first Century Printing, 1992.

Johnson, Janiece Lyn. "'Give It All Up and Follow Your Lord': Mormon Female Religiosity, 1831-1843." M.A. thesis, Brigham Young University, 2001.

Johnson, Melvin C. *Polygamy on the Pedernales: Lyman Wight's Mormon Villages in Antebellum Texas, 1845 to 1858.* Logan: Utah State University Press, 2006.

Jolley, Jerry C. "The Sting of the Wasp: Early Nauvoo Newspaper–April 1842 to April 1843." *BYU Studies* 22 (Fall 1982): 487-96.

Kenney, Scott G., ed. *Wilford Woodruff's Journal, 1833–1898.* Typescript, 9 vols. Midvale, UT: Signature Books, 1983–85.

Kimball, Heber C. *President Heber C. Kimball's Journal.* Salt Lake City: Juvenile Instructor Office, 1882. Grantsville, Utah: Archive Publishers, 2003.

Kimball, Stanley B. "The Saints and St. Louis, 1831-1857: An Oasis of Tolerance and Security." *BYU Studies* 13 (Summer 1973): 489-519.

————. "New Light on Old Egyptiana: Mormon Mummies, 1848-71." *Dialogue: A Journal of Mormon Thought* 16 (Winter 1983): 72-90.

————. ed. *On the Potter's Wheel: The Diaries of Heber C. Kimball.* Salt Lake City: Signature Books, 1987.

Kimball, Vilate, to Heber C. Kimball, Sept. 1837, Oct.-Dec. 1840, LDS Church History Library.

Larson, Stan, and Samuel J. Passey, eds. *The William E. McLellin Papers, 1854-1880.* Salt Lake City: Signature Books, 2007.

"A Late Mormon Miracle." *Gospel Herald,* Dec. 23, 1847, 186.

Launius, Roger D. *Alexander William Doniphan: Portrait of a Missouri Moderate*. Columbia: University of Missouri Press, 1997.

———. *Joseph Smith III: Pragmatic Prophet*. Urbana: University of Illinois Press, 1998.

Launius, Roger D., and Linda Thatcher, eds. *Differing Visions: Dissenters in Mormon History*. Urbana: University of Illinois Press, 1994.

LeSueur, Stephen C. *The 1838 Mormon War in Missouri*. Columbia: University of Missouri Press, 1987.

Lyon, T. Edgar. "Nauvoo and the Council of Twelve." In *The Restoration Movement: Essays in Mormon History*, eds. F. Mark McKiernan, Alma R. Blair, and Paul M. Edwards. Independence: Herald House, 1979, 167-206.

Mahoney, Timothy R. *Provincial Lives: Middle-Class Experience in the Antebellum Middle West*. New York: Cambridge University Press, 1999.

Marquardt, H. Michael, comp. *Early Patriarchal Blessings of the Church of Jesus Christ of Latter-day Saints*. Salt Lake City: Smith-Pettit Foundation, 2007.

"Married." *Nauvoo Neighbor*, July 2, 1845.

Marsh, Thomas B, to Brigham Young, Nov. 10, 1858. Brigham Young Collection, LDS Church History Library.

McLellin, William E., "The Successor of Joseph, the Seer." *The Ensign of Liberty, of the Church of Christ*, Kirtland, Ohio, Dec. 1847, 41-47.

———. to "Elder D[avis] H. Bays," May 24, 1870. *Saints' Herald*, Sept. 15, 1870.

"Meeting at Stand." May 4, 1845. Typescript in Leonard J. Arrington Papers, series 9, box 12, Merrill-Cazier Library, Utah State University, Logan.

Minutes of a Council of Twelve, May 24, 1845, LDS Church History Library. In *Selected Collections from the Archives of the Church of Jesus Christ of Latter-day Saints*, 2 vols. DVD. Provo, Utah: Brigham Young University Press, 2002, 1:18.

Missouri General Assembly. *Document Containing the Correspondence, Orders, &c. in Relation to the Disturbances with the Mormons; and the Evidence Given before the Hon. Austin A. King, Judge of the Fifth Judicial Circuit of the State of Missouri*. Fayette, MO: State General Assembly, 1841.

"Mister Editor." *The Prophet*, Jan. 15, 1845, 3.

Monroe, James M. Diary, 1841-1845. Coe Collection, Beinecke Library, Yale University.

"More Trouble in the Church." *The Telegraph*, Dixon, Illinois, Mar. 9, 1854.

"Mormon Inquest Testimony before Judge Austin A. King," Nov. 1838. Western Historical Manuscript Collection, University of Missouri, Columbia.

"Mormonism." *Carrollton Gazette*, Oct. 8, 1847. Rpt. *Davenport Gazette*, Nov. 4, 1847.

"Mormonism: A Letter from William Smith, Brother of Joseph the Prophet." *Illinois State Chronicle*, Decatur, June 11, 1857.

"Mormonism Again." *The Telegraph*, Dixon, Illinois. May 7, 1853.

"Mormon Times in Kirtland." *Cleveland Daily Plain Dealer*, May 17, 1859.

Mouritsen, Robert Glen. "The Office of Associate President of the Church of Jesus Christ of Latter-day Saints." M.A. thesis, Brigham Young University, 1972.

"New York Conference." *The Prophet*, Nov. 1844.

"New York Conference." *Times and Seasons*, Nov. 15, 1845.

Newell, Linda King, and Valeen Tippetts Avery. *Mormon Enigma: Emma Hale Smith*. 2d. ed. Urbana: University of Illinois Press, 1994.

Norman, Mary B. Smith, to Ina Coolbrith, Mar. 27, Apr. 24, 1908, p13, f955, Community of Christ Archives.

"Notice." *Nauvoo Neighbor*, May 28, 1845.

"Notice." *Times and Seasons*, June 1, 1844.

"Notice." *Times and Seasons*, Nov. 1, 1845.

"Notice to the Churches Abroad." *The Prophet*, May 10, 1845.

"Obituary," *Nauvoo Neighbor*, May 28, 1845.

"October Conference Minutes, City of Nauvoo, October 6, 1844." *Times and Seasons*, Oct. 15, 1844.

"Oliver Cowdery's Docket Book," January 17-19, 1838. Henry E. Huntington Library, San Marino, California.

Oliver Cowdery Sketch Book, Jan. 1-Mar. 27, 1836. LDS Church History Library.

"Opinions of the Smith Family." *Voree Herald*, June 1846.

Paden, Isaac, to James M. Adams, Apr. 1, 1846. James J. Strang Papers, Document 451, Beinecke Library.

Page, John E. "Forgetful Prophets." *Gospel Herald*, Dec. 9, 1847.

"Patriarch Bill Smith." *Warsaw Signal*, July 2, 1845.

"Patriarchal." *Times and Seasons*, June 1, 1845.

The People v. William Smith, Indictment for Rape." Signed by States Attorney William T. Miller, Lee County Criminal File Records, General number 12, Illinois Regional Archives, DeKalb.

"Petition of William Smith, Isaac Sheen, et al., of Covington, Kentucky, against the Admission of Deseret into the Union, December 31, 1849." *Journal of History*, Oct. 1914, 453-57.

Porter, Larry C. "The Odyssey of William Earl McLellin: Man of Diversity, 1806-83." In Jan Shipps and John W. Welch, eds. *The Journals of William E. McLellin, 1831-1836*. Urbana: University of Illinois Press, 1994, 291-378.

Post, Stephen. Journal, 1835-1875. LDS Church History Library.

Pratt, Parley P. *History of the Late Persecution Inflicted by the State of Missouri upon the Mormons*. Detroit: Author, 1839.

Proctor, Scot Facer, and Maurine Jensen Proctor, eds. *Autobiography of Parley P. Pratt: Revised and Enhanced*. Salt Lake City: Deseret Book, 2000.

"A Prophet Robbed and Deserted—Excommunication of Elder Sheen." *Daily Cincinnati Commercial*, May 20, 1850.

Quaiffe, Milo M. *The Kingdom of Saint James: A Narrative of the Mormons*. New Haven: Yale University Press, 1930.

Quinn, D. Michael. *The Mormon Hierarchy: Origins of Power*. Salt Lake City: Signature Books, 1994.

———. "'My Eyes Were Holden in Those Days': A Study of Selective Memory." In Larson and Passey, *William E. McLellin Papers*, 59-82.

Quorum of the Twelve Minutes, Dec. 6, 1847, typescript. Leonard J. Arrington Papers, Special Collections, Merrill-Cazier Library, Utah State University, Logan.

"A Record of the Transactions of the Twelve Apostles," Feb. 14-Aug. 28, 1835, LDS Church History Library. A transcription was published in Ronald K. Esplin and Sharon E. Nielsen, "The Record of the Twelve, 1835: The Quorum of the Twelve Apostles' Call and 1835 Mission," *BYU Studies Quarterly* 51, no. 1 (2012): 4-52.

"Reed Peck Manuscript," 1839. In Henry E. Huntington Library, San Marino, California. Printed as *Reed Peck Manuscript*. Salt Lake City: Utah Lighthouse Ministry, n.d.

Reid, Col. J. M. *Sketches and Anecdotes of the Old Settlers, and New Comers, the Mormon Bandits and Danite Band*. Keokuk, IA: R. B. Ogden, 1876.

Richards, Willard. Journal, 1836-1853. LDS Church History Library.

Rudd, Calvin P. "William Smith: Brother of the Prophet Joseph." M.A. thesis, Brigham Young University, 1973.

Russell, William D. "Portrait of a 'True Believer' in Original Mormonism." In Larson and Passey, *William E. McLellin Papers*, 105-36.

"The Salt Lake Banditti." *Melchisedeck and Aaronic Herald*, Feb. 1850.

Schaefer, Mitchell K., ed. *William E. McLellin's Lost Manuscript*. Salt Lake City: Eborn Books, 2012.

Seegmiller, Janet Burton. "The Mormon Succession Crisis: A Family View." *John Whitmer Historical Association Journal* 20 (2000): 94-110.

Sessions, Gene A. *Mormon Thunder: A Documentary History of Jedediah Morgan Grant*. Urbana: University of Illinois Press, 1982.

Sheen, John K. *Polygamy: The Veil Lifted*. York, NE: Author, 1889.

Shepard, William. "James Blakeslee: The Old Soldier of Mormonism." *John Whitmer Historical Association Journal* 17 (1997): 113-32.

Shipps, Jan, and John W. Welch, eds. *The Journals of William E. McLellin, 1831-1836*. Provo and Urbana: *BYU Studies* and University of Illinois Press, 1994.

"Since the first side of this paper ..." *Gospel Herald*, May 30, 1850.

"Slander Refuted," *The Telegraph*, Dixon, Illinois, Apr. 30, 1853.

Smith, Andrew F. *The Saintly Scoundrel: The Life and Times of Dr. John Cook Bennett*. Urbana: University of Illinois Press, 1997.

Smith, Eliza R. Snow. *Biography and Family Record of Lorenzo Snow*. Salt Lake City: Deseret News, 1884.

Smith, George A. "My Journal." *The Instructor*, Sept. 1948, 418-22, 444; Nov. 1948, 515-18.

Smith, George D., ed. *An Intimate Chronicle: The Journals of William Clayton*. Salt Lake City: Signature Books, 1991.

Smith, Joseph. Letterbook, 1829, 1837-43. LDS Church History Library.

Smith, Joseph, Jr., et al. *History of the Church of Jesus Christ of Latter-day Saints,* ed. B. H. Roberts, 2nd ed. 6 vols., 1902–12. Salt Lake City: Deseret Book, 1959.

Smith, Joseph Fielding, comp. *Life of Joseph F. Smith: Sixth President of the Church of Jesus Christ of Latter-day Saints.* Salt Lake City: Deseret News Press, 1938.

Smith, William. *Defence of Elder William Smith, against the Slanders of Abraham Burtis, and Others.* Philadelphia: Author, 1844.

———— to Heber C. Kimball, Dec. 21, 1844. Brigham Young Collection, LDS Church History Library.

———— to Brigham Young, May 7, 1855. Brigham Young Collection, LDS Church History Library.

————. *A Proclamation and Faithful Warning to All the Saints Scattered about in Boston, Philadelphia, New York, Salem, New Bedford, Lowell, Peterborough, Gilsom, St. Louis, Nauvoo, and Elsewhere in the United States.* Rpt., by Thomas Sharp. "A Proclamation and Faithful Warning …" *Warsaw Signal,* Oct. 29, 1845.

————. "To the Church of Jesus Christ of Latter Day Saints," July 28, 1846. *Zion's Reveille,* Dec. 1846.

————. *William Smith on Mormonism.* Lamoni, IA: Herald Steam Book and Job Office, 1883.

Speek, Vickie Cleverley. *"God Has Made Us a Kingdom": James Strang and the Midwest Mormons.* Salt Lake City: Signature Books, 2006.

Staker, Mark Lyman. *Hearken, O Ye People: The Historical Setting of Joseph Smith's Ohio Revelations.* Salt Lake City: Greg Kofford Books, 2009.

Stevens, Frank E. *History of Lee County Illinois.* 2 vols. Chicago: S. J. Clarke Publishers, 1914.

Strang, James J. "An Appeal." *Gospel Herald,* Aug. 21, 1848.

"Strang's Consistency." *Melchisedeck and Aaronic Herald,* Oct. 1849.

Taylor, John. *The Gospel Kingdom: Writings and Discourses of John Taylor.* Ed. G. Homer Durham. Salt Lake City: Bookcraft, 1987.

Temple Lot Suit, typescript. Inez Smith Davis Papers, p23, f47, Community of Christ Archives, Independence, Missouri.

"To the Saints." *Messenger and Advocate,* Nov. 1835.

"To the Editor." *The Prophet,* Apr. 5, 1845.

"To the Scattered Saints." *Zion's Standard: A Voice from the Smith Family.* Broadside, Mar. 24, 1848.

"To the Subscribers." *Elders' Journal,* Aug. 1838.

Turley, Richard E., Jr. *Victims: The LDS Church and the Mark Hofmann Case.* Urbana: University of Illinois Press, 1992.

U.S. Census, 1820, 1830, Essex County, Massachusetts; 1840 Howard County, Missouri; 1860 Jasper County, Missouri; 1850 Lake County, Ohio; 1870 Santa Clara County, California; 1860 Utah County, Utah Territory.

Van Wagoner, Richard S. *Sidney Rigdon: A Portrait of Religious Excess.* Salt Lake City: Signature Books, 1994.

Vital Records of Acton, Massachusetts, to the Year 1850. Boston: New England Historic Genealogical Society, 1923.

Vogel, Dan. "James Colin Brewster: The Boy Prophet Who Challenged Mormon Authority." In Roger D. Launius and Linda Thatcher, eds., *Differing Visions: Dissenters in Mormon History.* Urbana: University of Illinois Press, 1994, 120-39.

Walker, Kyle R., ed. *United by Faith: The Joseph Sr. and Lucy Mack Smith Family.* American Fork, UT: Covenant Communications, 2005.

Walker, Kyle R. "William Smith's Quest for Ecclesiastical Station: A Schismatic Odyssey, 1844-93." In *Scattering of the Saints: Schism within Mormonism.* Ed. Newell G. Bringhurst and John C. Hamer. Independence: John Whitmer Books, 2007, 92-114.

Watson, Elden J., comp. *Manuscript History of Brigham Young, 1846-1847.* Salt Lake City: Author, 1971.

———. comp. and ed. *The Orson Pratt Journals.* Salt Lake City: Elden J. Watson, 1975.

"We Have Received ..." *Gospel Herald,* Nov. 2, 1848.

Whitney, Orson F. *Life of Heber C. Kimball.* 2nd ed. Salt Lake City: Bookcraft, 1945.

"William At It Again." *Warsaw Signal,* Jan. 4, 1849.

"William Smith—Fornication, Adultery." *Cincinnati Daily Commercial,* May 22, 1850.

"W[illia]m Smith—The Imposter." *Daily Nonpareil,* Cincinnati, May 20, 1850.

Wood, Joseph. *Epistle of the Twelve.* Milwaukee: Author, 1851.

Woodruff, Wilford, to Brigham Young, Oct. 9, 14, 1844. Brigham Young Collection, LDS Church History Library.

Young, Brigham, to Parley P. Pratt, July 17, 1842. LDS Church History Library.

Index

Adam-ondi-Ahman, Missouri, 161, 169n19, 184

Adams, George J., 128, 209-13, 215-16n54, 231, 234, 351

affidavits, of Adam Black, 184; Orson Hyde, 188-89, 292-93; Thomas B. Marsh, 188, 292-93

alcohol, 23-24, 64, 66-67, 72, 149, 154, 217, 239, 245, 331-32

Aldrich, Hazen, 49-50

Alger, Fanny, 113, 119, 169

Allen, James B., 160-61

Ames, Charity, 48-49

Ames, Ira, 48-49, 140

Anderson, Lavina Fielding, 13, 351n150

apostasy, 353-61. *See also* belief; dissenters; excommunication

apostles, 3, 71-72, 79-95; character of, 5-6, 9, 12, 34-36, 57-59, 81, 92-95, 98, 102-04, 112-14, 119, 125-26, 130, 144, 148, 154-156, 160-61, 195, 212, 229, 232-33, 237-41, 262, 266, 276, 280, 284, 291-92, 295-96, 300-01, 322, 341n113, 355, 359-61; chosen, 80-83, 155-56, 180, 286-87; compared to Paul in New Testament, 29, 37-38, 55, 69, 112n48; criticized, 5, 10, 97-104, 124, 140, 152-54, 186, 192, 202, 217-18, 245-46, 293; evangelists, 9, 12, 20-21, 38, 41-49, 52, 57-58, 66, 83-84, 102, 145-46, 180-81, 198-99, 291, 353, 377-92; financial means, 34, 37, 53, 69, 73, 76, 100-02, 112n48, 124-26, 130, 136-39, 149, 153, 169-70, 209,

229n102, 233, 284, 292, 332, 381; lapses, 3, 8-11, 20, 30-31, 39-41, 52, 56, 78, 81, 97-101, 119, 146, 157, 193, 329-30, 346-47; "lost," 3-4, 157, 174, 183, 297-98, 354-55, 357-361; object lessons, 4-7, 182-83, 296-99, 353-54; requirements of, 9, 46-47, 57-58, 80-83, 90-91, 310; self-assurance, 18, 28, 39, 52, 59, 80-81, 84, 120, 246, 291; seniority, 3, 85, 103-04, 111-14, 123, 151, 189, 231, 340; speaking ability, 18, 28-29, 32-33, 40, 43-46, 52-53, 56-59, 75, 79, 83-84, 88-93, 128, 180-81, 228-29, 377, 389; steadying the ark, 86, 104-05, 109, 116-17, 141-42, 203, 206; voted on after death of Joseph Smith, 203. *See also* marriage; Quorum of Twelve Apostles

Archer, Abenade, wife of William Smith, 220n75, 329-30

Arrington, Leonard J., 158, 353, 359

Avard, Sampson, 177, 184, 193-94

Babbitt, Almon W., 105, 345n131

Backenstos, Jacob B., 243, 258

Barrows, Ethan, 88, 91

Bates, Sarah (Sally) Marinda, marries Orson Pratt, 21, 110

Battle of Crooked River, 183, 189. *See also* Mormon War in Missouri

Baxter, John, 255, 257

Beach, Rufus, 252, 253n57

beer, *see* alcohol

belief, 16, 32-33, 83, 104, 107-08, 114, 141, 205, 275, 291, 306, 311,

About the authors

William Shepard is a past president of the John Whitmer Historical Association. He has published in *Dialogue: A Journal of Mormon Thought,* the *John Whitmer Historical Journal,* and *Journal of Mormon History* and has presented research papers at historical conferences. He is a leader of the Church of Jesus Christ of Latter Day Saints (Strangite) in the Burlington branch founded by James J. Strang in the 1840s. After he finished his undergraduate and master's degrees in history and served in the U.S. Air Force, he worked as a teacher for the developmentally disabled in Wisconsin for nearly thirty years.

H. Michael Marquardt is an independent historian who has authored such books as *The Joseph Smith Revelations: Text and Commentary* and (as co-author) *Inventing Mormonism: Tradition and the Historical Record.* He is the compiler of *Early Patriarchal Blessings of the Church of Jesus Christ of Latter-day Saints* and its companion volume, *Later Patriarchal Blessings of the Church of Jesus Christ of Latter-day Saints.* Originally from San Francisco, he retired from the US Postal Service in Sandy, Utah. His lifelong passion has been Mormon history.

Lost Apostles was typeset by Jason Francis in Bembo, a humanist typeface based on punches cut by Francesco Griffo in 1495. It was first used for the book *de Aetna* by Italian poet Pietro Bembo and named after him. In 1929, the typeface was revived by Stanley Morison for the Monotype Coporation, which created a digital rendition in the 1980s for desktop publishing.

The jacket was designed by Ron Stucki and features the Gotham typeface by Tobias Frere-Jones. Created in 2000, it became famous for being used in Barack Obama's 2008 presidential campaign.

Printed and bound by Sheridan Books, Ann Arbor, Michigan.

MORE ADVANCE PRAISE

Lost Apostles carries us to the tumultuous founding days of Mormonism. Of twelve original apostles, six departed, disillusioned or excommunicated, their stories subsequently forgotten or intentionally ignored. They left because of internal conflicts that played out dramatically against the backdrop of the American frontier. Through meticulous research and clear writing, the authors bring these early church leaders out of the stereotype of "apostate" to full life in a transformed but chaotic world. I highly recommend this book.

> —**POLLY AIRD**, author of *Mormon Convert, Mormon Defector: A Scottish Immigrant in the American West* (Best Biography Award, Mormon History Association); co-author of *Playing with Shadows: Voices of Dissent in the Mormon West* (Best Documentary History Award, Utah State Historical Society)

We have all heard of the original members of the Quorum of Twelve Apostles who departed the church over different beliefs, priorities, and prerogatives. But until now we have not fully grasped their lives and careers, their strengths and foibles, their accomplishments and struggles. Authors Shepard and Marquardt have marshalled in-depth research to tell fascinating stories about individuals who once held prominence in the first-generation church but have been lost to history. This is a fine discussion of those six who dissented from the Latter Day Saint movement during its earliest years.

> —**ROGER D. LAUNIUS**, Associate Director, National Air and Space Museum; author of *Joseph Smith III: Pragmatic Prophet* (Best Book Award, John Whitmer Historical Association; Evans Biography Award, Mountain West Center for Regional Studies); *Space Stations: Base Camps to the Stars* (Publication Prize, American Institute of Aeronautics and Astronautics)